Rhetorics of Literacy

In memory of my mother

Rhetorics of Literacy
The Cultivation of American Dialect Poetry

Nadia Nurhussein

THE OHIO STATE UNIVERSITY PRESS · COLUMBUS

Copyright © 2013 The Ohio State University.
All rights reserved.

Library of Congress Cataloging-in-Publication Data
Nurhussein, Nadia, 1974–
Rhetorics of literacy : the cultivation of American dialect poetry / Nadia Nurhussein.
p. cm.
Includes bibliographical references and index.
ISBN-13: 978-0-8142-1216-5 (cloth : alk. paper)
ISBN-10: 0-8142-1216-6 (cloth : alk. paper)
ISBN-13: 978-0-8142-9317-1 (cd)
1. Dialect poetry, American—History and criticism. 2. American poetry—19th century—History and criticism. 3. American poetry—20th century—History and criticism. 4. Literacy in literature. I. Title.
PS323.N87 2013
811.009—dc23
       2012038435

Paper (ISBN: 978-0-8142-5668-8)
Cover design by James A. Baumann
Type set in Adobe Sabon
Typeset by Juliet Williams

contents

List of Illustrations	vii
Acknowledgments	ix

Introduction • "Mere Mutilation":
   Becoming Literate in Dialect Poetry — 1

Chapter One • The Difficulty of Dialect Poetry — 18
   Anthologizing Dialect Poetry — 26
   Marketing the Mass Poet — 32
   Performing Dialect Poetry — 36
   Silent Reading and Silent Film — 42
   Dialect and the Phonograph — 48

Chapter Two • Plain and Peculiar Dialects:
   Bret Harte and James Whitcomb Riley — 57
   Voicing Harte's Truthful James and Ah Sin — 59
   Riley's Child Writing — 71
   The Spelling Bee Poem — 82

Chapter Three • Lettered Dialect: Paul Laurence Dunbar I — 90
   Dunbar's Performances — 92
   The Epistolary Dialect Poem — 99
   Dunbar's Class in Spelling and Reading — 110
   The Spelling Bee Poem Redux — 114

Chapter Four • **Cultivated Dialect: Paul Laurence Dunbar II**   **117**
    The Ease and Labor of Dialect Poetry   121
    The Commerce of Magazine Verse   126
    Dialect, Advertising, and the *Century*   131
    The Cultivation of Dialect Performance   137

Chapter Five • **Gendered Dialect: Frances Ellen Watkins Harper and Maggie Pogue Johnson**   **143**
    Harper's Aunt Chloe and Her Literacy   147
    Femininity, Fashion, and Dialect   155
    Johnson's Education and Idleness   164

Chapter Six • **Annotated Dialect: Claude McKay and Langston Hughes**   **172**
    From Showman to Spokesman: The Unlettered Poet   174
    Hughes's Typography   179
    Hughes's Marginal Literacy   182
    McKay's Dialects and Poetic Diction   194

    Conclusion   **208**

Notes   215
Bibliography   259
Index   276

list of illustrations

Table 1.	Selected textbooks and anthologies, 1898–1935	27–28
Table 2.	Selected elocution and recitation manuals, 1885–1903	29
Figure 1.	Illustration of James Whitcomb Riley by Art Young, from *Authors' Readings* (New York: Frederick A. Stokes Company, 1897)	46
Figure 2.	Illustration of James Whitcomb Riley by Art Young, from *Authors' Readings* (New York: Frederick A. Stokes Company, 1897)	47
Figure 3.	Illustration from Bret Harte's *Heathen Chinee* (Rock Island and Pacific Railroad, 1872)	69
Figure 4.	Illustration from Bret Harte's *Heathen Chinee* (Rock Island and Pacific Railroad, 1872)	70
Figure 5.	An advertisement for *The Complete Works of James Whitcomb Riley*, published in the December 1917 *Biblical World*	78
Figure 6.	Paul Laurence Dunbar reading at the National Cash Register Company, 1904	140

acknowledgments

I am deeply indebted to a number of foundations and organizations for the fellowship support that aided the completion of this book: the American Council of Learned Societies, the Lilly Library at Indiana University, the Ford Foundation, and the Bancroft Library at the University of California, Berkeley. In addition, I have benefited from the assistance of librarians and archivists at the Lilly Library, the Houghton Library at Harvard University, the Rare Book and Manuscript Library at Columbia University, the Beinecke Rare Book and Manuscript Library at Yale University, the University of Virginia Library, the New York Public Library, the Boston Public Library, the Dayton Metro Library, the Ohio Historical Society, and the American Antiquarian Society, among others. The staff at my own university's Healey Library has been of enormous help, particularly Janet Stewart in the Interlibrary Loan department. Jeff Opt at the Archive Center at Dayton History, Jeff Codori, and Waltye Rasulala were exceptionally helpful and forthcoming with useful information related to Paul Laurence Dunbar, James Whitcomb Riley, and Maggie Pogue Johnson respectively.

It was my privilege as a student to work with such exemplary scholars as Christopher Nealon and Susan Schweik, who steered the development of the dissertation from which this book evolved and who have continued to be generous with their time and their mentorship in the years since. Other faculty in the English department at the University of California, Berkeley—especially Stephen Best, Anne Cheng, Samuel Otter, and George Starr—raised productive questions and problems that moved this project forward in unexpected ways. My year at Mount Holyoke College was also invaluable. Mary Jo Salter, Jeffrey Santa Ana, Michelle Stephens, Donald Weber, Elizabeth Young, and others helped to foster an environment that made my transition from graduate student to faculty member relatively painless, and I appreciated the precious time I had there that allowed me to make progress on this book before diving into full-time teaching.

The community to which I have been lucky enough to belong at the University of Massachusetts, Boston, deserves considerable thanks, in particular my colleagues Matt Brown, Bob Crossley, Sari Edelstein, Holly Jackson, Betsy Klimasmith, and Eve Sorum. Thanks, also, are due to my research assistant, Brad Smith. My students have provided me with a wealth of original thought and fresh readings of the literature discussed here. I have learned a great deal from those enrolled in my M.A. courses, especially those enrolled in the Spring 2012 "Poetry and Performance" seminar, who have been among my most valuable interlocutors and whose views on Riley's "The Phonograph" prompted me—first grudgingly, then gratefully—to revisit and completely rewrite that section of my first chapter.

Colleagues I have met over the course of my career, at conferences, symposia, and elsewhere, have offered extremely valuable feedback on my work. They are too numerous to list in any comprehensive way, but a preliminary list must include Robin Bernstein, Joanne Braxton, Mike Chasar, Brad Evans, Shelley Fisher Fishkin, Gene Andrew Jarrett, A. Yemisi Jimoh, Gavin Jones, Meta DuEwa Jones, John Lowe, Meredith McGill, Koritha Mitchell, Thomas Morgan, Stephen Railton, Arnold Rampersad, Joseph Skerrett, James Smethurst, Edlie Wong, and Richard Yarborough. As a graduate student, I had the great fortune to benefit from the friendship of and conversations shared with Elizabeth Chang, Mai-Lin Cheng, Sandra Lim, and Asali Solomon. Our writing group—short-lived and irregular though it was!—contributed to the shaping of many of the ideas driving this book.

At The Ohio State University Press, I have been fortunate to have the opportunity to work with Sandy Crooms, Malcolm Litchfield, Eugene O'Connor, and Laurie Avery, all of whom have been a pleasure to work with. Thank you also to Ed Hatton and his eagle eye. The anonymous readers of the book manuscript perused my work carefully and painstakingly, giving me insightful suggestions for improvement, seeing things in my work that I did not see myself. The editors and anonymous readers at *American Periodicals* and *African American Review,* journals in which earlier versions of chapters 3 and 4 appeared, also gave me generous comments and constructive criticism; grappling with those suggestions improved those chapters significantly. Thank you, too, to the employees and owners of the many cafés where I occupied valuable real estate, especially Caroline and Andy at Three Little Figs, who didn't seem to mind my sitting and reading and writing for hours on end.

This book has benefited immensely from the boundless encouragement of my father, Mohammed, my sister Siham, my brother Safy, and my entire extended family. Although my mother, Zahra, is not here to witness my finishing of this book, the traces of her loving guidance are present in it everywhere, and I dedicate it to her memory. Lastly, this project would have been inconceivable without the support and inspiration of Nicholas Nace, who has always been my greatest advocate when I couldn't or wouldn't be my own. He remains my best reader.

introduction

"Mere Mutilation"
Becoming Literate in Dialect Poetry

With a desperate thrust of his long fingers through his Bard of Avon locks the young man confronted the beautiful girl.
"Refuse me," he hissed, "and I shall do something that the whole world will regret!"
The beautiful girl shuddered.
"Oh, Archibald," she pleaded, "you—you are not going to write love poetry for the magazines?"
"Worse still. I shall start writing dialect poetry."
Thinking of the terrible calamity that could be thwarted by a woman's "yes," she accepted him on the spot.
—Anonymous, "Terrible Threat"

Around 1880 poetry turned into literature.
—Friedrich Kittler, *Gramophone, Film, Typewriter*

In the April 1897 issue of the *Century Magazine,* humorist Charles Battell Loomis published a short story titled "The Dialect Store." In it, a newspaper writer narrates a dream in which he shops at a store selling "[a]ll kinds of dialects . . . by the yard, the piece, or in quantities to suit." Browsing, he inspects their stock of Scotch, black American, Western, German, French-Canadian, Yiddish, Yankee, Irish, and English "dialects." All of the clerks assisting him are stereotypes of their ethnicities, repositories of exaggerated literary dialect in themselves: the black man selling black dialect is sycophantic and eager to please, the Jewish clerk obsessed with bargaining. The dialects are deliberately bad, and the story's central message is one about how formulaic contemporary dialect writing, an enterprise tried by many in their desperation to succeed in the late-nineteenth-century literary marketplace, can be. "The Dialect Store" satirizes dialect writers who approach composition in this mechanical manner, arguing that they are artistic failures, even if they are commercial successes. Tacking material—literally, because the dialect is sold as if fabric—to literary work is depicted as artificial and unnatural, and the "quill-drivers" who would patronize this storehouse are not creating genuine literature but manufacturing products. As the newspaper writer absurdly concludes, "I'd be the greatest dialect-writer of the age if I could get goods on credit there."

If this is bad dialect writing, good dialect writing, by extension, necessarily captures the essence or spirit of the particular speech represented. It must be natural; it must not submit to the kind of easy translation suggested by the black clerk of "The Dialect Store" when he urges his customer, "any tahm you want to fix up a tale, an' put in de Queen's English in black, come yer an' as' fer me."[1] One reviewer, for example, providing an explanation for why "references of the press to dialect poetry are in the main cold and unsympathetic," cited a partially successful dialect poem that ended unconvincingly, because "no man who is capable of writing ''neath a grassy screen' is capable of following it with 'Durn it all!'—except an amateur dialect poet."[2] Most serious dialect writers in late-nineteenth-century America conceived of their writing as sincere efforts to represent "nonstandard" speech, and demanded that literary dialect look like it would sound convincing if read aloud, without obstructing the reading process. A journal called *The Writer,* founded in 1887 with the subtitle "A Monthly Magazine for Literary Workers," frequently addressed the issue of how to write dialect effectively in the magazine's early years. A typical assessment was that "[o]rdinary dialect writing appeals merely to the eye, indeed, and its rules seem to be conventional or traditional. Really good work . . . must be read aloud to be appreciated."[3] Literary dialects that call attention to themselves visually were considered flawed because, as one writer argues, "[p]athos is not attained by the use of apostrophes to mark the omission of letters and syllables, nor by the use of extraordinary alphabetical combinations (though, to be sure, some spelling of so-called dialect *is* enough to bring tears.)"[4] And yet, the effects of punctuation and orthographical experimentation constituted a large part of the experience of reading dialect poetry. If we can accept that, as Jennifer DeVere Brody writes, "one of punctuation's many functions is to endow print with affect and emotion," it is possible that the apostrophes marking elisions that are found everywhere in dialect poetry somehow elicit an affective response in its readers.[5]

Despite the fact that so many found fault with dialect writing as it was commonly practiced, the genre was incredibly popular at the turn of the century, as illustrated by the dialogue in the epigraph above. The *Century,* like many other American magazines and newspapers, was able to sustain a special section in the late nineteenth century devoted largely to dialect pieces, along with other light and humorous literature and cartoons. ("The Dialect Store" shares a page, in a section titled "In Lighter Vein," with a poem by Paul Laurence Dunbar.) *Harper's Monthly Magazine* and the *Atlantic Monthly* also devoted a considerable amount of space to dialect writing, and in 1890 Edward Bok, editor of the *Ladies' Home Journal,* aggressively solicited James Whitcomb Riley for a dialect poem, believing that it would increase the magazine's circulation by "one or two hundred thousand subscribers."[6] The force of the dialect writing trend was so overwhelming that contemporary reviews frequently complained of it. Some complained simply of poor execution, as I've already mentioned. Others had more serious concerns about the impact of the genre itself on its readers. A reviewer for *Appleton's Journal* demanded that "the critics, in mercy to mankind, must avoid pointing out this easy path to fame, lest a new and devastating epidemic of dialect verse fall upon the land."[7] The supposed dangers of nonstandard language such as slang and regional and ethnic varieties of English, in speech and as represented in writing, were of grave concern to some lexicographers and philologists who were committed to the idea of preserving the American language against corruption, as Kenneth Cmiel, Michael North, Gavin Jones, and others have written. The dialect fabrics found at "The Dialect Store" may be sewn together to create something resembling the perfect dialect story, but the seams where these cloths meet are, for some, flaws themselves. As one critic grumbled, in a metaphor anticipating the conceit of Loomis's story, "Our literature seems bent on turning its wrong side out, and displaying to the world its seams and ravellings and tattered linings."[8]

Itself a patchwork of various tacked-on literary dialects, "The Dialect Store" becomes the type of easy dialect story it warns against, passing briefly through dialects as the protagonist passes through the space of the store. The visual effect for readers of the different dialects jostling against each other—here, in one heteroglossic story, but also in late-nineteenth-century literature in general—is one of constant disorientation and reorientation. As North and Jones point out, the linguistic diversity brought about by increased immigration posed a threat to the imagined purity of a still-developing standard American English language, and dialect literature, with all of its multilingual characters, served as documentation testifying to this "terrible threat," to quote the title of the first epigraph above. An essay in *The Bookman* articulates this sentiment:

> Of course the chatter of these types is nothing now to what it will be—when they all begin to intermarry and produce other types. If Johnny or Chimmie should be spared to wed a Hungarian lady, or Ole should become enamoured of Miss Li Sing, or one of Mr. Cahan's Poles should seek the hand of a Bowery "loidy," will any one vouch for the consequences? Surely the American novelist has taken on himself a tremendous linguistic burden.[9]

Needless to say, the mixture of races behind "this Babel of discord" is the unstated threat, not simply the mixture of languages undermining a centralized and standardized American English.[10] And the writer is somehow responsible for this intermarriage, in his assuming this "tremendous linguistic burden." Unmediated interaction between these ethnic types will doubtless "produce other types": miscegenated and potentially unreadable. Writers and readers will be faced, the *Bookman* writer fears, with dialects that are less distinct, exceeding definition, and both writers and readers will be forced to navigate unfamiliar waters. This is most assuredly not a picture of happy "melting pot" assimilation; it is one of surreptitious and menacing ethnic identity. Moreover, this charge, while here leveled at the novelist, was more effectively directed at the dialect poet. The circulation of dialect in periodical literature and in publicly displayed and disseminated ephemera, such as signs, broadsides, and advertisements, implicated poets—whose lyric verse is frequently understood to be monologic, and thus unmoored from any tempering and mediating narrative voice to control that menace—in this jostling.[11] The story of this book, therefore, is implicitly one of literary miscegenation, despite the fact that each poet discussed here is closely associated with one particular literary dialect.

However, no dialect writing—even if "pure"—can ever truly be familiar. Dialect had fascinating effects on the reading process, and writers exploited these effects formally and thematically. In this study, I explore the production and reception of dialect in late-nineteenth- and early-twentieth-century American poetry, examining the contexts in which dialect poetry was written, read, and performed. I am invested in both the formal mechanisms and the cultural history of dialect poetry, and, as a result, I bring something like what Caroline Levine calls a "strategic formalist" perspective and what Monique Morgan describes as "politically inflected formalism" to the study of dialect poetry. Levine's strategic formalism, a theoretical position acknowledging that "[l]iterary forms . . . trouble and remake political relationships in surprising, aleatory, and often confusingly disorderly ways," is part of a "new attention to form as a part of a politically aware historicism," and this position aligns with my intervention into dialect poetry as a genre. In fact, as Morgan writes, there may be something about "poems written in this period" that "invite[s] readers to view social perspectives and formal choices as inextricably linked, constantly influencing each other."[12] I consider my work here to be in conversation with that of Morgan and Levine, who represent a significant trend in Victorian poetry studies, and with that of Virginia Jackson, Yopie Prins, and other poetry scholars represented in the January 2008 *PMLA* special section titled "The New Lyric Studies" and in the groundbreaking collection *The Traffic of Poems: Nineteenth-Century Poetry and Transatlantic Exchange,* edited by Meredith L. McGill. In addition, the dialect poem presents us with a provocative case study when read through Virginia Jackson's illuminating study of the twentieth century's literary-critical drive to reduce all poetry to the lyric. As a type of dramatic monologue, one that more than any other poetic form defies John Stuart Mill's definition of poetry as something "overheard" (as opposed to "eloquence," which is "heard"), the dialect poem poses challenges to "lyric reading" as described by Jackson. As Jackson points out, Mill calls the book of poetry "a soliloquy in full dress," but also claims that, though "[t]he actor knows that there is an audience present; . . . if he act as though he knew it, he acts ill."[13] Dialect poems, on the other hand, explicitly require audiences, and they require actors to dramatize their acting rather than obscure it.

Unlike Gavin Jones, Richard Brodhead, and others, I focus exclusively on the use of dialect in verse rather than prose in part because the dialect poem was ready made for elocutionary use in a way that the dialect prose piece was not. It was easier for audiences to, on one hand, imagine that the recited dialect poem captured the unmodified voices of a disappearing culture, and, on the other hand, struggle through odd transcriptions of those voices. In this respect, the dialect poem resembles what Susan Stewart calls a "distressed" genre, one in which "the literary 'voicing' of folklore forms emphasizes their new textuality all the more," because "any genre that in literature attempts to 'pass itself as' the oral is destined to appear in ill-fitting clothing."[14] (The transcribed-speech-as-clothing metaphor resurfaces.) The intersections of the oral and textual aspects of the dialect poem, visible in both its composition and its reception, resulted in confusing and contradictory interactions with the genre.

As this book demonstrates, neither the cultural nor formal aspects of dialect poetry may be neglected if one wants to understand how the genre operated in late-nineteenth-century American culture. Like Shira Wolosky, who, in a section of the *Cambridge History of American Literature* dedicated to nineteenth-century poetry, "approaches poetry as a distinctive formal field on which the rhetorics of nineteenth-century American culture find intensified expression, concentration, reflection, and command," I find that dialect poetry offers a specialized case of this relationship between poetics and rhetoric; as Wolosky puts it, "far from negating the specifically literary nature of a poetic text, rhetorical context illuminates and affirms poetry's cultural importance and aesthetic power."[15] With similar goals in mind, I explore in this book dialect poetry's rhetorical interest in where sound meets literacy and textuality. My approach thus also shares ground with approaches like Garrett Stewart's "phonemic reading" and John Shoptaw's "lyric cryptography." Like the Victorianists cited above, Shoptaw states that his approach is concerned with "mak[ing] a historical and cultural reading of [a] poem textually specific."[16] In the lyric cryptography he observes, poetic meaning is produced as alternative senses hiding in words and in the relationships between words. These kinds of meanings, especially those resulting from graphemic and phonemic cryptography, are produced again and again in dialect poetry.

While some critical attention has been paid to the important role of dialect poetry in the United States—Wolosky, for example, addresses it in her contribution to the *Cambridge History of American Literature*—that attention is rarely sustained. Dialect poetry is often mentioned in passing and yet rarely discussed in depth. My goal in this book is to demonstrate that the profound influence of this popular genre stems not only from its use as an entertaining distraction from "serious" poetry, or as a force for standardization or caricature, but as a complicated pedagogical and rhetorically purposeful tool. In order to demonstrate this, I am concerned with the formal details, the mechanics, and the cultures of reading practices, and this is one respect in which my book differs from recently published books by Joshua L. Miller and Matthew Hart, studies that are concerned with the relationships between nonstandard language and modernist writing (American in Miller's case and transnational in Hart's).

Throughout this book, I use the terms "dialect" and "literary dialect" to describe the limitless ways in which writers evoke so-called nonstandard speech in written English and not speech itself. Written English does not correspond to a particular spoken dialect; thus, orthographical alteration wrongly suggests deviation from a correct standard. Because literary dialect differs qualitatively from spoken dialects, any dialect poetry—"good" or "bad"—calls attention to its inauthenticity. A poet's transcription of speech inevitably shows bias, recording some features which seem relevant to him or her while omitting aspects of his or her own.[17] Too frequently, dialect poetry has been read as an unsuccessful attempt to record speech, when it should be read instead as evidence of the difference between speaking dialect and writing it (or as Charles Bernstein puts it, "the yammering gap between speech and writing"[18]). The fact that so many readers and writers have failed to note that dialect poems could be driven and enriched by their visual effects, by their appeal to the eye in addition to the ear, has surprisingly continued to exert influence upon readings of dialect poetry over one hundred years after the period of its greatest popularity.

I use the term "dialect" rather than "vernacular" precisely to emphasize that any analysis focusing exclusively on the orality of literary dialect is necessarily limited, ignoring an entire field of activity. The visual and textual elements of literary dialect have been historically undervalued especially by African American literary criticism, devoting greater attention instead to dialect poetry's roots in an oral tradition. In a 2010 review, Tess Chakkalakal writes that all five of the recently published studies covered by her essay "document and supplement the turn away from vernacular and oral forms of African American expression that were once central to the formation and study of African American culture," pointing to a general trend toward illuminating African American literate practice.[19] My study joins, perhaps ironically, this recent work turning away from the vernacular and generally concerned with the literate dimensions of African American culture. Despite this trend, however, the most significant and lasting criticism of dialect poetry remains that of James Weldon Johnson, who called it "mere mutilation of English spelling and pronunciation," thereby rejecting the genre's visual and textual aspects.[20] I argue that, in fact, it is the interplay between suggestions of orality and literacy that gives literary dialect its interest, and much of the African American literary tradition depends upon this interplay to a degree that has still not been fully acknowledged. Henry Louis Gates, Jr., for example, argued a generation ago that dialect poetry generally "failed when it tried to cram a live, spoken form into a rigid, written one, oblivious to its internal logic, unaware of its linguistic possibilities, technically inadequate to preserve the poetry as spirit." Consequently, he writes, it "choked and wasted a spirit and produced a mediocre body of trivia."²¹ The tension produced by this imagined incompatibility and coercion is precisely what requires closer attention. The juxtaposition of elements that gesture toward orality alongside those exploiting literate forms does not necessarily impoverish the genre. Dialect poetry in the nineteenth century did not "waste" an existing form; it developed a new, productive, and strangely difficult one.

Because dialect poetry has been associated with orality, critics of dialect poetry have in most cases assumed that the genre succeeds best when attempted by a native speaker of that dialect. As a reviewer of Bret Harte's work wrote, "It is gravely to be doubted whether any rhymes written in dialect by men who are not in the habit of using that patois as their ordinary speech should be regarded as anything but literary curiosities, as *tours de force* of odd learning, precisely like the Greek verses of schoolboys and the anagrams of a century ago."²² The reviewer's comparisons are revealing. Gates's "mediocre body of trivia" appears here in the form of "literary curiosities." Both perspectives suggest that, unless dialect poetry comes naturally, it can only be a futile intellectual exercise. In fact, according to this reviewer, the new dialect poems (Harte and John Hay are considered in his review) are not the work of poets at all; instead, they "belong to the class of *jeux d'esprit* which poets have rarely written, but with which clever men have always amused themselves."²³

In response to readers' and writers' frustrations with dialect spellings that failed to evoke speech, representations of dialect in American poetry have moved, as several critics have noted, from primarily orthographical to primarily syntactical over the course of the last century. Unlike orthography, syntactical variety is as apparent aurally as it is visually, satisfying readers who are invested in preserving the impressions of orality in poetry. However, I argue that the poets discussed in this book alter orthography in order to encourage visual readings. It is not surprising, then, that poets interested in dialect were also interested in the illogic of conventional spelling. The author of "The Dialect Store" is also the author of humorous poems about spelling, including the well-known "O-U-G-H," which is included in the *Norton Book of Light Verse* under the section "Some Fun with the Mother Tongue." The poem's speaker, a French child whose speech is represented in dialect, attempts again and again, in stanzas escalating in absurdity, to determine how "-ough" as it appears in certain English words should sound. First, he rhymes "plough" with "through," only to be corrected by the schoolteacher; finally told that "lough" should be pronounced with the ending "-ock," he is driven to violence and threatens to throw a "rough" (a rock).

Strange spellings, in the forms of both dialect writing and orthographies encouraging phonetic spelling reform—with Loomis's poem being an example of both—reflected cultural dissatisfaction with the inaccuracy of written English and the desire to have American spelling correspond closely to the way people really spoke. Both nineteenth-century dialect poetry and spelling reform, then, emerged from the intersections of orality and literacy. Walter Ong describes the nineteenth century in America as a period of nostalgia for a primarily oral culture, in which oral performances, including lecturing and public novel reading, were popular. For example, Ong writes that, "[s]till yearning for the old orality, the nineteenth century developed 'elocution' contests, which tried to repristinate printed texts, using careful artistry to memorize the texts verbatim and recite them so that they would sound like extempore oral productions."[24] Lecturing in America was becoming big business for English novelists, essayists, and other belletrists, with Charles Dickens's 1867–8 reading tour "the first financial blockbuster."[25] The next two decades, the decades during which Bret Harte and James Whitcomb Riley—the subjects of my first two chapters—respectively made names for themselves, "seem to have been the climax of the business" of lecturing.[26] Despite the fact that dialect writing achieved some popularity earlier in the nineteenth century, most notably with the publication of James Russell Lowell's *The Biglow Papers*, Harte's "Plain Language from Truthful James" (also known as "The Heathen Chinee"), published in 1870, provides the chronological starting point for this study precisely because of the coincidence of the extreme, unprecedented popularity of the poem in both its print and oral incarnations.

The education of children, according to Ong, was influenced by this "yearning" for orality: "The famous *McGuffey's Readers*, published in the United States in some 120 million copies between 1836 and 1920, were designed as remedial readers to improve not the reading for comprehension which we idealize today, but oral, declamatory reading."[27] All of this interest in orality coincided, ironically, with increased literacy. Lee Soltow and Edward Stevens show that the second and third of three dramatic drops in illiteracy occur in the 1870s, corresponding with compulsory education in many states, and in the 1880s, corresponding with compulsory attendance.[28] By the turn of the century, literacy rates were high, certainly among whites. And, among African Americans, 70 percent were literate in 1910, up from 30 percent only three decades earlier, demonstrating "the slow but steady rise in black literacy in the United States in the decades of the late-nineteenth and early-twentieth centuries."[29] So, where

Ong emphasizes attempts to revive oral practices such as elocution, Shirley Brice Heath finds an invasion of print in the late nineteenth century:

> In what was termed the "age of reading," more people were literate than ever before, and wide varieties of information were available. Conversations and other oral forms of communication—even public oratory—were declining in favor of newspapers and other written means of exchanging knowledge and opinion. This extension of writing into formerly oral areas of communication, such as public lectures, debate series, picnics, stump meetings, and conversation clubs, influenced the increasing drive for standardization by grammarians and like-minded citizens.[30]

In fact, this mingling of writing and speech, of literate and oral modes, helps to explain the popularity of dialect poetry and to describe how it functions. The success of dialect poetry depended upon the environment provided by coexisting—and mutually enriching—oral and literate modes at the end of the nineteenth century. At the turn of the century, one could encounter poetry, as Joan Shelley Rubin points out, "not only in the intimate surroundings of a lovers' tête-à-tête, but also, for example, in classroom recitations, family gatherings, speaking choir concerts, Boy Scout campfires, religious services, celebrity performances, and, eventually, radio broadcasts. Each of those venues supported ideologies and behaviors (such as rereading, reading aloud, and reading in groups) that eluded ledgers and statistics."[31] And, yet, all of those oral reading practices were accompanied by pervasive silent reading, which was becoming more and more entrenched within and without the classroom, as I discuss in the first chapter of this book.

Reading dialect poetry as a phenomenon that requires of its readers a degree of competence with the features of both oral and literate art forms, I demonstrate in this study how the emergence of the figure of the silent dialect poetry reader in late-nineteenth-century America herself embodies a challenge to the perception of literary dialect as unequivocally oral. The reception of dialect poetry, as sometimes a silent reading experience and sometimes public declamation, was pulled in what were perceived to be opposing directions to create an entirely novel and experimental reading experience, one that was disquieting for some poetry readers. Many readers and writers thought that dialect poetry—even poetry in general—suffered if it was not read aloud. Readers such as John Harrington Cox, in a 1914 essay, expressed a commonly held view when he complained that the silent reading of poetry was "artificial" and that it was "a marvelous delight only when the subtle harmonies of the verse pulse through the reader's soul and his inward ear catches its stately tread or tripping measures."[32] In other words, even silent poetry reading, it was argued, should never be truly silent. Furthermore, even more than the silent reading of other subgenres of poetry, the silent reading of dialect poetry itself enacted the mingling of orality and literacy intrinsic to it, and contradicted understandings of dialect writing as simply a nostalgic attempt to recover an oral time in our culture's development.

Because late-nineteenth-century and early-twentieth-century dialect poetry is frequently about, and explicitly addresses, semi- and nonliterate people, they are presumed to be its intended audience. However, despite statements of poetics by dialect poets insisting that they see their dialect work as the mode of expression best suited to their roles as poets of the people, the mode that allows them to write inclusively to literate and illiterate alike, dialect poetry actually excludes readers who cannot engage successfully with the complex oral and literate components of the verse. In effect, dialect writers' experiments with spelling distanced them from less competent readers and impeded direct communication. Take, for example, Twain's assertion in the "Explanatory" for *The Adventures of Huckleberry Finn* that he "painstakingly" represented "shadings" of dialect in the novel, which, as Lisa Gitelman points out, "is equally a claim about his proficiency in spelling them. Orthography was one ground upon which literate English speakers negotiated their own identity and the identity of others while at the same time experiencing writing as artificial, glimpsing everywhere the potential failure of textual representation to recuperate aural experience."[33] That writers labored over their dialect spellings to such an intense degree suggests that they targeted an audience who would respond both to the elements that make dialect poetry easy to listen to and to those that make it difficult to read. Dialect poems intended for competent readers sometimes—as in the case of Riley's "child writing" poems—prompt readers to revisit childhood, when a reader is typically most aware of his or her efforts to process writing, with all of the attendant struggles, but to retain in the end the ability to move easily between oral and literate modes.

Ironically, though dialect poetry requires work from both reader and writer—not as semantic or conceptual complexity would, but as something like mechanical complexity—it has been dismissed by scholars and critics, then and now, largely because of its lack of complexity.[34] Oliver Wendell Holmes, a literary lion by Riley's time, damned him with faint praise by claiming that he "has done things, perhaps, which will outlast the more laborious work of some of the older and more pretentious poets."[35] While predicting an immortality (that Riley would not achieve) as a way of honoring the younger poet, he also assumes that his verse is effortlessly produced, that no labor has gone into it, and, by extension, that no work is required to interpret it. This was, of course, a common misconception. A journalist writing in 1871 of the popularity of Harte's poem the year before expressed the feelings of many when he wrote that "[i]t seemed that nothing was so easy as to write dialect poetry."[36] In response to this misconception, I intend for the "cultivation" in my subtitle to evoke the multiple senses of the word in Raymond Williams's etymology in *Keywords*, containing almost opposite meanings: cultivation shifts from describing a kind of work to describing a quality or temperament that is most easily fostered by a lifestyle free from work. As dialect poetry was actively cultivated in the late-nineteenth-century United States, its practitioners expose in various ways the labor involved in its reading as well as its writing. What critics of the genre attacked as a formulaic quality is alternatively evidence of its constructedness, as opposed to the ethereal and mysterious inspiration attached to other forms of lyric poetry. We see this distinction in an 1871 newspaper poem titled "A Recipe for a Poem 'In Dialect,'" published one year after Harte's "Plain Language from Truthful James," which compares writing a dialect poem to preparing a dish. After choosing a crude Western character, one needs only to "Pepper his talk with the raciest slang, / . . . / Seasoned with blasphemy,—lard him with curses." Once finished cooking, so to speak, the would-be poet may "Serve him up hot in your 'dialect' verses,— / Properly dished, he'd excite a sensation, / And tickle the taste of our delicate nation." Whether stitched together as in the fabric metaphor in Loomis's story or mixed together in a culinary metaphor, a dialect poem was thought to be—to add yet another metaphor—a creaky machine, assembled through formula.

The difficulties presented by dialect poetry, then, mean that it does not behave as much popular literature does. The nineteenth century saw a tremendous increase in the number of books, magazines, and newspapers published in the United States, including those of the seemingly effortless sort, such as dime novels, that high-brow readers considered detrimental. James Russell Lowell, himself once a dialect poet, complained that the increase of printed materials "has supplanted a strenuous habit of thinking with a loose indolence of reading which relaxes the muscular fiber of the mind."[37] While I would not argue that reading dialect poetry necessitates "a strenuous habit of thinking"—quite the opposite—it does require its readers to work through it before allowing them to relax. Popular literature, as Janice Radway argues, displays its essential conservatism "in its refusal to adopt the subversive modernist argument that meaning is the result of a complex collaboration between text and reader"; instead, she writes, "author and reader seem to understand each other automatically, naturally and without effort."[38] William Charvat's definition of popular poetry is similar:

> Ordinarily it is not conspicuously or radically experimental in form; it does not challenge the reader on grounds where he does not wish to be met; it is not intellectually daring or adventurous; it is not pervadingly cynical or pessimistic. More positively, it is, or seems to be, clear and lucid; its rhythms and rhyme patterns are unmistakable; its imagery and symbolism are exposed rather than hidden, functional rather than ends in themselves. Its subject matter, not its method or its devices, is its reason for existing. . . . To be professionally successful, the poet who produces it must have a "manner" that is his own and is as readily recognizable as a brand name, and a "matter" or "matters" that can be exploited without seeming repetitiousness over a long period of time.[39]

According to Charvat's definition, the poets discussed here certainly do display some of the aspects associated with popular poetry. They are certainly "brand name[s]," and most use "unmistakeable" rhyme schemes, even those writing during an era when free verse was the norm among most major poets. However, I would argue that dialect poetry is experimental in its way, and does challenge the reader in its labor-intensive manipulations of language. Nineteenth-century dialect poetry, as Bernstein suggests in his grouping of poets like Dunbar and Claude McKay with poets like Louis Zukofsky and Gertrude Stein, anticipates some of the experiments of modernist writing. It depends upon collaboration that is more or less translation: the interpretive work involved in decoding dialect.

The process of reading dialect poetry in late-nineteenth-century America was shaped by the writing practices of two of the most famous poets of the era, Harte and Riley. The cultural impact of their popular poetry is major, but few have taken it seriously; Angela Sorby, in her recent book chapter about Riley, and Gary Scharnhorst, in his substantial body of work on Harte, are notable exceptions. In my first two chapters, I argue that dialect poetry served contradictory educational goals—for example, supporting recitation but "corrupting" informal speech—in a multifaceted atmosphere of increasingly silent reading, of devotion to spelling, and of popular poetry performance. Harte's and Riley's public personae were developed in part by their performances, and in these chapters I discuss how audiences perceived the relationship between their physical presences on the stage and their dialects. Poetry performance, however, extended beyond the stage at the end of the nineteenth century: Riley's presence was also preserved on phonograph by the Victor Talking Machine Company and in film (he served as a narrator in a silent film adaptation of "Little Orphant Annie"), which I address here. As Margaret Linley writes, "Given that the nineteenth century was a time of tremendous and exciting proliferation of new industrial and communications technologies, there is much to be done by simply considering poetry in historical relation to the vast array of Victorian inventions such as the stereoscope, kaleidoscope, phonograph, computational machines, photography, and film."[40] In response to Linley and to Ivan Kreilkamp's suggestion that scholars of Victorian poetry, like those of Victorian fiction, understand poetry of the period "as one element in a much broader modern culture of mechanical reproduction, mass visual experience, [and] mediated print cultures," I propose the same for the dialect poetry of Victorian America represented most visibly by Riley. Dialect poetry—a subgenre viewed as particularly backward-looking, offering an even more exaggerated version of "Victorian poetry's own production of an often romanticized or nostalgic vision of the past"—can be understood anew through these modern technologies.[41]

In addition, I identify two distinct types of literary dialect developed in the last decades of the nineteenth century. The "plain language" dialect typified by Harte's "Plain Language from Truthful James" and the "peculiar language" dialect used in Riley's poetry, especially in his "child writing," represent distinct branches of American dialect poetry, each inducing particular effects upon the ways their original audiences read. In Harte's case, the satirical bent of "Plain Language from Truthful James," a poem that Scharnhorst calls "one of the most popular poems ever published," was especially subject to gross misreading because of its allegedly plain language, as I discuss in this book's second chapter.[42] Because plain language is less of a visual departure from written English than is peculiar language, readers interpreted the former as more transparent. Riley's peculiar language, in its deviation from conventional English spelling, invites readers to reenact childhood literacy acquisition. Dialect poetry frequently takes as its subject the process of becoming literate, and Harte and Riley both contribute to the subgenre of dialect poetry that I call the Spelling

Bee poem. These are poems that depend for their humor upon the false association of dialect writing with illiteracy, crowning a character whose speech is recorded to suggest illiteracy as the winner of a spelling bee.

My third and fourth chapters address the poetry of Paul Laurence Dunbar, who, I argue, uses cultivation's opposing senses to publish dialect poetry that points to both work and leisure in elite magazines such as the *Century* (usually relegated to a special section called "In Lighter Vein"). For Dunbar to attempt to place his publications in dialect in the *Century*, when most of the magazine's readers would have viewed dialect poems as necessarily uncultivated, is a deliberately political move, forcing these readers to labor while cloaking his poetry in an air of effortlessness and ease. Black and white readers and listeners alike chose to forget Dunbar's Midwestern roots and forays into Riley-like dialects because they compromised the effortless "authenticity" of his black poetic voice, which was grounded in an often stereotyped Southern culture. Dunbar's "inauthenticity," I argue, should be read in terms of both his failed emulation of Riley's performances and his pursuit of a dialect poetry shaped by literacy as much as orality. Critical focus on the oral elements of Dunbar's dialect obscures literate concerns, most notably in a subgenre developed in Dunbar's work: the epistolary dialect poem. In this variation on an existing form, Dunbar introduces the problem of how speech could be reflected in writing a letter. In his choice of the letter as a model for these poems, Dunbar responds to an emerging silent reading public for dialect poetry.

In James Smethurst's most recent book, *The African American Roots of Modernism: From Reconstruction to the Harlem Renaissance*, he argues that Dunbar "was the towering figure of black poetry who cast a huge literary shadow on all African American poets who followed him—and white, Asian American, and Latino poets, for that matter" and that his work has been "generally very poorly served by scholarship—at least until relatively recently."[43] Like Smethurst, I firmly believe that Dunbar's role in American literary history has been vastly underestimated and undervalued. For this reason, Dunbar is the central figure of this book, around whom the figures of the rest of the book directly or indirectly revolve and to whom I devote two chapters. Dunbar's example exerts a centripetal force that serves as an organizing principle for this book, gesturing forward to Maggie Pogue Johnson, Langston Hughes, and Claude McKay, and gesturing backward to Harte, Riley, and Frances Ellen Watkins Harper.

The book's fifth chapter addresses the relationship between women and dialect writing through the examples of Frances Ellen Watkins Harper and Maggie Pogue Johnson. As critics have pointed out, dialect writing at the turn of the century was written primarily by men, as the genre was considered culturally inappropriate for women. (The stylistically divergent careers of married poets Paul Laurence Dunbar and Alice Dunbar-Nelson illustrate this point.) In this cultural milieu, Harper and Johnson chose to write and publish dialect poems, two of a small number of female dialect poets. Harper, in her "Aunt Chloe" poems in *Sketches of Southern Life,* and Johnson, in several poems about education, dealt explicitly with the process of literacy acquisition in their dialect poetry. Using a variety of the "plain language" I identify with Harte, Harper's Aunt Chloe broaches subjects that are explicitly political and topical. Johnson's poems in *Virginia Dreams,* modeled closely after Dunbar's, were written (as the subtitle tells us) "for the idle hour," linking dialect poetry with leisure.

My sixth chapter investigates the effects of handling a genre that is available to readers but not listeners. Although McKay's and Hughes's poems in *Songs of Jamaica* and *The Negro Mother and Other Dramatic Recitations* respectively may urge their readers to perform them aloud, the apparatus accompanying each is a silent text. In this chapter, I consider the excesses of both Walter Jekyll's notes to McKay's book and Hughes's notes to his own collection. I argue that Hughes's notes effectively become parallel poems themselves, sustaining narratives that are independent of the text to which they are attached. Jekyll's notes reflect his perspective that the poet and his literary dialect must be mediated, being not sufficiently literary on their own. McKay's poems, however, emphasize the continuities between literary dialect and poetic diction, and expose Jekyll's stumbling attempts to distinguish between two kinds of "purity": that of black speech as it represented in the book and that of standard English speech.

As Charles Bernstein writes, "One of the extraordinary things about the poetics of the ordinary is that it can make poems that look so strange."[44] In fact, Bruce Andrews uses the materials of Riley's dialect poetry to this end in his recent experimental sound poetry project, *White Dialect Poetry;* his "Libretto," for example, repeats the word "o'" for more than a page, creating blocks of text that work to defamiliarize the dialect word by isolating it from its potential linguistic structures and suddenly rendering it graphic. In addition, Andrews juxtaposes the spellings "adzac'ly," "adzackly," and "adzactly"—three ways of getting to the same sound.[45] (He even includes, in a part of this project titled *WhDiP, a sequence,* Riley's punning "ortographts," a word that makes an appearance at the start of this book's first chapter.) Andrews' project exploits the fact that dialect poets must negotiate their ways through their distinctive alterations. Because there is no standard lexicon or orthography of dialect writing, a writer must develop his own "mutilated" spelling, to cite James Weldon Johnson's description of literary dialect.

Rather than drawing the audience in, which is the illusion of the talky raconteur's "gather round" type of dialect poem Harte and Riley especially were known for writing, literary dialect strains the intimacy between the writer and his or her audience. The loss of intimacy is a direct result of an intense focus—of reader and writer—on an unusual printed text. In relation to the "typographically centered" lines of poetry designed "for physiological reading ease" by German poet Arno Holz, who asked "why the eye should *not* have its particular pleasures in the printed type of a poem," Frederick A. Kittler argues that "[t]he aesthetics of reception had become quite different circa 1900: instead of communication and its myth of two souls or consciousnesses, there are numerical relations between the materiality of writing and the physiology of the senses."[46] Dialect poetry, more than other literary genres at the turn of the century, made readers aware of this lack of transparency. Whether or not they share the writer's ethnic, gender, or class identities, readers need to puzzle out or translate the poem into standard written English from the poet's spelling, which is peculiar to him or her. The dialect poems discussed in this book present themselves as rhetorics of literacy, demanding from their readers a silent reading experience alongside the performance-based aural reception usually associated with the genre. Dialect poetry's paradox is in its concurrent simplicity and difficulty, its familiarity and strangeness, its ordinariness and literariness. The approaches taken by these poets illustrate how dialect poetry becomes a barometer of the shifting relationship between orality and literacy in late-nineteenth- and early-twentieth-century American literary culture.

chapter one

The Difficulty of Dialect Poetry

"Another book of Riley's"—
    And now, on every side,
The folks who aim at dialect
    Take up their pens with pride;
They ring in "ef" and "ruther,"
    And "thist," and "shucks" and "haint."
The frost is on their dialect—
    The spelling, though, is quaint.

"Another book of Riley's,"—
    They lift their joyous song,
In which they show that dialect
    Consists in spelling wrong.
They're writing now from Portland
    Clear back to Sandy Hook
An endless stream of "dialect"
    On Riley's "nuther book."

"Another book from Riley"—
    They wreck the alphabet
To twist us out some dialect
    That ne'er was spoken yet.
Here's to you, Mr. Riley,
    Your book's a welcome guest,
It's good to read your dialect
    And then skip all the rest.

    —W. D. Nesbit, "The Rhymes of Riley"

When the speaker of James Whitcomb Riley's "The Rossville Lectur' Course" says that humorist Robert Burdette is too "busy writin' ortographs" to perform as part of a small-town Chautauqua-style lecture series, it is no accident that Riley's invented dialect term lies visually between "autograph" and "orthography."[1] Refusing to resolve itself, Riley's dialect spelling pun illustrates how dialect poetry could assume a contradictory role in literary education: "bad spellings" exemplified the dangers the popular genre ostensibly posed to everyday speech, but these dangers were often outweighed by the valuable possibilities opened up by its orthographical experimentation in the mastery of both oratory and, ironically, literacy.

Usually associated with orality, dialect poetry in fact often both thematized and cultivated literacy, finding a distinct place for itself in the increasingly silent classroom. In other words, the public performance and declamation of dialect poetry (disseminated in a manner consistent with its nostalgic vision of a lost, primary orality) was exceedingly popular, but the silent reading of dialect poetry—a seeming oxymoron—encouraged a new and challenging kind of literacy. Riley and other popular dialect poets published in various print media. And, complicating the perceived opposition between literacy and orality, some dialect poets were also presented to audiences by the end of the century in new visual media and media of secondary orality. A silent film in which Riley appeared, to which I turn at the end of this chapter, even reproduced the dialect spellings of his writing on the screen in order to provoke a viewing experience that mimicked the book-reading experience, combining the visual "autograph" of Riley's appearance with his peculiar "orthography."

In conflating "autograph" with "orthography," Riley's dialect spelling in "The Rossville Lectur' Course" participated indirectly in the debates surrounding the organized spelling reform movements developing in late-nineteenth-century America. First published in 1886, Riley's poem appears coincidentally during the same year that the American Philological Association and the Philological Society of England together compiled a lengthy list of words whose spellings they proposed should be improved (for example, *above* should be written *abuv,* and *addle* should be written *adl*).[2] Six years later, in a *Harper's Magazine* essay titled "As to 'American Spelling,'" Brander Matthews is one of many luminaries contributing to the attack upon conventional spelling, arguing that "our spelling, so far from being immaculate at its best, is, at its best, hardly less absurd than the haphazard, rule-of-thumb, funnily phonetic spelling of Artemus Ward and of Josh Billings."[3] The dialect writer-performers Matthews mentions, Ward and Billings, became famous through "cacography," with spellings that are meant primarily to indicate illiteracy and *not* mispronunciation; each, as William Dean Howells writes, "appeals to the grotesqueness of misspelling to help out his fun."[4] In fact, however, their spellings sometimes correspond to those of spelling reformers in their faithfulness to spoken English; for example, the *Complete Works of Josh Billings* lists the titles of its chapters in a "Table ov Kontents," spelled in a way that would please many spelling reformers. Nevertheless, Matthews's intended point is clear: the established orthography and the language of dialect poets resemble each other in their irrationality.

H. L. Mencken, on the other hand, argues years later in *The American Language* that one of the major impediments to successful spelling reform is precisely the fact that the new phonetic spellings recall comic dialect writing, and therefore will not be taken seriously.[5] It seems that there was no consensus in the last decades of the nineteenth century and the first decades of the twentieth, at the time of dialect writing's greatest popularity, about what dialect spellings in fact were doing. Literary dialect incorporated both the phonetically significant (in representing nonstandard speech) and the phonetically insignificant (as in cacography, which I am including under the rubric of dialect poetry, and as in eye dialect), and it recalled both conventional and reformed orthographic systems while destroying the illusion of perfect correspondence suggested by either system. For that reason, Matthews may use literary dialect as a negative example in order to support his argument against conventional spelling, and Mencken may use it to show the pitfalls of spelling reform.[6] The strange spellings of dialect poetry allowed popular writers of the late nineteenth century to trouble the relationship between written and spoken American English, alternately reforming and reinforcing conventional orthography.

In either case, dialect writing was closely associated with its orthography, at least for the obvious reason that literary representations of speech formally consisted in distortions of conventional spelling. Walter Blair describes the late-nineteenth-century mania for dialect writing as a kind of classroom misbehavior: "It was an age, too, when schoolmarms and dictionary makers were stuffy and stern about spelling, elegant diction, and grammar; therefore, assaults on all three seemed both naughty and funny."[7] All three, admittedly, could be attacked in dialect poetry, but assaults upon orthography were the ones to which readers seemed most sensitive. For example, in an 1895 letter to the editors of *Dial* magazine given the title "The Craze for Wrong Spelling," a frustrated reader from Texas, William Wanless Anderson, complains about what he calls "newspaper poems of good quality, marred only by the fault of bad spelling, intentionally bad spelling," used to indicate "vulgar pronunciation." He is concerned principally with spelling and not syntax in dialect poetry; he finds that the latter is usually "from first to last . . . faultless." He claims:

> There is no conceivable temptation that can justify the use of orthoëpic, orthographic, or syntactical irregularities, unless it be a desire for picturesqueness—such, for instance, as is found in the Scottish dialect, or the dialect which Tennyson musically portrays. . . . The common American half-dialect which is found in most of these poems is altogether unpicturesque and unbeautiful. . . . Dialect poems are, of course, sometimes so good as to be still good, though defaced in this manner; as are some of the pieces of the well-meaning James Whitcomb Riley, at present the chief offender. . . .

Anderson ends his letter with the pronouncement that dialect poets "should respect the English language, not degrade and deface it."[8] His attitude, including the Anglophilia reflected in his description of American English as "unpicturesque and unbeautiful," is not far removed from the attitude that Blair alleges typified schoolmarms and dictionary makers in the late nineteenth century.

However, American spelling reformers, most notably Noah Webster, had already begun their "assault" upon a less-entrenched orthography by the late eighteenth century. Webster's efforts to change American spelling were founded upon the desire to make it conform to his idea of actual American speech. Many nineteenth-century philologists, Gavin Jones points out, saw spelling reform "as a form of democratic social work," an effort to increase mass literacy.[9] Like spelling reform, dialect poetry's attention to spelling betrays in some cases a certain reverence for it and for its potential, as phonetic dialect poems attempt (at least in theory) to uncomplicate the relationship between speech and writing, providing greater access and creating more potential readers. Moreover, stereotypical schoolmarms and dictionary makers were hardly attacked in or by dialect poems. The dialect poem in fact ironically performs the work of the schoolmarm: it promotes literacy. By "writing orthographies" as well as "writing autographs," popular dialect poets of the period stimulated the public's interest in bad spelling and thereby in spelling in general, standing for contradictory positions in the debate, at a time when concerns about spelling on both sides were gaining more public notice.

As good spelling was fast becoming the cornerstone of a solid education,[10] dialect poetry's spellings, even if potentially useful as an aid to literacy, were certainly imagined to be exerting a negative influence upon the informal speech of its audience. The catchiness essential to most dialect poems enabled their lines to lodge in the minds of listeners and readers, and these lines were easily integrated into American phraseology at large. An anonymous reviewer in the November 1871 issue of *The Galaxy* certainly suggests as much when he writes of Bret Harte's "Plain Language from Truthful James," "It is not too much to say that it has sensibly modified the colloquial speech of the day."[11] As if recalling an epidemic, one journalist remembers a time when Harte's poems were "in everybody's mouth, from the codfish shores of the Atlantic to the golden sands of the Pacific, from the rustic regions of the Northern Lakes to the alligator bayous of the Gulf of Mexico—so to speak. . . . [I]t seemed impossible for any man to address another without lugging in the grotesque phraseology of the Californian humorist."[12] The influence of Harte's poem was transnational and, for a time, seemed destined to be transhistorical. In 1900, T. Edgar Pemberton could write—in England—that, "in spite of the thirty years that have elapsed since his creation, the doings of Ah Sin and the sayings of Truthful James are still as familiar amongst us as household words."[13] And, as late as 1911, a journalist cited an English writer who claimed that, with the exception of Pope's "Essay on Man," "there is no poem in our native tongue that has added so great a number of distinctive phrases and epithets to our everyday speech."[14]

The language of dialect poetry could be heard everywhere, but it is also worth noting that it was printed everywhere. In 1871, only a year after they were published, Harte's poem and John Hay's "Little Breeches," another popular dialect poem, had "probably been printed a million of times. They are copied and gravely approved by English reviews of the first class. . . . They are pinned up on the walls of gin-shops, and carried furtively in the portemonnaies of Doctors of Divinity."[15] Not only did copies of the poems seem ubiquitous in print culture, crossing all boundaries of social class, the language of the most popular dialect poems—especially "Plain Language from Truthful James"—had printed lives outside of the poems themselves. Reporters used Truthful James's words as if they were their own, leading the reviewer cited above to claim that "[n]o poem of its length in the language has furnished such a store of quotations to the newspapers as Mr. Harte's ballad of 'Ah Sin.'"[16] One newspaper writer, in the same year that saw the explosion of printed iterations of Harte's and Hay's poems, prematurely declared the end of dialect poetry, perhaps eager to be rid of "the most fearful swarm of poetical dialecticians" that followed in Harte's wake. "No newspaper was complete without one," he writes, but, because "the thing was overdone to an extent which has made people awfully tired of it," the newspapers stopped printing it. To paraphrase Mark Twain, these early reports of the death of dialect poetry were greatly exaggerated, as the amateur attempts to reproduce Harte's and Hay's (and, later, Riley's, as the epigraph to this chapter illustrates) work proliferated. As these imitations suggest, not only did readers of dialect poetry learn to read the orthographies of their favorite dialect poets, they also learned to reproduce them, assimilating new scripts in the process.

The impact of literary dialect in general, especially because of its ubiquity, was felt to be an especially great danger to the speech of children as they were struggling toward an understanding of the mechanics of the English language.[17] The vulnerability of schoolchildren is addressed indirectly in an acerbic poem called "A Recipe for a Poem 'In Dialect,'" also briefly cited in this book's introduction. The writer worries insincerely that he might be a "fogy" because

> . . . I can't help recalling an earlier stage,
> When a Poet meant something beyond a Reporter,
> And his lines could be read to a sister or daughter;
> . . .
> And we all would have blushed, had we dreamed of the rules,
> Which are taught us to-day in our 'Dialect' schools.
> . . .
> Well! 'twere folly to row 'gainst a tide that has turned,
> And the lesson that's set us has got to be learned;
> But I'll make one more desperate pull to be free
> Ere I swallow the brood of that *"Heathen Chinee."* (emphasis in original)[18]

In light of this poem, it makes sense that newspaper writers would have picked up the language of popular dialect poems. If dialect poems themselves are nothing more than a form of reportage, those journalists who quote from poems such as "Plain Language from Truthful James" would perhaps find Harte's language surprisingly consistent with journalistic discourse, if a bit more colorful. But the pedagogical power of dialect poetry is even more significant here. Essentially comparing the reading of newspapers to a passively received education, the poet regrets that "the lesson" taught in the contemporary "'Dialect' schools" is unavoidable. For better or for worse, to be well versed in dialect poetry was now a necessary part of being an educated American.

Evidently, however, dialect poetry's supposedly unfortunate influence upon speech differed from its influence upon elocution. While literary dialect was believed to corrupt everyday speech, and to frustrate any attempts to standardize spelling in one way or another (as the opposing views of Mencken and Matthews demonstrate), it could actually improve oratorical skills. Late in the nineteenth century, the recitation movement shifted noticeably, becoming more democratic and entertainment-oriented and less instructive, with recitations of dialect poetry becoming increasingly common and contributing to this shift.[19] In addition, at the turn of the century, elocution was evolving into a less formal, less artificial art, and dialect suited efforts to sound more natural when reciting literature.

But, somehow, just as the production and recitation of dialect poetry was rising, it appears that reading aloud was generally waning. In the 1880 *Every-Day English: A Sequel to 'Words and their Uses,'* a compilation of articles originally published throughout the seventies, Richard Grant White complains that "[r]eading aloud seems almost gone out of fashion. . . . It is no longer really taught in schools, or it is taught in very few. A single generation has seen it pass away." One of the reasons for its decline in the home and in public, White argues, is the rise of silent reading.[20] This demise was perceived as especially disastrous for the appreciation of poetry. In a journal article from 1914, John Harrington Cox, an educator and early scholar of folksong, insisted that poetry "must be *heard*. The printed page is able to impress the thought and the form, but the melody and the cadence must be sounded, and these are the things which touch the emotion and enliven the imagery. Silent reading of poetry is artificial." As a solution to this unfortunate occurrence, he proposes that "[t]here should be a return to the oral presentation of verse. . . . At home, by the fireside, in the school, in public everywhere, let poetry be read as *verse*."[21] In other words, both private and public reading of poetry must, for Cox, in essence be public, as he rejects reading practices that mute and, therefore, interiorize poetry. Silent reading was having a profound effect upon reading practices at home, at social events and, perhaps most important, at school. Shirley Brice Heath writes:

> By the . . . early twentieth century in the United States, exercise books, written examinations, and standardized tests silenced classrooms. Learning to read and write one's mother tongue depended on written practice to reproduce standard language norms, which at the lower levels were isolable mechanical features of the language (e.g. spelling, subject-verb agreement, vocabulary development, etc.), and at the higher levels relied on predictable responses to literature. Once students learned basic ter-

minology surrounding the identification of authors, genres, and literary conventions, they moved on to write the essay, the dominant productive genre in classrooms. For the instruction and testing of such learning, silence became *de rigueur,* and evaluation of a student's knowledge depended exclusively on the written record.[22]

More than other genres of poetry, dialect poetry had the ability to keep alive the tradition of reading aloud in this new era of the silent classroom. Its burgeoning popularity supported a fundamentally nostalgic and conservative impulse. Despite dialect poetry's reputation as a possible impediment to the improvement of children's spelling and colloquial speech, it was considered a pedagogically valuable instrument for the disappearing art of recitation.

Because it was one of the genres of literature most suitable for the revival of elocution, dialect poetry was well positioned to promote an alternative literacy, one steeped in what Walter Ong would call a culture of "secondary orality." The period of 1918 to 1925, according to one study, may have "marked . . . an exaggerated and, in some cases, almost exclusive emphasis on silent reading procedures"—with the transformative year of 1922 coincidentally being "particularly productive of books that treated different phases of silent reading"—but dialect poetry continued to counter these forces by nudging readers toward a new kind of print-influenced orality.[23] In addition to silent reading, another significant change in reading instruction ushered in during the early twentieth century (although it was also tried and promoted by some educators earlier) was the intense emphasis on "whole word" reading, or what Lillian Gray called the "look-and-say excess," as opposed to phonics, which was popular at the turn of the century, or the alphabet method, "which was nearly universal in the United States until about 1870."[24] Although there have been vociferous advocates on both sides of this divide since the early nineteenth century, the general shift in the early twentieth century was toward whole-word reading. It is easy to see how the dialect poetry reading experience presents a challenge to this shift. In encouraging readers to sound out words, dialect poetry supported prevailing reading instruction methods when "rigorous phonic programs were the rule . . . from about 1880 to 1915."[25] However, by the end of Riley's career, when his poems were introduced most aggressively into the classroom, dialect poetry worked against the emerging whole-word instruction and required an approach based in phonics that we might call reactionary and nostalgic in light of contemporaneous pedagogical innovations.

Anthologizing Dialect Poetry

Far from offending the traditional schoolmarm, then, dialect poetry complemented her efforts and soon entered the textbooks. As a matter of fact, in 1905, the Indiana State Teacher's Association honored Riley with a program of lectures and performances in tribute to him, the transcripts of which were published. Riley Day, a local and then national school holiday, was observed by students through performances of both Riley's work and their own modeled after Riley's, a testament to the didactic quality of his verse, which I will discuss in greater depth in the next chapter. At the level of higher education, he was awarded several honorary degrees.[26] Elizabeth J. Van Allen writes in her biography of Riley that "[s]tudents in classrooms on the prairie and in the Ivy League read Riley poems," indicating the wide range of students to whom his poetry was taught.[27] Not surprisingly, Harte and Riley are well represented in poetry collections like 1935's *You Know These Lines!: A Bibliography of the Most Quoted Verses in American Poetry* as poets whose "lines you *do* remember" whether or not "you *should*."[28] Their poetry, in other words, may be memorable, but it is hardly worth memorizing; it is rote knowledge that somehow entices and creeps up on its readers. In this way, dialect poetry functions as an extreme subgenre of lyric poetry; as Jonathan Culler writes of the lyric, "poems seek to inscribe themselves in mechanical memory, *Gedächtnis,* ask to be learned by heart, taken in, introjected, or housed as bits of alterity that can be repeated, considered, treasured, or ironically cited."[29] Like the poetry itself, the personality of Riley in particular looms large and mesmerizes students in their classrooms. The classroom influence of Riley and Eugene Field, another "children's poet," is compared by Walter Barnes to a type of thrall and hero-worship: "[w]e have hypnotized school-children into admiration of them; we celebrate their birthdays, hang their pictures in our schoolrooms."[30] In addition to choosing children as the subject for his poetry, Riley actively courted schoolchildren as a significant segment of his reading audience.

However, the poetry by Riley that was read in the classroom was not a representative portion of his oeuvre. It was most often less dialectal than the best known of his verses; that is, the dialect used is relatively intelligible and not visually intrusive. In Tables 1 and 2, I refer to this quality as "readability," borrowing loosely from Edgar Dale and Jeanne S. Chall's definition of the term to mean "the sum total . . . of all those elements within a given piece of printed material that affects the success a group of readers have with it. The success is the extent to which they understand it,

TABLE 1
Selected Textbooks and Anthologies, 1889–1935

Title	James Whitcomb Riley Poems	Readability, Based Upon Dialect Spellings[1]
Open Sesame! Poetry and Prose for School-Days, Vol. 1, Arranged for Children from Four to Twelve Years Old (1889)	"Little Orphant Annie"	Low readability
Library of the World's Best Literature, Ancient and Modern, Vol. 31 (1897)	"Away"	Standard English
	"When She Comes Home"	Standard English
	"A Life Lesson"	Standard English
	"A Song"	Standard English
	"Nothin' to Say"	Low readability
	"Knee-Deep in June"	Low readability
Lights of Literature (1898)	"The King"	Standard English
	"Knee-Deep in June"	Low readability
Best Things from American Literature (1899)	"A Life Lesson"	Standard English
The Literature of All Nations and All Ages: History, Character and Incident (1900)	"A' Old Played-Out Song"	High readability
	"Beautiful Hands"	Standard English
The New McGuffey Fourth Reader (1901)	"A Song"	Standard English
The Heath Readers, Fifth Reader (1903)	"The Child"	Standard English
	"A Song of Autumn"	Standard English
Wheeler's Graded Readers, A Third Reader (1904)	"The Brook-Song"	Standard English
	"The Land of Thus-and-So"	Standard English
Classics Old and New: Third Reader (1906)	"A Simple Recipe"	Standard English
Poems By Grades, containing Poems Selected for Each Grade of the School Course, Poems for Each Month and Memory Gems, Vol. II, Grades 5, 6, 7, 8 (1907)	"The Name of Old Glory"	Standard English
The Art-Literature Readers, Book Four (1909)	"Child-Heart"	Standard English
	"The Brook Song"	Standard English
	"No Boy Knows"	Standard English
	"The Yellow-Bird"	Standard English
	"The Boy Patriot"	Standard English
	"The Circus-Day Parade"	Standard English
	"Pansies"	Standard English
	"On the Sunny Side"	Standard English
	"The South Wind and the Sun"	Standard English
	"Extremes"	Standard English
	"The Nine Little Goblins"	Standard English
	"The Prayer Perfect"	Standard English
	"God Bless Us Every One"	Standard English
	"A Life-Lesson"	Standard English
Elson Grammar School Reader, Book One (1911)	"The Name of Old Glory"	Standard English

TABLE 1 (*Continued*)
Selected Textbooks and Anthologies, 1889–1935

Title	James Whitcomb Riley Poems	Readability, Based Upon Dialect Spellings[1]
The Riverside Reader, First Reader (1911)	"A Sea-Song"	Standard English
The Riverside Reader, Fifth Reader (1912)	"The Circus-Day Parade"	Standard English
	"The Name of Old Glory"	Standard English
	"Out to Old Aunt Mary's"	Standard English[2]
	"A Song"	Standard English
	"A Sudden Shower"	Standard English
Studies in Reading (1912)	"Let Something Good Be Said"	Standard English
	"A Life Lesson"	Standard English
Howe Reader, Book Eight (1912)	"Who Bides His Time"	Standard English
The Metcalf-Call Readers, Fifth Reader (1912)	"The Treasure of the Wise Man"	Standard English
The Young and Field Literary Readers, Book Four (1914)	"The Circus-Day Parade"	Standard English
Readings from American Literature: A Textbook for Schools and Colleges (1915)	"When She Comes Home"	Standard English
	"The Raggedy Man"	Low readability
	"The Days Gone By"	Standard English
American Literary Readings (1917)	"Afterwhiles"	Standard English
	"The Raggedy Man"	Low readability
Wheeler's Graded Literary Readers with Interpretations, Sixth Reader (1919)	"Out to Old Aunt Mary's"	Standard English
	"The South Wind and the Sun"	Standard English
Poems for Youth (1925)	"Little Orphant Annie"	Low readability
	"When the Frost is on the Punkin"	High readability
An Hour of American Poetry (1929)	"A Man by the Name of Bolus"	High readability
	"The Old Man and Jim"	High readability
How to Read Aloud: A Guide to Interpretive Reading (1935)	"Out to Old Aunt Mary's"	Standard English
First Appearance in Print of Some Four Hundred Quotations (1935)	"A Life Lesson"	Standard English
	"An Old Sweetheart of Mine"	Standard English
You Know These Lines!: A Bibliography of the Most Quoted Verses in American Poetry (1935)	"A Life Lesson"	Standard English
	"Little Orphant Annie"	Low readability
	"An Old Sweetheart of Mine"	Standard English
	"The Old Swimmin'-Hole"	High readability
	"Out to Old Aunt Mary's"	Standard English
	"The Raggedy Man"	Low readability

[1] High readability = more than one of five words is a dialect spelling; Low readability = fewer than one of five words is a dialect spelling; Standard English = no dialect spellings.
[2] I have categorized this poem as "standard English," because its only dialect spellings are "'em" and "babtizin'," the latter left in quotation marks.

TABLE 2
Selected Elocution and Recitation Manuals, 1885-1903

Title	James Whitcomb Riley Poems	Readability, Based Upon Dialect Spellings[1]
Elocutionist's Annual (1885)	"Out to Old Aunt Mary's"	Standard English
Elocutionist's Annual (1888)	"The Elf Child" ("Little Orphant Annie")	Low readability
	"An Old Sweetheart of Mine"	Standard English
	"The Old Man and Jim"	High readability
Standard Comic Recitations (1888)	"Chairley Burke's in Town"	Low readability
Elocutionist's Annual (1889)	"The Land of Thus and So"	Standard English
Emma Dunning Banks's Original Recitations (1890)	"The Elf Child" ("Little Orphant Annie")	Low readability
Werner's Readings and Recitations, No. 2 (1890)	"Waitin' Fer the Cat to Die"	Low readability
	"So I Got to Thinkin' of Her"	High readability
	"Old-Fashioned Roses"	Low readability
	"My Fiddle"	High readability
	"Lost"	Standard English
	"A Canary at the Farm"	Low readability
Readings, Recitations, and Impersonations (1891)	"The Elf Child" ("Little Orphant Annie")	Low readability
	"At 'The Literary'"	Low readability
Ideal Series: Select Readings and Recitations for Christmas (1891)	"Last Christmas Was a Year Ago"	High readability
Ideal Series: Select Readings and Recitations (1891)	"The Unheard"	Standard English
Ideal Series: Select Readings and Recitations for Young People (1891)	"The Baby"	Standard English
	"Curv'ture of the Spine"	Low readability
Ideal Series: Select Readings and Recitations for All the Year Round (1892)	"A Feel in the Chris'mas-Air"	High readability
Standard Recitations (1893)	"Little Cousin Jaspar"	Low readability
Good Humor for Reading and Recitation (1893)	"A Fall-Crick View of the Earthquake"	Low readability
	"Who Santy Claus Wuz"	Low readability
Ideal Series: Select Readings and Recitations for Christmas (1894)	"Mr. Foley's Christmas"	Low readability
Ideal Series: Select Readings and Recitations (1894)	"Let Something Good Be Said"	Standard English
Werner's Readings and Recitations, No. 20 (1899)	"A Liz-Town Humorist"	Low readability
Werner's Readings and Recitations, No. 23 (1899)	"Iry and Billy and Jo"	Low readability
Taylor's Popular Recitations (1903)	"A Life Lesson"	Standard English
	"An Old Sweetheart of Mine"	Standard English
	"As My Uncle Ust to Say"	High readability
	"Jim"	Low readability
	"Kathleen Mavourneen"	Standard English
	"Old John Henry"	High readability
	"Our Two Opinions"	Low readability
	"When the Green Gits Back in the Trees"	High readability

[1] High readability = more than one of five words is a dialect spelling; Low readability = fewer than one of five words is a dialect spelling; Standard English = no dialect spellings.

read it at an optimum speed, and find it interesting."[31] Because I argue that the most unintelligible feature of dialect poetry, the feature inhibiting our ability to "read it at an optimum speed" and the feature to which most detractors of dialect poetry objected, is spelling and not, for example, syntax, I use the number of dialect spellings as my measure of readability.

In his *Golden Multitudes: The Story of Best Sellers in the United States,* Frank Luther Mott writes, "There was a time when 'The Old Swimmin'-Hole,' 'An Old Sweetheart of Mine,' and 'Little Orphant Annie' were memorized and recited by thousands," but Mott does not mention just who was memorizing these poems (children or adults, for example), or in what contexts (school or home or some other place).[32] "Little Orphant Annie," a "low readability" poem and arguably Riley's most famous, rarely appears in textbooks. Of the selected textbooks and anthologies I reviewed, only three include it, one being *You Know These Lines,* a book that is not for school-use and is not geared toward children. In the commonly taught Riverside and McGuffey readers, none of the Riley poems included are in dialect. The group of late-nineteenth- and early-twentieth-century textbooks listed in Table 1 gives his "standard English" poems disproportionate weight.

In Table 2, which lists selected late-nineteenth-century elocution manuals, many not explicitly for school-use (including volumes of *Standard Recitations,* the *Ideal Series,* and *The Elocutionist's Annual*), we find the situation reversed: dialect poems outnumber non-dialect poems dramatically, with twice as many "low readability" (17) as "high readability" (8) texts. That Riley is best known as a dialect poet is not apparent in the textbooks and anthologies, but is clear in the elocution manuals. Although part of this shift can be attributed to the decline in the popularity of dialect poetry, it also indicates that the classroom was not the place for "low readability" poems. To cite Lesley Wheeler, "the canon of elocution—the most famous and most admired poems for recitation—is remarkably different from the literary canon that survived recitation's ubiquity," and, although none of Riley's poetry has been canonized, the choices of the anthology- and textbook-makers cited in Table 1 reflect a desire to create a distinct "literary" canon of Riley's work.[33] As his example demonstrates, dialect poets were valued in the classroom—and the hints of local color provided by the suggestion of dialect were considered constructive and instructive—but only so much dialect orthography was allowed. In other words, even the pedagogically valuable aspects of dialect poetry were exploited only with reservations, and dialect poetry was a contradictory educational tool.

In addition to serving elaborate and complex educational goals, much of dialect poetry, as we will see in the coming chapters, takes as its subject the *process* of becoming literate in one way or another, whether that process is illustrated through dueling paratactic and hypotactic constructions, the misspellings of a spelling bee, or the products of child writing. The act of reading these poems in effect breaks down literacy in order to rebuild it in unorthodox ways; hearing them performed does not have this effect. The competent reader, as a result of the poem's disruption of literacy through bad spelling, is returned to a state of virtual semi-literacy. As Gavin Jones puts it, dialect "transferred the difficulties of subliteracy onto 'sophisticated' readers."[34]

Of course, the act of reading dialect writing differs greatly from the act of reading most other types of literature. Jones paraphrases William James's argument regarding the effects of spelling reform upon reading in *The Principles of Psychology* that "[t]o emphasize single phonemes rather than the ideographic wholeness of words would work directly against reading's psychological mechanisms"; as Jones points out, dialect writing works the same way, disturbing "the natural process of reading, making it seem difficult for people of supposed linguistic competence, slowing them down."[35] However, literary dialect does more than slow the reading process; it forces some degree of articulation, making what would be silent reading a performance. Michel de Certeau writes in *The Practice of Everyday Life* that reading

> is no longer accompanied, as it used to be, by the murmur of a vocal articulation nor by the movement of a muscular manducation. To read without uttering the words aloud or at least mumbling them is a 'modern' experience, unknown for millennia. In earlier times, the reader interiorized the text; he made his voice the body of the other; he was its actor.[36]

Reading dialect, however, can require "uttering the words aloud or at least mumbling them." Not quite the articulation of oral delivery, but a bit beyond the subvocalization associated with reading in general, dialect poetry's voicing resembles more closely the "sounding out" of a reader in the early stages of literacy. As de Certeau writes, "the schoolchild learns to read by a process that *parallels* his learning to decipher; learning to read is not a *result* of learning to decipher: *reading* meaning and *deciphering* letters correspond to two different activities, even if they intersect."[37] The person becoming literate performs how the acts of reading and decoding happen separately. In "sounding out" words, the child and the dialect reader are not reading but merely translating from one medium to another: first, encountering words visually, letter by letter; and second, producing a phonetic interpretation of the marks on the page. Regardless of the many non-phonetic features of literary dialect, dialect poets often insist that their work must be read aloud, making readers of dialect poetry involuntary actors, as de Certeau puts it.

Late-nineteenth-century readers were not approaching dialect poetry as an imitation of oral art, but as a new and experimental generic experience combining the resources of orality and literacy. As a result, the links between dialect poetry performances and the appearances of dialect poetry in print (in textbooks, anthologies, magazines, newspapers, and other media) are necessary to an understanding of the ways in which literary dialect functioned psychologically and culturally.[38] In reading dialect, the nostalgic experience—aside from that supplied by the thematic material of the literature—derives from the fact that readers were able to re-enact the experience of becoming literate through the phoneticization of literary dialect. This obtains to some degree even for children, having recently become literate. This developmental nostalgia, of the early childhood reading experience, works in tandem with the historical nostalgia many associate with dialect poetry.[39] In practice, then, the competent reader and the semi-literate reader would differ in their approaches to literary dialect, because literary dialect (especially child writing, which I will discuss later) encourages a return to an orality similar to Ong's secondary orality, to a new form dependent upon elements of both print and oral cultures, mixing spelling errors that don't indicate phonetic differences with spelling errors that have phonetic accuracy as their goal.

Marketing the Mass Poet

To be sure, performed dialect literature idealistically appears to direct its appeal to both semi-literate and highly literate readers, and to the working and leisure classes.[40] William Dean Howells argues that Riley's audience exceeds Longfellow's in size because his poetry "reaches the lettered as well as the unlettered" and excludes no group from his potential audience.[41] Most treatments of dialect poetry, however, have emphasized the "unlettered" as its most significant audience. For example, Paul H. Gray claims that popular poetry of the "poet-performer movement" from 1870 to 1930, a movement in which dialect poetry played a major part, was "aimed unerringly at the *petite bourgeoisie*—farmers, merchants, salesmen, and housewives—people who claimed they hated poetry but flocked by the thousands to hear these poets perform and then bought their books by the millions"; Gray calls the poetry "self-consciously and deliberately 'low-brow.'"[42] A letter found in the James Whitcomb Riley Collection at Indiana University's Lilly Library would appear to support this view, as the letter writer alerts Riley to the fact that, while shopping just before Christmas, not only did he witness "a little boy poring over one of yr books his face all aglow & smiling & he utterly oblivious to the crowd jostling about him," he also observed "an old farmer (in his native costume clad) look around over the store, fingering now this book and that, & after much consideration finally he selected a big family Bible and Riley's works."[43]

However, Martha Vicinus in her study of nineteenth-century British dialect literature perhaps unintentionally admits one of the central paradoxes of dialect writing when she writes that, although an "average reader" may find dialect literature appealing in its subject matter, he or she "might have had difficulty in deciphering the irregular spelling of dialect works."[44] Because Riley's themes revolve mainly around lower and lower middle-class life, many mistakenly assume that his reading audience consisted mainly of members of these classes. In a statement about nineteenth-century regionalist writing, a statement that just as easily could have been limited to dialect poetry specifically, Richard Brodhead argues that it "was *not* produced for the cultures it was written about, which were often nonliterate and always orally based."[45] Similarly, Alan Trachtenberg writes that, before Twain's *Adventures of Huckleberry Finn*, "dialect either appeared within a grammatical framework or otherwise made clear it was intended for a grammatically proper reader."[46] Rather than courting an illiterate or minimally literate reader or listener, as an understanding of dialect poetry as oral or inclusive would suggest, the dialect poem targets a highly literate reader.

The notion that dialect poetry's supposed orality was a sign of inclusivity is implicit in much late-nineteenth-century American dialect poetry, particularly poetry written in the Riley tradition. As Paul Laurence Dunbar writes in his poem "James Whitcomb Riley," Riley succeeds as a dialect poet because "he puts the food so good an' low / That the humblest one kin reach it." Riley's poetry is described by critics (and describes itself) as low-brow, just as Gray alleges, but Angela Sorby's perspective in a recent study of Riley differs: she claims that his poetry in fact satisfied the reading appetite of a disappearing "middlebrow" culture, giving as evidence his *Rubaiyat of Doc Sifers*, "a piece that both parodies Fitzgerald's

Rubaiyat of Omar Khayyam as 'hifalutin" and yet assumes a knowledge of the *Rubaiyat*'s literary conventions."⁴⁷

Interestingly enough, Riley's decision to include a reference to the *Rubaiyat* in his title led to an extended argument with his publishers. The *Century*'s William Carey (the *Rubaiyat of Doc Sifers* was published by the Appleton-Century Company) worried that the title would "hinder the sale of the book several thousand copies," as even he "had to go to the Dictionary to find out the meaning of Rubaiyat but there are others who will not go. . . . They will never get beyond the word they don't understand & they will not recommend a book whose title they cannot pronounce."⁴⁸ (It is curious that the impediments to pronunciation *within* the book posed no problem for Carey.) Riley, resistant to the "gloomy forecast" predicted by his publishers and to requests that he "manage to get in the home idea somewhere in that title in place of the Rubaiyat," claimed to better understand the cultural capital with which his readership approached his books.⁴⁹ "How can the title fail," he asked Carey, "when it is the poem's very self—its life-thread—surely—surely—I argue, you are most strongly mis-reading your audience and mine in this one instance."⁵⁰ A few months later, the publishers were apparently proved right, as sales of the book were weak relative to Riley's other ventures.

As a matter of fact, the pun of the character's name—Sifers/ciphers—points, I believe, to Riley's deliberate efforts to make his dialects difficult to "cipher," despite his statements to the contrary. On the one hand, he writes to a correspondent in 1890 of his dislike of Thomas Gray for his inversions—"isn't it more like Algebra? There is positive evidence that the poet '*ciphered it out*'!—and yet, on the other hand, the linguistic convolutions of Riley's own *Rubaiyat* led one critic to write that it was "written in a dialect that is calculated to loosen the back teeth of the man who tries to read it aloud."⁵¹ Doc Sifers even reads the natural world as if ciphering: "bark o' trees 's a' open book to Doc, and vines and moss / He read like writin'—with a look knowed ever' dot and cross."⁵² (The character's practice recalls Madison Cawein's advice to Riley a few years earlier, in 1892: "Why, my dear boy, don't you do as I have done? Hunt out some delightful country homestead in the very heart of wild and picturesque hills where you have rusticity spread open before you like a unique schoolbook, full of facts & information, to study and peruse!"⁵³) Even though Riley's attack upon Gray's poetry cited above continues with the aphoristic advice that "*Clearness* is poetry's first virtue. . . . Readers would *read*—not *conjecture—speculate*—grope and be left groping" (emphasis in original), we cannot legitimately call the dialects of Riley's *Rubaiyat* clear or easily accessible to all.

Before buying books by Harte, Riley, and Dunbar, readers of dialect poetry frequently encountered their writing in magazines that were clearly targeted toward high-brow audiences.[54] These three dialect poets published much of their work in elite magazines, such as the *Atlantic Monthly, Harper's,* and the *Century;*[55] and, in 1870, Harte was famously offered a prestigious contract to write for the *Atlantic Monthly* exclusively for one year. Even abroad, Harte was "known to every cultivated man in Europe," which included readers of the *Moscow Gazette* and the *Revue des deux Mondes.*[56] This is not to say that these writers published exclusively in elite magazines. They were published—and were reprinted—everywhere. Riley certainly had "low-brow" readers, and had, as Sorby notes, a "middle-brow following between 1877 and 1915 despite the shifting and shrinking of the 'genial middle ground' that had supported midcentury poets such as Longfellow and Whittier," but his reading audience necessarily consisted of many readers who were considered high-brow.[57]

The instability of the cultural status of Riley's poetry is telling. As Lawrence W. Levine points out in *Highbrow/Lowbrow,* the nineteenth century saw operas and Shakespeare's plays as both high and mass art.[58] The poetry of Longfellow occupied the same stratum mid-century, but Riley—who, in terms of popularity, could be called the Longfellow of his generation—found his position much more complex and confused than his predecessor's. As the last decades of the nineteenth century initiated a downturn in the cultural legitimacy of popular poetry, Longfellow's work gained status as Riley's lost it, and the middle stratum essentially disappeared. But that does not mean that the "high-brow" were not reading Riley. At a time when distinctions between classes of entertainment were becoming more clearly defined, the idealized experience of reading and hearing Riley's dialect poetry encourages an internally stratified movement from an imagined low-brow speaker to a high-brow reader with the Riley persona designated as a middle-brow mediator, a translator, an everyman.

The "shifting" mentioned by Sorby (and identified by Van Wyck Brooks) is more significant in this case than the "shrinking of the 'genial middle ground'": distinctions between Riley's audience and Longfellow's can be attributed to the beginnings of the effects of mass production upon the literary world. This is what effectively leads William Charvat to distinguish between Riley and Longfellow, calling the former a "mass poet" and the latter a "public poet." He excludes Riley and his fellow mass poets from his outline of American literary history because they are "not artists but manufacturers—impersonal producers of a commodity."⁵⁹ Even Riley's origin myth, as described to Hamlin Garland, would appear to present Riley as a manufacturer, beginning with his apprenticeship as a newspaper writer producing "reams and miles" of "free doggerel advertising, for our regular advertisers," as if writing poetry was factory work.⁶⁰ When he graduated to publishing what he viewed as more serious poetry in the newspaper, not versified advertisements, he "gathered them together in a little parchment volume" and, because of positive reader response, "printed a thousand copies—hired 'em done, of course, at my own expense.'" And, when Garland asked Riley if he sold them, he replied, "'They sold themselves. I had the ten-bushel box of 'em down in the "Journal" office.'"⁶¹ One wonders what Charvat would make of Riley's weighing of his books in bushels and of his conception of books not only as objects to be sold but as objects that autonomously sell themselves, like hotcakes.

That Riley conceived of and marketed his poetry—both serious and frivolous, both commercial and nominally divorced from commerce—as a product, and that his poetry was extremely and widely popular, does not mean, however, that it was truly intended for everyone. Although the "Hoosier Poet" image and persona was mass-marketed through the use of his likeness on cans of fruit, vegetables, juice, and coffee, his poetry defined itself by the exclusion of readers who were not competent to translate the orthography of his dialect writing, or not distant enough from the acquisition of literacy. As Van Allen writes, although Riley's characters were frequently semi- and illiterate, "the end product was usually geared for a very highly literate reading public," and his books, in fact, were "a sign of taste to be displayed in the parlor."⁶²

Performing Dialect Poetry

Despite the elaborate processes involved in reading dialect, the perception that literary dialect is purely and straightforwardly oral speech delivered by the unlettered to the unlettered is deep-seated, and the extreme popularity of dialect poetry performances in the late nineteenth century stems from this perception. Those who attended performances by Riley expected to find the characters in his verse come authentically to life, and in many cases they found them. In a special issue of *The Book News Monthly* dedicated to Riley, Henry Van Dyke engages in phrenological praise of Riley's plainness used as a tool to inhabit his characters:

Look at his head. Every outline of it is clear-cut, distinct, individual, and seems to say: "Whatever you are, be that." This is no figure in a masquerade, no fancy sketch of a twentieth-century troubadour, no grotesque imitation of a backwoods bard in a red flannel shirt or a barnyard balladist with a billowy beard. It is simply, "the gentleman from Indiana," just as he feels and as he is.[63]

Those who attended Riley's readings frequently remarked upon the "blankness" of the performer. One reviewer's description of him as feature-less suggests his ability to fall into character: "a plain-featured, boyish-looking young man with colorless hair. . . . His face, too, is a blank."[64] Hamlin Garland notes a similar impression in *Roadside Meetings;* he writes that Riley's "face remained as blank as the side of a china bowl."[65] Decades earlier, Garland interviewed Riley for *McClure's* and described his face as "the face of a great actor—in rest, grim and inscrutable; in action, full of the most elusive expressions, capable of humor and pathos."[66] Sorby, in addition, cites several spectators who claim that he seemed completely "in character" when he performed a poem. Just as easily, he would fall out of character; between poems, he seemed a blank slate. Mark Twain was one of many who praised him for his unique talent for transformative reading which, as Harold K. Bush argues, "coincided perfectly with the emergence of radical new developments in the theory of acting and performance" that emphasized "absorbing character" and not reading directly from the book.[67] Twain and others believed that Riley absorbed character better than almost any other poet of the period. That Riley, when not in character, displayed no obvious markers of being either low- or high-brow was a significant element of his reception, and he became an invisible middle-brow mediator between audience and character. Here I differ from Sorby's characterization of the power dynamics embedded in Riley's dialect poetry. She writes that "[i]n Riley's most popular performance pieces, power relationships are made fluid by the complete absence of sober, middle-class, standard-English-speaking white men and women."[68] I would argue that Riley *is* that middle-class, standard-English speaker; his presence in performance makes him a necessary component of his audience's reception of his poetry. His poetry allows him to be, as Shira Wolosky writes, "peculiarly, if not impersonal, then unindividuated."[69] Furthermore, his middle-class character and his blankness are strangely equated, just as whiteness and blankness are strangely equated, meeting to instill in Riley a kind of bilingual or even ambilingual authority.

Riley's face and body did not convey expression or even features when not engaged in a performance, but this invisibility notably did not apply to his mouth. Of course, as he became his dialect-speaking characters, listeners naturally focused on his lips. Garland, for example, in his *McClure's* article called Riley's mouth "his wonderful feature: wide, flexible, clean-cut. His lips are capable of the grimmest and the merriest lines. When he reads they pout like a child's, or draw down into a straight grim line like a New England deacon's, or close at one side, and uncover his white and even teeth at the other, in the sly smile of 'Benjamin F. Johnson,' the humble humorist and philosopher." But, even during the interview itself, Garland notes, "The most quaintly wise sentences fell from his lips . . . ; scraps of verse, poetic images, humorous assumptions of character, daring figures of speech—I gave up in despair of ever getting him down on paper."[70] Even when Riley is not in character, his mouth and—by extension—his seemingly oral nature fascinate and elude an audience increasingly steeped in print culture.

As an "oral" poet, it is no surprise that Riley should appear to "come alive" to his audience in performance. Perhaps, too, it is no surprise that his audience might claim to find it difficult to capture him in writing even outside of performance. But, paradoxically, Garland *also* says of Riley that he "spoke 'copy' all the time."[71] And, in fact, despite the fact that Garland regrets his inability to get Riley "down on paper," he describes those elusive gems escaping from Riley's lips as peculiarly material "scraps." In other words, Riley's bits of wisdom are already imagined to be in print as they leave his mouth. As much as his audience wanted to think of him as an oral poet, they could not avoid the fact that the orality associated with Riley was ultimately born in a world of print. It is as if Riley's audience, Garland included, could not resolve what they perceived as an incompatibility between orality and literacy.

Eventually, Riley stopped performing and, when asked why, he complained, "If you had ever gone about as a lyceum entertainer and been invited to the homes of local celebrities in small towns—and if you'd had to sit and listen to the small daughter of your hostess while she recited one of your poems in sing-song fashion . . . well, I say, if you'd been through what I have you wouldn't ask such a question.'"[72] Mabel Potter Daggett anecdotally recalled that Riley didn't "at all enjoy having Mary or Johnny trotted into the parlor in best clothes to recite 'Orphant Annie' to him," and that, when asked if he would participate in a street fair in his neighborhood, Riley allegedly said, "I'll do anything you want, if only you won't make a show of me."[73] He refused to perform, but offered an incarnation of himself on paper: a printed pamphlet of an occasional poem written for the fair, which sold for a dollar. As this anecdote illustrates, Riley was moving late in his career away from the oral representation of his work (by which he had made his reputation) and toward securing a place for his verse in print. It is as if the oral reproduction of his poetry by his own readers ultimately drove him further and further from performance.

Unlike Riley's, Harte's stage presence failed to impress audiences. A contemporary review of one of Harte's lectures reports that "[t]hose who had expected to see a physical illustration of an 'Argonaut' were most grievously disappointed."[74] C. Lewis Hind's *Authors and I* gives a humorous account of Harte's foppish appearance and its failure to meet his expectations, depicting a caricatured Harte, with "hair too artfully curled," as an "attractive dandy [who] fingered his ring and then glanced meditatively, and with approval, at his manicured finger nails." When Harte adjusted his waxed mustache with one of those manicured hands, Hind marveled at the unlikelihood of the fact that this "was the hand that had written of Miggles, and Stumpy, and Kentuck."[75] Walt Whitman, too, called Harte a "sharp, bright fellow, but entirely cut off from what he writes about by having cultivated foppishness and superiority."[76] In fact, Harte complained of his audience:

> They always seemed to have mentally confused me with one of my own characters. . . . I think, even now, that if I had been more herculean in proportions, with a red shirt and top boots, many of the audience would have felt a deeper thrill from my utterances and a deeper conviction that they had obtained the worth of their money.[77]

Although Riley, late in his career, also was a "man of marked neatness of dress and delicacy of manner," a "faultlessly attired gentleman . . . with a gold headed cane and often with a white carnation in his buttonhole," audiences were apparently enough satisfied with the transformative nature of his performances to accept his paradoxical attire.[78] Harte's performance of his dialects, on the other hand, failed to conform to audience expectations. Gary Scharnhorst mentions a reviewer from the *Toronto Mail* who describes Harte's "down-east accent, betraying 'peculiarities of diction that he did not pick up between Poker Flat and Lone Mountain.'"[79] Twain claims that Harte was such a bad reciter that, at one performance, he felt compelled to seize Harte's story and read it for him. Their styles differed greatly; while Twain was interested in dramatic flair and entertainment, Harte was concerned with what he perceived to be realism and avoided exaggeration.[80] Associating the audience's pleasure closely with the performer's ability (or willingness) to become the dialect speaker, Harte points in the lengthy quotation cited above to a crucial condition of dialect poetry's success. He was extremely well known in 1871 due to the publication of "Plain Language from Truthful James," but his popularity waned with his move to the East Coast.[81] His disgust with the ubiquity of "Plain Language from Truthful James" meant that, "[t]hough Harte occasionally read it at the conclusion of his lecture, he usually tried to avoid exploiting what he considered its cheap popularity."[82] At times, he would consent to audience demands, but his refusal or inability to temporarily fall into the role of the low-brow speaker with accuracy left audience members without a clearly defined high-brow role to play. His resistance to the implied contract of dialect poetry performance confused, frustrated, and disappointed audiences.

Even so, a few were moved by Harte's lectures and readings, and even Riley, a decade before publishing his first book, found himself influenced by Harte's performance style after hearing him read.[83] Dialect poetry performances in general were extremely popular entertainment in the late nineteenth and early twentieth centuries; not only did audiences flock to hear poets read their own work, but amateurs and actors attempted performances of dialect poems at picnics, benefits, school and church functions, socials, and other venues. Like the poets themselves, performers tried to become the speakers of the poems, and to recreate the situations of the poems accurately. *Riley Readings with Living Pictures* gives instructions for performing Riley's poetry, down to building a set and choosing the lighting, and, in the case of "The Raggedy Man," urges the performer to do "anything to make it lifelike."[84] Alice Dunbar-Nelson's introduction to *The Dunbar Speaker and Entertainer,* which includes several poems by Paul Laurence Dunbar, similarly encourages performers to "make it a part of yourself, put yourself in the place of the speaker whose words you are memorizing."[85] In other words, these performers were instructed to "absorb character," and to emulate performers such as Riley in reading style. More than anything else, it was important to give an authentic performance.[86]

As performances of dialect poetry were becoming more popular, much of middle- and upper-class American society in the late nineteenth century condemned theatricality as essentially duplicitous (as it involved adopting a persona) or even immoral. The differences between parlor recitations, school recitations, public performances by poets, and public performances by amateur and professional readers (as in the lyceum and Chautauqua) are subtle, and these types of performance vary in their theatricality. Some forms of performance were considered legitimate and beneficial, while others were corrupt. But these boundaries between acting and elocution, for example, were permeable and unstable.[87] Strangely, dialect readings, though they fall under the heading of "reading" and not "acting," complicate the duplicity of theater: not only did the poet adopt a persona, his persona was one that was decidedly *not* two-faced. Alison Byerly asserts that "the solo voice was preferable to an entire cast because it seemed to signify the presence of a stable, sincere self behind the theatrical roles."[88] However, the sincerity of the character portrayed, coupled with the implied "sincere self" behind him, conspire to create a listening experience for audiences that is in actuality more duplicitous than theater itself, despite the fact that it appears to be completely genuine. A variation on the "vicious circle [that] characterized . . . the genteel performance" described by Karen Halttunen, the sincerity of the dialect poet's recitation was so formulaically sincere that it ceased to be sincere.[89] And, when we consider the multiplicity of characters presented by the dialect poetry performer, we are left with a theatrical performance that lacks the grounding stability normally associated with the one-man show.

The practice of silent reading in this cultural context, however, reveals as much about the nature of dialect poetry as the history of the performance of Harte's and Riley's work. As popular as Riley was as a performer, books of his poetry also sold extremely well. People not only performed his poems publicly, they read them at home. As Mott writes, "the Bowen-Merrill illustrated editions [of Riley's poetry] were on half the parlor center-tables in the land."[90] William Dean Howells goes even further, effectively calling Riley's impact historically unprecedented in his claim that "[p]robably the most widely read American poems in their time were Longfellow's 'Hiawatha' and Whittier's 'Snow-Bound;' but Mr. Riley's poetry is much more widely read than either."[91] One minor poet and fan of Riley's recognized (and regretted) that his time on the stage prevented him from producing new poems for print. In a poem titled "An Open Letter to James Whitcomb Riley," Nellie Frances Milburn wrote:

> Each month I scan the magazines,
>   And look for rhymes by Riley.
> No other poet takes the place
>   Of him I prize so highly.

On birthdays, too, my friends, I know,
    Receive with stifled curses,
The substitutes that I must buy
    In lieu of Hoosier verses.

O! Leave the platform's noise and glare,
    And trav'ling's mad confusion;
Your native state bids you return,
    And seek your home's seclusion.

There fancies new will flock around,
    And beg you not to slight them,
Let other readers speak your lines,
    Ah! You alone can write them![92]

According to Milburn, Riley's unique contribution came through his published work rather than performance. Readers of periodicals were similarly clamoring for work by Harte. Just days after the first periodical publication of "Plain Language from Truthful James" in *The Overland Monthly,* Scharnhorst notes, the poem "had been reprinted in dozens of newspapers and magazines across the country, including the New York *Evening Post* and *Tribune, Boston Transcript, Providence Journal, Hartford Courant,* and *Saturday Evening Post* (twice)."[93] In fact, the entry for "Plain Language from Truthful James" in Scharnhorst's bibliography of Harte, listing all of the newspapers, magazines, ephemera, and anthologies in which it appears, goes on for nearly four pages. Clearly, the print (and reprint) history of the most famous dialect poems—particularly of Harte's "Plain Language from Truthful James" and Riley's "Little Orphant Annie"— is as noteworthy as the history of the oral circulation of dialect poetry. Although Harte's and Riley's poetry was performed and heard by many, it was likely read silently by many more.

Silent Reading and Silent Film

If we consider print to be a silent medium in turn-of-the-century American culture, we must acknowledge and account for the oddly silent presence of dialect poetry, however counterintuitive it may be to call a genre so closely associated with performance silent. In Riley's case, the silent and voiced lives of his verse were complicated by the poet's appearance in the relatively new silent medium of film. In 1918, Selig Polyscope Company produced a feature film adaptation of Riley's most famous poem, "Little Orphant Annie."[94] The material supplied by a 32-line poem was, understandably, a bit thin for a feature-length film. Using some details from Riley's "Where is Mary Alice Smith?," a prose piece about the "real" Annie, a narrative was built around the character, played by ingénue Colleen Moore, in which she was neglected and abused by her aunt and uncle (who appear in her mind as the "gobbl'uns" of the poem) and rescued by a local farmer (who appears in her mind as the typical knight in shining armor). Later in the film, the farmer tragically dies in battle, and his death is soon followed by Annie's, before it is all revealed to be "just a bad dream." *Variety* called the "excellent" film "a sweet but pathetic little story which has lost none of its human touches upon the screen." The elaborate fantasy scenes and realistic scenery are noted by the reviewer, who praises the "[e]xcellent photography with unusual lighting effects" and settings that "are all homely and picturesque."[95]

What is most intriguing about the film for my purposes, however, is Riley's role as narrator opening and closing the film—a structural framing device not mentioned in this brief *Variety* review. Riley is pictured, surrounded as per usual by a throng of children, reciting his poem. Because this is a silent film,[96] his silent performance is followed by intertitles, printing bits of the poem's narrative for viewers to read themselves. Although familiar phrases appear as intertitles, the adapted poem loses its verse form and becomes a prose narrative, even when Riley performs it for the children sitting around him. The poem as it was transformed by the filmmakers provides viewers with "repetition with variation," resulting in "the comfort of ritual combined with the piquancy of surprise," as Linda Hutcheon describes the pleasures of adaptation.[97] At the close of the film, the intertitles are replaced by a more traditional and familiar verbal medium: the book itself. As Kamilla Elliott finds in her analysis of intertitles and other words incorporated into early films, late silent films (1918–1926, the period during which *Little Orphant Annie* was produced) often "increased the use of legible texts" that "double as pictorial and textual objects inside filmed scenes," and the appearance of Riley's book in this film illustrates this trend.[98] As viewers, we flip through the pages of *The Orphant Annie Book,* reading in the theater what we might have read in our parlors.

So, what do viewers gain by Riley's unvoiced performance? What does his appearance add to the film? It's possible that Riley could have attracted audiences to the film, simply by his celebrity. As Timothy W. Galow writes, in his discussion of the celebrity of high modernist writers (whose books, I might add, coexisted with Riley's in the early-twentieth-century literary marketplace), "authorial personae functioned as an important site of knowledge production that could ultimately displace the texts upon which a writer's fame rested."[99] Although Riley's work was certainly very well known, his popularity as a celebrated figure may have even exceeded the popularity of his poetry. In an account of celebrity worship that sounds strikingly contemporary, a book called *In Lockerbie Street* (named for the street on which Riley lived) describes the attention Riley and his house received:

> More than fifteen years ago a poet went there to live. There fame and the tourists have followed him. Now the soft brooding quiet of the little green lane is broken by the blatant bawling of the sight-seeing autos that announce, "Ladies and gentlemen, this is Lockerbie Street and Riley's residence!"
>
> Yes, and once on a sultry summer's day as, on the front porch he refreshed himself with a cooling glass of innocent lemonade, the climax of dramatic interest was reached when the megaphone boomed hysterically, "Ladies and gentlemen, behold James Whitcomb Riley drinking a high ball!"
>
> . . . So he retreats from the front porch where he loves to linger, but where lately
>
>   The cam-e-ras
>   will catch him
>   if he don't watch out!
>
> . . . [T]hey are coming to Indianapolis to bring him the laurel wreath of their admiration. That it is done in the curious vandal American way, that would crown him and then carry away a piece of the crown as a souvenir, makes the tribute not the less real. Only the staring glare of publicity shines a trifle unpleasantly in eyes that have loved so well just starlight and sunlight falling in flickering shadows in Lockerbie Street.[100]

With a terrifying account of the anxiety and imprisonment brought on by Riley's national celebrity—"it's frightful to be forever on parade as a superhuman. It's like a man wearing a dress suit every day and not daring to bend for fear his smooth shiny shirt front might crack"—this writer clearly pities Riley for what she perceives as the misery of an unceasing spotlight, a theatrical stage from which he can never exit.[101] The threatening camera of the tourist, however, was later replaced by the apparently welcome film camera.

Given that audiences would not hear Riley perform his dialect in the film as they would have if attending a poetry reading, some must have gone to the movies simply to see a representation of Riley's body, to watch his movements and gestures—to see him act, in the early-twentieth-century film sense of the word. However, his performance style generally did not rely upon movement for expression. Instead, observers noted that Riley "depended entirely for emphasis on a rising or falling inflection, never raising the tone and seldom making a gesture."[102] Illustrations of Riley in performance printed in a book titled *Authors' Readings,* show a physically inexpressive performer, with subtle movements of his head and arms and with his eyes obscured by eyeglasses.[103] The film opens, after an intertitle asserting that the film is "Dedicated by the Poet to 'The Children of the Old Times and of These'—'With Changeless Love,'" with a shot of "the late James Whitcomb Riley" (he died before the film was released) sitting casually and almost motionlessly in a chair, gently petting a dog.

We might consider Riley's stillness in light of Walter Benjamin's distinction between the imagery of painting and that of film: "No sooner has [the spectator's] eye grasped a scene than it is already changed. It cannot be arrested. . . . The spectator's process of association in view of these images is indeed interrupted by their constant, sudden change. This constitutes the shock effect of film."[104] The portions of this film that focus on Riley, on the other hand, are marked by very slow movement, and in their lack of film tricks these scenes resemble theatrical performance and therefore do not clearly exemplify the loss of aura Benjamin associates with reproducible art forms such as film. (Of course, the Annie narrative at the heart of the film depends heavily upon special effects and sometimes frantic movement.) That Riley's person would be used to this end—to infuse the film nostalgically with some degree of aura—is no surprise. There is no "shock effect" here. The love Riley offers is "changeless" and the children he addresses are both modern and ancient.

The next shot shows a reciting Riley standing stiffly and formally (again, almost motionlessly), now accompanied by a version of the poem's actual dedication: "INSCRIBED—with all faith and affection—'To all the little children. The happy ones—The sober and the silent ones, the sad ones!—And all the lovely bad ones!'" Then, a scene shows "[t]he poet's afternoon at home," with a throng of children swarming up the exterior stairs of his celebrated home. This very image of Riley with his dog on his lap and surrounded by children dressed in frilly white outfits would have been familiar already to many viewers as it was recycled footage from a now-lost documentary filmed for Indiana's centennial and also circulated as a still photographic version by Lester C. Nagley, reproduced in

Figure 1. Illustration of James Whitcomb Riley by Art Young, from *Authors' Readings* (New York: Frederick A. Stokes Company, 1897). Harvard University Library, Widener Library

Figure 2. Illustration of James Whitcomb Riley by Art Young, from *Authors' Readings* (New York: Frederick A. Stokes Company, 1897). Harvard University Library, Widener Library

postcards, books, and other printed material, that Elizabeth Van Allen calls "the best-known photograph of the Hoosier poet."[105] To these children, he says, "I will tell you children the story of . . . ," and this introduction is followed by the aforementioned shot of *The Orphant Annie Book,* published by Bobbs-Merrill in 1908. Riley reappears at the end of the film, leaving the children who surround him with the following conclusion: "And that is the story of Little Orphant Annie. Some day I'll tell you how she grew up and lived happy ever after. Now run along and remember The Gobble-uns 'll git ye—Ef you don't watch out." The intertitles mimic the staggered appearance of the last line in the printed versions of the poem. After he waves goodbye to the group of departing children, the camera focuses again on *The Orphant Annie Book,* and closes it ceremoniously. These opening and closing scenes encourage viewers to see the filmic experience as a substitute for the book-reading experience, complete with inscription.

Dialect and the Phonograph

Considering that tens of thousands had visited Riley's body as it lay in state at the Indiana State Capitol, the posthumous presence of Riley's barely animated (and reanimated) body on screen could have given viewers from other parts of the country the opportunity to view the recently departed poet as a form of mourning, using "technical reproduction [to] put the copy of the original into situations which would be out of reach for the original itself," similar to the ceremonial listening to Robert Browning's phonographic recordings at the one-year anniversary of his death, which John M. Picker calls "an unprecedented form of poet worship."[106] While Riley on film gave audiences the silent physicality of the poet, or at least the illusion of his physical presence, Riley in phonographic recordings gave them the opposite: the poet as disembodied voice. These recordings, many of which are now available in the James Whitcomb Riley Recordings digital collection at the Indianapolis Marion County Public Library website, also brought him back into the parlor. Riley was pursued as a natural choice for preservation, not only because of his popularity, but also, I would argue, because of his associations with both orality and familiarity. As Jason Camlot writes, the phonograph was understood "as an apparent transcendence of the 'technology' of reading (as decipherment), leading to an experience that was even more immediate and intimate than that of the reader with his book."[107] Riley, having achieved a literary reputation that placed him closer in the public's perception to the medium of the phonograph than that of the book, would appear to be well suited for preservation as a voice.

A 1912 *Indianapolis Star* article, with the fascinating title of "Records Taken of Riley's Voice. Poet Consents After Years to Read Choice Poems for Talking Machine Company. Noted Writer of Verse Hears 'Proofs' of Selections with Manifest Interest," describes Riley's response—giving in after repeatedly turning down offers to have his voice recorded—to hearing "his own voice repeating his own poems from the proof plates of a talking machine" for a "new, unseen audience." Riley stood with "his hands thrust carelessly into his trousers pockets and an amused smile on his face. He was interested immensely and deeply impressed with the weirdness of hearing himself read."[108] The man who recorded him, Harry O. Sooy, later wrote an unpublished memoir recounting his experiences as a Victor Talking Machine Company employee. Finding an elderly Riley at his home, Sooy

> found it necessary, and did, make the records there in his home by having him recline in an easy chair. This was accomplished by having the recording machine movable, permitting me to place the recording horn very close to his face while in a reclining position. Mr. Riley's voice was, of course, very weak, so much so that I felt the records would not have commercial value, which proved to be quite true after I had returned and they were manufactured. . . .
>
> After some discussion by the Company over these finished records of Mr. Riley's, he was informed they did not have commercial value owing to their lack of volume. Mr. Riley then requested having me come out again to Indianapolis to try again, so I was instructed to make over the records in June. . . .
>
> . . . I am very sorry to say he was too ill to make a good record of his voice. Although a few of Mr. Riley's records appear in the Victor Catalog, they are not as good as we aim to have Victor products, but very few people understand just why they are not good; the foregoing is self-explanatory.[109]

Fewer than half of the recordings produced were actually issued by Victor Talking Machine Company. From the company's standpoint, having so few viable recordings after two attempts—and those "not as good" as hoped—would have to be considered a failure. The failure of Riley's recordings is especially disquieting if we consider that the phonographic recording generally was, to use Camlot's words, promoted "as a synecdoche for the entire person" and the recorded "voice as an alternative to bodily presence."[110] If the phonograph intended to serve as a depository of the "author's immediate, individualized presence," and Riley's poetry depended upon his particular "immediate, individualized presence" more than almost any other poet, then we would expect the recordings to be a runaway success.[111]

And, yet, despite Sooy's assessment, Theodore Dreiser recalls enjoying the recordings immensely in his *A Hoosier Holiday*, published the year Riley died. He writes, "Three recitations by James Whitcomb Riley, 'Little Orphant Annie,' 'The Raggedy Man' and 'My Grandfather Squeers,' captured my fancy so strongly that I spent several hours just listening to them over and over, they were so delightful."[112] How can we reconcile these two dramatically different impressions of the quality of the recordings? Perhaps what Sooy believed to be "weak" recordings were simply less theatrical and more natural than the recordings to which he was accustomed. Incidentally, the Victor encyclopedic discography includes several recitations of Riley's poems by people other than Riley, such as Harry E. Humphrey, who recorded several poems between 1913 and 1916. Although Riley's recordings are faint, they are much more natural and charming than Humphrey's—which are hammy and overly dramatic—and therefore more consistent with contemporary elocutionary trends. In an article titled "Poetry and Speech," Charles W. Hibbitt "recall[s] with pleasure" Riley's recording of "Little Orphant Annie," praising "its honesty of interpretation, its straightforward statement of a child's impressions, its humor and pathos."[113] Turn-of-the-century elocutionary trends valued this sort of natural delivery.

It is worth noting also that Riley's rustic and casual bemusement by the recording process—"his hands thrust carelessly into his trousers pockets," as described in the newspaper article above—may have been part of the show, as innovations in sound technologies would not have been alien to the elderly poet. In fact, Riley's letters to Joel Chandler Harris frequently address his use of his own Zon-o-phone. The two writers even shared their recordings with each other.[114] In addition, William Lyon Phelps, editor of Riley's letters, recalled a dinner in Riley's honor given by a Yale professor of experimental psychology by the ironic name of E. W. Scripture, whose research used "methods of natural science in studying the nature of verse."[115] Scripture "got out his phonograph, and Riley recited into it his famous poem, 'Old Fashioned Roses'"; later, Phelps writes, "we 'turned it on,' and it was a magnificent record."[116] Given that Scripture taught at Yale from 1892 to 1904, and Phelps notes that the dinner was in New Haven (Phelps was also a Yale professor during this time), this recording must have preceded Sooy's by several years. Moreover, Riley wrote an autobiographical poem titled *The Boys of the Old Glee Club,* in which the aging members of a glee club gather to listen to phonograph recordings of their young voices. Although the speaker affects the same bemused reaction that Riley does in the *Indianapolis Star* article, hearing the voices of the deceased club members is ultimately a comfort to him:

> . . . Brush had got the Boys to sing
> A song in that-there very thing
> Was on the table there to-day—
> Some kind o' *'phone,* you know.—But *say!*
> When John touched it off, and we
> Heerd it singin'—No-sir-ee!—
> *Not* the *machine* a-singin'—No,—
> Th' *Old Glee Club* o' long ago! . . .
> There was *Sabold's* voice again—
> 'N' *Ward's;*—and, sweet as summer-rain,
> With glad boy-laughture's trills and runs,
> *Ed. Thompson's* voice and *Tarkington's!* . . .
> And *ah,* to *hear* them, through the storm
> Of joy that swayed each listener's form—
> Seeming to call, with hail and cheer,
> From Heaven's high seas down to us here:—[117] (emphasis in original)

As Ivan Kreilkamp and John M. Picker have pointed out, many early listeners were disgusted and disturbed by the phonograph's ability to store the voices of dead loved ones. Picker cites Browning's sister, who called the posthumous playing of Browning's records an "indecent séance," and, as Kreilkamp puts it, citing an 1877 article, "To hear a voice speaking when the body from which it emerged has 'turned to dust' is wonderful but also 'startling,' eerie."[118] The separation of voice from body is not, however, disturbing for Riley. Rather than finding the preserved voices of the dead horrifying, or at least profoundly unsettling, Riley is quickly able to hear a reassuring humanity in the sounds emitted from the machine. What seemed at first to be "the *machine* a-singin'" is soon recognized unproblematically as the singing of his departed friends. It is as if his friends have "thrown" their voices down to earth, an ordinary act of ventriloquism with which a dialect poetry performer would be familiar.

In a review of *The Boys of the Old Glee Club*, *The Independent* asked rhetorically, "Should not this be noted as the first attempt to bring the phonograph into the range of poetry?"[119] However, much earlier in his career, Riley wrote a poem titled "The Phonograph," published in his hometown newspaper *The Hancock Democrat* but never collected in any of Riley's books. It is unlikely that a man alienated by the "weirdness" of sound recording would write a poem that playfully anthropomorphizes the phonograph with such warmth and familiarity:

> Grandmother Phonograph, oh she's a busy body—
> Gossiping and chattering and tattling all the while;
> Jolly as an office seeker o'er a glass of toddy,
> With a friend to listen, nod his head and smile.
>
> She knows a thing or two nobody else can tell you—
> She can quote from Shakespeare to Mary's Little Lamb;
> Perpetrate conundrums that will pick you up and sell you
> At a rate that indicates she doesn't care a—clam.
>
> Wonderful advantages she has of other women,
> Some of which are serious I'm sorry to relate—
> Give her crank a yank or two and here she comes a jimmin'
> Like a human organ-grinder in the hands of Fate.
>
> Got a metal palate and a metal tongue to match it,
> And a fund of epithet it's harrowing to hear—
> Let her get her back up, and I really wouldn't stretch it,
> On a sixty thousand dollar salary, once a year.
>
> Wait till she lifts her voice in Woman's rights orations,
> And stumps around the commonwealth in politician style,
> And I'll bet, not to disappoint her sex's inclinations,
> She'll accept the Presidential office after while.[120]

As what is essentially a versified editorial in response to a small-town exhibition of the "most marvelous invention known to science" (as it was called in the *Hancock Democrat*'s announcement of the event), "The Phonograph" encapsulates Riley's sense of wonder and fascination inspired by this object. In fact, the poem was introduced with the following editorial note, which suggests that the phonograph acted as his muse: "Our home poet, after lavishing four complimentary tickets on the affair, felt constrained to cock his prophetic eye upon the early future and grind out the following impromptu."[121] In describing Riley's compositional process as a "grinding," the editor points to an affinity between Riley himself and the phonograph, who is, as Riley calls her, a "human organ-grinder." The metaphor prefigures Twain's remarks in introducing Riley at an 1889 joint reading with Bill Nye, remarks quoted by Sorby to introduce her chapter on Riley: If Riley "enchants your spirit and touches your heart with the tender music of his voice," remember that "[i]t's not his music. . . . He only turns the crank."[122]

Riley imagines himself turning the crank, too, in "The Phonograph"—"Give her crank a yank or two"—and the implied violence of the action suggests that the relationship between Grandmother Phonograph and he who would turn her crank might be a kind of power struggle. Her unlimited and unpredictable power, evident in her ability to "[p]erpetrate conundrums that will pick you up and sell you" and her "fund of epithet it's harrowing to hear," resembles the frightening ambitions of a liberated woman who could eventually make her way to the White House. Comparing her to a "human organ-grinder," in addition to expressing a commonality between Riley and the phonograph, suggests a gruesome crushing of humanity (both body and sound) akin to that of a meat grinder; the proximity of "human" and "organ" permits a listener to hear the hyphen, alternatively, between those two words. When she "lifts her voice," is her voice her own? Is it a human voice? When she meets with a friend, "[g]ossiping and chattering and tattling," is she speaking, or has her body been evacuated so that other voices may step in and possess her? Is gossip—things heard from other people and passed on—itself a medium reminiscent of the phonograph, and therefore what we should expect to hear from a phonograph's mouth?

The tensions between the phonograph's opposing qualities—she seems human at times, but at other times seems simply an apparatus or medium in which human voices drown—again points us directly back to Riley's identity in performance. Grandmother Phonograph's shifting registers, as she goes from quoting Shakespeare to "Mary's Little Lamb," finds a parallel in Riley's movement from one dialect persona to another, and he even compares himself directly to a phonograph in an 1879 letter to a friend.[123] Camlot, citing an early promotional recording that assumed the voice of the Edison phonograph, remarks upon the "high elocutionary style [used] to perform the true voice of the phonograph," which purported to "serve as the transparent medium for the performance of other (say, less pure) voices and characters without losing its own identification with the clear and natural." "The speaker who can mimic a range of sounds and voices convincingly," Camlot writes, "may then underscore the underlying transparency of his own voice, just as the phonograph's voice was inherently clean."[124] In light of this, Riley's renowned blankness, discussed earlier in this chapter, reinforces his affiliation with the machine and its supposed neutral transparency.

Despite his awe, Riley ultimately was not intimidated or unsettled by this technology; if anything, he found a kinship between his voice and hers, even with her cyborg "metal palate and a metal tongue to match it." Later, in 1900, he still views the emerging sound technology through corporeal metaphors; away from home, he writes to the Holsteins (the family with whom he lived) to ask whether his Zon-o-phone's "bronchial trouble [is] clearing up in the milder summer weather."[125] Riley does not find any incompatibility between phonographic recording and his verse, contradicting Frederich A. Kittler's example of the poet Ernst von Wildenbruch, whose 1897 "For the Phonographic Recording of His Voice," composed and performed for the phonograph, demonstrates in its "poetaster rhymes" what Kittler calls "an embittered competition between poetry and technological media."[126] Riley's position also contrasts strongly with that of Twain, who said of the phonograph, "you can't write literature with it, because it hasn't any ideas & it hasn't any gift for elaboration, or smartness of talk, or vigor of action, or felicity of expression."[127] Despite the poem's sexism and anxiety, Riley's picture of an interactive, progressive, and energetic Grandmother Phonograph expresses his view that she has all of these qualities. His identification with her does not mechanize him as much as it humanizes her.

Furthermore, in Riley's "An Old Sweetheart of Mine," one of the poems recorded for the Victor catalog, the speaker yearns for his childhood sweetheart only to be interrupted mid-reverie by his wife, who, in a twist, turns out to be the "living presence" of that sweetheart, a phrase rendered newly ironic by its utterance by a phonographic voice. Unlike Browning's famously disappointing recording of "How They Brought the Good News from Ghent to Aix," which trails off into forgetfulness and "preserves not the transcendence of poetic genius but the humanity of memory's imperfection," Riley's recorded voice was received by many listeners as a perfected animation of a dormant and vital poetic voice inaccessible in print and finally released.[128] For instance, Riley inserts laughs into his readings of "On the Banks of Deer Crick" and "Tradin' Jim" in a seemingly natural and spontaneous manner, and these laughs are the peculiar signature of his "immediate, individual presence," or—to quote "The

Rossville Lectur' Course"—his "ortographt." It is not surprising that Dreiser should have found his performances so satisfying.

Exactly half of the Riley recordings available on the Indianapolis Marion County Public Library website are of pieces written in dialect, and they are performed in a way that is consistent with reports of Riley's live performances. They are, just as Camlot writes of dialect monologists Cal Stewart and Russell Hunting, done "in an unstudied manner that does not reveal the source of the speech to be letters on a page." As exemplified in the non-dialect performance of "An Object Lesson," Riley's recordings, like the "Cohen on the Telephone" recordings discussed in Camlot's essay, imply an audience and "often position the listener as eavesdropper . . . upon his one-sided conversations with people he does not understand (and who, of course, do not understand him)." In overhearing these phonographic performances, members of Riley's listening audience again—as they did in attending his live performances—establish themselves as ironic participants in this high cultural activity. As Camlot argues, "The recorded monologue . . . complicates the audience's position in relation to dialect, for in this in-between space the monologue is both objectified and received from a distance, and yet it is also potentially something performed by the audience itself," leaving the question of "whether they laughed at the ethnic characters or, in a more familiar (if not familial) way, laughed with them—or both."[129]

Riley's dialects did not foreground ethnicity or race, but the racial dimension is a significant factor in recordings of Paul Laurence Dunbar's poetry. However, recordings of Dunbar's poetry did not exaggerate dialect as one might expect if reading Dunbar in the context of minstrelsy. Although there are, to my knowledge, no recordings by Dunbar himself, it is nearly as instructive to consider the many early performances of his work recorded by actors. According to Tim Brooks, the earliest Dunbar recordings, by Reverend James A. Myers of the Fisk University Jubilee Singers, are performed "without excessive exaggeration"; the 1913 recordings by Edward Sterling Wright are "intelligent and sensitive readings, without a trace of mockery," with the dialect "pronounced when it serves the scene, restrained otherwise."[130] Unlike Riley's recordings, it is worth noting that recordings of Dunbar's poetry rarely invited audience laughter at the expense of the speakers and worked to distinguish themselves from the "coon song" recordings popular at the time with which the poems often were conflated.

Although Dunbar was a popular performer of his verse, his particular manipulations of dialect demonstrate a strong commitment to the printed word, as we will see in later chapters. Riley, too, placed his dialect verse in dialogue with textual media familiar to his readers, especially in the case of the relationship of his "child dialect" to educational reading material, as I address in the next chapter. Beyond the versions of the poet presented in printed media, however, the two additional Rileys produced in film and phonograph—technological media new to turn-of-the-century America—combined to offer his listeners and readers a multimedia poetic experience. Riley's presence in these modern media would seem to problematize his association with a provincial simplicity of a time gone by, but, ultimately finding a compatibility between the poet and these modern media, audiences felt reassured that films and phonographic recordings were simply new repositories in which to preserve Riley and the world he represented safely in the past.

chapter two

Plain and Peculiar Dialects
Bret Harte and James Whitcomb Riley

Just as the cultural and formal importance of dialect poetry as a genre has been largely dismissed, so has the importance of its most prominent practitioners. The dialect poetries of Bret Harte and James Whitcomb Riley have been ignored by recent genealogies of American literary history, despite the fact that Harte and Riley cast considerable literary shadows, with the writings of numerous canonical authors bearing traces of their influences.[1] A good deal of recent work in American literary and cultural studies has addressed the significance of dialect as a discrete and secondary characteristic of regionalist and local color writing, but I argue in this chapter that granting primacy to the formal details of Harte's and Riley's forgotten verse can shed new light on the relationship of issues of race and class to the linguistic experiments of written dialect. Harte, whose dialect is fairly "plain," and Riley, whose dialect is more "peculiar," develop two quantitatively and qualitatively different ways of representing nonstandard speech, each used to distinctly political ends: in the service of political satire in the case of Harte and in the service of childhood literacy acquisition in the case of Riley. In this chapter, I also return to the late nineteenth century's valorization of proper spelling, the implications of which Harte and Riley explore in their poems. Before turning to Riley's "peculiar language," I will examine the effects of the "plain language"—a dialect less extreme in its departure from written English—used by Harte in his most famous poem, a poem that alerts its readers to the apparent plainness of its language in its very title.

Because several traditions of dialect poetry are dependent upon illusions of authenticity and sincerity, writing a successfully ironic dialect poem would prove to be difficult, as Harte discovered. His intentions in writing "Plain Language from Truthful James" have been well documented: the poem means to attack white racism, not Chinese immigrants. As Gary Scharnhorst has pointed out, how the poem was received is a different matter. The poem's seeming transparency allows it to have, as a critic writing in 1957 notes, "little more meaning than a Rorschach blot."[2] Readers used the poem to support hatred as if it finally gave, in its catchy phrases, a citable and metrical vocabulary to the anti-immigration sentiment that was growing in the West. Contemporary newspaper articles frequently cited "Ah Sin" or "the Heathen Chinee" in otherwise straightforward news articles as both historical and exemplary rather than a fictive creation. If, as Gavin Jones claims, dialect writing "was more than a humorous gimmick: it *enabled* certain types of political criticism . . . by creating another level of discourse in which deep ethical convictions could be safely represented," why did the second "level of discourse" so often fail to register with Harte's readers?[3]

Jones points to Finley Peter Dunne's Mr. Dooley as an example of a character who uses dialect in his "plain, common-sense criticism of weighty political problems," but reading Mr. Dooley's dialect is a much more complex process than reading Harte's is.[4] The same is true of the dialect of William Dean Howells's Berthold Lindau in *A Hazard of New Fortunes,* which, as Henry B. Wonham points out, functions to "cloth[e] his revolutionary ideas in a ridiculous idiom"; it is a "masking device that allows Howells to import socialist thinking into the novel, while ensuring that Lindau's ideas remain linguistically marginalized."[5] In other words, Mr. Dooley's and Lindau's views may be "plain," but their language is not. Although dialect can be a fitting vehicle for satire, it depends upon the type of dialect used. The "plain language" sort typified by Harte's "Plain Language from Truthful James" was, simply put, too plain to serve the satire he intended. Harte's poem succumbed to misappropriation more readily than it would have had it been written in a "low-readability" dialect.

The overt political humor of "Plain Language from Truthful James," whether understood by its original readers in a blatantly racist or blatantly anti-racist manner, actually facilitated its circulation. Because Harte's poem achieved such fame and was quoted everywhere, it was, to use de Certeau's term, aggressively interiorized by its performers. In fact, distance from the actual local conditions that gave rise to the poem drew readers to the poem even more, as a 1911 article from the *Charlotte* (NC) *Daily Observer* argues. Initially ignored in California, "where it should have been at once understood and appreciated," the poem made its way to newspapers in the Eastern United States and England, where it was received warmly by readers who enjoyed it despite the fact that they "missed a little of the fun that those who lived nearer the scene of their action derived from it"; "thousands of people who knew nothing of possible difficulties which the growing power of the Chinaman might create in the labor markets of California, were talking of Ah Sin."[6] Readers "absorbed" the character of Truthful James, and this character's perspective was sometimes absorbed to such a degree that "Plain Language from Truthful James," incredibly, was cited on the floor of Congress as if it were empirical evidence of the menace posed by Chinese laborers.[7]

From "Plain Language from Truthful James," the mantra "We are ruined by Chinese cheap labor" became a battle cry for those who feared the "Yellow Peril."[8] It seems, as Scharnhorst and many others have argued, Harte's irony was missed. In the poem, Truthful James and Bill Nye challenge Ah Sin, whom James also calls "the heathen Chinee," to a game of euchre.[9] Because Ah Sin claims not to understand how the game is played, James and Nye consider him an easy target. James says that he regrets duping the innocent Ah Sin, but Nye shamelessly hides cards in his sleeves with the intent to cheat him. Ah Sin, however, does understand the game and attempts to one-up the card sharp by hiding jacks in his own sleeves. Upon discovering this deception, Nye becomes furious and violent. The fact that he is "ruined by Chinese cheap labor" appears to be the basis of the offense. Our "reporter" Truthful James understates the brutal nature of the one-sided assault: he says only that Nye "went for that heathen Chinee" and a vague "scene . . . ensued."

Voicing Harte's Truthful James and Ah Sin

"Plain Language from Truthful James" recounts a hate crime not unlike the attacks happening across the West at the time. Scharnhorst writes that "[w]hile Harte may have meant to satirize prejudice, his poem had the opposite effect," in fact inciting or at least legitimizing racial violence.[10] Scharnhorst does not, however, propose why or how this misunderstanding might have happened. I argue that Harte's speaker's seemingly plain-spoken style especially contributed to both the popularity and the straightforward misappropriation of his text. In the first stanza of the poem, Truthful James's indirect language belies his epithet:

> Which I wish to remark,
> And my language is plain,
> That for ways that are dark
> And for tricks that are vain,
> The heathen Chinee is peculiar,
> Which the same I would rise to explain.

His complaint about the "peculiar" Ah Sin, whose "dark" ways and linguistic deception stand in stark contrast to his own "plain language," is that Ah Sin's language is not completely transparent and fails to reflect Ah Sin's thoughts. However, James's own language is hardly transparent. The obscurity begins with the first word: "Which I wish to remark—" appears to begin the poem *in medias res*, unconnected grammatically to any other clause in the stanza. The last line of the stanza repeats the violation, with "[w]hich the same I would rise to explain" reading as an unnecessary addendum (in the first version published in the *Overland Monthly,* where Harte was an editor, this last line is isolated, forming its own distinct, though fragmented, sentence). This last line poses as linear expository writing—i.e., "I will explain this below"—but its structure ends up confusing rather than clarifying James's point. Most conspicuously, however, the recurrent "which" leaves the earthy James strangely ungrounded, and it may be the most unusual and unintelligible (and yet most copied) feature of his "dialect."

What is perhaps the most obscure definition of "which" included in the Oxford English Dictionary's entry gives a quotation from Harte's Truthful James ("His Answer to Her Letter") as an example of usage. Ironically listed under "Peculiar constructions," this "which" is defined as "[h]ence, in vulgar use, without any antecedent, as a mere connective or introductory particle." Although the introductory "which" poses as a uniquely Western dialect feature—and Harte suggests his dedication to spoken American dialect when he attributes the realization of the American short story in part to "the inchoate poetry that may be found even hidden in its slang"—it appears that Harte may have borrowed James's verbal tic from English literature.[11] John O. Rees traces Harte's use of the introductory "which" to Joe Gargery of Charles Dickens's *Great Expectations*. After Harte adopted the expression in "Dow's Flat," Rees writes, "'Which . . . '

was clearly on its way from conscious humility to Gilded Age ostentation, and three months later Harte's most famous speaker, the exuberant Truthful James from Table Mountain, went on to fix the term firmly in the American imagination of his time as a Western flourish."[12] In fact, years later, a line remarkably similar to Harte's surfaces in fellow Northern Californian Gertrude Stein's *Stanzas in Meditation.* Stanza 38 opens with the line, "Which I wish to say is this."

The accusation that he derived his style from Dickens dogged Harte from the early days of his career. Twain claims that "Bret Harte was by no means ashamed when he was praised as being a successful imitator of Dickens; he was proud of it. I heard him say, myself, that he thought he was the best imitator of Dickens in America."[13] Harte's dialect, too, was said to have been lifted from Dickens; Howells was one of many complaining of Harte's "cockney-syntaxed, Dickens-colored California."[14] Generally, Harte was considered a poor dialect writer and "a benchmark against which writers claimed greater dialectal authenticity."[15] In the preface to *The Hoosier School-Master: A Story of Backwoods Life in Indiana,* Edward Eggleston says of Harte's stories that "the absence of anything that can justly be called dialect in them mark them as rather forerunners than beginners of the prevailing school," and Twain, too, claims that "no man in heaven or earth had ever used [Harte's dialect] until Harte invented it."[16] Many others, however, defended the authenticity of Harte's Western literary dialect against these complaints. "Which," in particular, was defended as authentically Western American. In an article assessing Harte, Warren Cheney says that "'which' is perfectly good Pike."[17] Henry Childs Merwin calls the charge against "which" "ridiculous" in his biography of Harte, claiming that "[t]he use of 'which' is indeed now identified with the London cockney, but it may still be heard in the eastern counties of England, whence, no doubt, it was imported to this country."[18] Even as influential a scholar of literary dialect as George Philip Krapp, in his 1925 *The English Language in America,* claimed that Harte's "use of *which* as a kind of demonstrative or coordinating conjunction is supported by other local American use."[19]

Nevertheless, the charge is a grave one for a writer so closely associated with his literary dialect. That Harte's speakers would habitually use any constructions that are distinctly and identifiably non-Western is enough of a problem for his dialect, but that such a prominent construction—one that came to define the literary American West—could have direct English literary antecedents undermines the poetry's claims to dialectal honesty, transparency, or "plain language." "Which" made the poem strange for most readers, as J. C. Heywood suggests in his 1877 collection of essays, *How They Strike Me, These Authors:*

> At the time when it was written the peculiar use of the relative pronoun "which"—a rhetorical figure borrowed from the slang of the London cockneys—and other characteristics in the style of this piece, could be seen in a comic paper published in Australia. But it was novel enough to be uncommonly attractive to staid people on both continents, who habitually heard only conventional forms of speech, and whose spirits were less active than those of explorers, to whom innovation is the rule of life.[20]

For Heywood, it is not Ah Sin but Truthful James, in his use of "which," who is "peculiar."

In the end, Ah Sin wins—by cheating—"the game 'he did not understand.'" Like Truthful James, Ah Sin, by feigning incomprehension, pretends to lack sophistication and facility with the language. However, when he uses this presumed lack to his advantage in his scam, Ah Sin's linguistic abilities are exposed. Significantly, the internal quotation marks setting off "he did not understand" serve as scare quotes, primarily to highlight the irony of the statement, but also may indicate either a paraphrase of Ah Sin's speech or a quotation from Truthful James, who speaks the same line earlier in the poem. To have James enclose his own statement, from a previous line in the poem, with quotation marks would be unnatural and awkward; therefore, the former reading seems to me more plausible.

Here is a difference between the facsimile of the original manuscript and the version first published in the *Overland Monthly*. The original line is "In the game he did not understand"; the quotation marks are absent. If we understand the words as spoken by Ah Sin, Harte's change acknowledges Ah Sin as a voiced participant in the poem, not simply a device or symbol, but the words enter the poem stealthily. The quotation marks are misleading; because the subject of the phrase is in the third person and the action in the past tense, we know that he is not being quoted directly here. Moreover, it is odd that, in a dialect poem that emphasizes Ah Sin's foreignness until this point, literary dialect is not used to represent his indirect speech. Ah Sin's speech is the opposite of Truthful James's "plain language" dialect: rather than inscrutable language parading as plain, unadorned speech, Ah Sin's presumed indecipherability is revealed to be intelligible. In representing *the representation of* Ah Sin's speech in standard written English, Harte expresses his refusal to estrange Ah Sin, without actually having to represent his speech in one way or another; he leaves that job to James. Harte gives Ah Sin one line of hidden, indirect speech in an attempt to alienate the reader from Truthful James more strongly than from Ah Sin.

But the line's workings are more complex than this. Even if James does not quote himself here, he is the one paraphrasing Ah Sin. The line, reported by James, passes through his dialect. Regardless of this fact, James's quotation marks suggest more of a fidelity to Ah Sin's words than an unmarked paraphrase would. Ironically enough, there is no difficulty in understanding "he did not understand."

Ah Sin's apparent silence in "Plain Language from Truthful James" prompted a curious literary response, one of many poems responding to Harte's, that put Ah Sin in James's place.[21] In a poem likely falsely attributed to Harte, "Ah Sin's Reply to Truthful James" (published originally in the January 22, 1871 *Chicago Tribune*), Ah Sin turns the tables on James, calling his deception the "sinfulest."[22] In this poem, Ah Sin's cheating is all a misunderstanding: the wax on his nails that facilitated the cheating in Harte's version is here revealed to be shoemakers' wax, because Ah Sin was "'prenticed on shoes"; the cards up his sleeve "got there by mistake." Most noteworthy, however, is that Ah Sin's dialect resembles James's closely. Ah Sin even begins with James's introductory "which." Because the poem is an imitation of Harte's original, this resemblance makes sense, but it is striking in light of the fact that everything surrounding Harte's original (including the illustrations, which I will discuss later) conspires to give Ah Sin an exaggerated Chinese pidgin literary dialect. In addition to restoring Ah Sin's integrity, "Ah Sin's Reply to Truthful James" treats Ah Sin's speech in "plain language" style. The traces of James's dialect—such as that introductory "which"—cannot be eliminated in a poem imitating a "Truthful James" poem without tampering with the poem structurally.

"Ah Sin's Reply to Truthful James" succeeds in giving Ah Sin a voice for the first time, because Ah Sin doesn't speak directly in Harte's "Plain Language from Truthful James." Richard Brodhead's discussion of American regionalist writing is helpful in understanding the popularity of Truthful James's manner of speech and the relative silence of Ah Sin. He explains what is at stake in regionalist writers' decisions to represent white American speech instead of the speech of the ethnically diverse immigrants populating the United States at the time, as white readers were able to "substitut[e] less 'different' native ethnicities for the truly foreign ones of contemporary reality: crusty Yankee fishingfolk for southern Italians or Slavs, Appalachian hillbillies for Russian Jews and Chinese."[23] However, "Plain Language from Truthful James" is an interesting case: it presents a moment of contact between a character of a "less 'different' native ethnicit[y]" alongside a "truly foreign" character only to mute the latter. To have Ah Sin speak in a way that is too "dark" or too "plain," just as James cannot speak in a way that is too "plain" or too "dark," would render the poem's argument about linguistic and moral transparency less subtle or defuse the irony of the poem. For a notable example of a dialect poem in which a non-white character's lack of voice is glaring, we may look to Dunbar's "When Malindy Sings." In a response to Gayl Jones's reading of the poem, Gavin Jones writes:

> Gayl Jones criticizes Dunbar for never representing Malindy's voice, for never letting her speak her own story, yet the very point of the poem is that her voice inherently lies *beyond* the written medium. By emphasizing the resistance of black voices to literary representation in a dialect whose purpose it was to capture this very voice, Dunbar creates a massive irony that highlights dialect as an inadequate literary convention. "When Malindy Sings" has a self-destructive logic that undermines rather than confirms the dialect stereotype.[24]

Gavin Jones's defense of Dunbar's silencing of Malindy could be extended, if problematically, to Harte's treatment of Ah Sin's voice. Dunbar, a black poet silencing the singing voice of a black woman, does not parallel our case exactly here, in which a white poet silences the speaking voice of a Chinese man. Although Harte works deliberately to avoid presenting stereotypes of the immigrant Chinese voice, at least in this poem, to the point of not representing the voice directly at all, racial difference makes his case necessarily different from Dunbar's. On the phenomenon of white writers assuming the voices of non-white characters, Michael Toolan writes, in an essay on literary dialect in South African writing, "Intent on avoiding perpetuating the insult of appropriation, not wishing to be seen attempting to confer legitimacy or worth on speech (since they would reject, as another version of ideological domination, the very idea of 'conferring legitimacy'), these authors have maintained a kind of problematic silence with regard to the voices of ordinary black people."[25] Toolan's explanation of the suppression of black voices in J. M. Coetzee's writing can also explain why Harte's representations of Ah Sin's voice are as convoluted as they are. Harte's indirect quotation of Ah Sin, giving him a half-voice, can be understood as an attempt to avoid the Scylla of insulting representation that dialect poetry's audiences often expected and the Charybdis of censored silence.[26]

As easy or as difficult as Ah Sin's and Truthful James's speech may be to understand, their relationships to written language are a separate matter. Truthful James and Bill Nye are characters that draw significantly from orally based cultures. James's recurrent "which" makes his language resemble more closely the repetition of oral storytelling than it does the linear structures conventionally associated with written narrative. The "Truthful James" poems read as if transcribed speeches and conform to a rhetorical shape that is conventionally oral. However, if, as Walter Ong and others claim, one of the features characteristic of orality is its emphasis upon parataxis and one of literacy its emphasis upon hypotaxis, then it appears that James exaggerates elements from both oral and literate composition in his speech. James's "which," regardless of the fact that his use of it may refer to a true dialectal use in some varieties of British or Western American English, seems in the context of the poem to belong to hypotactic discourse. It is not, however, the start of a syntactically subordinate clause. As for Ah Sin, there is little indication in "Plain Language from Truthful James" that he is either literate or illiterate in English but, in another poem featuring Ah Sin, he is one of a group of men producing a sign—a warning to Truthful James and his partners—"with letters in some foreign tongue."[27] Ah Sin, presumably, is fully literate in at least one language, and James is at least familiar with the structures of written discourse.

"The Latest Chinese Outrage" is a poem in which Ah Sin does speak—he speaks, in addition, in "Free Silver at Angel's," which did not have the popular success of "Plain Language from Truthful James"[28]—and, when he does, his divergence from standard English is made prominent. Harte's mercenary attitude toward his writing career may account for his decision to have Ah Sin's voice conform to popular views of it. Similarly, although Truthful James's speech is represented in conventional orthography in "Plain Language from Truthful James," James's language is marked in later poems such as "Truthful James to the Editor" and "The Spelling Bee at Angel's" as dialect through misspelling. Why would Harte use conventional orthography to represent James's speech and quote Ah Sin's only indirectly in "Plain Language from Truthful James," a poem that takes as the subject of its satire the supposed deceit and inscrutability of foreigners? and why would this fact make the poem more palatable to those who would use it unironically?

The misreading of "Plain Language from Truthful James" was facilitated by the fact that the "plain language" dialect—in other words, dialect that *doesn't* make itself visually obtrusive—encourages readings of the poem's voice as authentic. Although it is true that Harte's message may not have been in such danger of being misunderstood had he not emphasized the supposed sincerity and simplicity of his speaker, measured against the duplicity of Ah Sin, "plain language" dialect poetry is always defined in part by the sincerity and simplicity of the speaker. If an audience understands a poem to present the dialect as a lens through which truth can be glimpsed (that being Truthful James's unadorned "plain language"), then the ideas expressed through that medium, regardless of the author's distancing ambitions, will be read uncomplicatedly as authentic and sincere. If, on the other hand, an audience approaches a poem's voice as an encrypted space—passed through an author's phoneticization to be analyzed by the reader—it becomes too essentially duplicitous to be very effectively used as straightforward propaganda. Truthful James's "plain language" dialect was adopted as propaganda because it was not enough of a dialect to work as satire. The process of reading "Plain Language from Truthful James" is unlike the typical dialect poetry reading process: the poem does not require that its reader revisit semi-literacy through phoneticization. Its potential difficulties are due to syntactical differences, which could put readers whose speech patterns are depicted therein at an advantage, and not spelling distortions, which put readers who are highly literate—regardless of speech—at an advantage. Unlike Riley's literary dialect, which depends upon spelling distortions, Harte's literary dialect in "Plain Language from Truthful James" depends upon syntax in order to represent nonstandard language, and consists of few words whose spellings need deciphering. On the surface, the language of the poem is very "plain."

One year after the poem's initial publication, a reviewer for the *London Spectator* remarked upon the poem's vulnerability to misreading. Calling the poem's use of satire "subdued" and "restrained," he writes that it fought against racist attitudes on one hand and provided support for them on the other, giving the anecdote of a politician who thanked Harte for his anti-immigration poem:

> Of course, if the story is true, the politician in question must have been somewhat thick-headed, for it would not be easy for a moderately intelligent man to avoid seeing that Mr. Bret Harte wished to delineate the Chinese simply as beating the Yankee at his own evil game. . . . Still, the blunder, or it may be the rumor of the blunder, points clearly to the most striking characteristic of the humor displayed in this ballad, and in one or two others of the same kind which are published side by side with it in the volume from which we take it,—the extreme reticence of

style,—a reticence which if expressed in less vernacular language would indicate the reserve of cultivated indifference,—with which the writer glosses over what he desires to say. Mr. Bret Harte's genius is chiefly, as we have said, great in pathos; but in "That Heathen Chinee" there is no pathos, only banter and scorn of the outwitted Americans who raise the cry against cheap labor.

It would be impossible, we think, to conceive a more impartial and carefully subdued narrative. It has the air almost of "quietism," so scrupulously does it refrain from using strong expressions, or rather even seek for weak ones when strong would be justified . . . [29]

This "extreme reticence of style," coupled with the image of a manicured Harte discussed in the previous chapter, evokes the impression of a Flaubertian author as described by Stephen Dedalus, paring his fingernails from an impersonal distance. Although the reviewer stops short of blaming Harte's use of "vernacular language" for the misreading, he implies that the same poem written in standard English would have expressed a "cultivated indifference" that would have made the satire impossible to miss. Harte's unfamiliar hybridization—mild dialect mingled with an "extreme reticence of style"—effectively renders the poem unreadable to some. Many readers would find dialect to be at odds with subtlety, and in Harte's poem the "strong expressions" one would expect from a dialect satire are missing.

In fact, the central act of violence against Ah Sin is related in a surprisingly mild manner; it is not made plain by the poem itself. As Scharnhorst points out, the illustrations to "Plain Language from Truthful James" by Sol Eytinge in the Osgood edition—the "only illustrated edition of the poem published with the author's sanction"—and by Joseph Hull in the unauthorized Western News Company edition expose the violence that is veiled in the poem.[30] Hull even summons up an unmentioned crowd to include in his illustrations "a barroom brawl where Ah Sin is tossed up into the air by a gang of drunken hooligans wielding liquor bottles (and somebody's boot) and shooting off a gun," essentially "suppl[ying his] own solution to the 'Chinese Problem': mob violence against Ah Sin."[31] When the Eytinge-illustrated edition was published, newspapers across the country, including the *Cincinnati Daily Gazette,* delighted in the fact that, after so many unauthorized and "hopelessly inane" illustrated editions, readers would finally see the characters as they should appear, "according to Mr. Harte's own suggestions; thus furnishing what may be accepted as authentic portraits . . . and veracious representations of the different acts."[32] Despite the fact that the illustrations depict more than the poem states outright, Eytinge's illustrations were deemed to be accurate depictions of the poem's narrative.

An ephemeral illustrated edition of the poem Scharnhorst does not discuss—one that veers even further from the Hull edition in its unsanctioned feel—is a pamphlet advertising Western railroad travel on the "Rock Island Route."[33] Just as Yopie Prins says of Browning's poetry in a railroad edition of his work, the Rock Island edition allowed Harte's poem to be "incorporated into the body—individual and collective—of American readers, who knew [him] 'by heart' not only by memorizing and reciting his verse at home and in school, but by association with the rhythms of train travel."[34] However, unlike the other kinds of reading mentioned by Prins, train reading prohibits recitation. The expression of this incorporation, which we might associate with the interiorization discussed by de Certeau ("he made his voice the body of the other"), becomes awkward and inappropriate in a public train car. Railroad editions of poetry like Browning's and Harte's are ideally designed for silent reading, lest you risk disturbing the passenger sleeping beside you. Moreover, it is worth noting here that the transcontinental railroad may have, in fact, been a factor in accelerating the triumph of silent reading in late-nineteenth-century America, since passengers were traveling long distances in relative comfort, giving them the opportunity to read, but only to themselves. In fact, Tom D. Kilton calls the railroad "a leading secondary contributor to the spread of reading and learning among the masses through its various roles as publisher, bookseller, and librarian," and the railroad's relationship to reading practices in the United States remains an understudied topic of research in literary studies.[35]

Although most of the illustrations to Harte's poem in the Rock Island edition are accompanied by captions that are derived from the poem indirectly, such as "The inference that Mr. A. S. was soft" and "The smile that was pensive and childlike," one of the illustrations also introduces, in its captions, the dialect that is strenuously avoided in the text proper. The caption on the page depicting the discovery of Ah Sin's treachery reads "Mr. A. S. holds much'ee jacks." The next page, which presents the final stanza of the poem and an illustration of a violent attack upon Ah Sin, carries the following caption: "The language that was plain." In the first caption, Ah Sin's exaggerated foreignness—epitomized by an invented dialect—emerges, not surprisingly, just at the moment when Bill Nye and James discover the proof of Ah Sin's cheating (the cards in his sleeves and the wax on his fingernails). The illustration accompanying the final stanza of the poem depicts even more violence, unlike in Eytinge and Hull's

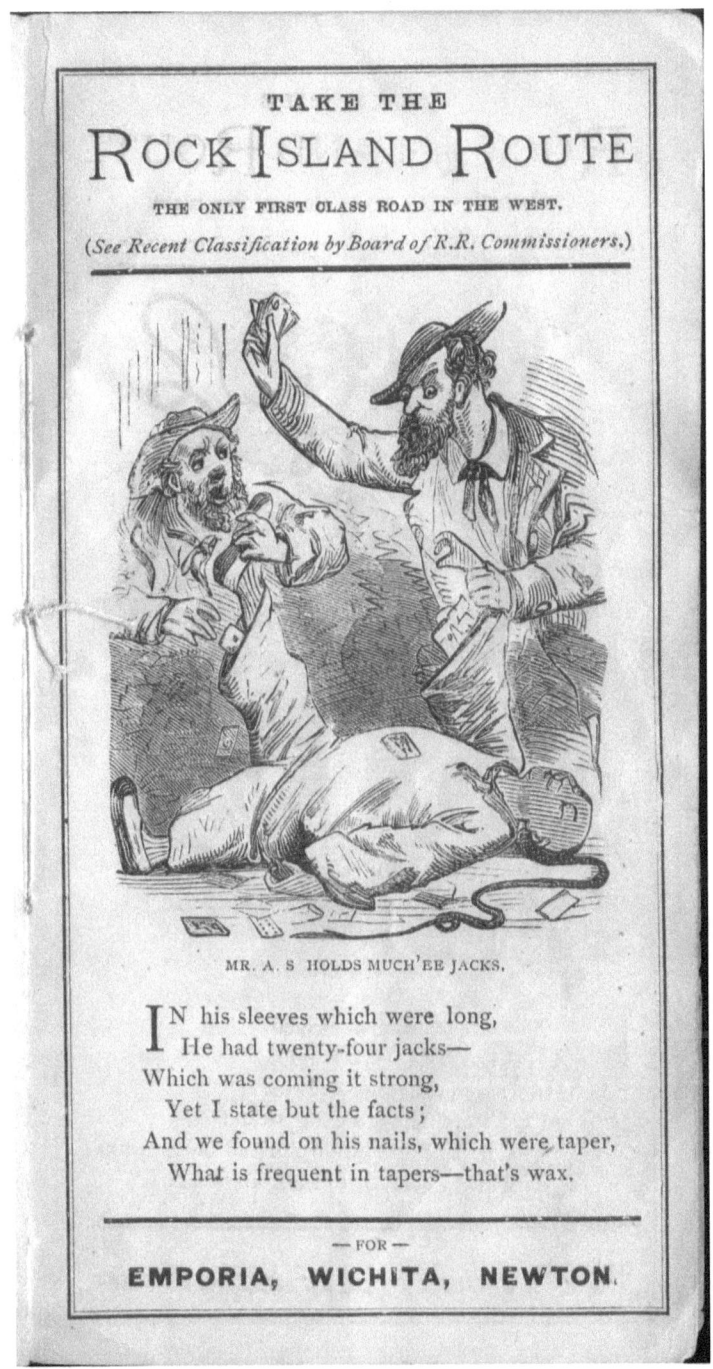

Figure 3. Illustration from Bret Harte's *Heathen Chinee* (Rock Island and Pacific Railroad, 1872). Albert and Shirley Small Special Collection Library, University of Virginia

Figure 4. Illustration from Bret Harte's *Heathen Chinee* (Rock Island and Pacific Railroad, 1872). Albert and Shirley Small Special Collection Library, University of Virginia

editions (where James stands alone, facing the reader), visually equating "The language that was plain"—"American" language—with a sort of basic and unrefined vigilante justice.

Harte's efforts to satirize white racism and to avoid putting Ah Sin's speech into literary dialect are especially undercut by this illustrator, and were easily defeated by the contexts in which Harte's work was published. Soon after the publication of "Plain Language from Truthful James," Ah Sin developed what became a firmly entrenched voice, used even in laundry advertisements, and it was not one of Bret Harte's making. Images of Ah Sin were made to conform to existing racist representations of the Chinese in popular culture, and "[c]heap reprints with caricatures of Ah Sin were vended on the streets of cities around the globe."[36] The fact that the poem was, in effect, popularly renamed "The Heathen Chinee"—even the official facsimile of the poem, published in 1871, adopts this title—illustrates the shift in the poem's message. The cultural moment into which Harte's poem was received had already determined that Ah Sin was a "pidgin dialect" character, despite the fact that Harte never gives him a full voice. Harte immediately became estranged from his universally adored creation.[37] Although a biographical sketch published in the *Overland Monthly* in 1902 claims that Harte "never would have succeeded as a 'space writer' on a newspaper; he was too conscientious and too scrupulous in his laborious composition," it is worth noting that the poem that made his reputation, published in the same periodical thirty years earlier, supposedly "was hastily written . . . to fill an unfinished column."[38] The poem "was always being altered and stippled up," but it was essentially written and published as ephemera, with a careless surviving typesetter's mistake and a collaborative composition history that includes contributions by the magazine's printer, proofreader, and a "literary friend," alongside Harte.[39] The fact that readers so often encountered dialect poetry as they went about their daily lives, outside of books and magazines but through ephemera such as an extended advertisement for a train line, must inform any examination of the publication and reception histories of dialect poetry.

Riley's Child Writing

Hamlin Garland called Riley the "poet of the plain American," but, unlike the plain language of Truthful James, the language of Riley's child-writing poetry is presented as Ah Sin's unspoken voice was: it is peculiar.[40] In calling Riley's child-writing poetry "peculiar," I also intend to reiterate Derek Attridge's reference in *Peculiar Language: Literature as Difference from the Renaissance to James Joyce* to William Wordsworth's use of the word in his Preface to *Lyrical Ballads* as a type of literary language that deviates from so-called ordinary language. By child writing, I do not mean representations of children's speech, although these are also part of his oeuvre.[41] An example of Riley's child writing can be found in a newspaper piece titled "Schoolboy Silhouettes—No. 1," in which the narrator is overcome by nostalgia when confronted by an old McGuffey's Reader and, more important, by the spelling mistakes of his childhood sweetheart in a letter contained therein:

> "My own true love, I seat myself to let you know I got your respected letter with much goy. I thought I would write you a few lines before I come to scool, so's I could get Annie to give you this before scool was took up. I herd pa say you was with those boys to Shivverree last nite at Mr. Joneses, and I node you wasent, so when he went to the store I cride. I also send those lines of poetry back as you sed. I think those lines is beautifull. Won't she be mad when Dan speaks those lines as you sed. I can have ma says a party when summer comes, and I want you to come to." [42]

Much of the language of "Schoolboy Silhouettes—No. 1" intended to represent spelling mistakes could, for a moment, be mistaken for the language of a dialect poem, representing nonstandard pronunciation. Similarly, part of Riley's "Lisping in Numbers" seems at first glance to be a phonetic dialect poem, but it is in fact an imitation of a child's written English. Implicit in this poem—and in the many others that rely on illiterate spellings for their effectiveness (or their "fun," as Howells puts it)—is the loaded suggestion that a child's apparent illiteracy and a nonstandard dialect speaker's English can be presented in the same written language. This is unsurprising, since much dialect writing, in its composition and reception, has allowed depictions of nonstandard speech to be confused with illiteracy. In order to suggest nonstandard speech, the writer deviates from written English, reinforcing the assumption that it represents only the standard prestige dialect. Like eye dialect, illiterate writing is often more accurate than standard orthography and demonstrates how illogical English orthography can be.[43] As Noah Webster argues, quoting Benjamin Franklin, "'those people spell best, who do not know how to spell;' that is, they spell as their ears dictate, without being guided by rules, and thus fall into a regular orthography."[44]

But Riley's speaker is not quite illiterate. Choosing a child on the cusp of literacy as his speaker, Riley performs the act or process of becoming literate in his poem. The language of "Lisping in Numbers" reflects the psychology of a speaker beginning to internalize the rules of literacy (which letters can go together, for example) and sometimes overcompensating and getting it wrong, as in "qute" for "cute." Unlike most literary dialect, child writing can record spelling errors that *don't* indicate a phonetic difference. These are "semi-literate" errors—errors produced in the acquiring of literacy—and a reader's understanding of the "joke" depends upon the reader's memory of that acquisition. The errors of child writing are usually phonetic simplifications. For example, in *Children's Creative Spelling*, Charles Read finds that "children represent syllables that consist of an unstressed vowel plus /l/ or /n/ with just L or N. . . . The similarity is not exact, in most such words there is usually no vowel in actual pronunciation, so that the children's spelling is simply phonetically accurate."[45] Children learning to read frequently expect our language to be more phonetically regular than it is, and they tend to reflect this regularity in their spelling.

The semi-literate child of "Lisping in Numbers" writes his own poem called "The Squirl and the Funy Litel Girl." Its language is remarkable in its resemblance to the languages of both dialect poetry and spelling reform:

A litel girl
Whose name wuz Perl
Went to the woods to play.
The day wuz brite,
An' her hart wuz lite
As she galy skiped a way.

A queer litel chatter,
A soft litel patter,
She herd in the top of a tree:
The surprizd litel Perl
Saw a qute litel squirl,
As cuning as cuning cud be.

She twisted her curl,
As she looked at the squirl,
An' playfully told it 'good day!'
She calld it 'Bunny'—
Wuzent that funy?
An' it noded an' bounded a way.[46]

Some of the alternative spellings here would please any spelling reformer. Although "brite" and "lite" call advertising language to mind, and many spelling reformers recommend against their adoption,[47] they do seem more phonetically accurate than "bright" and "light" as they are pronounced in modern-day American English. Moreover, the child writer's spellings of "calld" and "squirl" are consistent with Read's findings about simplification in children's spellings. Some of these phonetic misspellings essentially amount to eye dialect ("wuz," "hart," "herd," which represent standard pronunciations but are meant to visually suggest nonstandard ones), and have appeared in dialect writing as such. However, eye dialect in a dialect poem is phonetically insignificant; it does not succeed in representing nonstandard speech. Here, since the goal is to represent *writing* and not speech, what would be eye dialect elsewhere strangely becomes significant. The "dialect" of "The Squirl and the Funy Litel Girl," in the larger context of the dialect poem "Lisping in Numbers" in which it is embedded, exposes the traces of the vacillation between orality and literacy found in Riley's work. One critic, writing in 1937, inadvertently points to this vacillation. Praising what he sees as the oral basis of Riley's poetry, he criticizes, on the other hand, modern poets such as e. e. cummings for "the un-English appearance" of their writing. Cummings, he continues, "throws at the reader a series of 'unknown' words which must almost be taken into a laboratory to analyse," resulting in a poem that is "a puzzle to disentangle" and whose only virtue resides "in the cleverness of the typewriter keyboard." He seems unaware that his description of cummings's work applies to Riley's just as well, and that his praise of Riley's phonographic performance of "Little Orphant Annie"—"No one has ever read it so well as he, because he did not print on the page how it should be read"—only proves that Riley's poetry is as much of a "puzzle" as cummings's and does not offer up the secrets to its oral interpretation.[48] Although one would expect Riley to treat his poems as scripts for producing Hoosier dialect, there are elements in his work that resist this type of performance.

Issues of literacy emerge even more aggressively in certain inconsistencies. Rhyming "Bunny" with "funy," for example, seems implausible; "funy" would appear to rhyme with "puny," not "bunny." But Riley will not allow two rhyme words to be misspelled to the point of confusion. "Perl" and "squirl," both misspellings, rhyme in stanza two, but both also appear as rhyme words elsewhere in the poem, paired with words that are spelled correctly. Even more glaring is the presence of the apostrophe in this poem. Every use of the word "and" here ends with the omission of the "d" and the addition of an apostrophe, a spelling that suggests literacy. A speaker who pronounces the word as "an" would, of course, have no reason to mark the word as lacking something. Dale B. J. Randall writes of the "literate blunder[s]" found in other Riley poems supposedly written by semi-literate poets: "Benj. F. Johnson of Boone would never have written *whoopin'* nor *s'pose* unless he was far more wise in the ways of punctuation than his real-life counterparts."[49]

"Lisping in Numbers" deals directly with the writing process; many others of Riley's poems involve or take place in school, or describe scenes of reading and writing. These are typical subjects for children's literature of the period.[50] In his *A Child-World*, Riley writes of Almon Keefer:

> But the best
> Of Almon's virtues—leading all the rest—
> Was his great love of books, and skill as well
> In reading them aloud, and by the spell
> Thereof enthralling his mute listeners . . . [51]

And, in Riley's *Book of Joyous Children,* in a section of a series of poems titled "A Session with Uncle Sidney," Riley's child speaker extols similar virtues in "little Leslie-Janey," who is pictured writing at her desk in an accompanying illustration:

> Uncle Sidney's vurry proud
> Of little Leslie-Janey,
> 'Cause she's so smart, an' goes to school
> Clean 'way in Pennsylvany!
> She print' an' sent a postul-card
> To Uncle Sidney, telling
> How glad he'll be to hear that she
> "Toock the onners in Speling." [52]

The poem illustrates the relative importance placed upon spelling of all scholastic subjects. Unlike Leslie-Janey, Riley had some difficulty with spelling as a child, and the idea that his precise experiments with spelling as a dialect poet could have been motivated by this initial trouble with spelling is amusing to consider.[53] Of course, the irony of these lines is that the excellent speller Leslie-Janey makes several spelling errors in her postcard home. She leaves the "h" off of "honors"—an error to which I will return in my discussion of Dunbar—and even misspells "spelling." Like "The Squirl and the Little Girl" in "Lisping in Numbers," the line

'Toock the onners in Speling,' as it appears in a post-card, is not intended to reflect nonstandard speech but nonstandard writing. However, prefaced as it is by child dialect, the child writing begins to resemble that other sort of altered orthography.

A poem whose subject is on the cusp of literacy, as Leslie-Janey seems to be, invites its reader to put the maximum distance between himself or herself and the subject of the poem. However, Leslie-Janey says, inexplicably and comically, that she "[t]oock the onners in Speling." She has proven herself to be literate, but the poems' misspellings demonstrate that there is a "difference" between her literacy and our literacy. In the context of a poem that uses dialect spellings, the spellings in Leslie-Janey's post-card do not look all that out of place—just as the misspellings of "The Squirl and the Funy Litel Girl" did not look out of place in the context of "Lisping in Numbers"—and they trick readers into confusing her misspellings with Riley's. But what are the effects of this misspelling on readers who are only just becoming literate, as the likely target audience of *The Book of Joyous Children* would have been? Adult readers nostalgic for and charmed by creative misspelling would have no trouble identifying "onners," for example, as child writing and not dialect writing; a child, who may be encountering a version of his or her own failed attempt at writing, mingled with spelling errors he or she may recognize, would probably find reading these poems a very alienating and confusing experience.

A group of more conventional child-dialect poems (*not* child-writing) by Riley would have confronted adult readers of the *Century*'s December 1890 issue, in the "Bric-À-Brac" section of the magazine. These three pages, titled "Some Boys," included "The Raggedy Man" and "Our Hired Girl," two of his most well-known poems. He introduced the poems with the following statement:

> In presenting the child dialect upon an equal footing with the proper or more serious English, the conscientious author feels it neither his desire nor his province to offer excuse. Wholly simple and artless, nature's children oftentimes seem the more engaging for their very defects of speech and general deportment. We need worry very little for their futures, since the All-kind Mother has them in her keep. It is just and good to give the elegantly trained and educated child a welcome hearing. It is no less just and pleasant to admit his homely but wholesome-hearted little brother to our interest and love.[54]

The overly "elegantly trained and educated child" is only tolerated by him because it is "good"—not "pleasant"—to do so. The child whose speech and writing show "defects" is more interesting and endearing to Riley. Furthermore, he believes that his speech is more authentic, just as nonstandard dialects are believed to be more authentic than standard; Riley appears to understand the subcategory of child dialect through an application of recapitulation theory in his argument that "[t]o range back to the very Genesis of all speech, we can only rightly conjecture a dialectic tongue—a deduction as natural as that a babe must first lisp—the child babble—and the youth and man gradually educate away all preceding blemishes."[55] Apparently closer to the original source of language, the "uncultivated" child and the dialect speaker are less adulterated, and their defects and childhood lisps as represented in print are the visible marks of that purity.

Despite this clearly nostalgic perspective that seems to target adults, Riley's poetry was frequently marketed towards children. *The Riley Reader,* published in 1915 and described in its promotional materials as a collection of Riley's "choicest poems for children," also included "a program for observing Riley day and some model reading lessons based on poems in the book."[56] These announcements for the book were sent to school superintendents across the country, encouraging them to adopt the book, which was "suitable for use in the fourth and fifth grades." The publishers quickly ran out of examination copies; schools were apparently eager to include Riley's poetry in their curricula. In fact, an announcement for the Indiana School Journal Teachers Club (essentially an advertisement for Riley's *Homestead Edition Complete Works*) recommends the adoption of Riley's poetry as a solution to the teacher's difficulty "to secure material for school readings that is wholly applicable and healthy," and one teacher writes in response, "I know of no books more likely to leave a wholesome impression upon the minds and characters of teachers and pupils alike."[57] The Riley papers at Indiana University include letters from teachers and students, expressing admiration for and enthusiasm about Riley's presence in the classroom. Like Garland, one child praises Riley for using "plain language that every one can understand" rather than "'Flowery language' as most poets do." Another child, using misspellings reminiscent of Leslie-Janey's, tells Riley that his favorite of his poems is "the ragdiman" and that his "teacher rote poems on paper and told us to lurn them."[58]

In addition, Riley's poetry reached children in their homes. Just after Riley died, Harper and Brothers published a multi-volume set of his work, a set of "easy-to-read, comfortable sort of books that James Whitcomb Riley would have liked." *The Complete Works of James Whitcomb Riley* was apparently wholesome enough to be advertised in a magazine

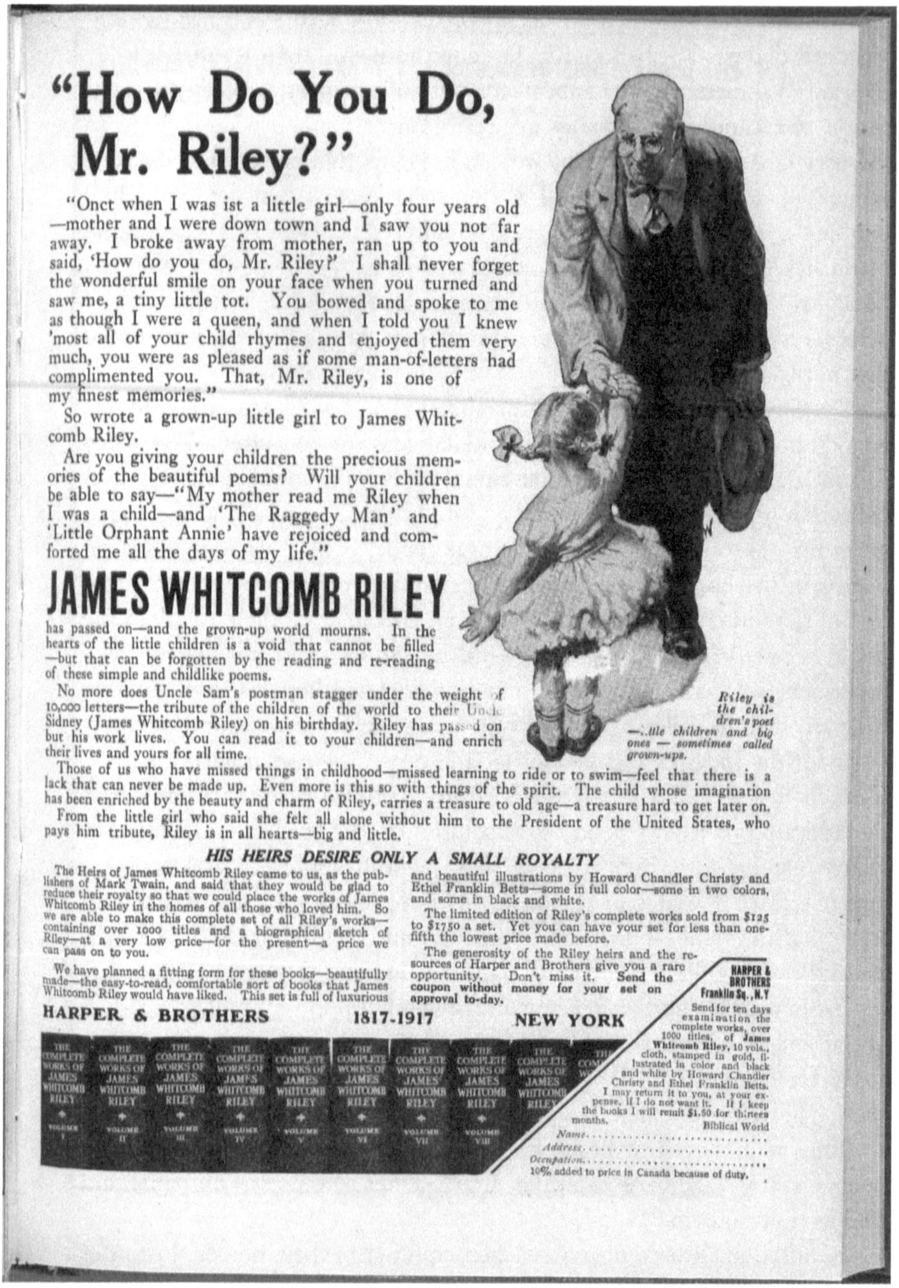

Figure 5. An advertisement for *The Complete Works of James Whitcomb Riley*, published in the December 1917 *Biblical World*. Harvard University Library, Widener Library

called *The Biblical World,* among others. In the advertisement, a little girl approaches the poet (whom she recognizes) to tell him that she knows "'most all of [his] child rhymes and enjoyed them very much," to which Riley responds "as if some man-of-letters had complimented" him. As an adult, she recalls the memory of this meeting in dialect fittingly modeled after Riley's—"Onct when I was ist a little girl." The woman's dialectal voice, however, is supplanted by the less charming voice of the adman, who points a finger at parents in an accusatory manner: "Are you giving your children the precious memories of the beautiful poems? Will your children be able to say—'My mother read me Riley when I was a child—and "The Raggedy Man" and "Little Orphant Annie" have rejoiced and comforted me all the days of my life.'" The message of the advertisement is that the failure to expose children to Riley at a young age is a "lack that can never be made up," like the inability to ride or swim; it does them a disservice because it is "a treasure hard to get later on." Luckily, unlike the bittersweet loss of childhood that comes with inevitable maturity, so perfectly expressed in the woman's memory that introduces this advertisement, Riley's loss eventually "can be forgotten by the reading and re-reading of these simple and childlike poems."

As early as 1889, *St. Nicholas* magazine was soliciting Riley for more verse for their Christmas issue ("Whatever special subject pleases you best is sure to be the one that will also please the boys and girls best"[59]). By 1894, Riley claimed *St. Nicholas* was "rebukeful over [his] long neglect of them."[60] In the interim, Riley had conceived of a distinct strategy for his child poems. Rather than publishing them in venues specifically for children, he approached their sibling magazine the *Century,* a magazine associated with cultivation, with the "elegantly trained and educated child" as opposed to his "homely but wholesome-hearted little brother." In 1890, Riley explained his plans to *Century* editor R. U. Johnson:

> I *believe* I've struck *a novelty in child literature,* and fear *Child Magazines* will erroneously interpret its effect on the juvenile mind—and mark this proof of *my* standpoint's undeniable truth, right here:—While I am aware of the rigid restrictions and responsibilities of the Editor's office, I feel certain that *my real* boy, if admitted to the literary realm, *with all his dialectic imperfections,* would in no wise *pervert* his more fortunate fellows; but, rather, *indirectly—wholesomely* and amusingly *instruct,* being at the same time in return, equally advanced and benefitted.-This theory's *truth,* again and again, I have *years* found *proved,* in public *audiences,* by *enthused parents* as well as children.—So, from

like evidences by steady mail, the most popular poem I have ever written—the most sought for in enduring form—is "Little Orphant Annie," with its awful, dire, and wholly lawless grammarless refrain of 'The Gobble-uns'll git you

>   Ef you
>   Don't
>   Watch
>   Out!

(emphasis in original)

Riley's pedagogical argument for his child dialect—that it would "instruct" rather than "pervert" cultivated children—he claims to find supported by his audiences of both adults and children, but he recognizes and anticipates resistance to his point of view. He frames his proposition to Johnson by admitting that he has "not had *dialect* encouraged by the juvenile magazines anyway" (emphasis in original) and asking if the *Century* would accept "a group of these little poems, which might be used, with some brief comment from the author."[61] When Johnson accepts the poems, Riley rejoices in the fact that "[n]ow *everybody* shall" (emphasis in original) love his child creations as much as he does, with the *Century*'s "sanctioning hand to lead the little rompers into full view of the public."[62]

Riley's uncertain place in magazines illustrates how his designation as a poet for children was constantly shifting, and how the boundaries between adult and child verse were increasingly gaining definition. Even among his "Hoosier Child Rhymes," E. L. Burlingame, editor of *Scribner's,* made distinctions between poems that "might seem to us too specially directed to children for our purpose," and "others, though of child-subjects, [that] are of wider appeal."[63] As a result of these shifting tectonic plates, much of his work fell between the cracks, as when *Century* editor Carey informed Riley in 1895 that the *St. Nicholas* editor "is afraid that 'A Homesick Memory' is too teary & adulty for St Nicholas & Mr Johnson feels it is too youthful for the Century."[64] Although Carey's response suggests a thematic basis for his distinction between child and adult poetry, Riley's letter to Johnson quoted above emphasizes the role dialect played in the children's magazines' reluctance to accept some of his poetry. It is precisely this dialect that Riley claims would educate his young readers, albeit "indirectly."

If we take on face value Riley's pedagogical goals for his peculiar writing as explained to R. U. Johnson in the quotation above, then Riley's elucidation of the differences between the "bad spellings" representing transcribed dialect and those representing illiterate writing also apparently has a pedagogical purpose:

> I've written dialect in two ways, first as a writer bringing to bear all the art he possesses to represent the way some *other* fellow *speaks* and second as a Hoosier farmer might *write*. Old Benjamin F. Johnson was supposed to have written the poems for the paper. They represent his way of writing, while the others are my interpretation of his speech. In either case it's the other fellow doin' it.[65] (emphasis in original)

By extension, according to Riley, child-writing poems should be considered in the same league as dialect poems like "Little Orphant Annie" and the "Some Boys" poems published in the *Century*. His statement reflects the inconsistencies in his own practice of literary dialect. On the one hand, he distinguishes between representations of speech and of writing ("I've written dialect in two ways"), but on the other hand he seems unaware of the fundamental differences between the modes ("In either case it's the other fellow doin' it"). Again, the assumption that dialect speaking and illiterate writing are somehow linked stems from certain practices of reading literary dialect as oral. Because standard written English does not correspond to the standard prestige dialect any more strongly than it does to nonstandard dialects, there's no reason why the way a "fellow *speaks*" should predict or determine the way he "might *write*." The two are unrelated, but the resemblance between "bad" writing and good transcriptions of "bad" speaking is so striking visually that the connection has become deeply entrenched. Riley's dialect has been attacked and defended by many in terms of its accuracy,[66] but, because Riley states his two goals as interrelated, even the phonetic dialect is loose enough to include non-phonetic elements.

As Donald M. Scott writes in an essay about the lecture system in mid- to late-nineteenth-century America, orality and literacy coexisted in forms that often present themselves as if exclusively oral or exclusively literate. Because most people attending lectures during this period were "both hearers and readers," with each role affecting the other, "it does not seem particularly useful to think in terms of oral *versus* printed media. Instead of construing print and orality as belonging to inherently separate social and cultural worlds, it might be more useful to approach them as different parts of an overall system of cultural expression, a system containing a variety of printed, oral, and visual genres."[67] Although the idea of dialect poetry as fundamentally oral clung to Harte's and Riley's dialects, the mingling of oral and literate modes in nineteenth-century American literary culture is evident in the misreading of Harte's attempt to ironize James's "plain language" as anything but plain, and in the confusion of representations of illiterate writing and representations of dialect by Riley himself and by his readers. The interplay of phonetic and nonphonetic elements in their work informs the reading process of silent dialect poetry readers, readers whose experiences with dialect poetry borrow from both orality and literacy.

The Spelling Bee Poem

In a May 17, 1905 newspaper article published in the *Bellingham* (WA) *Herald* titled "Ade's Literary map of Indiana," the journalist describes a speech delivered by George Ade in which Ade geographically divides Indiana, a state especially overrun by authors, by literary genre. "Go south and west of Indianapolis," he says, "and you will find the dialect poetry. Riley started it. Now no one seems able to head it off. Every man who can spell thinks he is an author."[68] Given the intricate and controlled manipulations of spelling found in Riley's child-writing experiments, as well as in other more conventional types of dialect poetry, it does make sense that Ade associates the ability to spell *correctly* with the ability to write a dialect poetry that defines itself through misspelling. Moreover, dialect poetry, like popular turn-of-the-century poetry generally, frequently addresses thematically the problem of correct spelling.[69] The obvious difference between dialect and non-dialect poetry that takes up the subject of spelling is, of course, that dialect poetry necessarily consists of misspelled words.

Harte's poem "The Spelling Bee at Angel's" belongs, as do the lines quoted above from Riley's "A Session with Uncle Sidney," to a subgenre of dialect poetry I call the Spelling Bee poem, one that demonstrates how literacy is problematized in dialect poetry. The "humor" in these Spelling Bee poems derives in part from the irony of the fact that a speaker whose language is recorded to suggest illiteracy could be the winner of a spelling bee. Harte's speaker (again, Truthful James) invites a group of schoolchildren to listen to his morbid tale of a bar-room spelling bee and its unrefined participants. One of these outlaws, Smith, proposes to the group a "new game . . . that ez far ez I can see / Beats euchre, poker and van-toon" and, after some initial resistance (one man insists that "the man who tackled euchre hed his education squar"), everyone joins in. Incongruously, a teacher is in the crowd, and, because he knows the rules, "high upon the bar itself the schoolmaster was raised." As the words become more difficult, the participants become more frustrated and aggressive. One of the words given even prompts a threat: "When 'phthisis' came they all sprang up, and vowed the man who rung / Another blamed Greek word on them be taken out and hung."[70]

As it turns out, strangely enough, the word "phthisis" was something of a lightning rod for spelling reform efforts.[71] On more than one occasion, Mark Twain (in "A Simplified Alphabet" and "Spelling and Pictures," at least) cites "phthisis" as a prime example of the problems with our orthography. In addition, this very word provokes the ire of spelling reformer Masticator B. Fellows in Owen Wister's *How Doth the Simple Spelling Bee*.[72] In this comic novel, Fellows stalks a professor and somehow sneaks a leaflet into his pancake breakfast asking, "Phthisis. How can you eat while a word like that is allowed?" As in "The Spelling Bee at Angel's," and in the poem by Loomis mentioned briefly in this book's introduction, the novel ends in violence over spelling. The national pride at stake in the argument over spelling is apparent in the ode of the Simplified Spelling committee assembled by Fellows:

> My spelling 'tis of thee,
> Sweet land of spelling-bee,
> Of thee I sing.
> Land of the pilgrims' pride,
> Land where my fathers dide.
> For spelling simplifide
> Let freedom ring.[73]

The ode's unmistakable message is that our current spelling is fundamentally unpatriotic. Poking fun at those spelling reformers who believe that social injustices could be resolved by simplifying written English, the satire reaches absurdity especially in changing the spellings of "died" and "simplified" to match their rhyme word "pride." Wister's Fellows embodies this sentiment: he urges his committee to "[r]emember the poor foreigners, remember the little children. It is for them that the English language exists; and for them we must, therefore, smooth our spelling's cruel path."[74]

Arguing to reform our language for the sake of foreigners and children was nothing new. Over a century earlier, in his *Dissertations on the English Language*, Webster asked,

> Would this alteration produce any inconvenience, any embarrassment or expense? By no means. On the other hand, it would lessen the trouble of writing, and much more, of learning the language; it would reduce

> the true pronunciation to a certainty; and while it would assist foreigners and our own children in acquiring the language, it would render the pronunciation uniform, in different parts of the country, and almost prevent the possibility of changes.[75]

Webster proposes here that not only would foreigners and children benefit from spelling reform, nonstandard English speakers would also learn "true pronunciation" (undoubtedly a dialect not dissimilar from Webster's). Moreover, one of the desired goals of Webster's reforms could be described as nostalgic, if not reactionary: to keep the language as it is and "prevent the possibility of changes." Unlike the Riley tradition of dialect poetry, Webster's ideal English language would need no preservation for future generations. While part of Riley's project was to use phonetic spelling to capture a disappearing language, Webster expresses in this passage his hopes that phonetic spelling would encourage American dialects to disappear without a trace and leave a strong centralized standard dialect in their place, one that would not and could not disappear.

In "The Spelling Bee at Angel's," phonetic spelling allows for a literate joke similar to the one from Riley's "The Rossville Lectur' Course." At the end of Harte's poem, James tells his audience that he is the winner and only survivor of a spelling bee that somehow turned violent, but then the dialect spelling in the poem continues, ironically, with the word "eddication." More of a malapropism than a dialect spelling—lying somewhere between education and edification—the word is a joke aimed over James's head, at his expense, and directed toward the reader. The moral connotations that "edification" brings to bear upon "education" are in keeping with the message of a poem that ends by insisting that children pray. Like Riley's "ortographt," Harte's "eddication" depends upon the visual effect of its hybridization to underscore the non-phonetic aspect of the poem's phonetic dialect; the visual joke is obscured in performance. Again, the poem targets a highly literate reader, and James's ignorance of the joke points to his semi-literacy. Truthful James's audience within the poem, too, is only semi-literate: he tells the children "from school . . . driftin' by" to "drop them books and first pot-hooks."[76]

During the fight that breaks out prompted by disagreements over the spelling bee, three-fingered Jack dies "with Webster on his chest and Worcester on his brain." In 1878, the year "The Spelling Bee at Angel's" was published in *Scribner's Monthly,* Noah Webster's was still the most popular dictionary, but J. E. Worcester's 1846 *Universal and Critical Dictionary* was also widely known. Many of the spelling changes Webster proposed in his original 1828 *An American Dictionary of the English Language* have been adopted in American English, such as the omission of the "k" in words like "publick" and "musick" and the "u" in words like "favour" and "honour." Worcester's dictionary and spellers were less revolutionary than Webster's in their approach, taking British English as the orthographical standard. The controversy surrounding the publication of Worcester's dictionary—in 1829, he was accused of plagiarizing from Webster—continued in the 1850s and 1860s through publishers of the then-deceased Webster.[77] Webster's certainly had greater cultural influence and, more often than not, was the authority used for spelling bees. In an essay on the history of the spelling bee, Allen Walker Read cites a nineteenth-century anecdote as evidence: "The schoolmaster . . . remark[s] that he . . . shall give out nothing that is not in the spelling book." In a footnote to this quotation, Read claims that "[t]his proviso throws light on the hold that Webster's spelling-book had on the public mind."[78] What is perhaps the most famous spelling-bee scene in American literature also features Webster's spelling-book. In Edward Eggleston's *The Hoosier School-Master,* the dialect-speaking teacher declares that he "put[s] the spellin'-book prepared by the great Daniel Webster alongside the Bible."[79]

However, as the quotation from *Dissertations* above reveals, Webster had more in mind than the improvement and consistency of written English; he wanted the standardization of writing to encourage the standardization of speaking. Webster writes, "Nothing can be so disagreeable as that drawling, whining cant that distinguishes a certain class of people; and too much pains cannot be taken to reform the practice. Great efforts should be made by teachers of schools, to make their pupils open the teeth, and give a full clear sound to every syllable."[80] And although, nearly a century later, Worcester allows for pronunciation differences in his 1879 *A Pronouncing Spelling-Book of the English Language* between American and British speakers, he too gives strict pronunciation rules together with his spelling rules that seem designed to privilege certain regional and class differences while vilifying others: "Sound the *r* clearly. Say *jar,* not *jah; charm,* not *chahm.* Do not pronounce *aw* as if ending in *r.* Say *jaw,* not *jawr.*"[81] In their discussion of literacy instruction in nineteenth-century North American schools, Suzanne de Castell and Allan Luke point out that "'provincial' speech codes were frowned upon as evidence of rudeness or ignorance; textbooks of this period advised students to cultivate the friendship of children of higher station, so that they might assimilate more cultured and aristocratic speech habits."[82] The fact that three-fingered Jack's last thoughts are of these two most significant forces for standardization—not only of American writing but, less overtly, of American speech—is a humorous moment but also a disturbing one. Although the spelling bee itself ignites a general riotous and rebellious refusal to give in to Webster and Worcester, questioning the validity of words like "phthisis," three-fingered Jack cannot in the end free himself of a rule-bound and prescriptive approach to written and spoken language.

The value placed upon proper spelling obscured the secondary goal of standardizing pronunciation and creating a narrowly defined and uniquely American language. In this light, the nineteenth-century devotion to the spelling bee, reflected in the dialect literature, is about more than simply spelling for spelling's sake. It is important to remember how crucial spelling was as a scholastic subject during this period.[83] We see this clearly in literary depictions of Midwestern towns and villages. Eggleston's narrator claims, condescendingly, that "[t]here is one branch diligently taught in a backwoods school. The public mind seems impressed with the difficulties of English orthography, and there is a solemn conviction that the chief end of man is to learn to spell." The same schoolteacher who states that he would put Webster's speller alongside the Bible also comically declares that "[s]pelling is the corner-stone, the grand, underlying subterfuge, of a good eddication."[84] Not only does Harte's blended "eddication" reappear here, but Eggleston humorously uses the word "subterfuge" to mean something like substructure while conveying something like its opposite.

In an 1876 article addressing the introduction of the spelling bee to England, an anonymous writer jokingly suggests that a spelling bee participant who misses a long word may not be familiar enough with small-town newspapers and their excessive use of "spelling-bee" words: "we shall expect soon to hear that an 'orthographical conglomeration' has been held in some provincial town." With short and familiar words, on the other hand, dialectal differences can become an issue, and some people stumble when they spell words phonetically; the writer complains that "[i]t cannot be too often impressed on American speakers that when they come to write they must add a 'g' to the word which they call 'fixins.'"[85] Perhaps more often, however, Americans are said to go too far in the other direction, toward overcorrection and dependence upon the text, and become victims of "spelling pronunciation." In *Every-Day English,* published in 1880, White writes that Americans "are trying to be exact, to talk like a book, to speak dictionary English. A word to them is not simply a sound which expresses a thought or a thing, but something which is spelled, and which they must carefully pronounce according to its spelling."[86] What else could motivate the anxious overcompensation behind spelling pronunciation but a desire to turn from orality and an accompanying desire to cleave to the written word?

Spelling bees in dialect poems sometimes end by implicitly forwarding the principles of spelling reform, but the characters of Harte's poem (like Eggleston's characters) nevertheless take proper conventional spelling very seriously. They regress to a child-like state of excitement about the bee, during which, Truthful James says, "'twas touchin' to survey / These bearded men, with weppings on, like schoolboys at their play." One participant bellows, "not one mother's son goes out till that thar word is spelled!" In their allegiance to Webster and Worcester, Harte's spelling bee participants in effect eliminate the possibility of reading literary dialect as signifying illiteracy. In other words, spelling-bee words—illogical or foreign spellings such as "phthisis"—rarely succumb to dialect spellings because they are so distantly related to their pronunciations. Few people, literate or illiterate, nonstandard- or standard-English-speaking, know how they should be pronounced. In other words, winning the spelling bee has nothing to do with "good" pronunciation. The man who spells "eiderduck" with an "I" recognizes the irrationality behind correct spelling and becomes violent for the sake of spelling reform.

As entertaining and eventful as the spelling bee could be—and a spelling bee could hardly be more dramatic than the one at Angel's—the bee's pedagogical value trumps its entertainment value. The education supposedly gained from correct spelling was not frivolous but necessary linked to morality. If spelling bees were entertainment, they were Christian, wholesome entertainment; "[t]hey became, naturally enough, a social event, although the name 'spelling school,' which clung to them, salved the Puritan conscience."[87] Nineteenth-century spelling books also emphasize the moral value of good spelling. As Shirley Brice Heath points out, "During the last three decades of the nineteenth century, grammar books and composition texts show increased collocations of terms such as 'good,' 'moral,' 'industrious,' 'hard-working,' with 'good language' or 'suitable compositions.'"[88] The message of spellers was that good spelling would ensure goodness.

At first Harte's poem seems in keeping with the ideology of the spellers, but ends by refuting it. The poem concludes with James's admonition to the schoolchildren:

O little kids, my pretty kids, down on your knees and pray!
You've got your eddication in a peaceful sort of way;
And bear in mind thar may be sharps ez slings their spellin' square,

> But likewise slings their bowie-knives without a thought or care.
> You wants to know the rest, my dears? Thet's all! In me you see
> The only gent that lived to tell about the Spellin' Bee!

The men of "The Spelling Bee at Angel's" are invested in good spelling and yet immoral. Regardless of their ends, the "sharps ez . . . slings their bowie-knives" are equally comfortable "sling[ing] their spellin' square." Truthful James even compares victory on the battle-field to victory in a spelling bee in the case of Pistol Joe: "For since he drilled them Mexicans in San Jacinto's fight / Thar warn't no prouder man got up than Pistol Joe that night." As charming a scene as grown men sitting down for a spelling bee might be, we never forget that they are violent men, and hardened criminals besides. For the spelling bee participants, morality and spelling are entirely unrelated. And this, I argue, is what is so discomfiting for the children who hear Truthful James's story. The children leave James with "downcast heads and downcast hearts—but not to sport or play / For when at eve the lamps were lit, and supperless to bed / Each child was sent, with tasks undone and lessons all unsaid, / No man might know the awful woe that thrilled their youthful frames." The story is a shocking one under any circumstances, but it is especially disturbing for children on their way home from supposedly edifying spelling lessons. They have been utterly changed by this experience, and now question the idealizing pedagogy of the late-nineteenth-century classroom. Is spelling still good? Even if the children pray, as James beseeches them to do, might they end as the participants of the spelling bee at Angel's?

Besides being a social event and a supposedly wholesome activity, the spelling bee performance, in educational value, falls somewhere between the popular poetry reading culture emerging in the late nineteenth century and the more high-minded elocution tradition that preceded it and continued, transformed, into the twentieth century. Even quotidian schoolroom instruction could be a performance. As W. H. Venable, a superintendent of Dayton, Ohio schools from 1874 to 1884—and, incidentally, friend and correspondent of Riley's—wrote in an 1892 memoir, spelling lessons, "always taught orally," allowed verbal communication to enter the increasingly silent classroom, as "all the noise that had been pent up for the day, like a dammed and swollen stream, broke forth in one impetuous torrent of mingled howls and screams, every scholar yelling out his lesson on his own hook, and in his highest key, making the little old school-house rock again."[89] In Eggleston's *The Hoosier School-Master*, the "spelling-school," as he calls it, "is the only public literary exercise known in Hoopole County. It takes the place of the lyceum lecture and debating club."[90]

That a public exercise in the spelling of obscure words could have served as a "literary" event seemed to some to run counter to the contemporaneous interest in dialect poetry. Joaquin Miller, for instance, found fault with the ever-expanding dictionaries entering the market and in the same breath praised poetry for its lexical simplicity. For him, poetry and words are strangely at odds:

> ... Dr Johnson, and a plague take him so far as poetry is concerned, made a dictionary of about 50,000 words. Then our Webster died with the boast on his lips that he had built a dictionary of 200,000; then came the "Century" with 250,000; then the "Standard" with 300,000! Why, at this rate, before long we might have more words and less poetry than China!
>
> All honor to the great and learned teachers who made these wondrous books! Science needed them, but poetry, no ...
>
> And this is Riley's secret. He uses only little bits of baby words, and as few, even of these, as possible. I dislike dialect, but I take the stand to say that James Whitcomb Riley has written more real poetry and will reach more hearts than all the rest of us put together.[91]

What Miller overlooks is that Riley's "baby words" are themselves exercises in spelling and therefore, in this moment of active spelling reform debate, exercises in wordplay of a sort.

Like spelling reform and the spelling bee, dialect poetry raises the question of what *is* good spelling: correct, or corrected? Riley's interest in spelling is essential to the practice of his poetry, despite the fact that Minnie Mitchell observes a separation between the two in her reminiscences of the childhood Riley, writing, "[i]t was a matter of amusement how quickly Bud would slump out of sight at the mention of a spelling match, but how interested he became in the literary part."[92] The spelling bee was both edificatory and popular, and occupied a unique position in American culture and in American dialect poetry, as we will see also in Dunbar's poems. In the spelling mistakes of their "plain" and "peculiar" dialects, Harte and Riley emphasized the literate dimensions of their apparently oral poetry. In light of this, their visual experiments in dialect poetry can be considered important predecessors to the visual experiments of modernist poetry, and this chapter constitutes an effort to make their dialect poetries visible once again and return them to American literary history.

chapter three

Lettered Dialect
Paul Laurence Dunbar I

When the Western Association of Writers convened in Paul Laurence Dunbar's hometown of Dayton, Ohio in 1892, he read a welcome address in verse to the group, from which the following lines come:

> So, proud are you who claim the West
> As home land; doubly are you blest
> To live where liberty and health
> Go hand and hand with brains and wealth.

Throughout the poem, Dunbar uses the second person in greeting the Midwesterners in the audience, leaving room to question whether he would include himself among them as a Western writer, but the poem ends with his offering his own "welcome warm as Western wine, / And free as Western hearts."[1] In fact, Dunbar saw his dialect work as belonging, at least in part, to a Western American literary tradition. Moreover, a conspicuously Western tradition of African American art and literature was beginning to develop in the last years of the nineteenth century.[2] Many of the African American poets writing at the turn of the century, such as James Edwin Campbell, James David Corrothers, and sibling poets Aaron Belford Thompson, Priscilla Jane Thompson, and Clara Ann Thompson, lived in the Midwest for most or all of their lives, and several looked to Riley as one of the most profound influences upon their work.³ Dunbar himself, in a letter to Dr. James Newton Matthews written early in his career, expresses his belief that "[t]here could scarcely be a better thing than the development of a distinctly western school of poets, such as Riley represents."⁴

After receiving an encouraging letter from Riley following the Western Association of Writers reading, Dunbar and his reputation would come to be associated with the then-established Riley and his reputation for decades to come. The poets became friends and correspondents; in an interview conducted when Dunbar was passing through Indianapolis in 1900, he said that a "gratifying particular of my Western trip has been the meeting of James Whitcomb Riley, whom I met in Chicago, and whose friendship I have enjoyed for several years. His introduction to one of my books with that of William Dean Howells has been a valuable impetus to a recognition of my work."⁵ And, in fact, Riley seemed eager to position himself as a mentor to the younger poet, claiming that he "was the first to recognize Paul Laurence Dunbar."⁶ In 1898, enthusiastic rumors were circulating that the two were collaborating on a comic opera. The fantasy pairing made sense: Dunbar and Riley were among the best-selling poets of the 1890s,⁷ and their dialect verse shares a nostalgic sentimentality as well as the Western sensibility suggested by Dunbar in his letter to Matthews.

Despite this shared sensibility, however, Dunbar's correlation with his invented Southern black voices was so strong that books and articles sometimes grouped him with southern writers although he never lived in the South.⁸ Dunbar's performance as a Southerner goes beyond the stance within his poetry of stock characters of the plantation tradition (such as the displaced Southerner yearning for his days in the South) to the stance without his poetry of Dunbar's perhaps accidental pose as a Southern poet. In retrospect, Dunbar's false Southernness now seems to us one of the most glaringly inauthentic elements of his poetry, part of a general inauthenticity that readers now find jarring.

Dunbar's inauthenticity can be understood as a consequence of two strategies. The first is his attempt early on to model himself after Riley not only in style, dialect, and theme, but also in performances—performances that, in Dunbar's case, were produced and reinterpreted in the imagined tension between regionalist and African American literature. The second is his innovative attempt to view dialect's perceived orality through the lens of literacy to an extent that Riley did not. The "mask" metaphor critics often invoke in discussing Dunbar's use of dialect (derived from his poem "We Wear the Mask") falls short of describing Dunbar's experiments with written language.[9] As James Smethurst writes, the complex performances of blackness throughout the nineteenth century turned Dunbar's mask into a metaphor of "endless regress, a sort of funhouse mirror stage in which the possibility of a double consciousness is asserted, but without the comfort of any absolutely stable features or 'natural' boundaries."[10] To treat dialect orthography as a mask under which authenticity can be found also simplifies the subtleties of orthographic experimentation, and what it can manipulate readers into doing. To say simply that Dunbar wears a mask in his "inauthentic" dialect poems and removes it for the "authentic" standard English ones merely reverses the positions of Dunbar's first critics, who faulted his non-dialect poems for their artifice. The reversal I will describe in the coming paragraphs should alert us to the capriciousness of trends of reading that depend upon treating one oeuvre as authentic because oral and another as inauthentic because literate. We might think of this problem in light of Gene Andrew Jarrett's recognition of "the broad ideological tradition of romantic racialism that anointed authenticity, both of authorship and textual representation, as the determinant of African American literary realism" and Henry B. Wonham's claim that "ethnic caricature performs an integral function *within* the political and aesthetic program of American realism."[11] In dismissing the turn-of-the-century valuation of authenticity that was grounded in romantic racialism or caricature, we have neglected to realize that a reversed valuation of authenticity still informs readings of Dunbar's poetry.

Before exploring the effects of Dunbar's introduction of literate modes of communication, such as letter writing, into what is ordinarily treated as an oral genre, let us look at the factors and conditions—including his reception in relation to Riley's—that effectively drove Dunbar to embrace inauthenticity and artifice.

Dunbar's Performances

For most of his readers in the 1890s and early 1900s, Dunbar's picture of the South seemed accurate, conforming to their idea of what Jarrett calls "minstrel realism."[12] Many critics valued Dunbar for recording faithfully an existing culture and language that, they anticipated, would disappear soon.[13] Reviewers for Southern newspapers, however, seemed troubled by Dunbar's depiction of the black Southerner. One reviewer in Atlanta faults

Dunbar for failing to capture the speech of African Americans, saying, "If Dunbar ever understood his own race he has become so immersed in the culture of the schools that he understands it no longer."[14] Curiously, even in taking Dunbar to task for his alleged ignorance of Southern black speech, the reviewer erases regional differences in the end, claiming that perhaps Dunbar's failure can be traced to his forgetting what it means to be black. This response emerges from the prevalent view that Southernness, as J. Martin Favor argues in his study of authenticity and the "folk" in African American literature, was integral to representations of true blackness.[15] Rather than blaming Dunbar's Midwesternness for his lapses in representing Southern speech, or simply ineptitude, the reviewer finds that the corrupting influence of "education," apparently, is the culprit. Needless to say, Dunbar's selection of the South as the setting for much of his work reveals, on some level, an attraction to the exotic, not a nostalgia for the familiar.

Moreover, as Peter Revell suggests, Dunbar's choice of subject was strategic: he viewed his representations of Southern black life as a means toward "enlisting the sympathies of white readers by putting the Southern black farm laborer in a category with Riley's Hoosier farm folk, as someone poor but attractive, simple but honest, to be protected and even cherished."[16] Contemporary reviewers often discussed the nature of the affiliation between the two poets; a 1914 *New York Times Magazine* review stated, "What Mr. Whitcomb Riley has done for Hoosier folk in Hoosier dialect, Dunbar has done for his negro fellows in their quaint negro English."[17] Reviews of Dunbar's work invariably mentioned Riley, and Dunbar was often referred to as "the colored Riley" or "the Riley of his race."[18] Even in Dunbar's poems that are about Southern life, much of his technique and many of his ideas about dialect poetry—if not the dialect itself—come directly from Riley.[19] In fact, of the dialect pieces in Dunbar's first major book, *Lyrics of Lowly Life* (1896), nearly half are written in a Riley-type Hoosier dialect. Dunbar's earlier work in *Oak and Ivy* (1893) and *Majors and Minors* (1895) was even more heavily influenced by Riley, with two-thirds of the dialect poems in the former and half of the dialect poems in the latter written in a dialect resembling Riley's.

As a writer appealing both to white and black audiences, Dunbar straddles in his poetry the late-nineteenth-century regional white literary dialect tradition epitomized by Riley on the one hand, and the early-twentieth-century—implicitly non-regional, though ostensibly centered in Harlem—black literary dialect tradition developed later by Langston Hughes on the other. Both a black writer and a local color writer, Dunbar belongs to categories that are treated as practically mutually exclusive, treated so in part because of Dunbar's original reception by both black and white readers.[20] As Carrie Tirado Bramen writes, citing the example of Massachusetts resident W. E. B. Du Bois's being encouraged to attend a Southern black college where he would feel at "home" as opposed to Harvard, "Region and race . . . were not always allied: they might in fact be perceived as antithetical in the determination of one's subject position."[21] I have discussed how Dunbar's Midwestern and constructed Southern identities were in conflict, but, as the article from the *Atlanta Sunny South* suggests, there is more to Dunbar's non-regionalism than this. Riley's contemporaries may not have been in agreement about the authenticity of *his* dialect, but dialect writing was, in Dunbar's case, often considered to be a natural articulation of his (non-regional) blackness. William Dean Howells thought him the first black poet "to feel the negro life aesthetically and express it lyrically," and most of Dunbar's reviewers followed suit, praising his dialects.[22] Those writing for, editing, and reading periodicals aimed at African American audiences, too, generally preferred his dialect poems to his poems in standard English.[23] Dickson D. Bruce claims that "[t]he best evidence indicates that black authors and audiences liked dialect literature," and that it is wrong to think that African American literary magazines "accepted such writing with any less eagerness than did their mainstream counterparts," the *Colored American Magazine* even dedicating a section of the magazine to verse in dialect.[24] In fact, Dunbar, Lorenzo Thomas tells us, "was beloved by the black community. Fraternal lodges and cultural organizations were named for him during his lifetime."[25] Clearly, Dunbar's dialect poetry was not universally seen to be at odds with gentility and uplift.

Although Dunbar alleged that his work was linguistically sound, not like the demeaning exaggerations of blackface minstrelsy, much of his dialect verse is written—as it is clear to us now—in an imaginary Southern black dialect of an idealized recent past, calling to mind and seemingly derived in part from white writers such as Thomas Nelson Page and Irwin Russell.[26] Only recently have critics truly emphasized Dunbar's actual lack of familiarity with the varieties of Southern black speech he was supposed to be representing. On the other hand, Riley's late-nineteenth- and early-twentieth-century critics and readers were very well aware of the disjuncture between his middle-class upbringing and the poor, rural Hoosiers he created in his dialect verse. Riley's pose as one of those characters was understood and accepted as just that: a dramatic character. Part of the audience's pleasure in attending a Riley reading seemed to come from his ability to inhabit character after character, remaining "blank" between poems. Dunbar's audiences, however, came to see the "Negro boy-poet." Of course, Riley, too, was saddled with epithets ("The Hoosier poet"), but these titles came with the trappings of early literary celebrity. Dunbar's title, on the other hand, preceded him; it created his career and shaped his reception. He became, as Jarrett writes, "an icon of black authenticity."[27] That a young African American man could or would write poetry was, in and of itself, enough to gain Dunbar publicity.[28] Because his dialect was essentialized, some of his dialect poems modeled after Riley's—along with his poems in Irish, German, and other ethnic dialects—have been mistaken for failed attempts at "black dialect."[29] One reporter attending a Dunbar reading writes that, after reading "The Cornstalk Fiddle," Dunbar proceeded to read a standard English poem, surprisingly "[l]osing all trace of what is known as dialect."[30] It was often assumed that Dunbar was not performing characters at all when he read dialect poems.

More recent attempts in the mid- to late twentieth century to place Dunbar in relation to Riley have only confused matters even more. Although Riley's stock certainly has fallen, Dunbar has in a sense *still* suffered in comparison to Riley, now not for producing work of lesser quality but for falling short of an authentic black voice. As Gavin Jones begins an analysis of Dunbar, "Questions of authenticity have always been central to criticism of Paul Laurence Dunbar," and the fact that Riley valued his own dialect for its supposed authenticity contributed to critics' evaluation of Dunbar's work according to that criterion.[31] Rather than simply transferring Riley's techniques to a different milieu, Dunbar, it was now argued, cannibalized Riley's dialects. In the 1939 *To Make A Poet Black,* J. Saunders Redding points to the fact that Dunbar's dialect is "modeled closer upon James Whitcomb Riley's colloquial language than upon the speech it was supposed to represent," notably calling it "a bastard form" and a "synthetic dialect" created from Dunbar's "scant knowledge of many dialects."[32] Decades later, Bruce writes, "The dialect of Dunbar's poetry seems to have had far more to do with literary traditions than with folk speech. It was based on many of the conventions that informed the works of both white and black dialect poets."[33] Dunbar's debt to Riley is ultimately and invariably seen as a weakness on his part. Revell writes in his 1979 biography of Dunbar:

> Even so well-known a poem as Dunbar's "When De Co'n Pone's Hot," with its celebration of the gustatory delights of a Southern black family's table, owes a good deal to such popular Riley items as "Worter-

melon Time," a Hoosier poem of appetite, and "When the Frost is on the Punkin," whose rhythm is exactly matched by Dunbar's poem.[34]

Tellingly, Revell argues that "Dunbar's efforts in this manner only approximate the *genuine* and carefully constructed Hoosier speech of Riley's work" (emphasis added).[35] This late-twentieth-century evaluation of the authenticity of Dunbar's and Riley's dialects strangely reverses their positions: according to Revell, Riley's dialect reflects his true "Hoosierness," but Dunbar's dialect does not reflect his true "blackness." In other words, Dunbar's dialect poems can be understood as a hodgepodge, cobbled together from literary sources, including Riley's poetry, and Dunbar's own written interpretations of dialects he barely knew. As a result—so the current thinking goes—Dunbar is valuable to us only in his role as a foundational poet of the African American literary canon, but his inauthentic dialect hinders his full acceptance into this canon.

Dunbar's experiments with dialect, despite being conceived by him as building in part upon the Riley tradition, of course had peculiar consequences for him that shaped his popularity and determined his status as a seminal figure for African American poetry. Listening audiences, black and white, were unwilling or unable to suspend belief in the way audiences did for Riley. Some black readers and listeners were growing more tolerant of dialect writing, believing that, as Bruce puts it, "Whatever the sources of black dialect writing, the most crucial aspect of this literature was that, in the hands of black writers, it became a black literature. . . . [T]hey took the form out of the hands of whites and made it their own."[36] This view, requiring an audience to adopt literary dialect as "their own," succeeds in making dialect legitimate only on the basis of its authenticity. For many white readers and listeners, on the other hand, Dunbar's face notably signaled his "pure African blood" (as Howells described Dunbar) and, as it was "colored," could not be perceived as "blank."[37] Howells describes Dunbar's physical features as if he is a caricature: he opened his book to the frontispiece to find "the face of a young negro, *with the race traits strangely accented:* the black skin, the woolly hair, the thick, outrolling lips, and the mild soft eyes of the pure African type" (emphasis added).[38] In addition to evoking caricature, Howells's words "strangely" and "accented" point, in their secondary meanings here, to the idea that Dunbar's dialect (or "accent") is linked to his exotic (or "strange") appearance. "Absorbing" more than one character, to use Twain's term, was not feasible for Dunbar because he was seen as a character, or even a caricature, himself. A 1900 *Boston Transcript* article praising Dunbar, attributed to "E. S. F.," maintains that the poet is no "burnt-cork minstrel" because he is "the genuine article, to the manner born; a poet born, not made; singing the songs of his people from a full heart."

In response to this reception, Dunbar may have tried to distance himself from his literary dialect but, strangely, he did not disprove the assumption that literary dialect was authentic and was the proper medium for expressing authentic blackness. As Alice Dunbar-Nelson writes in a Dunbar memorial, presumably speaking also for her deceased ex-husband, "Say what you will, or what Mr. Howells wills, about 'feeling the Negro life esthetically and expressing it lyrically,' it was in the pure English poems that the poet expressed *himself*."[39] The opposition Dunbar-Nelson makes between race and self deracinates the Dunbar who writes "pure English poems" in order to support the notion that Dunbar actually succeeded in representing authentic blackness in the dialect poems. It does nothing to dispute Howells's influential assessment.

As Dunbar famously told James Weldon Johnson, his first poems in dialect were attempted in order to "gain a hearing."[40] The hoped-for aural reception suggested by his choice of the word "hearing" reveals much about the foundation of Dunbar's success. It was his triumph at the Western Association of Writers reading mentioned at the start of this chapter that led to a string of events landing Dunbar's *Majors and Minors* in Howells's hands. Dunbar was known as "an excellent reader of his own verses" who "liked to present them from the platform."[41] Early in his career, Dunbar learned that it was best to read his public's favorite pieces during his performances. The African American poet Joseph Seamon Cotter, Sr., suggested to Dunbar in a letter (dated July 9, 1896, shortly after Howells's review of *Majors and Minors* appeared), "Why not make [Howells] a visit and recite 'The Party,' 'An Ante-Bellum Sermon' and 'Whistling Sam.' 'Whistling Sam' will carry New England." Cotter goes on to say, "If you can carry this point with Howells, your audience will be the whole of New England." When Dunbar strayed from his most popular dialect pieces, however, his audience did not respond well.[42] It is true that many writers of the period simply gave their audiences what they wanted during readings, as Daniel Borus points out: Twain, Howells, and George Washington Cable all "deliberately selected portions that they knew the audience loved," as Riley did.[43] However, for Dunbar, the tyranny of audience proved more limiting than for his white contemporaries.[44]

As with Riley, Dunbar's skill as a public reader contributed to his popularity, and the performance styles of the two poets were compared.[45] However, unlike Riley, Dunbar—facing audiences whose ideas of black performance had few precedents other than minstrelsy,[46] then in its heyday—ended up recalling the worst of racist stereotypes in his antebellum characters of joyful slaves and despondent ex-slaves. The aforementioned Toledo reporter goes on to say, "Last evening he became a typical 'jolly coon' upon the occasion of his recitation of the plantation dance." Yet another newspaper article illustrates just what is at stake in interpreting Dunbar's performances as these reporters did. In the *Bowling Green Daily News,* one journalist writes that, while "[i]n his serious language poems, he shows his culture in a voice so free of the dialect that one fails to detect a false note," in his dialect poems "he gives its natural limitation full sway and the negro is yours to command." Hearing the speaker of the dialect poems as a "negro [who] is yours to command," some audiences believed that the poetry gave them permission to return to an antebellum world where blacks had no "culture" to "show." Sometimes, inexplicably, Dunbar even gestured overtly toward minstrel iconography; as Gavin Jones points out, James Weldon Johnson notes that a performance of "The Colored Band," accompanied by Rosamond Johnson's adaptation on the piano, included a "one-man impersonation of the marching band [that] was, in the main, some cleverly executed cakewalk steps."[47] This performance was so successful that Virginia Cunningham claims an additional reading was scheduled "to appease those who had been turned away."[48]

Dunbar's popularity as a performer led to the popularity of his poems as recitation pieces, and they appeared often in elocution manuals and anthologies. Besides Riley and Eugene Field, wrote one reader in 1906, Dunbar's "poems are oftener recited than the works of any other writer."[49] Even in 1930, in an essay titled "Dunbar Thirty Years After," Benjamin Brawley reminisces, "Many of us still remember the first time we read 'The Ol' Tunes,' 'Angelina' and 'When Malindy Sings.' We recall too the ease, the eagerness with which we committed the lines to memory."[50] Comparing Dunbar's poetry favorably to "so-called modern verse," Brawley finds that the simple melodies present in the former somehow attach themselves to unwitting readers. As I mentioned in my discussion of Harte and Riley, Dunbar's are "lines you *do* remember" whether or not "you *should*" (emphasis in original).[51]

Considering that Dunbar's success was, and continues to be, dependent upon performance—both as poetry recitation by himself and by others, and as racial and regional impersonation—it is curious that Dunbar himself claims to doubt the viability of dramatic form for African Americans. In an essay titled "The Negro in Literature," he writes, "the predominating power of the African race is lyric." Later, he repeats the sentiment, even rendering this lyricism essential: "the black man's soul is lyric, not dramatic. We may expect songs from the soul of the Negro, but hardly much dramatic power, either in writing or acting." Leaving aside Dunbar's many attempts at dramatic form outside of lyric poetry (the 2002 publication of *In His Own Voice: The Dramatic and Other Uncollected Works of Paul Laurence Dunbar* includes the heretofore unpublished play *Herrick*, along with other dramatic fragments), we can easily find drama in the poems. Three of the six Dunbar poems identified by Henry Louis Gates, Jr. in the foreword to *In His Own Voice* as his best known, "When Malindy Sings," "An Ante-bellum Sermon" and "The Party," could be categorized as dramatic monologues. In any case, Dunbar's outlandish claims have not steered his readers away from seeing the dramatic potential in his work.[52]

Also, perhaps not surprisingly, five of the six poems identified by Gates ("When De Co'n Pone's Hot," "A Negro Love Song," as well as the three mentioned above) are in dialect.[53] These six taken together, Gates writes, are "among Dunbar's most accomplished poems, and his most frequently anthologized—'anthologized' by memorization, by word of mouth, by speakers."[54] Gates's redefinition here of the word "anthologized" to mean "most frequently memorized" is provocative: dialect and dramatic form both seem to work to make these particular poems more conducive to oral distribution. Just as audiences preferred hearing dialect poems to nondialect ones, performers of Dunbar's poetry in dialect and dramatic form apparently were able to memorize more easily and to inhabit their characters more fully, as Brawley's example makes clear. Dunbar's most noteworthy experiment combining dialect and dramatic form involves a distinct subgenre of dialect poetry, one that is impossible in theory. What appears to be Dunbar's innovation, signaling a departure from a Rileyesque dialect poetry, is his development of the epistolary dialect poem written by a fictional character, essentially a variation on the dramatic monologue. This form (which was taken up by Hughes and McKay, among others[55]) put pressure upon the concept of Dunbar as "the genuine article," as the *Boston Transcript* article calls him, allowing him to circumvent the authenticity trap of dialect poetry and expanding the dialect poetry genre to include literate navigations of orality.

The Epistolary Dialect Poem

Despite the fact that the letter is a literate form of communication, the intention behind the language used by the dialect letter-writer seems to be to represent his or her own speech phonetically.⁵⁶ As a result, the epistolary dialect poem serves as a microcosm of the issues involved in writing dialect poetry in the first place. In Dunbar's case, the incompatibility of using a literate form to express speech in a dialect letter invokes the larger-scale incompatibility in using a literate form to express speech in dialect poetry generally. The letter-writer stands in for the poet in a way that Riley's child writer could not: the latter makes errors that point to the writer's semi-literacy, the former makes decisions that mirror the dialect poet's. What Dunbar is doing, in essence, is making the speakers of his epistolary dialect poems into dialect poets themselves—in order to transcribe speech, these characters would have to be accomplished enough in written English to experiment with it and to recognize where speech departs from writing. Dunbar's choice to represent their writing not as illiterate (as Riley's child writer is) but as simultaneously dialect *and* highly literate resists the association of dialect-speaking with illiteracy fundamental to so much contemporaneous dialect poetry.

The reading experience Dunbar directs his readers to have is a conflicted one: readers cannot recite the epistolary dialect poem as a more conventional dramatic monologue because, simply put, no one can be speaking. Letters, as private communication, are usually written and read silently, in the absence of the addressee and writer respectively.⁵⁷ Dunbar's choice of the letter as a model for these poems highlights a tension between a traditional dialect poetry that is performatory and an emerging dialect poetry of silent literacy. His epistolary dialect poem forces its readers to experience an admittedly inauthentic performance, to sense the resistance between the inclination to read dialect aloud and the inclination to read letters silently. In other words, Dunbar effectively makes recitation of these pieces problematic. In so doing, he emphasizes the continuities and tensions between orality and literacy in dialect poetry in general.

Dunbar's reception, in its significant difference from Riley's reception (despite his being described repeatedly as a "colored Riley"), appears to have increased his awareness of the inauthenticity of dialect performance. But even before his emergence on the national stage, Dunbar was pushing his poetry in the direction of inauthenticity. The epistolary dialect poem became for Dunbar a subgenre that would make silent literacy both a crucial and an explicit part of dialect poetry. Although he derives much of his dialect and performance practice from Riley, Dunbar was able to break from him precisely for this reason: because Dunbar's imitations of Riley's dialects were perceived as artificial while his imitations of black Southern dialects were praised as authentic, Dunbar turned to making the artifice of the entire endeavor clear, projecting representations of speech onto literate forms in ways that Harte and Riley did not, and producing as a result a more complex dialect poetry.

His uncollected epistolary dialect poems, "Happy! Happy! Happy!" and "A Letter,"[58] demonstrate three interrelated features of Dunbar's innovative approach to literary dialect: the persistent intrusion of the dramatic in his lyric poems; the application of dialect in a letter and what it might mean for dialect writing; and the introduction of issues of literacy for African Americans. The last of these is broader than the other two and proves crucial in understanding Dunbar's sense of his African American reader—as also shown in essays such as "Is Higher Education for the Negro Hopeless?" (published in 1900 and reprinted many times)—and how this imagined reader might handle dialect poetry as a written form.

The first stanza of "Happy! Happy! Happy!," cited below in its entirety as it appears in *In His Own Voice*, consists of a letter written by a woman (Mandy) to her presumably less educated lover (Julius), ending the relationship. The stanza is followed by five lines serving as a curious transition in an ambiguous voice, and a third stanza, Julius's response:

"Dear Julius" I've been cogitating,
    Long before expatiating,
On the hopeless alterations,
    In our mutual relations;
Having mounted in position,
    To a loftier condition,
And because I cannot flattah
    I must say you are *"non grata."*

Happy, happy, oh my best of queens,
Makes me feel as mealy as a pot of beans!
    Tell you what's the matter
I'm my lady's own *"non grata"*
An' I'm happy, happy, happy cause I do' know what it means.

Dear Mandy I been readin'
    With a pleasure most exceedin'
All the pleasant bits of writin'
    Dat yo' han' has been inditin'
But you mo' dan fill my measure
    Wid de sugar-drip of pleasure,

> When you say without a flattah,
>   I's you' lovin' own *"non grata."*⁵⁹

Perhaps the first thing a reader would notice about the poem is that Julius's response is written in literary dialect, but Mandy's initial letter is not (with one exception, to which I will return in a moment). Mandy's vocabulary consists of Latinate words ("cogitating," "expatiating," "alterations"), ending finally in an actual Latin phrase (*"non grata"*). The excessive and often unnecessary commas end-stopping the lines of her stanza contribute to the exaggerated hypotaxis,⁶⁰ underscoring the relative paucity of commas in Julius's stanza. Although it looks "standard," her dialect should not be understood as neutral. The poem mocks the "educated" woman; she is parodied as a snob. Her dialect, including her pretentious word choice and her awkwardly complex grammar, may be due to her "[h]aving mounted in position / To a loftier condition," making Julius now *"non grata."* In other words, she finds her status new and unfamiliar, and her assumption of this self-important and affected persona, along with its language, fits imperfectly. As much as her language reveals a desperate desire for propriety, her letter writing defies the etiquette rules given in nineteenth-century letter-writing guides; the samples therein were "overwhelmingly statements of sincere and heart-felt sentiment: they included marriage proposals, acceptances, and rejections." Mandy's use of Latinate words in this rejection is an effort "to produce an effect through fine words [that], the manuals warned, should be abandoned for the simple art of expressing true feeling."⁶¹ Take, for example, these instructions from *Miss Leslie's Behaviour Book: A Guide and Manual for Ladies:* "The 'wording' of your letter should be as much like conversation as possible, containing (in a condensed form) just what you would be most likely to talk about if you saw your friend," and always avoiding a tone that is "affectedly didactic."⁶²

Mandy's affected language has dramatic consequences in the poem: we find in the third stanza that Julius apparently misunderstands her letter. He claims that reading her rejection gives him "pleasure."⁶³ In fact, the word "pleasure" appears twice in the stanza, along with its variant "pleasant," mimicking the triple repetition of "Happy" in the poem's title and in the last line of the second stanza. His letter mirrors Mandy's structurally, especially in its last couplet, but the words ending the lines here are fairly common ones, and three ("readin'," "writin'," and "inditin'") are, not surprisingly, terms related to literacy. As I mentioned in my discussion of Harte's and Riley's dialect poetry, literary dialect is frequently used to give a character the illusion of illiteracy; altering spelling in order to reflect a character's pronunciation can promote the misconception that standard spelling reflects the pronunciation of a standard English speaker. But altering spelling to represent neither a letter-writer's nonstandard speech nor his illiterate writing is what makes this poem substantially different from both conventional dialect poems and, for example, Riley's child-writing and Benjamin F. Johnson poems.

Again, the larger question looming over our readings of this poem is how a person's speech could be reflected in writing a letter. Just as the "author" of Riley's "The Squirl and the Funy Litel Girl" would not write "an,'" as I pointed out in my reading of Riley's apostrophes in the previous chapter, no letter-writer would sincerely write "readin'." "The Squirl and the Funy Litel Girl" and Benjamin F. Johnson's poems hardly foreground these slips, as Dunbar's epistolary dialect poems do. Riley attempts to distinguish between the representations of Benjamin F. Johnson's writing and speaking, but ultimately seems unaware of the differences between writing and speaking, demonstrating that he thinks of literary dialect as essentially oral. Dunbar, in "Happy! Happy! Happy!," experiments with this already-established dilemma in interesting ways. First of all, in producing a textual dialogue between Mandy and Julius that seems to stand in for a spoken dialogue, Dunbar allows the first and third stanzas to highlight the position of literary dialect as a medium that reflects orality through the lens of literacy.

In conceiving of literary dialect as representations of orality through literacy, Dunbar forces the "oral" elements of the poem to challenge the status of standard English.[64] Mandy's letter contains one word in literary dialect—"flattah"—and it is the only word repeated in Julius's stanza aside from its rhyme word (*"non grata"*). This is no accident. When the reader first encounters "flattah," in the context of Mandy's standard English stanza, we register it subconsciously as standard English. Because readers will think of the prestige dialect (that is, standard English) as corresponding with written English, we are coaxed into thinking that Mandy speaks it as well as "writes" it. Because of the social difference Mandy introduces as a means of defining her relationship with Julius, readers are led to perceive Mandy's "flattah" as something different from Julius's "flattah." However, our eyes tell us that this is not the case. Dunbar's approach to literary dialect grows out of his awareness of the prestige dialect *as* a dialect. Obviously, all ways of speaking belong under the rubric of orality, but dialect poetry, in its focus on nonstandard dialects, usually regards standard dialects as nothing more than the spoken articulation of written language. As such, standard dialects are presumed to be closer to writing. Although Dunbar rarely represents the speech of his standard-English-speaking characters phonetically, as he does here with Mandy's "flattah," his decision to represent Mandy's speech exactly as he represents Julius's (if only for a moment) in effect turns standard English into dialect.

The second stanza seems to be written in Julius's voice, but here the dialect is closer to standard ("I's" in the third stanza is "I'm" in the second). Significantly, "matter" is allowed to rhyme with "non grata." Instead of changing the spelling to "mattah," mirroring the phonetic "flattah" in Mandy's and Julius's letters, this stanza allows for nonstandard pronunciation to be represented by standard spellings. A manuscript located in the Paul Laurence Dunbar Collection at the Ohio Historical Society shows that, in a working draft of the poem, Dunbar toyed with the possibility of writing the line "Tell you what's de mattah," and the change is a major revision in terms of reading this stanza as transitional.[65] The change to "matter" in the typescript (the version reproduced in *In His Own Voice*) shows that Dunbar intended, through ridding the stanza of most visual markers of dialect, to lead his reader away from the thought that Julius or Mandy would be speaking in this stanza. Moreover, rhyming "matter" with "non grata" urges the reader to pronounce the word without a post-vocalic -*r*, a pronunciation that could signal any number of English language dialects, some socially privileged and some not. Our perspective shifts. If a reader pronounces "matter" without the -*r*, he or she will not balk at rhyming the two words. One who does pronounce "matter" with an -*r*, on the other hand, will become aware of the fact that the poem is treating what is usually, in the United States, the nonstandard pronunciation here as the standard.

Perhaps the strongest evidence of Dunbar's experimentation with dialect perspective is the ambiguity of the last line of this second stanza. If we understand the perspective of this stanza to belong to Julius, our most plausible choice, the line finally makes no sense: presumably he is happy *not* because of his ignorance, which is what the line means literally, but because he thinks it is a good thing to be "non grata." The second clause of the line—"'cause I do' know what it means"—makes a coherent reading of Julius's response even more difficult. Reading "do' know" as an elision of "don't know" leaves the poem comic, because Julius is portrayed as a fool. Reading it, on the other hand, as "*do* know" (with an extraneous apostrophe) may not explain Julius's happiness—unless he was eager to get out of the relationship—but it does mean that Julius is much more knowledgeable than he appears to be. Julius's knowledge of the fact that Mandy's letter *is* a rejection becomes clear, and this insight, of course, colors our reading of the tone of the final stanza. His letter to Mandy could be sarcastic, or it could be spiteful, but it is no longer foolish. The dialect speaker is not the fool of the poem; instead, it is Mandy, whose pretentiousness is satirized by both Dunbar and Julius.

In contrast to the complex structure of "Happy! Happy! Happy!," "A Letter" is relatively simple.[66] Most of "A Letter" conforms to the genre of the nostalgic poem so common in Riley's verse (such as "The Old Swimmin'-Hole" and "An Old Sweetheart of Mine") and in the plantation tradition. In the form of a letter, the speaker tells his mother how he pines for the life he left behind in the South and the "ol' plantation." Dunbar returns here to the theme of the displaced Southerner longing for the rural South while living in the urban North. The "mystery" of the poem is why the speaker is now happy, in spite of the longing described in the second, third, and fourth stanzas. We have to wait the length of the poem to find out why, as the speaker writes in the first stanza, he is no longer homesick:

> Deah Mammy I's a-writin'
>   Dis hyeah lettah full o' glee,
> An' I guess you'll be a-wondrin'
>   What on earf's a-ticklin' me.
> But you needn't try to guess it,
>   An' you needn't spread yo' eyes,
> Fu' I sholy gwine to hit you
>   Wid a moughty big su'prise.[67]

In the end, after some homesickness for the South, the speaker decides "de no'f, hit ain't so bad!" Thus, the poem is in marked contrast to Dunbar's "Goin' Back" and "To the Eastern Shore," sentimental poems more clearly fitting into the plantation tradition thematically. Unlike the old man in "Goin' Back," who was told "that things were better North, / An' a man was held at his honest worth" only to find the North lacking in "real ol' Southern heartiness," the speaker of "A Letter" overcomes his nostalgia and is not left yearning for the South at the end of the poem.[68] The theme of nostalgic sentimentality that Dunbar appears to share with Riley is challenged by poems such as "A Letter," which in the end makes light of nostalgia as shallow and inauthentic.

The speaker's memory of the South first surfaces in the third stanza, where he finds himself:

>   . . . . feelin' kin' o' lonesome
>   W'en I went to wo'k today,
>   T'inkin' 'bout de ol' plantation
>   An' de good ol' fashioned way
>   Dat we ust to hunt de possum
>   W'en de snow had kep' his trace . . .

The possum epitomizes his fantasy of the South, a loaded image considering its iconic value in blackface minstrelsy and other forms of caricature. (This focus on food is itself a feature of the plantation tradition.) His memory overcomes all of his senses, as his "mouf des sot fu' possum." Eventually his memory gives way to the reality of his sterile Northern situation: "But I say, 'now what's de use? / Ain't I no'f? Dey ain't No possums / In dis lan' a-runnin' loose.'" However, rather than ending with the speaker's hopeless longing for the products and lifestyle of the South, the poem reveals its surprise:

>   Den I mos' nigh drap wid trimblin'
>   At a somep'n' dat I see,
>   'Twere a possum, froze an' hangin'
>   In a winder des by me!

Missing the taste of possum, the speaker is surprised to find it for sale in the North. Claude McKay, thirty years later,[69] would publish a nostalgic poem similar to this one: "The Tropics of New York." In it, McKay's speaker happens upon some of the fruits and vegetables of his native Jamaica, now made exotic by being placed behind a window in a New York grocery store. As with "A Letter," the foods of his childhood lead the speaker of "The Tropics of New York" to memories of the landscape, idealized over time. Instead of a speaker who "mos' nigh drap wid tremblin'"—for joy and surprise—at the sight of something from home, we have here a speaker whose equally visceral reaction manifests itself as a "wave of longing" sweeping through his body. Michael North's excellent analysis of McKay's poem describes how the poem critiques the separation of the individual from the products of his country by imperialist forces: as North writes, the poem is "about the radically different fates of passenger and cargo in the global economy, the cargo assimilated as an exotic treat, the passenger cut off from both tropics and New York."[70] However, the most important difference between McKay's and Dunbar's poems is that, "[d]ough de buyin' seemed a sin," Dunbar's speaker *does* buy the possum and is able to recreate at least the culinary experiences he remembers from home. This is enough for him to be satisfied, and there is a depth of feeling in McKay's poem that is missing from Dunbar's. Unlike McKay's speaker, Dunbar's does not despair over his nostalgia, and the poem thus ends on an upbeat and comic note rather than a tragic one. The nostalgia depicted in "A Letter" is far from devastating.

Dunbar's poem argues that perhaps nostalgia is not as natural or authentic as poems of the plantation tradition would lead us to think. The plantation tradition, Gavin Jones writes, "worked by blurring the line between memory and reality; nostalgic stereotypes were politically powerful because they were so often taken as truths. In Dunbar's poems about slave life, however, there is a radical tension between the categories of memory and reality. Rather than a natural truth, memory is presented as a convention, a retrospective construction."[71] "A Letter" exposes reminiscing as a construction, in conforming to expectations early in the poem in order to upset them at the end. One of the conventional types of memory common to poems coming out of the plantation tradition is that of the old man looking back; the sentiment behind it is that, no matter how long one lives in the North, one will always be homesick. For example, Dunbar's character in "Goin' Back" says that "thirty years ain't wiped . . . out" his doubt about the virtues of the North. He continues:

> . . . year after year I worried along,
> While deep in my heart the yearnin' strong
> Grew stronger an' fiercer to visit once more
> The well loved scenes o' my native shore.

For the character in "Goin' Back," his nostalgia has only gotten more overpowering, but the nostalgia of "A Letter" is deflated with the realization that this longing, although it feels insubstantial and abstract, can be composed simply of the material goods that can be obtained anywhere in an industrialized world. Because poems in the plantation tradition frequently revolve around stereotyped scenes of food—stealing it, eating it, cooking it, and so on—Dunbar uses this obsession in order to expose the caricature and fantasy supported by this type of nostalgia: the myth of mindlessly happy slaves living at ease in the land of plenty. A 1904 *New York Times* review of Dunbar's *Li'l Gal,* determined to situate it squarely and unproblematically in the plantation tradition, claims that Dunbar's "negroes are filled with the joy of material life when food was good and easily got, and no one took thought for the morrow," and this is not an unusual contemporary review of Dunbar's work.⁷² In a memory that would appear to support the *New York Times* reviewer's impression of Dunbar's poetry, the speaker of "A Letter" never says he misses his mother, only that he'd have

> .... gin de whole creation
>   Fu' to hit yo' cabin do',
> An' to see de smoke a-risin'
> An' to smell dat bacon smell . . .

In the end, however, the nostalgia is finite and dissipates like the smoke pouring out from his childhood cabin. This critique of the nostalgia theme, a theme essential to dialect poetry in the Riley tradition and in the plantation tradition, for its emptiness and shallowness amounts to a refutation of stereotypes of black culture, and of the image of the displaced Southerner who can find no happiness in the North.

Again, just as "Happy! Happy! Happy!" does, "A Letter" introduces the question of how a letter might be written in dialect. The poem begins with a deictic expression—"[d]is hyeah lettah"—indicating that the letter is the poem itself, so it is clear that the poem is not a conventional dramatic monologue in which the person addressed is physically present. Strangely, there's a "—well—" in the poem, a clear signal of represented speech. That is, one doesn't *write* "well"; it is, especially surrounded by dashes, an unconscious interruption of thought. The authority of the dashes, however, is itself debatable. Of the three copies of the poem found in the Dunbar Collection, the two typescripts print the line as I have above, evocative of speech, but in the manuscript the line reads as follows: "But dat's ovah now, fu' well." The last two words of the manuscript version could be understood to mean "for good" or "full well," giving the line a completely different meaning.⁷³ In other words, Dunbar likely rewrote the poem to include *more* signals of represented speech.

Both "Happy! Happy! Happy!" and "A Letter" exhibit Dunbar's interest in showing how literacy, represented by letter writing, is constantly reshaping and restructuring orality, and vice versa, in a culture of secondary orality. As a poet who owed his career both to public performances of his poems (by himself and by others) and to impressive sales of his books, Dunbar saw the value of both oral and literate competence, viewing dialect as a vehicle to explore the space between the two modes. When Dunbar presented his work orally, it was received as an attempt to capture the true spirit and voice of African Americans in general. But, on the page, Dunbar's poetry is clearly interested in the inauthenticity of literary voice in general, and in how orality and literacy inform each other through dialect poetry. The oral elements that enter into written documents ("—well—" in a letter, for example) and the written reworkings of speech represented by dialect letters themselves belong to the same project.

That Dunbar's "A Letter" is preserved in both manuscript and typescript versions in the Ohio Historical Society microfilm of the Paul Laurence Dunbar Collection (the latter presumably typed using the typewriter preserved at the Paul Laurence Dunbar House in Dayton) allows us to see how a dialect poem that inhabits the space between orality and literacy changes as it travels from script to print and vice versa. Born just as the first typewriters were becoming commercially available—and in the same decade and town that saw the invention of the typewriter's cousin, the cash register—Dunbar was one of the first or second generations of writers to produce literature as type.[74] Dunbar's romanticism and apparent dedication to script in poems such as "A Garret," whose speaker writes verses with his "ill-rewarding pen," would suggest that he still views poetry writing as primarily scriptive (recalling Riley's romanticization of chirographic poetic composition and his fetishization of the pencil in his "A Worn-Out Pencil"). However, to examine the Dunbar archives makes it clear that part of the compositional process must have included typewriting, as it did for Riley.[75] The author of *Paul Laurence Dunbar: Laurel Decked* expresses what he perceives as the discontinuity between dialect writing and typewriting when he observes Dunbar's typewriter (a Remington Standard No. 6) as if talismanic, with a sense of awe and wonder: "There stands the typewriter which will never click to his wizard and industrious touch again. One wonders how any machine could be made to turn out his curious dialectic forms."[76] For Dunbar, however, the typewriter was in fact a generative tool.

Ironically, oral interjections like "—well—" (which we also find in Riley's poetry) translate into print more readily and more precisely than they do into script. As Charles Olson would write in "Projective Verse" decades later, the typewriter "due to its rigidity and its space precisions, . . . can, for a poet, indicate exactly the breath, the pauses, the suspensions even of syllables, the juxtapositions even of parts of phrases, which he intends. . . . For the first time he can, without the convention of rime and meter, record the listening he has done to his own speech and by that one act indicate how he would want any reader, silently or otherwise, to voice his work."[77] However, Olson's post-metrical conception of the printed poem as score cannot be applied exactly to Dunbar's use of type, with his regular rhyme and meter already determining the length of breaths and pauses. In any case, the turn-of-the-century typewritten poem foregrounds all of the "lines an' dots" (to quote Dunbar's "When Malindy Sings") and "ever' dot and cross" (to quote Riley's *The Rubaiyat of Doc Sifers*) of dialect poetry more dramatically than does the handwritten one. The typewriter makes more visually apparent the dialect poem's mingling of literacy and orality.

Dunbar's Class in Spelling and Reading

Dunbar's thoughts about illiteracy among African Americans, implicit in his poetry, become explicit in his essays, letters, and interviews: his interest in oral art forms represented in dialect writing did not extend to a respect for orality in and of itself, which he viewed as limited. As I have tried to show, Dunbar's poetry emphasizes what he sees as the shortcomings of both orality and literacy in and of themselves, but demonstrates, through the use of literate modes of communication and smaller-scale oral structures, how each can enrich the other. Bruce expresses the charges of many critics in his claim that "despite Dunbar's professed interest in folk life, the folk Negroes whose lives his dialect poems evoked were not the black people he most admired," pointing to Dunbar's 1901 essay "Negro Society in Washington," originally published in the *Saturday Evening Post,* in which Dunbar "praised the black elite's distinctive love of pleasure."[78] Signaling a departure from the "poet of the people" stance that Riley cultivated both within and without the literature, Dunbar's persona in his essay writing is certainly elitist. Despite writing affectionately of "the lower walks of life [where] a warmer racial color is discoverable" in "Negro Life in Washington," Dunbar goes on, in the same essay, to mark the lower classes as "of a different cast from that part of the Washington life which is the pride of her proudest people": doctors, lawyers, and professors. He calls the last of these "the acme of titular excellence," of whom there are more in Washington "than one could find in a day's walk through a European college town."[79]

Despite the favoring of a Du Boisian "Talented Tenth" that this essay reveals, with academics at the top of the hierarchy, Dunbar expresses in another essay views about what he considers the best type of education for African Americans. In "The Tuskegee Meeting," Dunbar argues that the pioneering black colleges and universities, founded in the late 1860s, were not well suited for African Americans, some of whom only recently were legally forbidden to learn to read. He writes of the first graduates of these schools that, when the "weight of classicity was placed upon them, they became mentally top heavy," resulting in the "pompous, half educated, big-worded negro who came on the stage of active life after the war."[80] Mandy of "Happy! Happy! Happy!" with her Latinate vocabulary seems to be a stereotype in this vein. Tuskegee's approach, he argued, was proving more successful, producing graduates better equipped for individual and racial progress. This is despite the fact that, elsewhere, he expressed disapproval of the Tuskegee model and worried that a fundraiser in Boston where he was to appear alongside Booker T. Washington and W. E. B. Du Bois would "destroy any future power Dubois [sic] and I may have by bringing us before the public in the character of speakers for the very institution whose founder's utterances we cannot subscribe to."[81] The inconsistency in Dunbar's views of African American education is reflected in the split in his work between classical and folk influences.

According to Dunbar, literacy was the key to the sort of education, whether vocational or liberal, that would benefit the race—a familiar theme in the African American tradition that preceded Dunbar. As Robert Stepto writes, "One does not have to read very far into the corpus of Afro-American letters to find countless examples of the exaltation of literacy and the written word."[82] A poet dependent upon book sales, Dunbar of course had personal motives for wanting to increase the number of black readers, already a significant number in the 1890s. However, the question of "Negro Education," often understood as simply literacy education, was still a much-debated one in the last decade of the century: Dunbar himself wrote "Is Higher Education for the Negro Hopeless?" in response to an essay that argued in the affirmative to that question. In addition, only four years before Howells's review of Dunbar's *Majors and Minors* appeared in *Harper's,* the *Atlantic Monthly* published an article by W. T. Harris called "The Education of the Negro," in which the writer's respondents (mostly white Southerners, often arguing with him[83]) addressed the points of the essay in footnotes. Lida Keck Wiggins recalls a conversation with Dunbar that is worth mentioning in light of Dunbar's essays about African American education, and the historical context in which these questions were circulating:

> Before I left him that afternoon, he took occasion to tell me that he was to have his "class" that night, and that he must rest a bit before the pupils came. I asked in amazement what class he meant, and he said, with an enthusiasm which left no doubt as to his heart-interest in the work:

"Why my class in spelling and reading. Some people think our people should be nurses and boot-blacks, but I am determined that they shall not make menials out of all of us." This class he taught for weeks, giving literally of his very life for the betterment of the race.[84]

Dunbar-the-teacher, according to Virginia Cunningham, "still had his own McGuffey's Readers" and he "bought himself a history of pedagogy and a book on methods of education."[85] Dunbar's determination to increase literacy and promote primary and secondary education among African Americans was linked in his mind to decreasing the ranks of menial workers in African American communities: he himself had been one; after graduating from high school, the only work he was able to get was as a janitor or an elevator operator.

The value of primary and secondary education, for Dunbar, was indisputable. His own mixed feelings about the value of higher education, which I discuss in the greater detail in the next chapter, are colored by the fact that he was unable to attend college; Brawley calls this one of the biggest disappointments in Dunbar's life.[86] Dunbar may have been resigned to becoming an autodidact himself, but he clearly promoted the general value of higher education of the few for the many, in African American communities. He writes, in "Is Higher Education for the Negro Hopeless?":

> Every graduate from a Negro college, it is true, does not become a Moses in the community where he is settled, but, on the other hand, in every section where a Negro college is located, and where there are Negro graduates, it is proven beyond dispute, whatever detractors may say to the contrary, that the moral, social, and industrial tone of the people has been raised. They have gone into the districts where the people did not even know how to live, and by their own example taught the benighted the art of life, which they have learned in the schools for higher education.

The *Atlanta Sunny South* review I mentioned earlier in this chapter, which attacked Dunbar for "becom[ing] so immersed in the culture of the schools that he understands [his race] no longer," reflected the views many held—including Dunbar at times—that the more educated an African American became, the further he or she was from black culture. In "Negro Life in Washington," Dunbar writes that the African American of the middle classes, particularly the college-educated, "has imbibed enough of white civilization to make him work to be prosperous. But he has not partaken of civilization so deeply that he has become drunk and has forgotten his own identity. . . . He has retained some of his primitive ingenuousness."[87] For Dunbar, "civilization" and blackness are apparently at odds, but he thinks that there is some value to keeping the two in balance. The so-called primitiveness, the inability to "even know how to live" that Dunbar links to African American culture, can be saved by the forces of "civilization."

In asserting his familiarity with the high as well as the low,[88] Dunbar was again attempting to distance himself from the "lowly" linked with dialect. Howells writes, of Dunbar's work in *Majors and Minors*, "I do not think one can read his Negro pieces without feeling that they are of like impulse and inspiration with the work of Burns when he was most Burns, when he was most Scotch, when he was most peasant."[89] But, in response to this dictum, Emeka Okeke-Ezigbo claims that Howells "unwittingly offended Dunbar by associating him with the very things he wished to avoid; for Howells was saying by implication that 'Dunbar was the most "Negro," the most Southern, and the most peasant.'"[90] And it does seem to be the case that, as much as his career depended upon the association, Dunbar resented being grouped with the black lower classes.

Several critics have pointed to this ambivalence as the driving force behind Dunbar's repudiation of the dialect poetry that was so profitable for him. Okeke-Ezigbo claims that Dunbar "considered himself superior to the uneducated slaves and freedmen" and that his "condescending attitude toward the black folks conditioned his stance on 'Negro dialect.'"[91] Jean Wagner, too, traces Dunbar's approach to his own dialect poetry to a condescending and disdainful attitude toward poor blacks. He writes, "we need not summarily dismiss the possibility that Dunbar, by rejecting his dialect works that identify him with the people, was also rejecting his lowly social origins. In a certain sense, he may be considered as belonging to the developing black bourgeoisie which, in its urge to climb the social ladder, feels obliged to deny everything it might share with the lower class."[92] There is certainly much truth to this. And, in fact—although Charles T. Davis claims that Dunbar "opposed the rampant materialism the dominated the age"—Dunbar did seem very concerned with making money and with upward mobility, having struggled financially during his first years as a poet and perhaps trying to achieve financially what Riley, famously, accomplished in his career.[93] The letter from Joseph Seamon Cotter, Sr., who also considered Riley one of his "literary idols,"[94] to Dunbar that I mentioned earlier in this chapter reveals something of the strategic opportunism and commercial-mindedness that the two young poets may have shared with Riley:

You and Gov. McKinley are close together in Harper's. Do you see the point? If he is made President get your friends to speak for you. It may bring you a position in Washington worth $1000 or $1200 a year.

If you can get some New York house to bring out your book, a little fortune will be yours.

By all means arrange and give some readings in New England.

If Howells hears you read he will say something that will mean thousands in your pocket.

The public readings of dialect poetry, upon which Dunbar's financial success depended, had the somewhat ironic effect of linking Dunbar with the lower classes from whom he may have wanted to distance himself. The larger his audience became (as Cotter projected, "'Whistling Sam' will carry New England") and the richer Dunbar could become, the more "lowly" he would appear to his audiences.

The Spelling Bee Poem Redux

Dunbar's practical interest in literacy extends, as I have said, to his poetics in dialect writing. Nowhere is this as evident as in Dunbar's spelling bee poems, a subgenre introduced in the previous chapter and to which I briefly return in closing this chapter.[95] Revell calls Dunbar's "The Spellin'-Bee" the poet's "tribute to Riley's 'At "The Literary,"'" a story of courtship conducted in the exchanges of a village literary meeting, with much use of Riley's characterization of village types, lawyer, parson, miserly farmer, and the usual crop of village beaus and belles."[96] The prize for winning the spelling bee is a "little blue-backed spellin'-book with fancy scarlet trimmin'," which is clearly Webster's.[97] A gathering revolving around acts of literacy—not only the act of "spelling down" one's opponent, but the act of competing to win a spelling book—would prove an ideal subject for Dunbar's dialect poetry. Strangely enough, the speller seems to entice adult members of the community to participate in the spelling bee. In an essay about the history of spelling bees in the United States, Allen Walker Read cites a historian who points out that, as spelling bees became more social, "the rest of the community would join in." The mature nature of these nineteenth-century spelling bees is suggested by the fact that "the small children did not come: it was for those boys and girls who were in their teens and who were old enough to enjoy and appreciate 'a good time.'"[98]

As if contagious, "folks 'ud miss the very word that seemed to fit their cases." The town's miser joins in and, fittingly, misspells "charity." The most suggestive misspelling, however, is that of the lawyer who forgets the "h" in "honest." This error has deep implications for literary dialect. The "h" in "honest" is never pronounced, so spelling it correctly, with an "h," identifies the speaker as literate. Moreover, there are several English words beginning with "h" the aspiration of which marks someone as a Standard English speaker or not. Dropping the "h" in *spelling* "honest" calls to attention the common (mainly English) mistake of dropping it in *speaking* other words. Although dropping the "h" in speaking "honest" is consistent with most varieties of English, in *Pygmalion* the "reformed" Eliza Doolittle "[p]urposely drop[s] her aitches to annoy" the professor who has taught her to speak as he does: "Thats done you, Enry Iggins, it az."[99] The "h" is used as a weapon by Eliza Doolittle, who, by the end of the play, is fluent in two English dialects. Elocution manuals, such as *The Popular Elocutionist and Reciter* (published in 1894 in both London and New York), caution reciters about the "h": "Above all things, mind your *aitches*—an aitch dropped or wrongly aspirated, is to an educated ear what a note played out of tune is to a musician's."[100] In addition, two essays published in the *Atlantic Monthly*, "The H Malady in England" by Richard Grant White and "The Misused H in England" by Richard A. Proctor (appearing in January and May 1885, respectively) addressed the "h" issue, venturing answers to questions such as why the "h" is not dropped in America. The controversy over "h" in spoken English made it a vexed letter to exploit in literary dialect.

As I mentioned in my discussion of Harte's spelling bee poem, this subgenre serves as an implicit argument for spelling reform: the fact that spelling "honest" without an "h" would mark one as illiterate, whereas pronouncing it *with* an "h" would mark one as an imaginary dialect speaker (and hence "illiterate" in the world of most dialect poetry) places the reader in an uncomfortable paradox. Dunbar—as a Westerner posing as a Southerner, as an urban dweller posing as a rustic, as one of the high-society set posing as one of the "lowly"—seems drawn to these linguistic paradoxes even as he is frustrated by them.

Dunbar addresses the dilemma raised by Harte's and Riley's dialects—that is, the dichotomy between Harte's "plain language" and Riley's "peculiar language"—by foregrounding the confusion implicit in dialect poetry's dual identity as oral and literate. Although Dunbar builds upon their work, as we see in his use of the Spelling Bee subgenre, Harte's and Riley's dialects were essentially two methods of getting to the same place:

their dialects effectively became cautionary examples of the nonsensicality of attempting to force orality into a literate form. Riley dangerously conflated speech with illiterate writing and, in the nostalgia-inducing properties of his child writing, forwarded a progressive model of orality and literacy; Harte developed a type of literary dialect associated with transparency, which, despite his good intentions, dangerously propped up and provided fuel for racist views of Chinese Americans. Dunbar's attempted solution to the misuse of literary dialect was to experiment with including representations of speech in literate modes of communication, such as letter writing, allowing the dialect speaker to become a dialect writer by proxy. Although Dunbar's dialect poetry is considered either thematically reactionary or subversive now, supporting or rejecting racial stereotypes respectively, I would argue that Dunbar's innovation is a linguistic one, located in his buttressing of literate subgenres with oral structures and vice versa. His awareness of the racial stereotypes to which he and his work fell prey, resulting in part from the condescension a primary orality received in a culture of emerging secondary orality, prompted him to revise Riley's and Harte's views of the relationship between orality and literacy. That he did so by emphasizing the labor of reading and writing dialect poetry will be the subject of the following chapter.

chapter four

Cultivated Dialect
Paul Laurence Dunbar II

> One day when me 'n' Dunbar wuz a-hoein' in de co'n,
> Bofe uv us tried [*sic*] an' anxious foh to heah de dinnah—ho'n.—
> Him in his fiel', an' me in mine, a-wo'kin' on togeddah,
> A-sweatin' lak de mischief in de hottes' kine o' weddah.
> A debblish notion tuck me 't Paul wuz gittin' on too fast:
> But, thanks I: "Wait untwel he git 'mongst all dem weeds an' grass,
> 'N' I'll make him ne'ly kill his se'f, an' den come out de las'."
> . . .
> De sun shone on us br'ilin' hot: but, now an' den de breeze
> Blowed fresh, f'om 'cross de maddah lot, de fragrance ob de trees
> In de ole orchard, jes' beyon'. De birds sung clear an' sweet:
> De tree toad wuz a-callin' out his 'pinion ob de heat:
> De fahm-house looked invitin', an', erbout a mile away.
> De town gleamed white—across de road, de fahmers made dey hay:—
> But me 'n' Paul was hustlin': 'ca'se dat wuz ouh "busy day."
>
> —James Corrothers, "Me 'N' Dunbar"

In the February 1897 issue of *Current Literature,* Paul Laurence Dunbar's early poem "The Poet and His Song" appeared as one of several chosen to introduce his poetry to their readership, on a page given the title "Lays of a Negro Minstrel." His first major poetry collection, *Lyrics of Lowly Life,* had been brought out by Dodd, Mead and Company the year before, bolstered by a strong endorsement from William Dean Howells.[1] A poem about the practice of a working poet, "The Poet and His Song" opens with the following stanza:

> A song is but a little thing,
> And yet what joy it is to sing!
> In hours of toil it gives me zest,
> And when at eve I long for rest;
> When cows come home along the bars,
>   And in the fold I hear the bell,
> As Night, the shepherd, herds his stars,
>   I sing my song, and all is well.[2]

This imagined idyllic life—balanced between a hearty appreciation for labor and the relief from it provided by the soothing effects of art—gives Dunbar the terms for his georgic poem, one of his most celebrated. It is easy to see why, in its celebration of the pleasures of art, it has been called a "credo-like lyric."[3] At the end of the day, the speaker sleeps feeling "joy," but the sentiment of the poem darkens with the last two stanzas. The labor becomes more grueling and realistic, and his art becomes less effective at relieving the suffering that labor brings. One would think that this working poet would become embittered about the difficulties of his life in relation to the ease of the lives of "others [who] dream within the dell," but, as he says toward the end of the poem, when "with throes of bitter pain / Rebellious passions rise and swell," he simply sings "and all is well." It's hard to know whether we should believe the quick dissolution of this near rebellion at the close of the poem. The outburst is stifled with a "but—" and a too-pat, axiomatic conclusion: "life is more than fruit or grain."

Poetic composition is first viewed in this poem as an escape from drudgery; as he puts it, "In hours of toil it gives me zest." But, even though he whistles while he works, he must admit that his "days are never days of ease [because] I till my ground and prune my trees." The poet's work is to cultivate, in both the pastoral and literary senses: first, in a literal, agricultural sense, but also metaphorically, as his writing is pruned through revision. Metaphorically linking harvested fruit or grain with "harvested" verse is, of course, nothing new.[4] (In fact, James Corrothers would use the metaphor in "Me 'n' Dunbar," a teasingly competitive dialect poem published in the July 1901 *Colored American Magazine* in which he challenges Dunbar to a race—"Him in his fiel', an' me in mine"—to see who can hoe the most corn.) In light of the metaphor's pervasiveness, Dunbar's reworking of it appears so overwrought that the product of his physical labor, a plain "ripened gold" as he tends to it, demands to be read also as the product of poetic labor. This blurring of the work and the work song exposes the fantasy of poetic production—the idea that it is joyous—as a fantasy that ultimately cannot be sustained. Yet a third, self-reflexive sense of cultivation adds to the confusion. The mind and manner, in other words, may be cultivated; this is the sense of cultivation most distant from toil. When Dunbar writes to Dr. Henry A. Tobey, one of his early supporters, of his desire to "spend the coming year in college, chiefly to learn how and what to study in order to cultivate my vein," it is this third sort of general cultivation of the self that he seeks, rather than the second sort directed externally toward the improvement of his poetry.[5] It is the desired end result of refinement, along with the rigorous but invisible and apparently leisurely process of achieving it.

I argue in this chapter that Dunbar's poems shape him as a new brand of cultivated writer, as he was measured against shifting definitions of nineteenth-century authorship through his reception as a writer and performer of dialect verse. The paradox at the center of the concept of literary cultivation—the writer emphasizes the work that goes into making literature while also maintaining that it is an activity signifying leisure—is a productive one for Dunbar, allowing him to carve an ironic place for dialect in the cultivated literature so closely associated with elite magazines such as the *Century*. Although "The Poet and His Song" is written in standard English, more than half of the poems chosen by *Current Literature* are in dialect, despite the fact that, in the book from which they were chosen, non-dialect poems outnumber dialect poems nearly three to one. Dunbar's first few pieces in the *Century* were a mix of dialect and non-dialect, but soon nearly all of Dunbar's poems appearing in the magazine were in dialect. Just as Shelley Fisher Fishkin argues that readers should consider Dunbar's innocent love poems "against the backdrop of prominent stories running in the *Atlantic* and other leading publications in the 1890s about the sexual immorality of black women,"[6] I propose that we read his *Century* publications in dialect as attempts to accomplish a kind of oppositional political work. Dunbar clearly viewed these poems as a means of countering the convention, presented in the dialect work of his contemporaries, that dialect poetry is by definition uncultivated.

Of course, Dunbar was far from the first to publish dialect verse in the *Century*.[7] He was, however, likely the first African American to do so, and was presumed by many readers to be writing in his "natural" mode.[8] Within his chosen subgenre, he was, as Gene Andrew Jarrett and Thomas Lewis Morgan argue regarding Dunbar's short fiction, "expected to conform to the accepted literary norms in ways that did not affect white authors, at least if he wanted to remain in the good graces of editors and his reading public."⁹ These limitations led Dunbar to innovate the form in response to his reception in ways that his predecessors could not. Michael Cohen describes the appeal of Dunbar's dialect when he points out that his poetry "circulated as the fantasy of difference, seeming to come from the illiterate and inarticulate folk, but also available to literate and articulate readers";[10] I would add, however, that Cohen's "available" implies ease when in fact there is considerable labor involved in reading Dunbar's dialect. Dunbar's poetry forces those "literate and articulate readers" to do active work rather than passively receive the labors of the "illiterate and inarticulate" as they imagine they do in their idealized dialect reading experience.

Dunbar's dialect poetry, easy and full of ease in its sentiment, compels readers to reenact the literacy acquisition process, and forces them to do work just to plow through it, just as Dunbar has done work to plow through it. The poet has performed the necessary cultivation, and the poem's appearance in cultivated media such as the *Century* means that he expects that it will do its work on his readers, but only if those readers also join in the active cultivation. To ask *Century* readers of the 1890s to do this work was no small task. For example, an exemplary turn-of-the-century American reader, Brander Matthews, complained of reading in which "the joyless toil that went to its making oppresses the reader, forced to share the sore travail of the author."[11] Matthews assumes that if something is hard to write, there will be evidence of that effort that will make it hard to read. If the reader senses the work behind the composition of a poem or novel, he is likely to reject it out of hand. Paradoxically, however, it is also possible that, if an author exerts effort to find *le mot juste,* the reading process can be made easier, as the author meets the reader more than half-way (this is what Edward Bok argues, in an anecdote about discussing proofs with Robert Louis Stevenson, whose scrupulous revision made him realize "the truth of the maxim: 'Easy writing, hard reading; hard writing, easy reading'").[12]

What Dunbar accomplishes through his mastery of dialect poetry is the promotion of a reading experience that completely bypasses Matthews' and Bok's stark formulae: Dunbar makes it *seem* as if it does not ask the reader to share in the work. To use Bok's language, it is "hard writing" but it is *both* "hard reading" and "easy reading." For most readers, the necessary effort will not be apparent. Dialect poetry does not appear to require much but, surprisingly, it does require its reader to read intensively and thus requires cultivation. Rather than "reading as poaching," a metaphor Michel de Certeau uses to describe readers who "move across lands belonging to someone else, like nomads poaching their way across fields they did not write" in contrast to writers "working on the soil of language," readers of Dunbar, following in his path, are not offered this freedom of exploration.[13] Advertisements, such as a poster for a July 9, 1901 poetry reading by Dunbar that praised the "ease with which Dunbar pictures the genuine negro," belied the labor involved in creating that effect of ease.[14] Dialect poetry's ease paradoxically masks its difficulty, just as cultivation conceals the labor at its heart.

The Ease and Labor of Dialect Poetry

Early in his career, Dunbar began to see himself as a literary worker. He viewed his writing (verse and prose both, but especially prose) as commerce. As he writes to James Newton Matthews in 1893, "I am just beginning to realize what a busy work-a-day old world this is anyway. It used to seem all a universal holiday, even when I was drudging I thought that all beyond the limits of my elevator was rest and enjoyment."[15] The writing life that once promised, as in "The Poet and His Song," to be a leisurely life quickly lost that potential. The account given by Bok, editor of *Ladies' Home Journal* from 1889 to 1919 (a magazine in which Dunbar published and that he held "in high estimation"), of the current-day writer's plight—he is "in a feverish race: he needs keep in the procession and as near the head of it as he can"—turns out to be an apt description of the situation in which Dunbar found himself.[16] By 1897, he wrote in a letter to Alice, "I am myself writing very hard and very steadily, the last few evenings past having seen me do sixteen thousand words in prose and about half a dozen poems. This is hustling."[17] So, somehow, just as in "The Poet and His Song," the work and the song—once the means by which the poet can escape work—come to mean the same thing. There is no escape, "Be thou toiler, poet, priest," as Dunbar puts it in another poem, "Keep A-Pluggin' Away."

Dunbar's letters are, as are the letters of so many writers, full of references to payments received, sought, and expected. And, yet, when his intimate friend and frequent correspondent Rebekah Baldwin wrote to him in 1894, she seemed to think that any talk of money would be beneath him, that the poet's rarified and lofty position would seem to demand that he not concern himself with finances. She writes:

> I pray kind fortune scatter dollars (not roses) in your way. The "almighty dollar" is the open "sesame" to all things, even to the indulgence of poetic inspiration. If the very unpoetic ending of this scrawl offend you dear, "pluck it off" (I mean *cut* it off) and cast it from thee; for what indeed have poets to do with anything so vulgar as *money?* . . . No doubt if kindly Fortune obeyed my invocation and showered "filthy lucre" in your way, you would cry out in scorn, "A *poet's* path way is be [*sic*] strewn with *flowers,* he stoops not down to gather up base *coins!*" (emphasis in original)[18]

Baldwin's playful caricature of Dunbar only echoes a perspective presented by Dunbar himself in his verse about the profession. It's a perspective that could be described as both rustic and genteel. In a poem about James Whitcomb Riley, for example, the speaker lauds his subject for many reasons, not least of which is the fact that Riley does not write in order to make a living.[19] But neither does he write for pleasure. As Dunbar puts it in "James Whitcomb Riley," "Now in our time, when poets rhyme / For money, fun, or fashion," Riley puts serving his reader first.[20] Dunbar claimed to be skeptical of paths "strewn with flowers," to use Baldwin's phrase. In an 1892 letter to James Newton Matthews, he writes, "I have always had a desire to go to college, but must confess to having little faith in the 'on flow'ry beds of ease' method."[21]

The alternative, or an alternative, to the Riley model is the Dilettante ("The Dilettante: A Modern Type" appeared in the July 1895 issue of the *Century*):

> He scribbles some in prose and verse,
> And now and then he prints it;
> He paints a little,—gathers some
> Of Nature's gold and mints it.
>
> He plays a little, sings a song,
> Acts tragic roles or funny;
> He does, because his love is strong,
> But not, oh, not for money!
>
> He studies almost everything
> From social art to science;
> A thirsty mind, a flowing spring,
> Demand and swift compliance.

> He looms above the sordid crowd,
> At least through friendly lenses;
> While his mama looks pleased and proud,
> And kindly pays expenses.[22]

Unlike Dunbar's Riley, who is personable and "gives us" songs, the dilettante impersonally sends his written work out into the world and "prints it," as if only to satisfy himself. When he does make his work available, it is only "now and then"; he does not feel the responsibility to avail himself to his reader as Riley does. Of course, the dilettante is not just a writer. He paints, plays, sings, and acts. But, strangely enough, Riley also paints ("He paints our joys an' sorrers"), and he plays ("His heart keeps beatin' time with our'n / In measures fast or slow"), and he sings ("he sings simple songs"). What he doesn't do, however, is act. His is "honest passion," as sincerity was considered the true virtue of Riley's work by his devoted readers. A direct attack upon the refinement he associates with the dilettante, Dunbar ends "James Whitcomb Riley" with the following lines: "So let the others build their songs, / An' strive to polish highly, / There's none of them kin tech the heart / Like our own Whitcomb Riley." The "polish," together with the "trim an' skillful phrases" Dunbar disparages earlier in the poem, cannot make up for the dilettante's lack of substance.

As Lawrence Buell points out, the American literary milieu was dominated until 1835 by writers who were effectively dilettantes. Despite the ascendancy of the professional writer later in the century, the shadow cast by what Buell calls "genteel amateurism" extended beyond Henry Wadsworth Longfellow's generation, and appears to have influenced Dunbar's view of what an author could and should be.[23] However, the modern dilettante's lack of focus, for Dunbar, now outweighs whatever advantages come with dilettantism. The dilettante may be cultivated, but that cultivation lacks depth, in part because he reads extensively rather than intensively.[24] He "studies almost everything" and has a "thirsty mind," but he isn't exactly a paragon of scholarly behavior; for all his studying, he doesn't seem to know any one thing deeply. Riley, though not a scholar, may be a "genius" (to quote Dunbar) who delves more deeply into his art and into his reader's soul, and allows his reader to reciprocate. His didacticism is a kind of public service: "If there's a lesson to be taught / He never fears to teach it." The dilettante's "thirsty mind" absorbs knowledge passively, but Riley's student must actively "reach" for a collaborative knowledge. Here, the metaphor is not an agricultural one but something akin to mining, as the model of teaching and learning in "James Whitcomb Riley" is a kind of excavation in which his sentiment "thrills" us and "[t]hrough the core the tears go tricklin'."[25] Riley labors to penetrate the core, to get beneath the surface, but the dilettante can only refine and polish what he finds. To read "James Whitcomb Riley" alongside "The Dilettante" uncovers the ambivalence Dunbar felt about dilettantism: on one hand, it represents ease and leisure; on the other, it makes the artist capricious, impractical, and effete.

The satirical wallop of "The Dilettante" comes in the line addressing the impetus behind his art. Just as Riley does not "rhyme / For money," the dilettante turns his nose up at the suggestion. His art is driven by the love for it, "[b]ut not, oh, not for money!" The joke, of course, is that he has no need to worry about money; his mother supports his habit. The dilettante does not concern himself with earning an income, as he simply "gathers some / Of Nature's gold and mints it" rather than working to cultivate a plain all "ripened gold" as the speaker of "The Poet and His Song" does. These are two very different ways to describe metaphorical harvesting, one marked by struggle and the other free from it. It is worth noting here that "The Dilettante" was included in Dunbar's *Majors and Minors,* one of his two self-published collections. In other words, these were books he himself had "printed," but not without difficulty. Although the poem is satirical, the dilettante expresses Dunbar's submerged (and sometimes not-so-submerged) desire to make the writerly life approximate the idealized and now anachronistic poet life represented in Rebekah Baldwin's letter: unsullied by financial concerns, free from labor, full of strewn flowers and leisure. In this way, the poem ends up being something like self-mockery. But this leisurely existence is not in fact the writer's life, and especially not the life of a popular sentimental and "easy" poet at the turn of the century, whose job included making his poetry seem effortless, fluent and full of ease, concealing the labor that goes into its creation. Dunbar did not have the luxury to publish "now and then," as the dilettante does; he published furiously in his short career. He was, as he wrote to Alice, "hustling."

Dunbar presumes that dilettante writing goes hand in hand with dilettante reading, that one who "scribbles" will also read everything indiscriminately. The dilettante reader, as Dunbar depicts him, was essentially an idealized magazine reader. A generation later, in a 1928 article titled "The Rise of the Negro Magazine," Charles S. Johnson, editor of *Opportunity,* made the following claim: "Broadly considered, newspapers are expected to be informative, magazines cultural. . . . Mere literacy will not support a magazine, although it does more for a newspaper. A mellowed literacy is required for the appreciation and support of the Negro magazine."[26] But what is a mellowed literacy, and what distinguishes it from mere literacy? In his assertion that "mere literacy will not support a magazine," is Johnson suggesting that a degree or quality of literacy inheres in the text itself (i.e., the magazine's content should be more than merely literate) or in the reader (i.e., the reader approaches the magazine in a manner more than merely literate)? The passive constructions running through Johnson's pronouncements leave both possibilities: if "a mellowed literacy is required," of whom is it required, text or reader? In any case, Johnson's remarks send the message that the cultural value of the magazine necessarily excludes or wishes to exclude certain readers, or at least certain reading practices. Although this magazine-newspaper distinction had been made generally, Johnson in his literary-historical overview upholds this distinction for potential audiences of African American literature in the first third of the last century, a century inaugurated by Dunbar's formidable literary presence. Dialect poetry, the subgenre for which Dunbar was and is best known, occupies an unusual position in periodical literature: despite the fact that magazine readers would consider verse to be the most "mellowed" of literary genres, for many readers the intrusion of dialect compromised the mellowness of that verse. Dialect was the mark of literature that was not serious.

With the word "mellowed," Johnson invokes a cluster of related senses, most having to do with ripeness (of fruit or wheat, for example), maturity, gentleness, or softness. In the context of reading, duration is also a factor, as mere reading happens almost instantaneously, but mellowed reading takes time and requires leisure. But, despite the time spent, mellowed reading does not demand great effort; it is not profound or vigorous reading. Every sense of the "mellowed" of "mellowed literacy" points us back indirectly to another polysemous word often applied to literature that I have used throughout this book: "cultivated." The act of bringing crops to fruition yokes "mellowed" and "cultivation" to the concept of developing a sophisticated appreciation of the arts. "Cultivated" differs from "mellowed," however, in containing almost opposing meanings. Like "culture" (which, as Raymond Williams writes, underwent semantic shifts from "a noun of process: the tending of something; basically crops or animals" to "a process of human development" in the early sixteenth century, and then to the "independent noun, an abstract process or the product of such a process" in the late eighteenth and early nineteenth century), "cultivation" moved "from a physical to a social or educational sense."[27] In other words, cultivation originally described work but evolved to describe a status marked by the absence of work. Dunbar's poetry exploits this paradox of cultivation: his verse aims to combine the depth of excavation he associates with Riley with the refinement and elitism he associates with the Dilettante.

The Commerce of Magazine Verse

Poetry, deemed a mellowed genre by magazine readers, appeared to them to be less compatible with the commercial world of postbellum periodical publishing than prose, but this was not the case. Of course, as Ellery Sedgwick observes, "making a living was probably harder than in the previous generation of Longfellow, Whittier, and Lowell"—according to *Scribner's* editor Roger Burlingame, poets could expect maybe a dollar per line, and Dunbar's payment for his verse was not exceptional in this regard.[28] In a November 10, 1901, letter to his literary agent, Paul Revere Reynolds, Dunbar expresses disappointment at the fact that Reynolds has sold some of his work at fifty cents a line, which, Dunbar writes, "is less than I usually get for them myself, though I sell mostly but to two place [*sic*], the Saturday Evening Post and the Century. For a poem the length of 'The Haunted Oak' the Century gave me thirty-five dollars, and for another of twenty-four lines, fifteen dollars. This is the about the way my prices run. . . . The serious pieces usually bring higher prices."[29] However, although poetry at the turn of the century had little market value (unlike prose fiction writing, which could be a money-making venture for a few authors), poets found their writing to be in close dialogue with the commercial dimensions of the modern magazine. Magazine layout decisions had the potential to move poetry into a paratextual role similar to that of advertisement text commonly found in magazines like the *Century* in the 1890s. Advertising manager George H. Hazen—known, along with Francis A. Wilson of the *Youth's Companion,* as one of the "two bright particular stars in the advertising firmament"—was "a trusted adviser in all departments," indicating an editorial hand in both the marketing and creative aspects of the magazine.[30] Years earlier, William W. Ellsworth, who was in charge of the magazine's publicity with advertising manager Charles F. Chichester and was later president of the Century Company, believed that "[t]o write an advertisement is n't quite like writing a sonnet, but there is a satisfaction in doing it well."[31] The staff of the *Century* clearly saw some comparative relationship between poetry and advertising aesthetically, spatially, and affectively. Finding the correlation between poetry and advertising space even more explicit in the case of some African American magazines, Dunbar denounces "a certain prominent negro journal which supplements its statement of terms with the announcement that all poetical contributions must be accompanied by payment for publication at regular advertising rates. Rare encouragement, indeed, for that proverbially impecunious class, the poets."[32]

The generic boundaries between verse and advertising copy were becoming increasingly fluid at the edges, with light verse and jingles sometimes interchangeable. In fact, Bok proclaimed that advertising, at its best, could serve as a model for the sort of economy that literary language should strive for: it "meant to him the capacity to say much in little space" and it appreciated "the value of white space."[33] In an 1890 issue of *The Critic*, the "Lounger" (Jeanette Gilder) responds to a letter from an "amateur 'jingler'" who asks "where she can find a market for her wares,—sonnets or dirges, advertisements or puffs. Cash, not fame, is her present need." Her "wares"—she also calls them "commodities" later in the letter—include both high and low art, and she does not discriminate between them. Gilder gives her the following practical advice: "the writing of 'sonnets and jingles' never yet kept the wolf from the door of the amateur. There is a larger and more fruitful field to be cultivated by the writer of 'advertisements or puffs.'" Finally, she lectures her: "'Jingling' ought always, however, to be regarded as a relaxation or amusement, not as a means of livelihood."[34] (Her response suggests that "jingle" was not yet used to refer to advertising slogans.) Gilder demands that she make a sharp division between her "wares" on one hand and her verse on the other. She should remain an "amateur" or dilettante when it comes to her serious poems, written only to please herself, but she should work to "cultivate" a place for her advertising verse.

In 1895, Bok claimed to lament the changes to literary production he was witnessing. He reminisced about what he called the "pastoral days in literature," when the "'needs' of the publisher, the 'requirements' of the public, were far from the mind of the writer when he wrote, and yet his work invariably met both needs and requirements." Furthermore, he complained that "the products of some of our authors have simply become a mechanical annual crop, suggesting the fact that the writers are making all the hay they can while the sun of their prosperity is shining."[35] Bok's metaphor of writing-as-crop, along with his use of "pastoral" to describe a writing past viewed nostalgically, reveals an anxiety about the stability of "cultivation," a fear that the literature of cultivation might revert to the earliest stage of its etymological history. What had been grueling work and was now enjoyable leisure was in danger of becoming grueling work again. This interchangeability was exactly what eminent American Victorian Brander Matthews (who, Susanna Ashton argues, "epitomized the last stand of writers who sought the cultural status of 'the artist' even as they participated in the marketplace") found problematic in his 1899 essay "Literature as a Profession." In distinguishing the ideal man of letters from the journalist, he writes that the former "toils joyfully, without haste and without rest, never quitting his work till he has done his best by it." Furthermore, Brander Matthews's ideal man of letters "is never in a hurry"—unlike Dunbar, who was "hustling."[36] "Good writing is laborious writing," Bok insisted in his autobiography, *The Americanization of Edward Bok*, "the result of revision upon revision."[37] Bok and Matthews do not question the validity of the comparison of poetic output to fruit and grain, but they imagine the writer's exertion as something more akin to working leisurely in a garden than toiling in a field. No surprise, then, that the final photograph illustrating Bok's autobiography was captioned, "Where Edward Bok is happiest: in his garden." It was to the emerging literary culture exemplified by the careless "amateur 'jingler'" mentioned above, crowded with anonymous would-be poets eager to participate in the literary marketplace, that Bok and Matthews objected.

Although Brander Matthews argued that the medium in which a piece of literature is published is no indication of its literariness, William Dean Howells unsurprisingly observed trends that favored the elite magazine. At the turn of the twentieth century, Howells stood at the gateway of belletristic magazine reading, and he insisted in his 1893 "The Man of Letters as a Man of Business" that the quality of magazine publications in fact exceeded that of book publications. In addition, he argued that the reading audiences for magazines were more discriminating than book-reading audiences. As he put it, "at present the magazines . . . form the most direct approach to that part of our reading public which likes the highest things in literary art. Their readers, if we may judge from the quality of the literature they get, are more refined than the book readers in our community; and their taste has no doubt been cultivated by that of the disciplined and experienced editors."[38] Howells presents it as a perpetual cycle: refined readers are drawn to refined literature, and these readers are further refined in the process of reading the literature, carefully chosen by such "disciplined and experienced editors" as Howells himself. Soon readers would come to expect literature they would find in elite magazines to be more refined than literature they might come across in either books or newspapers.

Where does all of this interaction among magazine editors, readers, and text in the apparently most rarified sphere of publishing leave the writer? Howells proposes that the serious magazine author must consider the financial worth of his work just as other workers do. Despite the fact that the professional author was coming into being, supplanting the dilettante whose income came from other sources, few nineteenth-century American authors could became wealthy from their literary earnings alone.[39] Howells writes, "I wish that I could make all my fellow-artists realize that economically they are the same as mechanics, farmers, day-laborers." Of the writer, he argues,

> He is really of the masses, but they do not know it, and what is worse, they do not know him; as yet the common people do not hear him gladly or hear him at all. He is apparently of the classes; they know him, and they listen to him; he often amuses them very much; but he is not quite at ease among them; whether they know it or not, he knows that he is not of their kind. Perhaps he will never be at home anywhere in the world as long as there are masses whom he ought to consort with, and classes whom he cannot consort with.[40]

This confusion regarding the writer's stance as Howells describes it—seeming of the classes though he is not, and not seeming of the masses though he is—was central to the nineteenth-century writer's implied contract with the cultivated reader, especially the reader of the elite magazine. The writer's unease in his milieu, all the while seeming to be "on flow'ry beds of ease," and to be depicting his subject with ease, can prompt him—as in Dunbar's case—to produce easy literature that hides labor in plain view. In producing work that encourages and invites a mellowed reading, the literary artist assumed an identity mimicking that of the mellowed reader, an identity determined by elite cultural status. Just as readers were cultivated by the elite magazines, the writer who published in these magazines was also indirectly cultivated by them.

Many nineteenth-century writers may have built careers by presenting themselves as belonging to an elite class, but those who were themselves "of the classes" often presented themselves as if they were not. Longfellow, one of Dunbar's literary models, is an example of the latter; Charvat lists "toil" as one of the "endlessly reiterated words" found in his poetry.[41] A retired professor by 1854, Longfellow represented cultivated writing in the mid-nineteenth century in more ways than one. His verse was the very expression of the leisurely life, cultivated in the final sense of the word. But the imprint of work—residue of the first sense of the word—can be found throughout his writing, as Matthew Gartner points out.[42] In other words, Longfellow's poetry seems mellowed but is in fact cultivated, as the product of a writer who is a worker (or at least a writer who positions himself as one). This is not, however, how nineteenth-century authors' relationships to literary work have most often been understood. Most writers, it is commonly argued, worked to conceal their labor. In other words, the false veneer of literary cultivation in the last sense is a direct result of literary cultivation in the first sense. As Gartner writes:

> Whereas socially ambitious writers of the period found it advantageous to affect an aristocratic leisure, a socially privileged writer like Longfellow could affect a laborer's industriousness while actually enjoying great leisure and nursing a tendency to lassitude. . . . Longfellow frequently reminded his readers of the "long days of labor, / And nights devoid of ease" ("The Day Is Done," 1844) that go into the songs of even a humble poet, battling the perception of poetry as an effeminate art and underscoring its "democratic" qualities by insisting that the poet, too, is a worker.[43]

Longfellow's poetry, along with that of Robert Burns, John Keats, and James Whitcomb Riley, significantly influenced Dunbar's work. Following Longfellow's example, however, had an ironic effect for Dunbar: he attempted to "affect a laborer's industriousness" *in order to* "affect an aristocratic leisure" like Longfellow's. Although Howells contends that those who were attempting to distance themselves from a past life of labor would resist the subject in their writing—"The life of toil! It is a little too personal to people who are trying to be ladies and gentlemen of elegant leisure as fast as they can. If we have had to dig, or if we are many of us still digging, that is reason enough why we do not want the spade brought into the parlor"—this turns out not to be the case for Dunbar.[44] Before succeeding as a poet, Dunbar was an elevator operator, and lamented his fate in a letter to Dr. Tobey: "I am tied down and have been by menial labor, and any escape from it so far has only been a brief respite that made a return to the drudgery doubly hard."[45] Similarly, in a letter to James Newton Matthews, he writes, "your letter found me still chained to the ropes of my dingy elevator."[46] His language here is as transparent as it is adamant: "tied down," "chained to the ropes." He thought of his employment at the Callahan Building as a type of wage slavery. But in his poetry Dunbar—who, as Kevin K. Gaines writes, "lived at the margins of the black leisure class"—often presented himself as the worker he wished he weren't.[47]

Unlike Longfellow, Dunbar faced an additional challenge in presenting his poetry as an expression of mellowed literacy: he had a split literary personality, which was perceived by audiences as half-cultivated and half-uncultivated. This dichotomy is, of course, not inconsistent with the rhetoric of American literary identity in general;[48] however, when the rare poet's oeuvre exhibited both tendencies, audiences were driven to expose which was the more natural and authentic mode, a response most famously represented in Howells's review of Dunbar, as I discussed in the previous chapter. Newspaper reviews of Dunbar's readings illustrated how confounding the split could be for some audiences. Upon hearing Dunbar recite his poetry, journalists tended to apply separate methods of evaluation to his performances of dialect (or what they perceived as unrefined) poetry and standard English (or what they perceived as refined) poetry.

This was markedly different from how Dunbar, a cultivated dialect poet, saw himself. Dunbar famously told James Weldon Johnson, "I've got to write dialect poetry; it's the only way I can get them to listen to me."[49] But, he also famously wrote to Alice Ruth Moore, during the early stages of their courtship, "I want to know whether or not you believe in preserving by Afro-American—I don't like the word—writers those quaint old tales and songs of our fathers which have made the fame of Joel Chandler Harris, Thomas Nelson Page, Ruth McEnery Stuart and others! Or whether you like so many others think we should ignore the past and all its capital literary materials."[50] Dunbar saw dialect writing not as a side project to cultivation, but as an opportunity to develop a new and unexplored field of literary cultivation, one rooted in the work of predecessors such as Longfellow.

Dialect, Advertising, and the *Century*

Many historians have pointed to 1893 as the year that inaugurated a magazine "revolution" in the United States, when *Munsey's, McClure's,* and the *Cosmopolitan* lowered their prices to ten cents and began to depend on advertising more than subscriptions for revenue, resulting in huge circulations.[51] This change was happening precisely as Dunbar began to publish his poetry. However, he rarely published in this emergent "middle-class" of magazines. He sent his poetry to the magazines requiring a mellower literacy: *Harper's,* the *Atlantic Monthly,* and especially the *Cen-*

tury.⁵² His first nationally published poem did appear in *Munsey's* in 1894, but the following year he published three poems in the *Century* (April, May, and July) and apparently never published in *Munsey's* again. Roger Burlingame argues that, early on, "there was resistance to the cheap magazines by the more sensitive authors, who did not like to see their best work in the company of so much trash. There was talk in literary circles about writers 'selling their souls' or 'prostituting their talents.'"⁵³ This may have been what Dunbar believed. He did, in fact, claim that "the Century had always been the goal of [his] ambitions," and several biographies mention that he carried a copy of the magazine with him when working in his elevator.⁵⁴

While early biographical accounts of Dunbar make it clear how much the *Century* meant to him, it is worth pointing out also how much Dunbar meant to the *Century*. That the *Century* published a black writer at this time is remarkable, given what Janet Gabler-Hover in her discussion of the magazine during the 1880s describes as "a pathological attitude toward the African-American race and its place in America."⁵⁵ As Reynolds J. Scott-Childress argues in an essay about the poet's role in the magazine, the editors viewed Dunbar's serendipitous emergence as an opportunity to repair damage done by their publishing Thomas Nelson Page's "Marse Chan," which "became the basis for a whole new school of 'darkey' literature."⁵⁶ The *Century*'s editors also turned to Dunbar to ask what he thought of the magazine's articles on race and whether he thought the magazine "overdid the Negro as a comic character" (his answer: no).⁵⁷ Between 1895 and 1905, Dunbar published thirty poems in the *Century*—far more than he published in any other magazine—which averages to an appearance in one of every four issues during that decade. This decade, between 1895 and 1905, follows what Arthur John, author of a history of the magazine, identifies as precisely the period during which "the *Century* reached a pinnacle of prestige and influence unprecedented in American magazine history." And one of the signs that the *Century* appealed to an elite readership was the fact that it "carried more verse than its new competitors."⁵⁸

But how does an anonymous dialect poet writing in the 1890s become a cultivated *Century* poet? Dunbar began as a slush pile poet, sending unsolicited poems to the *Century* from the age of fourteen or sixteen, depending on the source.⁵⁹ Finally, in December 1894, the *Century* accepted three of Dunbar's poems, including "The Dilettante." His acceptance letter read:

We are inclined to accept the contributions you are good enough to offer us for the "Lighter Vein" department. May we therefore ask you to refer us to some person known to us, which reference shall be in the nature of a voucher for your good faith, as you are a stranger to us. This is in accordance with the rule of the magazine. Perhaps it would make this easier to you if I say that a note from my cousin, Charles U. Raymond of your city, vouching for you, would be sufficient.[60]

His provisional acceptance into the world of the *Century* changed the path of Dunbar's career. I would argue, in fact, that Dunbar's career breakthrough came not with Howells's 1896 review of *Majors and Minors,* usually cited as the event that "made" him, but with Dunbar's 1895 *Century* poems. But the provision—the stamp of approval by someone already within the inner circle—almost renders the acceptance meaningless. Without the necessary connections (without, in other words, prior cultivation), the elite periodical proved impenetrable for most writers. (Fortunately, Dunbar had made enough connections at that point that he had no trouble finding luminaries to "vouch" for him.[61])

In an article coincidentally published the same year Dunbar's first submissions were accepted, the president of the Century Company defended his magazine against charges of exclusivism:

> I know there is a popular idea that all magazines are run by cliques, that the articles are all written by a few of the editor's personal friends, that the manuscripts of new writers are returned unread or thrown into the waste-basket.... The twelve numbers of *The Century Magazine,* ending with the issue for April, 1894, contain 394 separate signed articles, and I find that these have been written by 326 different authors, so that only a few authors could have appeared more than once, except in the case of serials. Certainly, this does not look like the work of a small clique, especially as 94 of them were new contributors who had never written for the magazine before and were presumably unknown to the editor.[62]

Considering that the *Century* published so few authors more than once over the course of a year, Dunbar's achievement of thirty poems in ten years is all the more remarkable. Despite the protestations of the Century Company president, getting into the magazine as an unknown was statistically very competitive.[63] As David Perkins argues in his history of modern poetry, it was "not easy to break into print at this time, especially for the unconventional."⁶⁴ As we will see, Dunbar's manipulations of written dialect are in fact "unconventional" and very strategic, but his verse appeared superficially to be conventional. Ironically, there was always room for dialect poetry in the *Century*.

But, of Dunbar's many poems published in the *Century*, most, including "The Dilettante," appeared in a section to which the magazine's last pages were devoted. This department, which started as "Etchings" and then "Bric-À-Brac" before settling on "In Lighter Vein," included light verse, isolating and containing writing that did not qualify as genteel. The titles of this department grew increasingly oppositional to the other contents of the magazine: "Etchings," as artwork, can stand alone; "Bric-À-Brac," as ornament, positions itself as a decorative addition to the main text; "In Lighter Vein" finally defines itself *only* in subordinate relation to the main text. Even the *Century*'s table of contents in the late 1890s illustrates the relative anonymity of the "In Lighter Vein" author, whose name (in both italics and parentheses) is less prominently displayed than those of poets featured in the magazine proper. In an 1895 letter to Alice Ruth Moore, Dunbar called three recent poems taken by the *Century* "little things for 'The Lighter Vein' department"—just as the song of "The Poet and His Song" was "but a little thing"—suggesting that, although he had reached his goal, the accomplishment was diminished by his relegation to this section.⁶⁵ These songs may have been "little things," but they were not inconsequential for Dunbar, and he was, Addison Gayle, Jr., claims, "not pleased with this designation for his poems."⁶⁶

Although these light poems were considered less prestigious than the poems in the rest of the magazine, this is not to say that they were judged to be of lesser quality. This appreciation, though, was tinged with, as we might expect, more than a bit of condescension. According to Arthur John, it was the "best regular feature" and "consistently good." Reading it, he argued, produced an effect similar to that of "a lecturer sending his audience home smiling."⁶⁷ The entertainment provided by the department was useful for the magazine, but the further the work published there veered from the cultivated literature upon which the *Century* built its reputation, the more dangerous it became. Richard Watson Gilder, editor of the *Century* during Dunbar's career, once wrote to Hamlin Garland,

> People who are trying to bring up their children with refinement, and to keep their own and their children's language pure and clean, very naturally are jealous of the influence of the magazine—especially of the *Century Magazine*—in this respect. . . . [W]e at least think a dialect

story—especially . . . where all sorts of vulgarisms occur,—should very strongly recommend itself before being sent into almost every cultivated household in the United States![68]

In other words, dialect writing (if good) was permitted to appear in the *Century*, but only if sequestered or quarantined, or titled with a proper warning, so that readers would expect that they might get the chaff with the wheat. The so-called vulgarisms of dialect writing interfered with the *Century*'s project of edification. So, while Dunbar was afforded access to this world, his work was mainly bound to the "In Lighter Vein" department; it could not seep through. For all his success, Dunbar continued to be a "lighter vein" poet after his death, as three of his poems were included in an anthology titled *The Humbler Poets: A Collection of Newspaper and Periodical Verse, 1885 to 1910* in a section titled "In Lighter Vein," among poems by mainly unknown and anonymous writers.

After placing his work in the most cultivated of printed media, Dunbar could not control the editorial context in which he'd appear and the conditions of his periodical reception. The liminal position of the "In Lighter Vein" material—situated between the rest of the literature and the advertising—testifies strongly to its perceived commercial status. Moreover, this decade (1895–1905) that both immediately follows the highest point of the *Century*'s literary–cultural status and corresponds with the boundaries of Dunbar's career also marked an explosion of advertising verse. In an observation about the "sudden outburst of rhymed advertising, or 'jingles' in 1900–1905," Frank Luther Mott writes, "Copy writers had occasionally given way to the wiles of the muse throughout the nineteenth century, but perhaps there was more doggerel in the advertising of the nineties than previously."[69] For example, the popular Sapolio "Spotless Town" campaign, with its running narrative about the inhabitants of a town cleansed by Sapolio soap, reached its potential customers through simple rhymed verse. (The company also commissioned Harte to write a versified parody of Longfellow's *Excelsior*.) Versified advertisements in fact "did much for the growth of advertising."[70] With the prevalence of poetry that was really advertising, coupled with the light verse section's proximity to the advertising section, readers of the *Century* could have encountered Dunbar's verse as something less legitimate than the rest of the magazine's text.

Conversely, the *Century*'s advertisements attempted to borrow whatever artistic legitimacy had been bestowed upon the adjacent poetry. Jonathan Culler gestures toward this symbiotic relationship when he calls the advertising jingle "parodic support" for the lyric.[71] The Pears soap advertisement published in the same issue of the *Century* that introduced the world to Dunbar, just a few pages after his "Negro Love Song," features a jingle in ballad meter, placing its product in "ancient" history, in an authentic world predating the crass advertising world to which it would appear to belong. But, not only does this beloved product have a past, it has a future (it will "still be foremost / Another hundred years"). Not one of these "new wares" or flash-in-the-pan fads you might find elsewhere in the advertising section, Pears is treated as an intrinsic part of our culture. And, as if mutually devoted lovers, those "beauties of the ancient days / . . . / Kept faithful to their faithful PEARS," and this reciprocity and constancy distinguish the product from others. The second stanza of the advertisement could have come from a love poem, as it attempts to step outside consumer desire; in fact, it depicts a simple love story—between consumer and product—oddly similar to that in "A Negro Love Song."

Through this ad, Pears—which, as Ellen Gruber Garvey argues, "was particularly enterprising in annexing high culture to its advertising"—attempts to absorb the high-brow air of the medium in which it published, encouraging the reading that having Pears in your life was a sign of cultivation, just as the *Century*'s poetry was. The soap is said to appeal, in fact, to those supposed paragons of cultivation—"princes"—while still remaining democratically within reach of rustic "cottagers." The *Century* may have, as Janice Radway writes, "railed against popular magazines such as *Munsey's, Cosmopolitan,* and the *Saturday Evening Post* for embedding fiction and poems among ads for soap and crackers . . . , thereby revealing their commercial orientation," but the shared marginal status of the "In Lighter Vein" poetry and the advertisement verse allows this sort of intermingling in the *Century,* too.[72]

It may seem odd to compare advertising copy to periodical verse, but perhaps it would not seem as strange for magazine readers of the 1890s. As Garvey has pointed out, "Readers learned . . . to look to [advertisements] for some of the pleasures of fiction," and some magazines, through advertisement-writing contests, "encourage[d] readers to disregard distinctions between advertising and fiction."[73] And the formal similarities between the Pears poem and Dunbar's *Century* poem in the same issue—in fact, all of the poems included in the April 1895 "In Lighter Vein"—are striking when compared to the rest of the magazine's poetry. Three of the four poems in the main part of the issue are Petrarchan sonnets, but the "In Lighter Vein" poems are, like the Pears poem, in ballad meter. The sharp contrast between pentameter on the one hand and ballad meter on the other shows how strongly, as Antony Easthope wrote, the "hegemonic form" of pentameter in the Anglo-American tradition "includes and excludes, sanctions and denigrates, for it discriminates the 'properly' poetic from the 'improperly' poetic, Poetry from verse. . . . [A] poem within the metrical tradition identifies itself (in Puttenham's words) with polish and reformed manners as against poetry in another metre which can be characterized as rude, homely, and in the modern sense, vulgar."[74] Although the relationship between Dunbar and the *Century* editors was mutually beneficial, their ambitions for Dunbar's poetry were dramatically different: Dunbar aspired for high art, whereas Gilder apparently viewed work like Dunbar's as transitional, mediating and transitioning the reader between cultivated and vulgar (but increasingly necessary) modes of writing. "When Malindy Sings," for example, demonstrates well Dunbar's unconventional project of treating dialect poetry as a cultivated subgenre, celebrating the complexity of vernacular expression and reversing the subordinate position of the supposedly uncultivated; it was predictably rejected by the *Century*. It was only when Dunbar performed the poem to a strong audience response at a *Century* dinner in his honor that an embarrassed Gilder offered to take it.

Dunbar's "A Negro Love Song," on the other hand—his first dialect poem for the magazine—apparently fit seamlessly into the *Century*'s predetermined space for dialect poetry and appeared at first glance to be almost as conventional as the advertising verse following it. It even strongly echoes a poem by Joel Chandler Harris published in the same section of the *Century* thirteen years earlier (when a precocious Dunbar could have been reading the magazine[75]) *also* called "A Negro Love Song," with an almost identical form. This familiarity contributed to the effect of ease that allowed some *Century* readers to miss the cultivation behind the poem. Dunbar's project of cultivated dialect poetry, which he expected to further by publishing in the *Century*, suffered from the editorial guidance of readers' expectations. The juxtaposition of Dunbar's verse with advertising verse gives new meaning to two of the most celebrated lines in his poetry: "But ah, the world, it turned to praise / A jingle in a broken tongue."

The Cultivation of Dialect Performance

So, even as Dunbar mocks the pretensions of the dilettante, there is some envy hidden in the mockery. In 1897 he complained to William Dean Howells of having to perform at "vulgar" readings when in London, "put in upon programs between dancing girls from the vaudeville and clowns from the varieties," perhaps suffering in person the same indignity as his dialect verse, which was lost among the bric-a-brac.[76] Unlike the dilettante, he was not, as a performer, permitted to "loom above the sordid crowd." Dunbar declared that, if the novel he was working on proved a success, there would be "no more readings for me—forever. I have had my fill of readings and managers. If I can make my living by my pen I will not use my voice."[77] The public readings of poetry, upon which his financial success depended, often had the paradoxical effect of linking Dunbar with the proletariat from whom he may have wanted to distance himself. The larger his audience became and the richer Dunbar could become, the more "lowly" he would appear to his audiences; he would appear to *be* his "lowly" subject.[78] And it does seem to be true that, as much as his career depended upon the association of the poet with the subject, Dunbar resented that association.[79] He makes an effort, in essays such as "Negro Society in Washington," to distinguish himself from the most pretentious of elite black society, mocking the "severe high and mighty intellectual set" (just as he mocked Mandy in "Happy! Happy! Happy!"), "one which takes itself with eminent seriousness and looks down on all the people who are not studying something, or graduating, or reading papers, or delivering lectures, as frivolous." However, he writes, in the very same essay, "it is hardly to be wondered at that some of us wince a wee bit when we are all thrown into the lump as the peasant or serving class," grouping himself—in his use of the first person plural—with the ostensibly over-educated group he has been dissecting.[80] Signaling a departure from the folksy "poet of the people" stance that Riley projected both within and without the literature, Dunbar boasts, in a letter to his mother in 1896, that he is socializing with "the very cream" in Washington: his company includes "one high school and one college professor, one teacher (lady)[,] one lady who is the daughter of the wealthiest man in the district, a doctor, a banker & his wife and yours humbly."[81] Dunbar's writing about social interaction with the "classes" reveals just how deeply divided he was regarding cultivation. He was torn between the competing desires to separate himself from the crowd and, as the poem "James Whitcomb Riley" advocates, to build a personal relationship with the general reader.

During his poetry performances, dialect appears to have been the main factor in audience interpretations of Dunbar. Listening to dialect poetry, performed well, audiences may identify what they hear as the authentic speech of the poet, coming easily to him. As much as observers identified Dunbar with the rustic characters presented in his poetry, as I discussed in the previous chapter, reviews of Dunbar's readings also frequently remarked with surprise upon what they considered to be a cultivated demeanor.[82] A brief article in the *Dayton Evening News* described a reading Dunbar gave for the employees of the National Cash Register Company, where he had been a janitor years before. At that time, he had worn "the white suit of the janitors," but "[t]his time he was faultlessly dressed with an air and mien that bespoke education and culture."[83] Similarly, a *Washington Post* journalist, giving an account of a reading Dunbar gave for the blind, wrote, "There is an air of refinement about him which immediately singles him out for special attention." This journalist also notices that Dunbar opens his reading with "The Poet and His Song," which he calls "a dainty and touching little piece":

> The style of the poem surprises you, for it is not written in dialect. The English is as pure as though it came from Oxford or Cambridge. The sentiment rings true. It is the song of a workingman, who, whether at work in the field or in the forest, sings his song and all is well. Mr. Dunbar read this beautifully, with sincere feeling and perfect enunciation. The blind, who could not see him, might well have reasoned that this deep, rich, and melodious voice, coming to them in the darkness, belonged to one of the foremost English scholars of the day.
>
> This serious introduction was well chosen, for from strangers it immediately obtained for Mr. Dunbar respect and admiration. His dialect poems are songs of the people, yet this little serious bit proved that he could write for the few as well as for the masses.

As this reporter's response makes clear, audiences still thought of the dialect pieces as crowd-pleasers, designed not for a cultivated elite but for the "people," but there is no question that "The Poet and His Song" requires less of its reader than does, for example, "A Negro Love Song," which was Dunbar's first *Century* poem. The latter's difficulty effectively makes it a poem for the few. Take, for example, the poem's middle stanza:

> Heard de win' blow thoo de pine,
> Jump back, honey, jump back.
> Mockin'-bird was singin' fine,
> Jump back, honey, jump back.
>   An' my hawt was beatin' so
>   When I retched my lady's do'
>   Dat I could n't b'a' to go,
> Jump back, honey, jump back.

Figure 6. Paul Laurence Dunbar reading at the National Cash Register Company, 1904. The NCR Archive at Dayton History

When the poem appeared in as "A Negro Love Song" in *Majors and Minors,* Dunbar had altered the dialect spellings:

> Heahd de win' blow thoo de pines,
>   Jump back, honey, jump back.
> Mockin' bird was singin' fine,
>   Jump back, honey, jump back.
> An' my hea't was beatin' so,
> When I reached my lady's do',
> Dat I couldn't ba' to go—
>   Jump back, honey, jump back.[84]

The dialect spellings in the earlier *Century* version are much more alienating. The transformation of the first word in the revised version might be most immediately noticeable, but there are other changes—"hawt" into "hea't," "retched" into "reached," "could n't b'a'" into "couldn't ba'"—that point in the other direction toward careful and painstaking revision intended to soften and moderate the visual effect of the dialect for what Howells would call the less cultivated medium of the book. Another early dialect poem for the *Century* was also modified for book publication: the almost inscrutable "sec'uts" is restored to "secrets" in "Discovered."[85] Similarly, Dunbar originally wanted to use the antiquated spellings of "gaol" and "gaoler" in his non-dialect "The Haunted Oak," published in the December 1900 issue of the *Century,* in order to "give an added to [*sic*] touch to the form which I do not seem to get in the modern spelling."[86]

It is no accident that "The Poet and His Song" was included in many of Dunbar's reading programs, as it reflected his own idea of mellowed literacy. However, through the challenge presented by the dialect reading process, Dunbar taught his readers that his dialect work, too, required a mellowed literacy, albeit a new and differently inflected one. Not only did Dunbar consider dialect poetry, as I mentioned earlier, to be a subgenre that could expand to carry literary cultivation, he cannily manipulated the reception of his split literary personality by performing dialect poems alongside standard English poems in order to demonstrate for his audience the difficulty of dialect poetry. In addition, Dunbar's decision to publish in the elite magazines of the period, such as the *Century,* allowed his poems—and his reputation—to absorb the mellowness of the medium in which they appeared. As Hamlin Garland put it, to have one's work appear in the *Century* "was equivalent to a diploma."[87] The *Washington Post* journalist may have found Dunbar's standard English poem to be for the "few" and his dialect poem to be for the "masses," but in the end both modes were designed for the few.

Dunbar's early desires to "learn how and what to study in order cultivate [his] vein," as he wrote in his letter to Dr. Tobey, reflect his sometimes contradictory views about cultivation as it comes in contact with his poetics, particularly his early Riley-influenced poetics grounded in the "low." But, what stands out most in Dunbar's remark is the odd phrase "cultivate my vein." It would not be strange to want to cultivate a particular vein: say, poetry writing. But, for Dunbar, the cultivation is total. He is seeking complete cultivation of his self and not of a specific area residing outside of himself. And, because it is "my vein" and not "this vein," it becomes strangely corporeal, as if an intravenous injection would supply the cultivation he desires. The "my" is also proprietary, as if asserting that cultivation—though it may lie dormant or remain unrecognized—is part of who he is, how he would define himself. (As the speaker of "The Poet and His Song" says, "I till my ground and prune my trees.") Elite magazines such as the *Century* served an important role in his literary project of cultivation. His *Century* poetry, however, usually entered households through a "lighter vein," rather than the cultivated vein he sought.

chapter five

Gendered Dialect
*Frances Ellen Watkins Harper and
Maggie Pogue Johnson*

>Don't criticize my writing
>>'Cause I ain't well trained you know
>
>I hab al-ways been so sickly
>>Dat I haben had much show.
>
>Don't laff and ridicule me
>>Cause 'twill make me feel ashamed,
>
>For I knows dat I ain't great
>>Nor neither have I fame.
>
>Some of dese poems you'er reading
>>Was written long ago,
>
>When I was jist a little kid
>>Of thirteen years or so.
>
>Don't criticize my poems,
>>'Cause I wrote 'em all for you;
>
>I ain't had much training
>>'Tis de best dat I can do.
>
>And if you find's my book
>>Ain't good as t'ought to be,
>
>Jist leave it to my ignorance
>>And don't you laff at me.
>
>—Christina Moody, "To My Dear Reader"

This defensive proem opens Christina Moody's 1910 *A Tiny Spark*. In a dialect style that shares some features with Riley's child writing, full of eye dialect and cacography (such as "laff"), Moody emphasizes her

• 143

modest, self-deprecating, and almost servile ("I wrote 'em all for you") approach to poetry writing. She warns her reader that, because she "ain't well trained," he or she should not expect the verse that follows to show the effects of any education. Although versions of this rustic humility can be found in Riley's and Dunbar's poetry, the fact that Moody is a woman writing dialect poetry complicates how a contemporary audience would have understood that stance.

Despite the fact that the last decade of the nineteenth century and the first of the twentieth were unusually productive years for black women writers—it has, in fact, often been called the "Black Women's Era"—relatively few women dared enter the realm of dialect poetry.[1] When critics have addressed this silence, they have usually claimed that dialect writing was not an acceptable domain for women, and that it was seen as an affront and challenge to black womanhood. For example, Caroline Gebhard argues that, "[a]s partners in racial uplift, black women could ill afford to dispense with the prerogatives of genteel femininity. For black women, so often caricatured as hypersexual and ignorant, language associated with a lack of proper decorum or education carried a double risk."[2] So, for instance, when Paul Laurence Dunbar asked Alice Ruth Moore "whether or not [she] believe[d] in preserving by Afro-American . . . writers those quaint old tales and songs of our fathers which have made the fame of Joel Chandler Harris, Thomas Nelson Page, Ruth McEnery Stuart and others!," her response made it clear that she wanted nothing to do with conventional dialect writing.[3]

In addition to the threats it posed to "genteel femininity," dialect writing often espoused ideologies that ran counter to working-class women's interests. In an essay about poetry by working-class British women, Susan Zlotnick ultimately comes to a conclusion similar to Gebhard's—that women's writing and dialect writing were at odds—but she focuses on gender divisions within social class rather than race in her argument that dialect literature is a working-class genre that is exclusively male. In fact, according to Zlotnick, "dialect discourse was itself inimical to female self-expression. . . . [W]orking-class women were silenced by the dialect tradition, which, in its adherence to the ideology of domesticity, made it difficult for working women to write of their own experiences as women who worked."[4] What Zlotnick discovers about British working-class dialect poetry generally obtains for African American dialect poetry. And, moreover, what becomes clear in the meeting of Zlotnick's and Gebhard's arguments is the revelation that black women were driven from dialect poetry from both sides: black working-class women would turn from dialect poetry for its promotion of a lifestyle they didn't recognize as true, and black bourgeois women would turn from dialect poetry that was not consistent with racial uplift. In other words, both those who did and did not conform to the ideology of domesticity mentioned by Zlotnick would avoid dialect poetry.[5]

In this chapter, I take up the question of why so few women wrote dialect poetry, or rather why so few women were successful dialect poets (very few books of dialect poetry by women reached the literary marketplace), and what those women who did publish dialect poetry hoped to accomplish by doing so. In response to pressures that excluded women from the field, some women explicitly and directly confronted gender restrictions in their dialect poetry, particularly through the topic of the theatricality of clothing. I focus on the work of Frances Ellen Watkins Harper and Maggie Pogue Johnson, one known primarily as an activist and author of a novel and the other not known much at all. Although Harper's *Sketches of Southern Life* was first published in 1872 and was reprinted throughout the '70s, '80s, and '90s by Merrihew & Son and Ferguson Brothers, Johnson's *Virginia Dreams* and *Thoughts for Idle Hours* were published in 1910 and 1915 respectively in relative obscurity.[6]

According to Elizabeth McHenry, it is important to recognize that African American literature in the early twentieth century, a period "for which we have no real literary bearing, for which there is no catchy name or useful grouping of writers or works," has been characterized mainly by remarkable political, sociological, and otherwise nonfictional writing.[7] As such, many productive black writers—especially women, though it was still their "era"—were silenced in the sphere of fictive writing. McHenry singles out the unsuccessful (because unpublished) fictive work of Mary Church Terrell, and I extend McHenry's claims about black "literary failure" during this period for the purposes of my examination of Johnson's poetry. We could say, as McHenry says of Terrell, that Johnson's poetry in particular "is not 'great,' nor was it popular, and as such it fits in neither of the two primary (if vague) categories we have most often used to identify literature and comprehend literary history."[8] My work on Johnson's poetry intends to make her visible as one of many writers during this period—particularly African American women writers—whose literary production has not been examined closely precisely because they do not fit easily into the categories of "amateur," "coterie," or "professional" poet; in fact, this liminal status allows Johnson's poetry to serve as a case study of a fascinating, underexamined path in the development of African American poetry.

If prescribed gender roles at the turn of the century prohibited most black women from writing books of dialect poetry, why were they so often eager readers of them, and how can we reconcile this significant readership with those few dialect poets among them? As McHenry and others have discovered, Dunbar's dialect poetry was apparently especially well received by members of African American women's literary clubs at the turn of the century.[9] In addition, newspaper coverage of literary club events shows that black bourgeois women were avid consumers of dialect poetry, reading and celebrating and even performing it. For example, in 1914, a few years after Dunbar's death, a *Chicago Defender* article titled "Miss Lois C. Simmons Entertains" describes a mysterious event that piqued the curiosity of "[m]any people living in the 54th block on Dearborn St.," who were "pulled to their wit's end to know what the cause of so many beautifully dressed young ladies calling at the Simmons, 5424 Dearborn, autos driving up unloading, going away, some autos staying and a perfect stream of the smart set." After an elaborate dinner, this "smart set" of guests performed poems by Dunbar, "after which the young ladies left well pleased with a well spent afternoon."[10] Bourgeois women could be consumers and reproducers of dialect poetry without compromising their status—in fact, their participation in a popular literary trend signaled their inclusion in the "smart set"—even if they usually would not and could not be producers of it.

Because black bourgeois women such as those attending the Simmons event could afford the luxury of leisure, and could therefore devote time to reading, they made up a valuable readership for mainstream writers, which included many writers of dialect during this period. In fact, William Dean Howells's advice for writers emphasized the important presence and influence of female readers in general at the turn of the century:

> The man of letters must make up his mind that in the United States the fate of a book is in the hands of the women. It is the women with us who have the most leisure, and they read the most books. They are far better educated, for the most part, than our men, and their tastes, if not their minds, are more cultivated. Our men read the newspapers, but our women read the books . . . As I say, the author of light literature, and often the author of solid literature, must resign himself to obscurity unless the ladies choose to recognize him.[11]

Because many of the books on the newly established best-seller list were written in dialect,[12] it stands to reason that women were frequently the purchasers of these books. It stands to reason, also, that, if she was buying books of dialect poetry, the female reader during this period was a silent dialect poetry reader as well as a performer of it. Despite the fact that women sometimes performed poetry in settings such as the Simmons event and literary club meetings, the practice of reading aloud to a crowd of listeners, which many historians claim shared space with silent reading in Western reading culture at the turn of the century, was mainly reserved for men and performed in male-dominated places of employment or amusement. As a result, "female readers of the nineteenth century can be associated with the development of silent, individual reading, which relegated oral reading to a world that was disappearing."[13] The paradox of the figure of the silent dialect poetry reader—reading without articulation a phonetic transcript of speech, one that is *supposed* to work best when performed—recalls the tensions behind Harte's, Riley's, and Dunbar's approaches to dialect poetry, which in various ways spotlighted the intersections of orality and literacy in dialect poetry when the two modes seemed to be in opposition. Harper and Johnson were both interested in literacy, and they were interested in dialect at the same time, and found no contradiction in this position.

Harper's Aunt Chloe and Her Literacy

In her biography of Harper, Melba Joyce Boyd contends that she composed *Sketches of Southern Life* as a "practical function of her literacy campaign."[14] Through the use of the persona of Aunt Chloe, a recently freed and newly literate African American woman, Harper's book enacts the process of literacy acquisition with which many of her readers were just becoming familiar. Aunt Chloe expresses her opinions in a variety of the "plain language" dialect made famous by Bret Harte a few years earlier, a dialect defined mainly by its syntax rather than its spelling. According to Boyd, Harper avoided an "overapostrophied dialect" in favor of "accessible language" in order to allow for greater ease in reading; somehow plain-language dialect would engender in its semi-literate readers "a positive psychological response to learning."[15] Some critics, however, question whether the Aunt Chloe poems qualify as dialect poems at all. For example, J. Saunders Redding, in his influential *To Make a Poet Black,* describes Harper's dialect thus:

> In the volume called *Sketches of Southern Life* the language she puts in the mouths of Negro characters has a fine racy, colloquial tang. In these poems she managed to hurdle a barrier by which Dunbar was later to

feel himself tripped. The language is not dialect. She retained the speech patterns of Negro dialect, thereby giving herself greater emotional scope (had she wished or had the power to use it) than the humorous and the pathetic to which it is generally acknowledged dialect limits one.... [16]

Redding's subtle distinction between "dialect" and a "racy, colloquial tang" and his ready acceptance of the association of dialect with humor and pathos show the unmistakable influence of James Weldon Johnson's attack upon dialect (even echoing Johnson's use of the word "racy" to describe an acceptable modern alternative to dialect). Decades later, Elizabeth A. Petrino similarly argues that "Harper's regional and colloquial expressions veer away from dialect toward a broader, more inclusive representation of African-American speech."[17] Less extreme than Redding and Petrino, Boyd finds what appears to be a middle ground, calling Aunt Chloe's voice an invention intended to "bridge the cultural distance between standard English and black dialect."[18] However, what lies between these two poles sounds suspiciously like Redding's "colloquial" voice. Furthermore, in 1977, Gloria T. Hull could write that, during the Reconstruction years, "there are no women dialect poets," with a parenthetical qualification: "(Although Harper wrote dialect poems in her 1872 *Sketches of Southern Life,* she is not studied in this period or considered a part of the dialect 'school')."[19]

It is worth considering why so many readers want to dissociate Harper from dialect. When Paul Lauter claims that Aunt Chloe does not speak in dialect and that her "language is, I believe, designed to legitimate her keen political commentary," he is indirectly refusing the possibility that dialect can be used effectively by Harper as a political tool.[20] Although the Aunt Chloe poems are written in a "high-readability" dialect, there is no question that they are in fact dialect poems, and that Harper intended for them to be read as such, as part of that tradition. The fact that the Aunt Chloe poems are not limited to expressions of humor and pathos does not, as Redding suggests, prove that they are not dialect poems; instead, it proves only that dialect is a more elastic medium for poetry than he supposes. Boyd argues of Aunt Chloe, "Her literacy has modified her dialect," but I contend that Harper chooses to write the Aunt Chloe poems in dialect in order to prove precisely the opposite, implicitly responding to dialect poems that associated their speakers with illiteracy: that there is no relationship, and therefore no incompatibility, between dialect speaking and literacy.[21]

Here is "Learning to Read," one of Harper's Aunt Chloe poems, in its entirety. While the dialect spellings are not extreme ("agin'," "'Twould," "'em") and are kept to a minimum, "Learning to Read" functions, as do many of the dialect poems examined in this study, as a didactic presentation of a reading experience. In it, the aging Aunt Chloe enthusiastically sets herself to the task of acquiring literacy after a lifetime of having it withheld from her:

Very soon the Yankee teachers
    Came down and set up school;
But, oh! how the Rebs did hate it,—
    It was agin' their rule.

Our masters always tried to hide
    Book learning from our eyes;
Knowledge didn't agree with slavery—
    'Twould make us all too wise.

But some of us would try to steal
    A little from the book,
And put the words together,
    And learn by hook or crook.

I remember Uncle Caldwell,
    Who took pot liquor fat
And greased the pages of his book,
    And hid it in his hat.

And had his master ever seen
    The leaves upon his head,
He'd have thought them greasy papers,
    But nothing to be read.

And there was Mr. Turner's Ben,
    Who heard the children spell,
And picked the words right up by heart,
    And learned to read 'em well.

Well, the Northern folks kept sending
    The Yankee teachers down;

> And they stood right up and helped us,
> > Though Rebs did sneer and frown.
>
> And, I longed to read my Bible,
> > For precious words it said;
> But when I begun to learn it,
> > Folks just shook their heads,
>
> And said there is no use trying,
> > Oh! Chloe, you're too late;
> But as I was rising sixty,
> > I had no time to wait.
>
> So I got a pair of glasses,
> > And straight to work I went,
> And never stopped till I could read
> > The hymns and Testament.
>
> Then I got a little cabin
> > A place to call my own—
> And I felt as independent
> > As the queen upon her throne.[22]

The first reading experience that appears in the poem—some would "put the words together / And learn by hook or crook"—signals that something odd has happened to reading. It is ambiguous, as it is difficult to determine whether word fragments are being put together to form words, or complete words are being put together with others to form phrases and sentences. It may seem like a minor distinction, but it is a significant difference: if the former, the poem describes phonics and something similar to a literary dialect reading experience; if the latter, the poem describes a whole-word reading process, as I discussed briefly in this book's first chapter. If the poem presents the former, as I believe the poem does, that presentation would be perfectly in keeping with the project of dialect poetry.

Another unusual depiction of the reading process involves Ben, who simply "heard the children spell," then "picked the words right up by heart," and finally "learned to read 'em well." He begins in a position similar to that of a spectator at a spelling bee before memorizing the words he hears spelled, absorbing knowledge by rote just as one declaiming a poem might. But then, miraculously, his oral knowledge is transferable to the written page, and he is able to read the words whose letters he has learned without being taught what those letters look like. He is the owner of what Frederich A. Kittler calls, in reference to the illiterate Prophet Muhammed whose encounter with the Archangel Gabriel prompts him to read the scripture revealed to him, "miraculously alphabetized eyes."[23]

We learn nothing about how Uncle Caldwell learned to read. Uncle Caldwell, whose reading material is cleverly integrated into his wardrobe, is able to convince his master that the papers in his hat are no cause for alarm. Apparently, the master observes a distinction between writing and literature: the papers, once dirtied and disguised (perhaps used to line the hat?), no longer represent "book learning" and no longer pose a threat. They are "nothing to be read." The passive voice in this line raises the question of just who is doing the reading. From the master's perspective, the papers are "nothing to be read" by the slave, whom the master persists in believing to be illiterate in the face of overwhelming evidence to the contrary. In addition, the slave master decides that the papers are also "nothing to be read" by him, nothing to be examined or interpreted. In any case, the sentence is conditional: "*had* his master ever seen . . . "; Uncle Caldwell manages to successfully avoid even raising suspicion. Uncle Caldwell's secreting of his papers parallels an earlier concealment by the masters themselves, who "always tried to hide / Book learning from our eyes," but the masters' efforts—the negative obstruction of knowledge rather than the positive pursuit of it—are in vain where Uncle Caldwell's are successful.

Early in the poem, Aunt Chloe presents the furtive attempts of those in her community to learn to read as theft, saying that "some of [them] would try to steal / A little from the book." In an essay on *Iola Leroy,* Patricia Bizzell describes Robert's reading skills as the result of "stolen literacies," because his mistress, in illegally teaching him to read, "stole literacy for him" and Robert in turn "has stolen this literacy away from the mistress" by applying his skills in ways she did not foresee or sanction.[24] What is most interesting about the theft described by Aunt Chloe, however, is the degree: they would only "steal / A little," as if the stolen reading were a quantifiable material good; this differs from the wholesale theft implied in "stolen literacies." Stealing a little, without eliciting notice, recalls instead Michel de Certeau's concept of "la perruque" ("the wig"), cited productively by Charles Bernstein in "Poetics of the Americas." "La perruque" is the "worker's own work disguised as the work of his employer. . . . [T]he worker who indulges in *la perruque* actually diverts time (not goods, since he uses only scraps) . . . for work that is free, creative, and precisely not directed toward profit."²⁵ Bernstein applies de Certeau's concept metaphorically in order to describe Claude McKay's use of dialect writing in pentameter as "a running double play of ingratiation and defiance," as I will discuss in the next chapter, but here the example of Uncle Caldwell's scraps is a literalization of the metaphorical theft that typically lies behind a slave's (or even an ex-slave's) acquisition of literacy.²⁶

Hiding papers under one's hat for the purpose of sneaking literacy is not unique to Uncle Caldwell. Heather Andrea Williams cites several cases: "Some slaves hid spelling books under their hats to be ready whenever they could entreat or bribe a literate person to teach them. . . . As a young enslaved boy, Richard Parker . . . carried a primer under his hat to be ready for class at any time. . . . 'Uncle' Charles, a former slave in North Carolina, recounted that he also carried a primer under his hat and challenged white boys to tell him what a letter was, until he managed to learn to the alphabet."²⁷ In none of these cases did the slave learn to read spontaneously or independently. Similarly, in *Iola Leroy,* Harper tells stories of literacy acquisition resembling those in "Learning to Read," but she fleshes out some of the details. We learn of Tom Anderson, who "can read a little":

> He used to take lessons from a white gardener in Virginia. He would go between the hours of 9 P.M. and 4 A.M. He got a book of his own, tore it up, greased the pages, and hid them in his hat. Then if his master had ever knocked his hat off he would have thought them greasy papers, and not that Tom was carrying his library on his head.

Another man is described in the same paragraph, one who sounds much like Ben:

> One day he had an errand in the kitchen, and he heard one of the colored girls going over the A B C's. Here was the key to the forbidden knowledge. She had heard the white children saying them, and picked them up by heart, but did not know them by sight. . . . He got the sounds of the letters by heart, then cut off the bark of a tree, carved the letters on the smooth inside, and learned them. He wanted to learn how to write. He had charge of a warehouse where he had a chance to see the size and form of letters. He made the beach of the river his copybook, and thus he learned to write.²⁸

These stories hardly make learning to read seem effortless, as the poem does. In fact, *Iola Leroy*'s Tom "never got very far with his learning," despite his Herculean efforts. Although, regarding Tom, Boyd remarks that "the oral orientation of the culture can become a pedagogical technique for literacy," the problem with this model is that orality and literacy are not transferable skills, and we see this in the case of the girl who mediates the unnamed *Iola Leroy* character's acquisition of literacy.[29] After hearing white children reciting letters, she can imitate them orally, but has no means of understanding those letters as writing. The acquisition of literacy described in "Learning to Read" would have to qualify as almost miraculous.

Harper devotes several stanzas to Aunt Chloe's learning to read (she is, after all, the center of this series of poems), but by the end of the poem we are no closer to knowing how she does it. We know that she wants to learn primarily in order to read her bible, a desire that was not uncommon during the postbellum years.[30] Interestingly, Chloe wants to read the bible for "precious words it *said*" (emphasis added), as if she understands the book to represent a voice locked in text, invoking the "talking book" trope.[31] She already knows what the Bible *says,* from having heard it, but she expects that approaching the Bible through literacy will provide a different experience, a different sort of knowledge. Chloe says only that she "begun to learn it" and, later, she tells us that she "got a pair of glasses" and went "straight to work," understanding learning to read as a process and comparing it to a kind of labor. Ultimately, she "never stopped till [she] could read." In the end, like Ben—although Chloe's learning presumably took time—her literacy is, again, nothing short of miraculous.

Why would Harper want to describe these acquisitions of literacy as spontaneous and almost magical, even if they are (as Chloe's was) laborious? If she truly intended for these poems to serve as aids in increasing literacy, it is strange to leave the process so shrouded in mystery. Ironically, it is likely that Harper left the process vague because she did not want any part of the poem to discourage beginning readers. Chloe is, as Paula Bernat Bennett points out, "a singularly hard act to follow"; she is Harper's model for progress, but "not one to which many ex-slaves, especially those suffering direst poverty in the deep South, could easily relate."[32] The poem is, however, entirely uplifting: Aunt Chloe overcomes the doubts of the naysayers, and she is happy in the end. Not only is she happy, the poem draws a causal link between her literacy and her success.[33] The last stanza begins with a conditional "Then," as if learning to read necessarily leads to wealth ("I got a little cabin") and autonomy ("I felt as independent / As the queen upon her throne"). This is a fantasy of unlikely achievement, but the step that initiates Chloe's climb is literacy, a step that the ideal reader of Harper's poems is in the process of achieving. The Aunt Chloe series straddles the war years, with some of the poems taking place during the period leading up to the war and some after. "Learning to Read" depicts a doubly free Aunt Chloe. She is a freedwoman, but she believes that it is only through literacy that she achieves self-government and becomes her own master and her own "queen." It is also worth noting that, in terms of sequence in *Sketches of Southern Life* (taking the "Aunt Chloe" poems as a chronological narrative series), the poems following "Learning to Read" are still dialect poems, emphasizing again that Aunt Chloe's newfound literacy does not transform her into a standard-English-speaking character.

The character of Aunt Chloe has often been compared to Aunt Linda, a similar character who appears in *Iola Leroy*.[34] James Christmann claims that Aunt Linda (unlike Aunt Chloe) "rejects Western education . . . , instead basing her judgments on standards and values indigenous to her culture and class."[35] And, throughout most of the novel, she does turn away from reading. When Iola asks Aunt Linda, "Won't you get a pair of spectacles and learn to read?," she replies, "Oh, yer can't git dat book froo my head, no way you fix it. I knows nuff to git to hebben and dats all I wants to know." In fact, her attitude toward reading, according to the narrator, is not one of resignation but one of stubborn defiance: "Aunt Linda was kind and obliging, but there was one place where she drew the line, and that was at learning to read."[36] Aunt Linda seems content to "read" her environment for the same knowledge others get from print. Early in the novel, she says, "I can't read de newspapers, but ole Missus' face is newspaper nuff for me."[37]

However, Aunt Linda reveals a violent association with literacy that explains her reluctance. She admits that she "allers wanted to learn how to read," that she "once had a book, and tried to make out what war in it, but ebery time my mistus caught me wid a book in my hand, she used to whip my fingers. An' I couldn't see ef it war good for white folks, why it warn't good for cullud folks."[38] Aunt Linda's early traumatic reading experience echoes Douglass's and many other slaves' throughout the African American literary tradition and beyond.[39] A more picturesque and encouraging scene of adult literacy acquisition in *Iola Leroy* involves nameless elderly freedmen and women, and they are closer descendants of Aunt Chloe than Aunt Linda is. Iola's new school receives students "ready and anxious to get some 'book larnin'.'" Some of the old folks were eager to learn, and it was touching to see the eyes which had grown dim under the shadows of slavery, donning spectacles and trying to make out the words."[40] The students' difficulty in "making out the words" can be attributed not only to their obscured vision but also to the labor involved in literacy acquisition, a labor similar to that of "putting the words together," to borrow Chloe's language.

Even during the Reconstruction period represented in the Aunt Chloe poems, when the immediate challenges of everyday life meant that former slaves could not always afford to be concerned with reading instruction, education was still highly valued. As Harper observed in an 1870 letter,

> I rather think from what I hear that the interest of the grown-up people in getting education has somewhat subsided, owing, perhaps, in a measure, to the novelty having worn off and the absorption or rather direction of the mind to other matters. Still I don't think that I have visited scarcely a place since last August where there was no desire for a teacher; and Mr. Fidler, who is a Captain or Colonel, thought some time since that there were more colored than white who were learning or had learned to read.[41]

Harper intends through the Aunt Chloe poems to show, as Janet Gray argues, to "the distanced white audience and to educated black readers the urgent need of the newly freed communities for educators, as well as the dangers that they face."[42] The minimal literary dialect of the Aunt Chloe poems serves her purpose well in this respect: in challenging (but only slightly) her already literate audience to reenact the process of achieving literacy, she connects them directly with her subject and with the non-literate and semi-literate audiences she urges them to serve. As for those semi-literate readers for whom *Sketches of Southern Life* was intended to act as a pedagogical tool, their reading experience would be one not of re-enactment but enactment, and the aim of increasing literacy was attempted not only in thematizing that process but in actively ushering readers down Aunt Chloe's path.

Femininity, Fashion, and Dialect

In another 1870 letter, Harper noted that some accused her of disguise: "I don't know but that you would laugh if you were to hear some of the remarks which my lectures call forth: 'She is a man,' again 'She is not colored, she is painted.'"[43] Of course, behind the charges of cross-dressing and "blacking up" is the implication that Harper would not be capable of her thought were she truly a black woman. In addition, to appear at a lectern during this period would be to surrender one's femininity. As Frances Smith Foster writes, "Women who spoke in public to mixed audiences were considered by most people to lack good sense and high moral character."[44] If women were the keepers of moral virtue, then lecturing women—who represented compromised morality—were not really women. Appearing on stage as Harper did "paradoxically at once sexualized her . . . and masculinized her."[45] "Painted" not only suggests that her race is a guise, it also links her to the cosmetically enhanced and morally suspect world of the theater. The word, Carla L. Peterson argues, "resexualizes her, and dangerously so, as an actress, and perhaps even a prostitute. In fact, these women lecturers needed in some sense to become actresses in order to negotiate their public exposure in front of 'promiscuous assemblies.'"[46]

Despite this questioning of Harper's femininity and character as she appeared on stage, some of her audience, conversely, remarked upon an observable refinement that marked her unmistakably as ladylike, noticing "her 'slender and graceful' form and her 'soft musical voice,'" and describing her as "a quiet, slender looking, matronly mulatto woman, the structure of whose sentences and purity of diction were at once a surprise and revelation to her audience."[47] As with Dunbar, many articles refer to her unexpected "purity of diction" (she is, in other words, not a "dialect" speaker); another notes that Harper spoke "fluently, earnestly and used excellent language, after which display Miss Susan B. Anthony was led in remark to Miss [Frances E.] Willard: 'I'd like to see a white woman who could speak any more concisely than that.'"[48] However, what I would like to focus on here is the overwhelming attention to Harper's body. The refined demeanor remarked upon by so many journalists may have been presented and accentuated by Harper as a calculated attempt to counter criticism that directed sexual and inappropriate attention to her person—in other words, part of Harper's "acting strategies," according to Peterson, included the desire "to decorporealize the body from the outset and present the self as a disembodied voice."[49] Alternatively, however, in an essay titled "Frances Ellen Watkins Sings the Body Electric," Michael Bennett proposes that we consider Harper the true "poet of the body" of the mid-nineteenth century, not her contemporary Whitman, because her "poetic performances put her work and her self on display" and she "bodied forth her poetry on the stage."[50]

As a means of resolving these seemingly opposed views of Harper's physicality, I argue the obvious point that we must attribute Harper's success as an acclaimed orator to the effective combination of her verbal and physical skills. She did not shy away from using her body to good effect on stage. One of her best known poems, "Free Labor," in fact depended upon her audience noticing her body. As she celebrated the fact that her garments were not produced by slave labor, she repeatedly and deictically drew attention to her dress ("lightly shall it press my form").[51] As it happens, the entire description of a lecture by Harper in an 1888 Chicago *Daily Inter Ocean* article consisted only of the observation that Harper wore a "plain brown cloth dress," in which she "spoke to the most cultured and fashionable audience of the whole conference."[52] To note this plainness, of course, means to clearly distinguish between Harper and her presumably white and female audience—to suggest that Harper is not "cultured"—but Harper chooses to put forward a distinctly rustic figure, drawing attention to her costume's unfashionableness as well as its asexuality. This description of her appearance even suggests that the coarseness of her costume may have intended to evoke the coarseness of the typical slave's spartan wardrobe. This strategy stands in stark contrast to that of black male lecturers such as Frederick Douglass, who, as Richard J. Powell writes, "dressed in what would have been considered 'white men's clothing'—a formal suit, vest, dress shirt, and cravat—and thus challenged [his] audiences even before uttering a word."[53] In countrifying her costume in both print and performance, Harper embodies the homely dialect-speaking characters like Aunt Chloe in her fictive writing. Even the appearance of *Sketches of Southern Life* itself seems intended to contribute to this message of plainness. Boyd describes the book's "beige covers" which "were simply, but attractively embroidered around the borders, accented by an elegant, but unpretentious design in each corner."[54]

Maggie Pogue Johnson, on the other hand, often chooses to present her dialect poetry not in a cloak of blank asexuality but in a deliberate and emphatic masculine disguise; her speakers are often men. This move is not uncommon among African American women poets who wanted to take advantage of dialect poetry's popularity and goals at the turn of the century without sacrificing the appearance of bourgeois gentility. Clara Ann Thompson, for example, used a male persona, Uncle Rube, throughout her 1908 *Songs from the Wayside* (in one of these poems, "Uncle Rube to the Young People," the speaker even repeatedly enjoins his audience to "act like men").[55] In general, however, this phenomenon is relatively rare, as Siobhan B. Somerville points out in an essay that addresses the "dearth of examples of cross-gender impersonations by African American woman," in part because black women "have been granted limited access to the very category of femininity (from which one would presumably cross to a masculine persona)."⁵⁶ An essay by Tavia Nyong'o, in which he compares literary performer Mary Webb and the fictional Emily Garie (a character in *The Garies and their Friends* by Frank Webb, who was Mary's husband), provides a surprisingly useful way into approaching Johnson's poetry. Garie, Nyong'o writes,

> achieves [racial] solidarity through a retreat into the coverture of marriage and the social reproduction of a black bourgeois household . . . ; her nonfictional analogue, by contrast, established her racial solidarity by transgressing woman's sphere and publically [sic] performing racial and crossracial identifications, unmediated by either husband or marriage. She did not, after all, only perform women's roles from *Uncle Tom's Cabin;* she also assumed the voice of Uncle Tom and other male characters. In Hiawatha, dressed in the feathers of an Indian warrior, she similarly performed all the voices. These crossdressed performances were not interpreted as transgressions of propriety. By embodying multiple races and genders, however, Webb established a relationship among them that hinged upon her durational presence, her performance, and her body.⁵⁷

Johnson's first two books of poetry are projects of racial uplift that, like the actions of Webb and Garie, express her racial solidarity, but Johnson's poems are both deeply domestic in their marital conventions and subversive in their cross-dressing, combining Webb and Garie's positions, careers, and ideologies.

The most anthologized of Johnson's poems, "What's Mo' Temptin' to the Palate," has a male speaker.⁵⁸ One of the few critics to address Johnson's work, Ajuan Maria Mance points to the irony of this fact, arguing that, despite the poem's apparent focus on the male speaker's labor, the poem ends up presenting and celebrating his wife's labor in the domestic sphere.⁵⁹ The husband, tired from work, returns home to find pots and pots of food prepared for him, with no evidence of the cook until the end of the poem, when she enters with a pot of coffee. Mance calls the list of foods mentioned by the speaker "a detailed audit of both the duties and products of woman's domestic work," but is this a real meal?⁶⁰ The husband's list is conditional—a compilation of foods that *would* be "temptin' to de palate"—and includes possum, sweet potatoes, chicken, dumplings, baked beans, greens, and corn cakes. It seems unlikely that all of these foods would be eaten at once, but even if we accept that they would, the list continues with potential Thanksgiving and summer-time meals: turkey, cranberry sauce, celery, and watermelon. Then comes another list, unattached to any holiday: pork chops, lamb, ham, veal chops, and mutton chops. At this point, it should be clear that the speaker doesn't find all of these foods greeting him when he returns home. If it is an audit, it's an annual and not a daily one. In the penultimate stanza, he returns from his mythic gastronomic fantasy to find himself grounded in the post-work scenario, and "eat[s] dar by de fiah" a vague and unspecified "supper" of "plenty good to eat." His wife has not in actuality prepared those foods for which he "pines," but, significantly, it seems as if she has.[61]

The husband of "What's Mo' Temptin' to the Palate" is invested in this idealization of domestic life, and the idea of being greeted in this unrealistic manner is deeply satisfying. The successful marriage, as it is defined by the degree to which the wife meets her husband's expectations, affirms his sense of his social status.[62] Another poem by Johnson depicts a troubled marital situation: it records the alcohol-fueled fantasies of a man who dreams of killing his wife and child. "The Drunkard's Dream," however, turns out to be uplifting temperance propaganda, as the man is awakened (in both senses) by his wife and subsequently vows to change his ways, telling her, "I'll worship Thee only."[63] In this poem and in "What's Mo' Temptin' to the Palate," the suffering women in the background are supernaturally good and capable; in this case, the drunkard's wife is a goddess worthy of worship. From the perspective of behavior that is presented as aggressively masculine (dining as leisure, alcohol-fueled violence), the behavior of the women is understood by their husbands to be saintly and self-sacrificial (dining as work, victimhood or martyrdom). Behind female dialect poets' attempts to inhabit male characters lies the desire to "act like men" not as a convincing performance of masculinity but as an artificial and theatrical exaggeration of masculinity.

It is, I argue, because of this desire to expose the ways in which gender is performed that so many poems in Johnson's oeuvre revolve around the details of clothing, a visual index of gender identity. Johnson's recognition of the dramatic potential of clothing emerges from a personal interest in fashion: as a child, she sold her poems for straight pins to use in sewing; as an adult, she owned a millinery shop and enjoyed sewing clothes.[64] "Krismas Dinnah," apparently modeled closely after Dunbar's "The Party," describes from the perspective of an implied male speaker a social event similarly marked by excess.[65] At the celebration, both men and women are wearing their best. Three stanzas are devoted to masculine dress, including the following lines:

> Dey wo' dese long jimswinger coats,
> Wid big leg pantaloons,
> High silk hats wid broad red bands . . .

Only two stanzas, however, are spent detailing women's dress. Even then, the details are vague, and it is clear that the speaker is describing them from a masculine point-of-view: "Der dresses had sich great long trains, / We stood back wid de res'." The "we" who "stood back wid de res'" is clearly a masculine speaker, but it isn't until late in the poem that the "we" is absolutely characterized as a man: "De wimmen folks was helped fus' / To all de kins ob meat, / En den we men was helped." The sexes are separated as they enter the party, when they receive their food, and when they eat ("De wimmen dey was near de stove"), and their elaborate and distinct clothing styles facilitate that segregation.[66] Unlike Harper's plain brown dress, which resists both sexualization and gendering in its plainness, the men's and women's apparel in Johnson's poem, in its frippery, moves men and women more decisively toward their socially determined gender roles. A version of Harper's plain brown dress, however, is advocated in Johnson's "De Men Folks ob Today" by an older speaker who, complaining of the behavior of contemporary young men, focuses her critique on clothing. She warns the men that

> . . . when you courts de wimmen,
>   Dey don't lub you fo' yo' clo's,
> Dat wud be a sinnin',
>   En ebery body knows.
>
> Dey lubs you fo' yo' winnin' ways,
>   En not fo' dressin' fine,
> Lub fo' clo's dese days don't pay,
>   Is what's been on my min'.
>
> You stylish dudes who's settin' roun',
>   Ef you wants to marry,
> Take off dem stylish frocks en gowns,
>   Use common sense, don't tarry.
>
> Put on some good ol' wukin' clo's . . . [67]

The stripping down (as well as the dressing down) of these "stylish dudes" not only removes all pretense, it effectively diminishes the decorative differences between men and women. The "good ol' wukin' clo's," male and female, are humble and also equalizing in their simplicity. A similar charge is raised against the young people's elaborate fashions in Johnson's "De Wintah Styles," when an older woman claims that "way back in my time / No sich styles as dese, / Ever cums befo' de folks,— / We dressed den as we pleased." The old-fashioned and simple styles have evolved into "hiferlutin fine" styles so complex that they are buffoonish and exaggerated:[68]

De hats dey am so bery high,
    Wid feathers all aroun',
You can't tell what dey's made of,
    Or eben see de crown.

En chicken feathers, too,
    Dyed blue, red and green,
En folks wid hats a struttin'
    De same as eny queen.

De wimmen walkin' fru de streets,
    Wid diamon's in dey har,
En on dey hats ol' tuckey tails,
    A danglin' in de air.[69]

This extravagance, she fears, has the potential to cross into the taboo of transvestism. Ironically, "good ol' wukin' clo's" that are effectively genderless are unassuming and therefore not disruptive to the social order, but gender-specific costumes, in their neverending complexity, no longer can be trusted to reinforce gender difference as they did in "Krismas Dinnah" and are becoming increasingly difficult to read. The men of "De Men Folks ob Today" wear "frocks en gowns."[70] Young women in "De Wintah Styles," already wearing "coats like long jimswingers, / Vest, too, like de men," will soon complete the transformation: "I'se lookin' fer de time to cum / When dey will w'ar men's pants, / Dey's settin' back a lookin', / En waitin' fer de chance." This supposed abomination will inevitably be answered by God, who "will say 'enuf,' / En take dem up on high, / Whar he kin set de fashions."

Unlike her older female speakers, however, Johnson rejoices in the newfangled and complex performances of fashion even as they trouble gender categories. In fact, although Johnson's "I Wish I Was a Grown

Up Man" appears to be written from the perspective of a young boy, it is worth pointing out that he waits—just as the women in "De Wintah Styles" do—to "get a chance, / To wear those great high collars, / Stiff shirts, and nice long pants."[71] When republished decades later in Johnson's 1951 *Fallen Blossoms,* the poem resolves this ambiguity by gaining an epigraph that makes it clear that the speaker is a boy—her son, in fact—and not a woman ("written for Walter W. Johnson, Jr., to be recited when he was Four years old") but the context of the poem's first publication highlights the fact that the boy's sartorial initiation into manhood is the exact same performance that the woman's cross-dressing is.

But even when women wear conventional women's clothes in Johnson's poetry, it is usually in a manner that draws attention to their theatricality. Perhaps the most interesting of her poems about women's wear is "Aunt Cloe's Trip to See Miss Liza Kyle," one of Johnson's most popular poems and one she performed frequently, sometimes reciting it accompanied by a woman who pantomimed the events of the poem.[72] Johnson's Aunt Cloe lives in the country, and the poem humorously recounts her preparations for a visit to a city-dwelling friend. Not wanting to seem rustic and unsophisticated, she asks her friend about the latest fashions so that she can have a seamstress sew her a dress that will make an impression and won't be "called so countrified." In a manner reminiscent of Dunbar's "Happy! Happy! Happy!," the poem contains two letters in distinct registers; the first, from Aunt Cloe, is in dialect, and the second, from Liza Kyle, is in a supercilious mode of standard English:

> "You must wear a hobble skirt,
>   Your hair in puffs must be,
> With a band of ribbon round your head,
>   Where a bow you'll fix, you see.
>
> "Your shoe heels must be very high,
>   And make yourself look small;
> Be careful, too, just how you walk,
>   Or else you'll have a fall.
>
> "You'll have to take short steps
>   In your hobble skirt, you see,
> But that's the latest thing,
>   And in style you must be.

"Your hat must be extremely large,
    With a feather quill behind,
And then you'll be a model sure,
    Aunt Cloe, you'll just look fine.

"I enclose a picture here,
    Cut from a fashion book,
To show exactly how
    The hobble skirt will look.

"Now imitate the picture,
    The skirt looks rather tight,
But lace your stoutness down,
    And then you'll be all right."

Liza Kyle uses the imperative throughout her letter, even grammatically mirroring the strictures of female dress. Unfortunately, Aunt Cloe's simulation is a complete failure. Following the instructions of a "fashion book," she orders four yards of fabric—two yards of red and two of green—even though it is only barely enough for the seamstress to piece together the different colors to manufacture an unflattering motley construction. Because of Cloe's failure to reproduce the fashionable look, Liza refuses to even acknowledge her friend when she steps off the train. One of the messages of the poem is that Cloe has not been successfully initiated into the world of feminine clothing, which necessitates the woman's restriction and discomfort. Thus, when she chases an embarrassed Liza in order to force acknowledgment, Cloe commits crimes of both fashion and propriety by removing her high-heeled shoes and ripping the back of her skirt to lengthen her stride and add to her comfort. When initially invited to visit by Liza in order to "joy de city life, / De pleasure en de style," little did Cloe know that her own style, or lack of it, would be sufficient reason for her friend to snub her.[73]

In Harryette Mullen's "Off the Top," a brief essay appended to *Trimmings* (a series of prose poems most of which revolve around clothing as a learned aspect of feminine identity), she writes, "I don't think there is necessarily any 'feminine language' except in the sense that there is feminine clothing," and Liza Kyle's letter to Aunt Cloe demonstrates how learning an exotic vocabulary is necessary in order to induct women into a socially accepted version of womanhood.[74] We see this also in the aforementioned

"De Wintah Styles." Although Johnson celebrates frippery, some women who are attempting to be stylish only succeed in embarrassing themselves because "[d]ey don't know de dif'rence" between the turkey feathers they wear and "[d]e fines' ostrich tips." Even if we consider Aunt Cloe to be "the sympathetic character," as Dickson D. Bruce argues, claiming that "Johnson turned the rhetoric of the dialect tradition upside down, implying a kind of falseness in the assimilated black American" represented by Liza Kyle, Johnson still depicts Cloe as a fool in her failure to interpret the city style.[75]

Just as fashions dictate whether or not one belongs to a social or cultural group, dialect—as a fashion of speaking—can create generational and regional schisms between those who are deemed in style and those who are not. Even Cloe's name, familiar not just to readers of Harper but also to readers of Harriet Beecher Stowe, marks her as a dialect-speaking caricature of unfashionability. To borrow from the language of a couple of texts discussed in the introduction of this book, Loomis's story "The Dialect Store" and the anonymously published essay "The Pike Poetry," Cloe buys a cosmopolitan dialect "by the yard," but the dress she makes of it shows "to the world its seams and ravellings and tattered linings." In fact, Cloe's patchwork visually illustrates her inability to move effortlessly—seamlessly—from one dialect to another. She is as unnatural as a dialect story made from purchases from the Dialect Store would be. In Harper's *Iola Leroy,* the rural black dialect speaker is similarly contrasted against an urbane bourgeois character who speaks standard English but, as James Christmann argues in an essay about *Iola Leroy,* the two speech styles "occupy discrete spaces and yet interact and intersect in community-building exchanges"—at first.[76] Even if one would argue, as Deborah E. McDowell does, that the language of the dialect speakers of *Iola Leroy* "must be mediated and legitimated by the more accepted language of the major characters," one would likely concede that Harper does not mock the dialect speakers.[77] However, unlike Harper's novel, the success of "Aunt Cloe's Trip to See Miss Liza Kyle" depends upon mocking her failed attempts to master not one but two styles, despite the fact that Johnson herself attempts the same mastery as she alternates between poems in standard English and in dialect.

Johnson's Education and Idleness

The title page of Johnson's first known book of poetry, published in 1910, reads:

VIRGINIA DREAMS
Lyrics for the Idle Hour.
Tales of the Time
Told in Rhyme

The preface that follows justifies the publication of the collection: "At the solicitaion [sic] of a few friends, I have selected several of my poems, and if the perusal of them brings pleasure to you, dear reader, the object of this volume will have been accomplished." In part, this is an all too familiar mock-humble move, similar to Christina Moody's in "To My Dear Reader," although Johnson is casual and cultured where Moody is embarrassed and lacks "training."[78] Johnson's language in these prefatory materials, among the first paratexts a reader will encounter, points toward leisure. These poems are written "for the Idle Hour," some free time shared happily by both writer and reader. (A second book, published in 1915, reinforced the idea with the title *Thoughts for Idle Hours*.[79]) Her readers are friends and her friends are readers. Furthermore, the poems are intended for her reader's "perusal," and to bring him or her "pleasure." To peruse a book implies close examination or study, but to be simply pleased by it brings to mind the shallowness Dunbar associates with the dilettante. The implied tension between perusal and pleasure sets the stage for *Virginia Dreams*, from the start seemingly unable to decide whether it will be a tool of education or idleness, two ideals between which it observes a difference. Ultimately, however, even apparently passive education is always achieved through labor in this book, whether through "representative" black characters (Booker T. Washington, for example) or "non-representative" dialect-speaking black characters, and, although the reading experience she claims to encourage is one of leisure, Johnson's ideal man of culture would not choose to devote his time to leisure activities.

As I argue in a previous chapter, Dunbar was ambivalent about higher education, associating university study with "flow'ry beds of ease," and we can trace this ambivalence in part to his own lack of opportunity. Johnson was educated at the Virginia Normal and Collegiate Institute; taught school for two years; was President of the Literary and Debating Society in Covington, Virginia; and, as the wife of a physician, we can assume that she lived relatively comfortably.[80] In the 1930s, she wrote a pageant titled *Lifting as We Climb* for the Virginia State Federation of Colored Women's Clubs that was also performed at Hampton Institute and the National Federation of Colored Women's Clubs.[81] In addition, her poetry reflects her commitment to the ideology of racial uplift, which entailed university education. Johnson describes the historically black university in a feminine and messianic manner, conflating the classical image of the open-armed *alma mater* with the description of Ethiopia in Psalms 68—"Ethiopia shall soon stretch out her hands unto God"—a line that reverberated through much African American writing, including Harper's.[82] Johnson's "The Negro Has a Chance" personifies the college with a similar line: "With outstretched arms the college stands." Another poem, "The V.N. and C.I.," also describes the school as if a woman, recalling those "[w]ho've toiled within her walls," and proclaiming, "Her situation is beautiful, / As loftily she stands / Facing the Appomattox, / So picturesque and grand."[83]

But, although the landscape pictured in Johnson's book is dotted with feminine black colleges and universities, it is also dotted with great men.[84] Johnson honors in her poetry all manner of educated black people, and Washington, partly for his role as leader of an educational institution, is the brightest star in her firmament. Another college professor is lauded in a poem titled "James Hugo Johnston," as Johnson guides her reader geographically, leading us directly to the home of the president of her alma mater, Virginia Normal and Collegiate Institute (now Virginia State University): "On a hill near Petersburg, / Facing the old historic town, / There lives a model Negro— / One who's won renown." His example serves as a beacon, leading students to him "thro' the land" and encouraging them to his "paths . . . retrace," avoiding the "deepened mire / Of folly and disgrace," as if following his example would amount to a physical journey through a treacherous but character-building landscape.[85] He is exemplary in the way that Harper's Aunt Chloe is; both serve as models of educational achievement and moral strength for readers to follow.

A book titled *Evidences of Progress among Colored People* devotes a few revealing paragraphs to a brief history of the Virginia Normal and Collegiate Institute. Following a description of the school and its aims is an engraving and brief biography of Johnston, "president and Professor of Psychology and Moral Science." Johnston is described as "a self-made man," whose "first work in life was that of a newsboy on the streets of Richmond"; he even "kept his paper route for some time after he began teaching in the public schools of that city."[86] Clearly, Johnston was far from idle. He serves as a strong example for Johnson of what it means to belong to an elite social class that is committed to hard work. The examples of Johnston and other "great men" like him serve, in themselves, a purpose for Johnson similar to the education they represent. In *Up from Slavery*, Washington advocated the idea of an education consisting of discourse with great men, with General Armstrong as his "perfect man." "The older I grow," he writes, "the more I am convinced that there is no education which one can get from books and costly apparatus that is equal to that which can be gotten from contact with great men and women. Instead of studying books so constantly, how I wish that our schools and colleges might learn to study men and things!"[87] Likewise, Johnson's poem to Johnston demonstrates her belief that simply being in the presence of great men can, as if through osmosis, benefit the student.

In other words, Johnston is Johnson's idea of a representative man of the race. To cite Dunbar's essay "Representative American Negroes," "To have achieved something for the betterment of his race rather than for the aggrandizement of himself, seems to be a man's best title to be called representative." It is worth noting that most of Dunbar's examples of representative men in his essay are educators, and he in fact addresses this imbalance:

> It may be urged that too much time has already been taken up with the educational side of the Negro, but the reasonableness of this must become apparent when one remembers that for the last forty years the most helpful men of the race have come from the ranks of its teachers, and few of those who have finally done any big thing, but have at some time or other held the scepter of authority in a school. They may have changed later and grown, indeed they must have done so, but the fact remains that their poise, their discipline, the impulse for their growth came largely from their work in the school room.[88]

Not surprisingly, Dunbar's representative men are, as Kenneth Warren points out, "members of the turn of the century black elite"; representative men "would not ever include . . . many of the figures whom he represents through the means of dialect verse."[89] What is unconventional about Johnson's books of poetry is that she goes back and forth between representative men as Warren characterizes Dunbar's definition, such as Washington and Johnston, and "non-representative" dialect speakers, treating both types as inspiring and allowing the types to mingle within poems.

Johnson's attempt to aggrandize her professorial subject stands in stark contrast to, for example, Longfellow's desire to downplay a perceived class difference between himself and his general audience. Although "literary commentators frequently referred to him (sometimes flatteringly, sometimes pejoratively) as 'Professor' Longfellow," Charvat writes, "in his works he avoided reference to his specific academic status. 'Poet' and 'Scholar' are common symbols in both his verse and prose, but not 'Professor.'"[90] Johnson, not being a professor, neither faced the same personal dilemma nor benefited from the same racial privilege or fame, and partly for these reasons she took the opposite stance, choosing to emphasize her bourgeois standing by selecting university professors as the subjects of so many of her poems. Take, for example, "To Professor Byrd Prillerman":

> Dar's a skool in West Virginny,
> Dat I hears dem call de Farm,
> Whar dey raises ebery t'ing to eat,
> En has de bigges' barns,—
> Whar de ho'ses en de cows,
> In restin' spend de night,
> And w'ar away de hours,
> To dey own heart's delight.
>
> 'Tis dar dey teaches eberyt'ing
> In de wuken line,
> As much as folks kin well take in
> Upon de common min';
> Dey l'arns you how to cook,
> Dey l'arns you how to sew;
> In fact, dey teaches eberyt'ing
> Dat you wants to know.
>
> Has you eber seed de president
> Ob dat skool, de Farm?
> De man who bosses eberyt'ing,
> From de skool room to de barn;
> I tell you he's a great man,
> To meet him you kin see
> De 'telligence beamin' from his face
> As blossoms from a tree.
>
> He's hammered on de chillun's heads,
> Fo', lo, dese thirty years,
> Poundin' knowledge in dem
> 'Mid dumbness en 'mid fears;
> He's bro't dem from de dunce stool
> Ob ignance en disgrace,
> En trained dem in his skool
> To lead folks ob de race.

He's one de oldes' teachers,
In West Virginny State,
En what dat man don't know
Ain't worthy to relate;
So, when you wants to go to skool
To be sho to l'arn,
Go to dat Cullered Institute
Dat some folks call de Farm.⁹¹

Not only is Professor Prillerman a "great man," intelligence is said to be "beamin' from his face / As blossoms from a tree." The "'flow'ry beds of ease' method" through which Dunbar was reluctant to gain his education is reconfigured here: Professor Prillerman is depicted as if he generates and emanates flowers, as if his education manifests itself in flowery beds of ease on his person. But, while these blossoms can be conceived of as university laurels, hence signifying masculine achievement (and Johnson uses flowers in this way in a poem about Dunbar titled "Poet of Our Race": "Thy victor's crown is won"), there is no avoiding the association of floral decoration with femininity, especially considering the choice of the word "blossom," which carries the connotation of fruit-bearing and girlish development. The professor's flowery words, according to Johnson, resemble the efflorescence of Dunbar's verse, whose "words, as sweetest flowers, / Do grow in beauty 'round us here / To cheer us in sadest [sic] hours." And the "flow'ry beds of ease" Dunbar claimed to want to avoid coincidentally resurface in Johnson's poem to him, which addresses him as "thou, adored of men, / Whose bed might been of flowers." Johnson's Dunbar is surrounded by flowers, speaks in flowers, and interprets the flowers for us ("The language of the flowers, / Thou hast read them all").⁹² Although masculine "great man" poems appear throughout Johnson's books, the men at the center of these poems are often festooned with the feminine signs of cultivation. It is not only the fashionable young everyman, then, wearing "stylish frocks en gowns," who feminizes himself in order to advance socially, but also the great man. Unlike Harper's public persona, that a segment of her audience had to perceive as masculine in order to see or hear her, Johnson argues that it is only when these men are "feminized" by education—by the university that is coded female—that they achieve public greatness.

The emanation "beamin'" from Professor Prillerman resembles the transformative glow associated with Booker T. Washington in "To See Ol' Booker T.," an account of an old man's journey from Virginia to Tuskegee for the sole purpose of seeing the great man, who takes on the proportions of a messianic figure, similar to James Hugo Johnston and the figure of the *alma mater*:[93]

> So I pray de Lawd to keep
> Bof me en my ol' mule,
> En spar us till we git
> To dat Cullered Skool.
>
> En gib our eyes de light,
> Dat we can cle'rly see,
> Dat Alabama lan' so bright,
> En dear ol' Booker T.

Later in the poem, the same sentiment is expressed:

> . . . I'll set en look at him,
> En he will look at me,
> En fo' my eyes get dim,
> While I kin cl'erly see.

Including the title, the words "see" and "seen" are used fourteen times in the poem, the words "look" and "eye" used two and three times respectively; clearly the spectacle of university life is what's important here. Even the dialect spelling helps to emphasize that association: the word "expect" is written as "specs," and it is used twice.

The transformative effects of seeing the great man and the educational institution he represents are equivalent, in this poem, to having done actual labor. The most idle-seeming aspect of receiving instruction, sitting and looking, is seen as real work rather than idleness. The speaker is aware of the school's curriculum and offerings—"Dey teaches you all kin's ob wuk / En how to write en read, / En figger in de 'rithmetic / En ebery t'ing you needs"—but he needs only to see Washington to receive his education. Once one has seen, one can die: "I's seen dis great, great cullered man, / I's ready now to go" and "So now my eyes clos' to res'." The old man has "stood de tes'," as labor (or "tas'") becomes education (or "tes'") by the end of the poem.

The transformative touch—along with the power of his reciprocal gaze, the second extraordinary physical sense Washington possesses and offers as generously to his pupils as he does to world leaders—is another part of the education the old man hopes to receive. As he puts it:

> Dat eben kings en queens so great
> Did strive to shake his han'
> En welcome Booker T.
> To der native land.
>
> Now, you know he mus' be great . . . [94]

The old man feels sure of Washington's greatness in part because it has been confirmed physically by world leaders. He wants to "shake [Washington's] willin' hand'" and "take his gracious han' / Widin my trimblin' grasp," just as Washington himself advocated the study of "men and things." (The physicality of teaching and learning appeared also, if more violently, in "To Professor Byrd Prillerman," as the professor "hammered on de chillun's heads, / . . . / Poundin' knowledge in dem.") The speaker of "To See Ol' Booker T," whom Dunbar would likely not have characterized as "representative" because he speaks in dialect, qualifies for Johnson as a valued model and inspiring product of education (or, rather, *potential* product of education, since the poem is written in the conditional mood).

Both Harper and Johnson attempted through their dialect poetry to emphasize the value of education without detracting from the value of dialect, as many readers would have believed education and dialect speech to be at odds. The "great man" poem used by Johnson in order to make this argument also ironically emphasizes the cultivating effect of feminization in producing representative men, both dialect- and standard-English-speaking. As I will discuss in the following chapter, the dialect poetries of Claude McKay and Langston Hughes go even further in their scrutiny of dialect performance and its relationship to education and silent reading.

chapter six

Annotated Dialect

Claude McKay and Langston Hughes

The move from Maggie Pogue Johnson's dialect poetry to the dialect poetries of Claude McKay and Langston Hughes is admittedly a difficult one. For most readers, still influenced by James Weldon Johnson's pronouncement, the early work of McKay and Hughes represents a dramatic rupture, a change from dialect-as-artifice to dialect-as-natural-expression, or, to put it another way, a change from the mask of dialect to the true face of vernacular. If these modern dialect poetries reveal at last a true face, however, why do McKay and Hughes produce so much multiplicity not only in the form of dramatic monologue (as Dunbar, Harper, and Maggie Pogue Johnson did before them) but also as editorial intrusion? Through my treatment of the notes to Hughes's *The Negro Mother and Other Dramatic Recitations* and to McKay's *Songs of Jamaica,* I argue in this chapter that the divided condition of these books, a presentation that Charles Bernstein calls "schizophrenic" in his reading of *Songs of Jamaica,* is symptomatic of the continued and deliberate interplay between suggestions of orality and literacy found in earlier dialect work such as Dunbar's and Maggie Pogue Johnson's.[1] As such, the work of McKay and Hughes is more of a continuation of work begun by the earlier poets than a complete change of direction.[2] Although the notes to *Songs of Jamaica* are appended by McKay's patron Walter Jekyll and the notes to *The Negro Mother* by

Hughes himself, the effects of the division are nevertheless comparable: in separating the main text from the marginal text, the dialect poem assumes an even more pronounced air of orality, and the apparatus, in framing it, is designated literate. This chapter will address the effects and purposes of designing these books in such a manner; that is, how McKay and Hughes direct their readers to engage with the divided presentation of their work, and how the reception and publication histories of these books were determined by their use of dialect.

When Hughes and McKay began their careers, the practical importance of Dunbar's example had not yet been completely devalued for most readers. In fact, an advertisement for *The Negro Mother* declares that the book presents "widely known and well-beloved Negro characters delineated in a broadly popular manner not associated with Negro poetry since the death of Paul Lawrence [sic] Dunbar." Readers, editors, and publishers were on the lookout for the next Dunbar. McKay, too, was compared to Dunbar in reviews of his work. The two poets responded to Dunbar's example in different ways: McKay quickly turned away from dialect writing altogether; Hughes contended with the figure of Dunbar more assertively.

As a public poet, Hughes stands stylistically and thematically between Walt Whitman on one hand (perhaps his clearest literary predecessor[3]), and Dunbar on the other. Many readers have pointed to Hughes's indebtedness to one side or another of this heritage without mentioning what an uncomfortable position this puts him in, considering the inherent incompatibility between these two distinct branches of American poetry. True, both branches share what they would characterize as a popular, demotic approach; both use, or aim to use, language that is plain or common.[4] But Dunbar (and his model James Whitcomb Riley) exceeded Whitman in popularity, and the two rigidly metrical and rhyme-conscious poets expressed strong disapproval of what they considered Whitman's unrefined verse.[5] As Riley and Dunbar's significance waned—in fact, as their poems became, to different degrees, relegated to the status of literary-historical curios—Whitman loomed larger and larger into the early twentieth century, auspiciously when American literature was becoming more and more an acceptable subject for university study and for collection in anthologies.

By the 1920s, Dunbar's dialect writing was no longer treated as the graphic trace of his authenticity (as it usually was during his lifetime) but as a marker of his inauthenticity. James Weldon Johnson, after turning away from the Dunbar-like dialect writing he practiced early in his career, denigrated "the artificiality of conventionalized Negro dialect poetry" and declared repeatedly that it was capable only of "two emotions, pathos and humor, thereby making every poem either only sad or only funny."⁶ By the time he published the revised 1931 edition of his *Book of American Negro Poetry,* the shift away from artificial dialect was definitive, with Hughes and his contemporaries ushering in a new era of representing speech in American verse. Johnson could claim, two years later, that "[n]o Negro poets are today writing the poetry that twenty-five years ago was considered their natural medium of expression."⁷ The artifice of the previous generation, the supposed mask under which the authentic poet was crafting his lines, gives way in the 1920s to the true "natural" dialect poetry written by Hughes, which was barely marked by apostrophes, strange orthography, and other visual manifestations of the attempts to represent speech by poets before him. Johnson's attitude toward artificial dialect poetry betrays his faith in the possibility of an authentic or natural dialect poetry, neglecting the fact that any dialect poetry that depends upon visible manipulation automatically calls attention to its inauthenticity, whether it is as difficult to read as Dunbar's or as relatively easy to figure out as Hughes's.

From Showman to Spokesman: The Unlettered Poet

Hughes's twin lineages of Dunbar and Whitman result in a body of work that is unprecedented in American literature, providing a hybrid sense of what it means to compose poetry in a Wordsworthian "language of men." Was writing in dialect to be understood as entertainment, produced and manufactured by a writer seeking popularity above all, or was it to be understood as educative, seeking to draw audiences in order to instruct them, whether through advocating literacy or through reproducing or channeling authentic cultural expression in order to assert the value of orality? Although turn-of-the-century dialect poetry usually strove for both goals, Hughes's didactic intentions are closer to the surface. In fact, in a 1926 review of *The Weary Blues,* Alain Locke articulates the view, soon to become the commonly held view, that the major difference between Dunbar and Hughes, aside from their artificial and natural voices respectively, concerns the former's frivolity and the latter's substance. The former is critically insincere for his studiedness and his artfulness; the latter, by extension, sincere for his spontaneity and his artlessness. "Dunbar," he writes, "is supposed to have expressed the peasant heart of the people. But Dunbar was the showman of the Negro masses; here is their spokesman."⁸

A spokesman's position requires him to be sincere and transparent, a mouthpiece for those he represents; a showman is marked by his artifice. However, Hughes's status as earnest spokesman, "express[ing] the peasant heart of the people," was already compromised by the fact that he was composing his poetry in dialect orthography in the first place. As much as he may have seemed to be a departure from Dunbar to readers such as Locke, many readers (including Locke himself, elsewhere[9]) saw Hughes as continuing in the Dunbar tradition, even if he was modernizing it and even if his representation of dialect appeared to be more firmly grounded in speech. As poet and novelist Kenneth Fearing argues, in a review of Hughes's verse, "[d]ialect of any kind, it seems, automatically reduces a poem from the adult to the miniature plane, to a state of unreality. Paradoxically, though the language may be straight from life, a work in dialect is always slightly stagey, a tour de force."[10] This paradox, it turns out, is at the heart of the spokesman/showman distinction that Locke makes. A dialect poet—especially the dialect poet who embarks on a reading tour to "perform" his work, as Hughes did to promote *The Negro Mother*—is inevitably both spokesman *and* showman. Through his control of the production and reception of this book, Hughes attempted to distinguish between performance (with its attendant connotations of artificiality and theatricality) and recitation (which intends to have some edifying purpose) in order to conform to his own and Locke's assessments of him as more spokesman than showman. Recitation could allow him not only to serve as a mouthpiece, or representative voice, of a community, but also to serve as a model for other representative voices who could enact his verse.

To put it another way, Hughes conceives of himself as the type of poet William Charvat would describe as a "public poet": "Representativeness *in his time* . . . is the differentiating quality of the public poet, and it is the quality that makes the fundamental difference between his verse and that of the private poet. For to be a spokesman he must speak in a vocabulary and syntax familiar to his audience in his time."[11] For a lyric poet, Hughes strongly asserts the topicality of his poetry and often eschews the particularity of the private lyric voice even as he maintains the specificity of his subject. For instance, the dramatic monologues of *The Negro Mother* each require the embodiment of a culturally specific emblematic figure belonging to what Hughes would call the "great masses": "The Colored Soldier," "The Negro Mother," "The Big Timer," etc. They are types. This is remarkably different from the way Dunbar understands what it means to be representative, to speak for a people, as expressed in his essay "Representative American Negroes," cited in the previous chapter. For Hughes, the opposite is true: the people make it possible for the poet to speak, as he makes clear in "The Negro Artist and the Racial Mountain," in which he proposes that the "low down folks" or the "common people will give to the world its truly great Negro artist."[12]

Although the work of Hughes-the-spokesman assumes educational value, Hughes is wary of aligning himself with traditional educational institutions. As he wrote in a 1925 letter to Carl Van Vechten, "If I ever get in the school books then I know I'm ruined."[13] This critical attitude toward higher education may sound familiar following my discussion of Dunbar, but the change in perspective from Dunbar's ambivalently critical and Maggie Pogue Johnson's favorable positions to Hughes's contemptuous one (or, to generalize, from the turn of the century to the 1920s and 1930s) derives in part from the development of the black middle classes and the success of the ideology of uplift during the first few decades of the twentieth century. As Michael Fultz writes, "By the 1920s, . . . when the middle class was more secure in its leadership position in the black community, the highly prescriptive discussions of education so characteristic of 1900–1910 had virtually disappeared."[14] Dunbar's contradictory stance toward African American institutions of higher learning was in some ways the product of a cultural atmosphere in which criticism of the values of uplift was almost tantamount to siding with reactionary arguments against educating African Americans, such as the one published in the *Atlantic Monthly* that I mentioned earlier. In the 1920s and 1930s, when Hughes was beginning his career, the black middle classes censured literature deemed "unrespectable" and, because middle-class respectability was a distinct and easily recognizable ideology, challenges to it were more precise. In 1930, Sterling Brown, for example, mocks the predictability of the reactions of "respectable" African Americans to literature that does not depict the "best" of the culture: "These are sample ejaculations: *'But we're not all like that.' 'Why does he show such a level of society? We have better Negroes than that to write about.' 'What effect will this have on the opinions of white people?'* . . . *'More dialect. Negroes don't use dialect any more.'* . . . *'Negroes of my class don't use dialect anyway.'*"[15] As Henry Louis Gates, Jr., writes, noting how Hughes's attitude toward the respectability of the black bourgeoisie shaped his approach to dialect poetry, Hughes "undertook the project of constructing an entire literary tradition upon the actual spoken language of the black working and rural classes—the same vernacular language that the growing and mobile black middle classes considered embarrassing and demeaning, the linguistic legacy of slavery."[16] Dunbar was determined to distinguish himself from the "lowly," despite the fact that the success of his career was dependent upon that association, but the cultural tenor of the 1920s and 1930s permitted Hughes to openly embrace the so-called common man.

Hughes's early essays show that he was disturbed by some of the effects of higher education upon African Americans, believing that it encouraged schisms within the race. Like Dunbar, Hughes published an essay that focuses his criticism through a study of the residents of Washington, D.C. "In no other city," Hughes writes in "Our Wonderful Society: Washington," "were there so many splendid homes, so many cars, so many A.B. degrees, or so many people with 'family background.'" Everyone seemed college educated.

> She is a graduate of this . . . or he is a graduate of that . . . frequently followed introductions. So I met many men and women who had been to colleges,—and seemed not to have recovered from it. Almost all of them appeared to be deeply affected by education in one way or another.[17]

Behind the neutral sense of the word "affected" to mean "influenced" lurks the negative sense of "pretentious" or "full of affectation." We are reminded of Dunbar's Mandy, who, after "[h]aving mounted in position / [t]o a loftier condition," has been "deeply affected" by her implied education and middle-class respectability.

Many historically black colleges and universities in the early twentieth century, especially in the South, were fairly conservative, with disproportionate emphasis upon manners and refinement. Hughes, himself a graduate of a historically black university, argued that as a result they were "doing their best to produce spineless Uncle Toms." In a 1934 essay titled "Cowards from the Colleges," he complained of the archaic and anachronistic environments they fostered, claiming that "[t]o set foot on dozens of Negro campuses is like going back to mid-Victorian England" and that "Negro schools rival monasteries and nunneries in their strictness." While the restrictions enforced by many early-twentieth-century black colleges were put forward in the name of refinement,[18] Hughes argues instead that the collegiate culture facilitated a top-down transmission of submissiveness from administration to faculty to student body, like a virus from which it was difficult to recover (to borrow his term in "Our Wonderful Society: Washington"), and few who were exposed were spared. As he puts it, "both teachers and students of Negro colleges accept so sweetly the customary Jim-crowing of the South that one feels sure the race's emancipation will never come through its intellectuals."[19]

Hughes's distaste for college graduates, expressed so scathingly in essays such as "Cowards from the Colleges" and "Our Wonderful Society: Washington," leads him to turn to the uneducated—or, in his view, the unindoctrinated—as the true representatives of the race. Pointing to the need for schools to produce men and women who would serve "as an antidote to the docile dignity of the meek professors and well-paid presidents who now run our institutions," Hughes proclaims that "American Negroes in the future had best look to the unlettered for their leaders."[20]

The "unlettered" to whom Hughes refers certainly would include those who haven't read the "right" books, and perhaps those who haven't read any books—the so-called culturally illiterate. This is the primary sense of "unlettered" here. As Hughes himself writes, "I seek to employ colloquial Negro speech as used in some strata of colored life, but *not* in the educated classes" (emphasis added).[21] Not surprisingly, his poetics appear to be informed partly by his unfavorable opinion of those whom he calls the "cowards from the colleges." However, "unlettered" here also means "illiterate" in the conventional sense; in referencing oral-based art forms in his work, Hughes directs his appeal to those who cannot read or write at all.

Having attended Columbia and Lincoln Universities, Hughes was of course well educated. But, in a manner reminiscent of Riley, he cultivated this persona of the unlettered poet, speaking for and to the unlettered masses as ambassador, and this pose was upheld by his critics. A 1927 review that grouped *Fine Clothes to the Jew* with poetry collections by Ezra Pound, John Crowe Ransom, and Mark Van Doren, distinguishes between Hughes and the others, unsurprisingly pointing to the educational background that the reviewer says the white poets share, an education that she claims is patently visible in their work. They are "all three learned and, for the most part, urbane gentlemen, whose poetry is fed in almost equal streams by literature and life." On the other hand, the reviewer notes, "[t]he verses of Langston Hughes are completely unliterary, often willfully illiterate," pointing in her choice of "illiterate" to the absence in Hughes's work of literary tradition, as T. S. Eliot uses the term in "Tradition and the Individual Talent," more than to the dialect spellings that readers sometimes associated with illiteracy—in other words, to the primary sense of "unlettered" rather than the secondary.[22]

This group of three terms ("unlettered," "unliterary," "illiterate")—the first Hughes's own and the other two imposed upon him by a reviewer—and the distinctions between them, form a kind of background for my discussion of *The Negro Mother*. Although the three are etymologically (but not connotatively) almost identical, and all three can oppose the word "learned" used by the reviewer to describe Pound, Ransom, and Van Doren, the various senses of "literacy" informing these three negative constructions, as they are commonly used, bear upon Hughes's work in distinct but related ways.

McKay's *Songs of Jamaica,* which preceded Hughes's book by twenty years and which I will address later in this chapter, serves as a provocative comparison to Hughes's *The Negro Mother* in its use of accompanying notes; McKay's notes, however, consist largely of footnotes appended by Walter Jekyll. Hughes's notes to *The Negro Mother* compete with the poem for primacy, and the reading experience generated by this competition signals a departure from the idea of dialect poetry as an exclusively oral art form. The innovation of *The Negro Mother* comes from its vision of what an instructive collection of poems—one that strives to build upon orality and literacy separately—should look like. The key term of this chapter's penultimate subtitle, "marginal literacy," points both to Hughes's apparent attitude toward poetry that presented itself as literary or literate, and to a generic division or boundary separating the main text from its margins—perhaps the most immediately visible textual feature of *The Negro Mother.*

Hughes's Typography

Before approaching *The Negro Mother,* let us turn to Hughes's other early formal experiments that work against any implications that orality is more essential to his poetry than literacy. Hughes's later experiments with visual elements, such as in *Ask Your Mama* and *Montage of a Dream Deferred,* have been subject to numerous studies of late.[23] But, in the 1920s and 1930s, Hughes manipulated typography to create texts that appear to work as scores for performance, texts that seem "oral" and yet are in fact impossible to perform—the essentially unreadable poem "Wait," for example, published in 1933, consists of a main text which is flanked by two marginal lists of repeating words in capital letters (such as "SCOTTSBORO," "COMMUNISTS," "STRIKERS") and is followed by a detritus-like paragraph of the same words at the bottom of the page. In addition, "The Cat and the Saxophone (2 A.M.)," which appears in *The Weary Blues,* alternates between lines of lowercase and capital letters; Countee Cullen wrote of it, "This creation is a *tour de force* of its kind, but is it a poem [?]":[24]

EVERYBODY
Half-pint,—
Gin?
No, make it
LOVES MY BABY
corn. You like
liquor,
don't you, honey?
BUT MY BABY
Sure. Kiss me,
DON'T LOVE NOBODY
daddy.
BUT ME.
Say!
EVERYBODY
Yes?
WANTS MY BABY
I'm your
BUT MY BABY
sweetie, ain't I?
DON'T WANT NOBODY
Sure.
BUT
Then let's
ME,
do it!
SWEET ME.
Charleston,
mamma!
![25]

The capital letters, read fluently, are the words to the popular 1924 song "Everybody Loves My Baby" by Jack Palmer and Spencer Williams. Hughes's incorporation of such a familiar and ubiquitous song is purposeful; he wrote in a 1925 letter to Carl Van Vechten that "a man died in front of [him] at the theatre," and jokingly cites the reason of death as "[h]eart failure, caused doubtless by having to hear, for the ten thousandth time, 'Everybody Loves My Baby.'"[26] The song is interspersed with dialogue between two lovers, or potential lovers, who end the poem dancing the Charleston. The poem's structure forces a comparison between these lovers and those who make up the love story related in the song, but the two couples end up being fairly dissimilar. The song lyrics are fluent, easy to follow and repetitive, consisting of one speaker's very assertive declarations of belovedness, whereas the accompanying conversation (with the lover present and participating) is choppy even read separately, and full of questioning. The assertiveness of the song is accentuated by the capital letters, while the implied furtiveness and whispering of what might be masking an indecent conversation is reflected in the lowercase. Moreover, the pet-name featured in the song, "baby," is never used in the conversation, but the lovers refer to each other instead by every other slangy pet-name: "honey," "daddy," "sweetie," and "mamma."

In approaching the first half of the poem, the reader has little difficulty determining what is going on, but the second half is much more visually radical—without the benefit of having read the first half, a reader would be puzzled. The lines (especially the last nine) become much shorter and more fractured, some consisting of monosyllables and one consisting only of an unpronounceable exclamation point. The separate threads begin to merge at this point, as neither one is able to sustain an independent narrative for long. Although the poem begins with a line from the song, the Charleston couple's dialogue takes up more space early on in the poem, only to succumb later to the dominance of the song. Just as the poem is ending, however, the Charleston's couple's dialogue begins to take precedence once more. The dialects of "The Cat and the Saxophone (2 A.M.)" are treated as if equivalent languages; neither dialect is meant to represent standard English, but neither is visually off-putting or jarring, and neither is framed by the other.

Because of this alternating technique, "The Cat and the Saxophone (2 A.M.)" is much more easily read silently than aloud. Although it incorporates a song, it doesn't "sing" itself, as one reviewer says of Hughes's dialect poems.[27] Visually, a reader may understand each separate narrative thread (the song and the Charleston couple) as well as the way both work together. The typographical shifts, from capital letters to lowercase, indicate that the two threads come from different sources. Despite the fact that the shifting cases reflect the respective assertiveness and secrecy of the song lyrics and the Charleston couple's conversation, they do not indicate any increase or decrease in volume or intensity, as we might expect in a score for performance. Neither does the exclamation point at the end of the poem correspond to sound or attach to a word: were there no exclamation point after "mamma" in the penultimate line, we might chalk up the lone exclamation point to an unconventional line-break. Were there no period at the end of the last line from the song—"SWEET ME"—we might consider the exclamation point to be the final resurfacing of the song. Instead, we are left with an exclamation that intensifies nothing and carries no sound. In isolation, it exists as a visual mark of exclamation only, or a signal of affect, as Jennifer DeVere Brody might argue. In a discussion of Poe's "The Gold Bug," Walter Ong argues that punctuation marks "are even farther from the oral world than the letters of the alphabet are: though part of a text, they are unpronounceable, nonphonemic."[28] Besides being unpronounceable, the exclamation point, as a physical and nonverbal gesture, may refer to the unrepresentable act for which the Charleston—risqué enough itself—substitutes.

Hughes's Marginal Literacy

The visual elements upon which "The Cat and the Saxophone (2 A.M.)" depend, isolated punctuation marks and alternating cases among them, make it look at first very different from the poems of *The Negro Mother*. Easily identifiable as a collection of recitation pieces, *The Negro Mother* was published in 1931 in part as an attempt by Hughes to reach audiences through public readings. He turns to recitations when only a few years earlier he complained to Van Vechten, "My own poems are about to bore me to death, I've heard them so much in the mouths of others recently. I didn't think free verse was quite so easy to remember." Furthermore, he claims to doubt the value of his own poetry performance and poetry performance in general, telling Van Vechten, "Don't bother about coming to my reading. Readings always bore me sick, just like church, and I am forever amazed at the people who go to them."[29] He even recalls, in his autobiography *The Big Sea,* two childhood experiences with poetry recitation—one his mother's and the other his own—that he deliberately ruined in order to deflate the pompous and theatrical atmosphere surrounding them. *The Negro Mother,* then, represents a clear shift in Hughes's strategies for his reception, aiming to make readers into performers—into representative voices—and giving them the opportunity to participate in his didactic mission. Although it is a minor book of poems, *The Negro Mother* is one of several so-called minor books of poetry that were brought out, significantly, between a pathbreaking collection of dramatic monologues (*Fine Clothes to the Jew* in 1927) and what Steven Tracy calls Hughes's explicit invitation to "performance and audience participation" (1942's *Shakespeare in Harlem*). I call it a "minor book" but at the same time I propose revising that distinction; according to a 1938 letter from Knopf, *Fine Clothes to the Jew*—which is perhaps the book most closely associated with Hughes today—sold only a few hundred copies more than *The Negro Mother* managed to sell even without the benefit of the Knopf imprimatur.[30]

The book consists of several declamatory poems, in the form of monologues, all with black speakers, and alongside several of these poems runs a set of notes ostensibly designed to guide the person reciting. These notes don't, however, quite qualify as stage directions. Stage directions, because they are notes for performance, cannot be characterized as paratextual, according to Gerard Genette. In *Paratexts,* he introduces an example of a note from *Tartuffe* that is not really a note but a stage direction: "It is a scoundrel who says this." He writes, "The 'note' in *Tartuffe,* which evidently serves as commentary, is nonetheless provided—in parentheses between two lines of verse—as a direction for the actor: please deliver this monologue in such a way that the public clearly perceives the speaker to be a scoundrel and not the gentleman and truly pious person he claims to be."[31] And in so doing Genette effectively dismisses the possibility of paratext in dramatic literature. Although there are many examples of the *Tartuffe* sort in *The Negro Mother*—for example, the notes to "The Big-Timer" direct the performer to "[a]ssum[e] a false and bragging self-assurance, and a pretended strength he doesn't really feel"[32]—there are also several moments that cannot be ascribed fully to the author's intention to direct his performer. These moments resemble more closely an example from *Faust* cited by Frederich A. Kittler as the "first unperformable stage direction in European theatrical history": "he seizes the book and mysteriously pronounces the sign of the spirit."[33] (Goethe gives no indication of what this pronouncement might be.)

Hughes's set of notes, or the apparatus (as I will call it, in order to include all of the paratextual material that appears alongside the poem), essentially competes with what we would think of as the substantial part of the text. Hughes's glosses in effect become parallel poems themselves, running alongside the poems proper, with the two texts using interdependent parallel headings. What is most significant here about the apparatus is its availability to the reader, not the listener—strange, given the intention of the book to build upon orality. The poem, in other words, may present itself as oral, as many have argued about Hughes's poetry in general, but the apparatus does not. It is a silent text. The listening audience hears the poem, but has no access to the notes used by the performer to present it. The prefatory note may be read before the recitation—at risk of disrupting the dramatic illusion or of being redundant—but nothing can be done to incorporate recitation of the notes along the side of the text without producing an unorthodox listening experience. Hughes's notes to *The Negro Mother,* then, complicate the book's posture as belonging strictly to an oral tradition. The reader ends up with something very different from what the listener ends up with. The book as it is designed produces in readers the disruptive experience of processing competing silent and performed texts simultaneously, processing the "literate" alongside the "unlettered."

To all appearances, though, Hughes expected and hoped that much of his audience would encounter his poetry through hearing it read aloud. In a promotional letter apparently sent to reviewers along with the book,[34] Hughes stated clearly his intentions:

> In recent Negro poetry, I have felt that there has been a distinct lack of rhymed poems dramatizing current racial interests in simple, understandable verse, pleasing to the ear, and suitable for reading aloud, or for recitation in schools, churches, lodges, etc. I have felt that much of our poetry has been aimed at the heads of the highbrows, rather than at the hearts of the people. And we all know that most Negro books published by white publishers are advertised and sold largely to white readers, and little or no effort is made to reach the great masses of the colored people.
>
> I have written "THE NEGRO MOTHER" with the hope that my own people will like it, and will buy it.

As this letter demonstrates, *The Negro Mother* is born as the book that most clearly exemplifies Hughes's poetics of accessibility. Carl Van Vechten sent the book to Gertrude Stein, writing, "Langston one day bemoaned to me the fact that Negro elocutionists had nothing to recite like Kipling, or The Boy Stood on the Burning Deck."[35] Elizabeth Davey points out that *The Negro Mother* was written with this hope in mind:

> The distinctly dramatic presentation of the poems of *The Negro Mother* suggests that Hughes thought that a mass black audience for black literature would be built through public readings, rather than the private consumption of books. Even after his tour ended, by using *The Negro Mother* as a script, Hughes's readers could continue to nurture audiences in economically and educationally marginalized black communities.[36]

It was the first of two books published by Golden Stair Press, a small press founded by Hughes and artist Prentiss Taylor. Because the books were self-published, Hughes and Taylor had control over their content, appearance, advertisement, and distribution, to a much greater degree than Hughes did with his two previous Knopf collections (so we can assume that the advertisement comparing *The Negro Mother* to Dunbar's work, although written by Van Vechten, was essentially Hughes's own assessment). Selling a cheap pamphlet edition of *The Negro Mother*—the book sold for twenty-five cents, and broadsides of individual poems with illustrations for ten cents—he managed to reach large numbers of readers and listeners. It may seem that the "ripple-effect" strategy of reading performance (in other words, Hughes's strategy of selling books to his listening audience, who would then read the poems aloud to still other listening audiences) is designed to exploit the orality of Hughes's work, but his impressive book sales during his tour tell another story. The idea for the 25-cent *Negro Mother* came from Hughes's decision that the occasional one-dollar printing of *The Weary Blues* that Knopf put out for Hughes to sell on tour might be too expensive for his Depression-era audiences.[37] In the end, he managed to sell over 1700 copies total of the 25-cent pamphlet,[38] indicating that in fact he was also spreading the ideals of literacy along the way; he ends up advocating the "private consumption of books" that he would otherwise seem to repudiate. (One can only speculate, after the dismal sales of *Fine Clothes to the Jew* a few years earlier, what may have motivated Hughes to market his pamphlet so well.[39])

If Hughes launched his reading tour through the South in order to reach the "unlettered" by reading his poems aloud to them, then who bought these books?[40] Who were Hughes's reading (as opposed to listening) audiences? Hughes himself contends that "few white people bought [the] book. But to Negroes [he] sold three large printings," with seven printings in total.[41] The census taken one year before *The Negro Mother* was published indicates that, though African Americans were behind whites in literacy rates in 1930, it is highly likely that most of Hughes's black listening audience would have had the basic literacy skills necessary to read Hughes's undemanding diction. Furthermore, most of his readings during this tour were at the same historically black colleges and universities Hughes had attacked in "Cowards from the Colleges" and "Our Wonderful Society: Washington," where, he writes, "Thousands of students heard me, and I sold many books."[42] Effectively, "thousands of students heard me, and [therefore] I sold many books." Presumably, he was not reading to the "unlettered."

African American readers were not an insignificant demographic in the early twentieth century. Elizabeth McHenry emphasizes how much the African American literate culture that was cultivated in the nineteenth century has been overlooked.[43] Literary societies were being formed in significant numbers as early as the 1830s, by secular groups and by churches. In fact, McHenry and Shirley Brice Heath cite an 1892 issue of the *Brooklyn Eagle,* in which the reporter claims, "Almost every church in Brooklyn had a literary society. There was no class of its city's citizens fonder of literary pursuits than the Afro-American."[44] Nationwide, the postbellum period saw significant decreases in African American illiteracy.[45] Specifically, Penelope L. Bullock writes that in 1870—the year Harte's "Plain Language from Truthful James" was published—"79.9 percent of the Negro population ten years of age and over was recorded as illiterate. By 1900 this figure had dropped to 44.5 percent and by 1910 to 30.4 percent."[46]

Hughes's 1931 tour included Virginia, North Carolina, South Carolina, Alabama, and Michigan—states with comparatively high rates of illiteracy (all three or more percentage points higher than the national average for African Americans at that time).[47] However, it is also important to consider the remarkable *change* in literacy rates, particularly in the South. The percentage of literate African Americans in the South was less than 50 in 1890, but it had grown to more than 80 in 1930. While the number of Southern whites who could read increased only 32 percent during this period, the number of literate Southern blacks almost doubled, as Henry Allen Bullock points out in *A History of Negro Education in the South*. As he puts it, "long before mid-century the charge that Southern Negroes supplied the South with massive illiteracy had become statistically less justifiable."[48]

Hughes's desire to tour the states with the lowest rates of literacy, regardless of the fact that they were states with the most dramatic increases in literacy, reflects his dream—whether or not it was the reality—of reaching and educating people who rarely encounter literature. He makes this clear in his autobiography *I Wonder as I Wander,* writing that his "audiences ranged all the way from college students to cotton pickers, from kindergarten children to the inmates of old folks homes."[49] Where just a few pages earlier he had chosen to emphasize the fact that "thousands of students heard [him], and [he] sold many books," he now emphasizes the all-inclusive range of his audience: they are of all ages, all educational backgrounds, all socio-economic groups. His sentence could be extended, presumably, to include the literate on one hand and the illiterate on the other—the lettered and the unlettered. This desire to address his poetry to illiterate as well as literate audiences is also curiously consistent with his efforts to tap into, and enact, the oral features of African American artistic culture. Operating under the conceit that his audience's appreciation of his poetry is dependent upon aural and not literate reception goes along with a poetry that pretends to be exclusively oral.

As much as Hughes's dedication to orality seems to encourage the inclusivity and collectivity implied by public performance, the performance of Hughes's work is restricted to his interpretation of it. Strangely, Hughes's position as annotator becomes didactic and textually bound in a way that reaches back to an elocution tradition from a century before: guiding the reader through a proper enunciation of the poem, and framing an oral work with the literary apparatus deemed necessary to understand it. Hughes-as-annotator is anachronistically rigid and prescriptive in his instructions for performance.

Take, for example, Hughes's prefatory note to *Shakespeare in Harlem,* which, Steven C. Tracy writes, illustrates the importance of orality for Hughes. This note states that the poems should be "read aloud, crooned, shouted, recited, and sung. Some with gestures, some not—as you like. None with a far-away voice."[50] Superficially, this directive does suggest that Hughes envisions his readers performing the poems as they see fit. However, what's strange here is that Hughes seems to offer his reader some freedom in interpretation ("*Some* with gestures, some not—as you like") but immediately follows this offer with a restriction ("*None* with a far-away voice"). Of course, the "far-away voice" likely refers to an outmoded elocution voice a modern poet would want to avoid, but the parallel structure set up by Hughes seems intended to spotlight, even if ironically, the opposition between freedom and restriction in performance. Beginning the book in this way may be intended to open up multiple possibilities, but—determining the terms for its recitation ahead of time—the book leaves little room for spontaneity.

One of the few critics to address *The Negro Mother* in any depth, Davey mentions Hughes's glosses, but only to say that using them in performance enriches the poems, providing aural enhancement as guides for performance: "Although the language of these poems is simple in both diction and rhyme patterns, Hughes's scripting—the layout of the text, illustrations, and directions for the performance at the head of each poem and running down the outer margin—would have produced musically and emotionally complex performances."[51] We know something about one such performance because Hughes describes it in *I Wonder as I Wander.* At one reading during his reading tour, Hughes tells us that he "closed with 'The Negro Mother' from my new booklet. 'Imagine,' I said, 'a black woman of old in her starched white apron and bright bandanna.'"[52] Following this prefatory statement, Hughes then proceeded to read the poem. Hughes read some instructions for performing the poem; he did not actually perform them. And because he did not attempt to assume the persona of the Negro Mother, nothing prohibited him from reading all of his notes, but for some reason he did not. The notes included in the book for use in performing "The Negro Mother" read, "A poem to be done by a woman in the bandana and apron of the Old South—but with great dignity and strength and beauty in her face as she speaks. The music of spirituals may be played by a piano or an orchestra as the aged mother talks to her modern sons and daughters."[53] It appears that he neither read nor performed these notes in full, despite the fact that the notes, Davey claims, "would have produced musically and emotionally complex performances." In neither case would these prefatory notes have had the optimal desired effect upon Hughes's audience. The audience could see or could imagine, from the start, the woman's dress, but neither see nor imagine the more powerful aspects of her appearance—her "dignity," "strength," and "beauty"—and the interregional and intergenerational import of the poem indicated by the mention of "the Old South" and by the distance between "the aged mother" and the "modern sons and daughters."

Hughes's notes aren't simply subordinate to the poem. Contrary to Genette's claim that "No matter what . . . a paratextual element is always subordinate to 'its' text," the notes to *The Negro Mother* do not exist simply to support the text.[54] Neither are they really part of the text. "The Colored Soldier," for example, contains parallel narratives in "The Mood" and "The Poem"; by the end of the reading experience, "The Mood," as literature, often rivals "The Poem." These narratives coexist and entwine, like the interwoven discourses of "The Cat and the Saxophone (2 A.M.)," but they diverge on occasion and, in so doing, assert their autonomy. We might think of "The Mood" and "The Poem" as rivals for our attention, and Prentiss Taylor's illustrations add an additional medium that demands our notice.

In "The Colored Soldier," the first poem of the collection, the "mood" offers information not available in the poem proper. The poem tells the story of a young man who returns from war overseas having lost his brother in battle, and realizes that the democratic values for which they fought do not extend to black people in America.[55] The third stanza begins with the speaker, disgusted with present social conditions, telling us of a dream in which the spirit of his brother appeared to him. In fact, "The

Mood" tells the reader that he should be representing a speaker "[q]uietly recalling the vision."[56] Throughout most of the text, "The Poem" and "The Mood" appear to be synchronized: the recitation of particularly poignant and tragic lines should be delivered as if "remembering with a half-sob," and, when reading lines clearly reflecting the speaker's frustration, the reader should become "suddenly fierce and angry." However, the final stanza breaks from this expectation.

Then he sadly recalls the rows of white crosses in France.	Then I woke up, and the dream was ended— But broken was the soldier's dream, too bad to be mended. And it's a good thing all the black boys lying dead Over There Can't see! And don't know! And won't ever care!

It is strange that delivery of the last couplet here should not also be "suddenly fierce and angry," considering the impassioned exclamation marks. Instead, these lines should be uttered, inexplicably, while "sadly recall[ing] the rows of white crosses in France." This is the first disjuncture between notes and text that is anticipated by the line, "The dream was cruel—and bitter—and somehow not right." What is "not right" about the dream, clearly, is that the brother's naïve hopes about the racial situation in the United States following the war have now been turned into nothing but delusions. But, what is also "not right" about the dream, in the structural context of the poem, is its duality: the brother's hope for equal rights (his "dream") and the speaker's vision coincide at this point in the poem to form one "dream," only to separate in the first and second lines of the poem's final stanza. "[T]he dream was ended" refers to the speaker's vision; the "soldier's dream" to the brother's expectations. Two dreams are shattered at once. True, the speaker's dream simply and anticlimactically "ends," while his brother's is violently broken, "too bad to be mended." But, it goes without saying, the brother's dream is also, or was also, the speaker's dream. The "colored soldier" of the poem's title is not only the brother, but the speaker, too.

The crosses remembered by the speaker in "The Mood," although mentioned briefly earlier in the poem, are not featured in the corresponding part of the text proper; they are, however, realized in the illustrations on this page and the first page. How Taylor's stylized illustrations (or "decorations," as they are called on the title page) might have contributed to the production of "musically and emotionally complex performances," as Davey writes, is unclear. Are speakers expected to reproduce the scenes depicted in them regardless of the fact that they do not exist in the poem? Hughes's preliminary directions only specify how the performer should look, what the lighting should be like, and if there should be musical accompaniment—nothing about visual setting and backdrop.

Framed, like his first vision, by the word "recalls," the speaker's vision of crosses sparks what might be the most dramatic and profound disjuncture between the "Poem" and "Mood." They effectively oppose each other: in the former, the "dream was ended" but, in the latter, the second vision is just beginning. Unlike the first vision, which is the memory of a memory ("Quietly recalling the vision"), the second vision can be described as a sort of waking dream, and recreates an actual scene as memory ("recalls the rows of white crosses"). Hughes's treatment of memory shifts: images, as immediate experience, enter into the "Poem," as in the line, "I saw him standing there, straight and tall"—rather than, for example, "I imagined (or remembered) him standing there, straight and tall"—but the "Mood" consists mainly of indirection, re-creations of or emotional reactions to memory, as in the note, "remembering with a half-sob." They refer to events in the text proper. With the introduction of the crosses, an independent image—an image of a cemetery the speaker may never have seen in life—enters into both Mood and illustration, bypassing the text itself.

All of the words signaling memory, such as "recalls" and "remembers," occur in the "Mood," not the "Poem." And to include memory in a text designed to function exclusively as a recitation note is problematic because it cannot be presented: the audience will register the "half-sob" but not what, exactly, is being remembered. Even more problematic, however, is the inclusion in the Mood of recollection not experienced across the page, as is the case with the recollection of white crosses.

Aside from the fact that many of these directions are impossible to carry out literally—how can a speaker convey to his audience that he is imagining visiting a cemetery without telling them?—the fact that "The Mood" at this point carries and conveys more narrative information than the narrative proper complicates the poem's stance toward oral communication. Because the directions contain information impossible to relay in performance, "The Mood" is only really accessible to readers, and *The Negro Mother* is then designed for silent reading as well as performance.[57]

As a book that is written for recitation, *The Negro Mother* intends to participate in a history of elocution and performance traditions, but it's a confused history. Early in the nineteenth century, elocution was a tool used in moral education, but poetry performance became more closely associated with entertainment by the end of the century. As I mentioned earlier in this study, this shift coincided with the increase in performances of dialect poetry, by professionals and amateurs, and by readers and poets. Although the late-nineteenth-century debasement of the recitation movement would seem to render Hughes's effort less ambitious than he intended, the larger audiences that came along with this debasement can situate Hughes's attempt as a more expansive revision of the earlier recitation tradition that saw reading aloud as a means toward edification. In fact, Hughes's effort to keep dialect to a minimum, for the most part, in *The Negro Mother* could be ascribed partially to a desire to sidestep the qualities many associated with dialect poetry performance.[58] In other words, Hughes was trying to move his recitations away from the frivolity linked with entertaining dialect poetry, while still maintaining the more popular and less elitist audience that these entertainments could attract. As Cary Nelson notes, Hughes similarly uses a "rather mild form of dialect" for his "Letter from Spain," another "Colored Soldier" poem written a few years later, perhaps with the same intentions.[59]

In this negotiation, Hughes's efforts echo those transitional efforts in the mid-to-late nineteenth century to maintain the illusion that recitations were purely educational in the face of growing theatricality. In an essay about reading aloud and Victorian theater, Alison Byerly writes that, "[a]lthough readings became increasingly theatrical in the course of the nineteenth century, the Victorians continued to consider them—or conveniently pretended to consider them—educational as well as entertaining."[60] After recitation had lost much of its currency as moral instruction, but before it was relegated to the realm of entertainment through dialect poetry, readings were understood as a less corrupt alternative to the theater, as Byerly, Mark Morrisson, Philip Collins, and others point out.[61] However, the theatricality of presentation, which was precisely the problem for many nineteenth-century Americans, was picked up by Hughes as something valuable about recitation. What he rejected, in *The Negro Mother,* was *content* that was not explicitly related to education. He would borrow, piecemeal, the elements he wanted from the turn-of-the-century recitation tradition—for example, its break from elitism—but revert to an earlier recitation tradition in his intent to educate his listeners: part showman, part spokesman.

The silent form of *The Negro Mother*'s apparatus ends up overshadowing the book's voiced (and implicitly oral) poetic text as a whole. Moreover, the depictions of knowledge in the individual poems themselves, represented through the most inspirational and respected figures of the collection, also privilege literacy. In the titular poem, "The Negro Mother," the speaker recalls a preliterate state very negatively: "I couldn't read then. I couldn't write. / I had nothing, back there in the night." The speaker of "The Black Clown" serves as a negative example, beginning his address to the audience by saying that he is:

> Not the same as you—
> Because my mind is dull,
> And dice instead of books will do
> For me to play with
> When the day is through.

Finally, the last poem of the collection, "Dark Youth of the U.S.A.," begins by positioning the poem's speaker as a student and reader: "Sturdy I stand, books in my hand," with books thus becoming necessary props in performing the work. Later in the poem, he declares that "[t]o be wise and strong, then, studying long, / Seeking the knowledge that rights all wrong— / That is my mission." In other words, the knowledge that is accorded the power to right all wrongs is found in literate and not in oral information, and the student's purpose—his "mission"—is linked inextricably to his literacy. Of course, gaining strength individually and collectively through literacy was, as I mentioned in the previous chapter, a longstanding subject for the African American literary tradition that preceded Hughes. Hughes's emphasis on the value of orality only gives the appearance of a turn from this tradition: literacy, and the results that would flow from it (to quote Frederick Douglass), are still depicted in *The Negro Mother* as the "mission" of the characters presented in the book. And in having performers embody these characters, Hughes was imagining them and their audiences not as unlettered but as literate. When the Black Clown, who will have nothing to do with books, says that he is "[n]ot the same as you," he is addressing his listening audiences as readers.[62]

Hughes was certainly more concerned with preserving the impression of orality in his poetry than, for example, Dunbar was, as he revised his earlier dialect poetry to reduce what Stanley Schatt calls the "Dunbar-like dialect that [he] had enjoyed using in his late teens and early twenties."[63] Generally, he turned away from Dunbar's reliance upon orthographical peculiarity and toward syntactical dialect features that could be perceived by a listening audience just as well as a reading one. Hughes revised his poems more frequently than one might think, as several of his readers have pointed out.[64] Van Vechten's introduction to *The Weary Blues* suggests that the naturalness of Hughes's work is only the semblance of naturalness; he says of his poems, "[t]hey are the (I almost said informal, for they have a highly deceptive air of spontaneous improvisation) expression of an essentially sensitive and subtly illusive nature."[65] The "spontaneous improvisation" suggested by Hughes's verse is, of course, designed to look spontaneous and improvised, and Hughes's interest in oral art forms leads him to try to approximate the spontaneity often fundamental to the composition of those forms.

Although reading aloud was still a common activity through the late nineteenth century and taught in schools, by the time *The Negro Mother* was published, silent reading—and more specifically silent *educational* reading—had become more or less entrenched in the United States. This development, of course, has important consequences for Hughes's composition of a book of recitations at this time. Reciting poetry, especially as a travelling bard, did not feel modern; as Charles Chesnutt wrote to Hughes about his performance tour of the South, "It suggests the wandering minstrel of medieval times."[66] The various formats of *The Weary Blues, Fine Clothes to the Jew,* and *The Negro Mother* suggest that Hughes wanted to think of his poetry as belonging to an oral tradition, and that his strategies for exploiting that connection were constantly evolving. His early books figure as responses and challenges to the shifts in reading culture that, by the early twentieth century, were privileging silent reading, but they were also subject to these shifts. In a book titled *The Applied Psychology of Reading: With Exercises and Directions for Improving Silent and Oral Reading,* published in 1926 (the same year coincidentally as Hughes's first book, *The Weary Blues*), psychologist Fowler D. Brooks writes, "Silent reading is far more important for the adult than oral reading. This fact is so widely recognized now that we need not discuss it at any length." Poetry, however, has always been the exception. Brooks claims that poetry is peculiarly resistant to silent reading, and that it is "almost impossible" to read poetry without oral reading. He writes, "The reader may observe his own silent reading of poetry and see the importance of inner articulation. One may begin by reading silently a poem which he enjoys, but as he proceeds he often reads it aloud, or with noticeable vocalization."[67] One can't help it, or so he would have us believe. Even early-twentieth-century educators who strongly urged against oral reading, such as Herbert G. Lull and H. B. Wilson in their 1921 *The Redirection of High-School Instruction,* permit the qualification that "inner articulation habits developed by good oral reading which involve feelings of inflection, pitch, tone quality, and rhythm have some value for silent reading, especially the silent reading of poetry."⁶⁸

This understanding of the process involved in reading poetry—as distinct from other kinds of reading—persists today, as most poetry in general appears to require the use of oral models of reading, reception, and composition. The divergent modes in *The Negro Mother* that encourage readers to respond to it as both oral and literate reflect not only Hughes's dual concerns, but a larger cultural shift that had been happening for decades in silent reading practices. Subvocalization, or "inner articulation," functions as something like a loophole in the less-than-total triumph of silent reading, and allows the silent reading of poetry to exist with still some trace of performance. This is true to an even greater degree in the reading of dialect poetry. In *The Negro Mother,* the difficulty of reading the poems aloud arises from the perceived discordance of and tension between competing oral and literate modes of communication, and Hughes's appeal to poetry listeners, by distancing the oral and literate parts of the book from each other, ends up ironically reasserting their combination as indispensable to an appreciation of the book. Today, Hughes is recognized more than he is read and, when he is read, his work is treated as a celebration of orality. Ironically, in a book of recitations, we find a complementary celebration of literacy.

McKay's Dialects and Poetic Diction

Like Hughes's *The Negro Mother,* Claude McKay's early work in *Songs of Jamaica* was surrounded by an apparatus framing the book. McKay's apparatus confirmed that the book contained "the thoughts and feelings of a Jamaican peasant of pure black blood."⁶⁹ Readers are thus instructed to think of all of the characters presented in *Songs of Jamaica,* male and female, young and old, to be versions of McKay. Hughes stipulated how dark- or light-skinned performers of the *Negro Mother* poems should be, giving instructions that "The Black Clown" be done by "a pure-blooded Negro" and "The Colored Soldier" by a "young brown fellow," but the intraracial diversity of the characters effectively creates space for a community of readers to step in and out of the text rather than presenting one archetypal character through which to understand the book's various speakers. The diversity contained in McKay's book, on the other hand, is leveled by Jekyll's introduction. Jekyll, McKay's patron early in his career, writes an introduction to *Songs of Jamaica* that is notably not evaluative in a literary sense; it is clear that only authenticity and purity of expression matter to him. In an essay titled "Boyhood in Jamaica," McKay recalls that, upon meeting Jekyll and asking his opinion on a group of poems that were all in standard English but one, Jekyll disliked the poems in "straight English" but of the dialect poem he told McKay, "this is the real thing."[70] As Michael North points out, "McKay came to him already speaking and writing perfect standard English, which Jekyll urged him to drop, at least on paper, in favor of the Jamaican dialect," because "[i]t was vitally necessary to his white patrons and readers that he be 'real.'"[71] An English folklorist living and collecting tales in Jamaica, Jekyll impressed upon McKay the importance of presenting himself as "the real thing" in his poetry.

In response to Jekyll's rejection of his "straight English" poems, McKay wrote mainly dialect poems for *Songs of Jamaica,* a book that Heather Hathaway calls "an act of mediation."[72] Similarly, Charles Bernstein writes that, "[l]ike Dunbar's *Complete Poems,* McKay's dialect poetry is a schizophrenic presentation, foregrounding two unequally powerful readerships, black and white"; one is constantly reminded of "the controlling hand of white editorial authority [that] is always present on the page."[73] Robert Stepto's treatment of slave narratives and their structures provides a set of terms that prove helpful in understanding the relationship between McKay's text and the "authenticating" material appended to it by Jekyll. Although the generic differences and historical distance between nineteenth-century slave narratives and an early-twentieth-century book of dialect poetry make the application of Stepto's terms inexact in this case, his categorizations at least heighten our awareness of the anachronicity of Jekyll's appended introduction. Bernstein's comparison to Dunbar might be slightly more appropriate, as Howells's authentication also revolves around the "purity" of Dunbar's blackness. Although this comparison should take into account the sixteen years and the national borders that separate the publications of *Lyrics of Lowly Life* and *Songs of Jamaica,* it is also worth noting that *Songs of Jamaica* was actually published one year *before* the first edition of Dunbar's posthumous *Complete Poems* (the former in 1912, the latter in 1913).

Before Hughes, McKay was treated as yet another first real black literary "spokesman" and as a significant departure from Dunbar. Max Eastman, in an introduction to *Harlem Shadows* that is often outrageously racist, writes that "[t]hese poems have a special interest for all the races of man because they are sung by a pure blooded Negro. They are the first significant expression of that race in poetry. We tried faithfully to give a position in our literature to Paul Laurence Dunbar. We have excessively welcomed other black poets of minor talent, seeking in their music some distinctive quality other than the fact that they wrote it."[74] These remarks by Eastman, coupled with Jekyll's introduction, even in attempting to distance McKay from Dunbar, ironically amount to a retreading of the authenticating material Howells provided for Dunbar's *Lyrics of Lowly Life.*

At first, in *Songs of Jamaica,* Jekyll extends the "purity" of McKay and his countrymen to their language: "What Italian is to Latin, that in regard to English is the negro variant thereof. It shortens, softens, rejects the harder sounds alike of consonants and vowels; I might almost say, refines."[75] This perspective reflects what North points to as a common view that saw dialect as "'purer' than the standard written language because it was less affected by printing, education, and 'elocution masters.'"[76] Ultimately, however, the pronunciation differences Jekyll points out ("d" for "th," for example) are to him evidence of linguistic laziness, and only two pages later the implications of "refinement" are very different. Jekyll writes, "The negro has no difficulty whatever in pronouncing it clearly: it is merely that he does not, as a rule, take the trouble to do so. . . . And here let me remark, in passing, that in one breath, the black man will pronounce a word in his own way, and in the next will articulate it as purely as the most refined Englishman."[77] "Refinement"—he could have alternatively written "cultivation"—shifts here from the province of the black man to the province of the white, specifically Englishman, reminding us of the hesitancy behind Jekyll's "I might almost say" in his original statement. His assertions that Jamaican English is more "refined" than "English," and yet those who speak it are necessarily less "refined" than those who do not, produce a critical contradiction.[78] In other words, as nonsensical as it sounds, articulating a word in a refined way must differ, for Jekyll, in some way from articulating a word as if one is refined.

The idea behind Jekyll's second statement, that the black man can switch from speaking "in his own way" to speaking as "the most refined Englishman," stands in marked contrast to the assumptions that drive poems such as Harte's "The Spelling Bee at Angel's" or Johnson's "Aunt Cloe's Trip to See Miss Liza Kyle," in which the "refined" conditions of the event of the spelling bee or a visit to the city respectively find the characters unable to shift registers. In fact, the most basic level of humor in Harte's and Johnson's poems comes from the fish-out-of-water situations in which the dialect speakers find themselves, from the unlikely fact that the characters are not able to alter their speech or behavior at all depending upon their circumstances. But in Jekyll's remarks we get a hint of what seems to be the threatening underside of dialect poetry and its "charms": the dialect speaker is essentially duplicitous and inscrutable. This perceived threat is at the heart of Jekyll's shifting sense of "refinement."

Like the dialect in which the "unrefined" black man expresses himself, by association considered now to be *un*refined and *im*pure, the speaker of the poem is essentially illegible and refuses to be fixed. Why else include such extensive pronunciation notes and appendices, longer than McKay's poems in some cases? A note to "Quashie to Buccra," North writes, "conjures up a dramatic scene before the first-time reader thinks to ask why there *are* notes."[79] And, as Bernstein points out, *Songs of Jamaica*'s "many compromising aspects" include "running translations and glosses at the foot of each page, providing unnecessary and misleading translations of dialect words."[80] It is certainly true that many of the glosses are unnecessary. For example, Jekyll's treatment of the final stanza of McKay's "Heartless Rhoda" consists of a summary longer than the text itself. Here is the final stanza, followed by Jekyll's accompanying note:

> Life I only care to see
> >In de way dat udders live;
> I experiment to be
> All dat fate can mek o' me:
> >Glad I tek all whe' she give,
> For I'm hopin' to be free.

> A free paraphrase will best explain the meaning of these six lines. Rhoda sees other girls marry, and out of pure curiosity she wants to find out what married life is like. So she makes the experiment,—though this [marriage] is only one of the things that Fate has in store for her. And she takes gladly whatever Fate gives, always hoping (and meaning) to change the present experience for another.[81]

In addition to this lengthy note, Jekyll offers his readers a note translating "udders" as "others." This is in case, I suppose, readers should think that the poem's speaker would like to live as a cow's udder!

Many notes, moreover, call attention to redundant words that seem to improve rhythm, as does "say" in the line "But I can tell you say" from "Fetchin' Water." Occasionally, though, Jekyll will make his estimation of the poetic value of extraneous words explicit in a way that he never does in his introduction, as he does in his note to the line "Joanie, when you were me own a true sweetheart" from McKay's "Pleading." Jekyll writes, "There is a delicious caressing sound about this intrusive 'a.'" Even so, the notion that this language might be "literary" is never admitted, despite the fact that redundancies are also a common strategy in heightened poetic diction (think of, for example, the semantically extraneous second "and go" of "I will arise and go now, and go to Innisfree" from William Butler Yeats's "The Lake Isle of Innisfree," a poem whose archaic structures never really cross over into dialect writing). The excesses of Jekyll's apparatus serve a purpose for him, and for the audience he imagined for McKay. Any trace of inscrutability that might remain in the text would threaten the standard-English-speaking reader, who imagines that the language of the poem would be perfectly accessible, legible, and natural to any black reader.

The apparatus' presence in *Songs of Jamaica* can be attributed to Jekyll's insistence that the poet and his invented dialect speakers must be interpreted. It is clear from Jekyll's introduction that he thinks of literary dialect as insufficiently literate on its own. This is not to say that Jekyll did not value the Jamaican dialect; clearly, he did. But Jekyll has something at stake in directing McKay toward dialect writing: the resultant text depends upon Jekyll's perception of the division between ordinary language (that of the dialect poems) and literary language (that of the apparatus). Bernstein is right to say that the most obvious of Jekyll's notes are his translations, but a significant number guide pronunciation; for example, a footnote to the word "do'n" reads, "'Down' is pronounced very short, and is a good rhyme to 'tongue.'"[82] In fact, Jekyll's entire introduction, save the paragraph about McKay's "purity," is comprised of directions for pronunciation. Jekyll's notes indicate, in other words, that he understands *Songs of Jamaica* as a profoundly oral composition, and his notes as a literate companion.

Jekyll's consistent and determined treatment of *Songs of Jamaica* as the awkward transcription of oral poetry amounts to an attempt to force McKay into the paradoxical role of an illiterate writer. Stepto claims, in his reading of Henry Bibb's narrative as an "eclectic narrative" (or, a first-phase narrative, in which the authenticating material is appended to and not integrated into the text), that "Bibb's removal from the primary authenticating documents and strategy (that is, from the 'Introduction') weakens his control of the narrative and . . . relegates him to a posture of partial literacy."[83] This is also true, to some extent, in McKay's case; his literacy is obscured by Jekyll's introduction.

Of course, McKay was ill-equipped to fill the role Jekyll prescribed for him. The poems themselves smack of a culturally specific and Anglophilic kind of literary artifice. In his introduction to *Harlem Shadows*, McKay describes the kind of education he received in the British colony, pointing out that "the language we wrote and read in school was England's English. Our textbooks then, before the advent of the American and Jamaican readers and our teachers, too, were all English-made."[84] In fact, Bita's poetry-inspired reverie in *Banana Bottom* could have been modeled after McKay's own childhood educational experiences. When she comes across "some of those verses that had been prescribed during her elementary-school days as 'recitations to develop the love of poetry in children'" and "the 'memory gems' that did service as 'little moral lessons in short poetic flights,'" she sits, "shut entirely off from her surroundings and was back in school again, absorbed in the blue-covered reader and the poems (how she did love to prattle them!)."[85] Bita's absorbing reading brings to mind the literary appetite of the young McKay, whose reading material included "anything that was thrilling": first, mainly novels, and then, "with [Jekyll's] excellent library at [his] disposal, . . . *Childe Harold, The Dunciad, Essay on Man, Paradise Lost*, the Elizabethan lyrics, *Leaves of Grass*, the lyrics of Shelley and Keats and of the late Victorian poets."[86] The speaker of McKay's "Old England," one of the poems included in *Songs of Jamaica*, gushes at the prospect of visiting Westminster Abbey to see Milton, Shakespeare, Wordsworth, and Gray. Although Bernstein believes that "Old England" "overplays the sentiment" and therefore can be read ironically, McKay himself, in *A Long Way from Home*, writes, "In my young poetic exuberance in the clean green hills of Jamaica, I had chanted blithely and naively of 'chimney factories pouring smoke,'" apparently referring to this poem.[87] The product of British instruction, McKay valued the English literary canon—Whitman stands out as an odd and unexpected exception—and his writing as a result privileged the oral elements Jekyll wanted only with difficulty.

As Hathaway writes of *Songs of Jamaica*, the "language . . . does not ring true. Frequently, what appears to be McKay's voice, that of one who speaks in the 'cultivated' tongue of 'straight English,' interrupts the mood and tone of the dialect that is intended to characterize the peasant speaker."[88] To this I would counter that the language of written dialect poetry, in any case, can never "ring true," because readers must decode each writer's invented dialect. Hathaway's use of the words "voice" and "tongue" in the sentence above reveal an unproblematized association of dialect writing with orality. Words such as "whe'" in McKay's "Heartless Rhoda," although they may make contextual sense, render the poem for a moment less legible. The reader must figure out, even if for a split second, what "whe'" might signify, while "o'er"—another contraction that represents a similarly nonstandard pronunciation—would cause no such problems and would be instantly recognizable, being already part of our literate inheritance. "Whe'" is not, on the other hand, a word English language readers are used to seeing in print.

Using Charles Dickens, Thomas Hardy, Herman Melville, and Mark Twain as examples, Michael Toolan writes that readers "negotiate those pages . . . where some other dialect than the familiar standard is rendered in a spirit of enforced labour. No doubt there are effects of charm and quaintness achieved, but by and large the sense of alienation predominates."[89] In many cases, ironically, the more phonetically precise the dialect is, the more difficult it is to read. In reading a linguistically detailed dialect poem by the nineteenth-century African American poet James Edwin Campbell, Mark Balhorn decides, "Except for the eye dialect, there is a lot to recommend this piece from the standpoint of linguistic accuracy, but as is evident when one first tries to read it, as literature, it is not very effective. Since the rendering is difficult to process, the resulting voice sounds inarticulate, even inscrutable." Like McKay's "whe'," Campbell's dialect "[s]pellings such as 'lib' for 'live,' 'hunner yurs' for 'a hundred years,' and 'ebbry tings' for 'everything,' are not automatically recognized and the reader must consciously analyze the string in order to retrieve lexical meaning. . . . [R]eading of the text remains a labor."[90] That both Toolan and Balhorn describe the dialect reading experience as "labor" demonstrates just how thoroughly readers abandon phonics as they achieve competency, making the processing of unfamiliar written words hard work. In other words, readers would recognize "o'er" instantly, but "whe'" produces an instance of defamiliarization that requires some degree of exertion to figure out. As Bernstein puts it, "[t]ranscribed speech, for example, may seem more unnatural than the idealized conventions for representing speech. . . . The ordinary erodes and resists the standard, just as standard English and normative verse forms exoticize and defamiliarize the ordinary."[91] Or, to put it in terms outlined in an earlier chapter, "whe'," like Riley's child-writing, forces the reader to revisit the phoneticization and subvocalization of early literacy. "O'er," however, does not. Reading it effortlessly is an indicator of familiarity with the English poetic tradition.

Because Jekyll reads McKay's dialect as "the real thing" and implicitly argues for literary dialect as the most "natural" medium for McKay's poetry in his introduction, while McKay's poetry necessarily presents dialect writing as just as artificial as the standard English writing, both literary dialect and poetic diction strain legibility in McKay's case. This seems to me distinct from "code switching," the oral practice that Lee M. Jenkins invokes to describe the shifting registers in McKay's "Sukee River" (the only dialect poem, Jenkins points out, that McKay translates later into standard English).[92] Moreover, like Dunbar's early poetry collections, the poems in *Songs of Jamaica* are written in several different dialects, all straining legibility to different degrees and in different ways, demanding that readers shift registers constantly. In other words, McKay poses a challenge to the writer cited in this book's introduction who claimed that "no man who is capable of writing ''neath a grassy screen' is capable of following it with 'Durn it all!'—except an amateur dialect poet."[93] "To E.M.E.," for example, is one of several poems in a less obtrusive dialect (the poem begins, "You see me smile: but what is it? / A sweetened pain—a laughin' fit—," with only "laughin'" being a dialect spelling, and a conservative one at that).[94] Another poem, "A Country Girl," is a dialogue of two distinct dialects, both distinctly Jamaican. Those poems not in dialect are almost invariably written in such self-consciously poetic diction that they call attention to themselves, such as "A Dream," with the lines, "Day broadens, and I *ope* the window wide" and "I lightly *gambol* on the school-yard green" (emphasis added).

Rather than thinking of these artificial standard-English poems as failures, as Jekyll might, we can think of McKay's approach to poetic diction as a variation of his approach to dialect poetry. As Donald Wesling writes, "In principle, reading [dialect] poetry is the same kind of literary experience as reading a heavily elaborated diction in Alexander Pope."[95] McKay recognized this. In his introduction to *Harlem Shadows,* McKay defends his habitual use of heightened poetic diction. He writes:

> I have not hesitated to use words which are old, and in some circles considered poetically overworked and dead, when I thought I could make them glow alive by new manipulation. Nor have I stinted my senses of the pleasure of using the decorative metaphor where it is more truly and vividly beautiful than the exact phrase. But for me there is more quiet delight in "The golden moon of heaven" than in "The terra-cotta disc of cloud-land."[96]

McKay's remarks, published in 1922, read almost as a rebuttal to the sort of Imagist prescriptions favoring precision to abstraction set forth by Pound. Pound's "A Few Don'ts by an Imagiste" warns writers, "Don't use such an expression as 'dim lands *of peace.*' It dulls the image. It mixes an abstraction with the concrete. It comes from the writer's not realizing that the natural object is always the *adequate* symbol."[97] In fact, "A Dream"'s embrace of the "poetic" extends beyond word choice to inversions of word order: for example, "Sadly the scenes of bygone days I view."[98]

According to definitions of poetic language that distinguish it from ordinary language,[99] dialect verse is paradoxically both: literary dialect claims to represent speech almost as closely as a phonetic transcription might, but, as literature, it is initially off-putting and illegible to the reader. Stanley Fish argues that "the very act of distinguishing between ordinary and literary language, because of what it assumes, leads necessarily to an inadequate account of both," and dialect poetry would provide Fish with a peculiar case study: dialect writing as "ordinary" language defines itself against literary conventions, but requires all of the labor associated with literary language.[100] On one hand, dialect writing is plain and prosaic. On the other hand, it becomes—almost despite itself—literary, appealing to its readers on a visual and literate level. In its attempted closeness to orality, with its seeming phonetic accuracy, literary dialect ends up even more literary (i.e., extraordinary) than "o'er" is. In his analysis of Gerard Manley Hopkins, Cary H. Plotkin claims that Hopkins's use of dialect "heighten[s] current language into poetic language . . . by virtue of the attention that dialect words draw to themselves as words rather than as transparent vehicles of meaning," thus "making the components of language obtrude into the foreground of the poem." As a result, dialect words "constitute a supplementary resistance to reading."[101] Literary dialect, then, seems to have it both ways, being both natural and unnatural, ordinary and poetic.

Many of the features associated with poetic diction are just as present in dialect verse as they are in "poetic" verse, and are used to the same end. Perhaps most notable among these features is elision. Like his use of inversions and poetic diction generally, McKay's use of poetic elisions is deliberately antiquated.[102] For example, the omitted "v" in "o'er," a "poetic" elision, is visually equivalent to the present participle's omitted final "g," a common "dialect" elision. This is an obvious and readily apparent point *visually,* but it is also almost counterintuitive. In fact, Otto Jesperson's brief genealogy of poetic elisions in his 1905 *Growth and Structure of the English Language* provides an historical reinforcement to this perhaps unexpected parallel: "*howe'er, e'er, o'er, e'en* were at first vulgar or familiar forms, used in daily talk. . . . [T]he short forms were branded as vulgar by schoolmasters with so great a success that they disappeared from ordinary conversation while they were still retained in poetry. And now they are distinctly poetic and as such above the reach of common mortals."[103] The cultural capital attached to poetic elisions obscures their origin as so-called ordinary language and their connections to dialect elisions.

Because literary dialect is the genre of poetry thought to be closest to speech and poetic diction the furthest from it, the two modes would seem to be at opposite extremes. McKay's poems, again, emphasize the continuities between the two types of language. Unlike poets who conceive of literary dialect as a deviation from poetic diction, McKay demonstrates that literary dialect and poetic diction are not in opposition. Literary dialect's resemblance to other types of literary language in its strangeness leads McKay to conceive of writing sometimes in dialect and other times in the most elevated poetic diction as parts of the same project. This is a different way to look at what Daniel T. McGee writes of as "McKay's lifelong interest in the possibility of an alternative to both dialect and standard, a language that would neither imprison the poet in the stereotypes of minstrelsy nor force him to adopt the pose of a white poet"; in seeking an "alternative," McKay's dialect and standard English verse lay bare the similarities between the two modes.[104] His poetry reflects an awareness of the shared resources of literary dialect and literary language. Despite valuations of dialect poetry as dependent upon its naturalness, McKay demonstrates that writing in dialect can never be natural.

In addition to the continuities and apparent alternation between dialect and nondialect writing in *Songs of Jamaica,* many of the poems' elisions are at once literary conventions and literary dialect. The strained legibility to which I referred above often manifests itself as a mingling of poetic diction and dialect writing in poems that are difficult to categorize as either dialect or nondialect. For example, Hathaway discusses a poem, "The Hermit," in which "words of dialect and formal English clash against one another." She points out that sometimes the diction (including the word "pelf") and the word order ("the inversion of 'ever are'") "appear artificial in the context of the surrounding dialect."[105] However, rather than keeping the linguistic resources of dialect and poetic diction discrete and in conflict, McKay makes it difficult for his readers to determine whether a particular elision or archaism is meant to indicate a speaker's use of dialect or poetic diction. It is not unusual, for example, for McKay to use "o'er" in a dialect poem. "Old England" contains the lines "I would view Westminster Abbey, where de great of England sleep / An' de solemn marble statues o'er deir ashes vigil keep." The Oxford English Dictionary claims that "ope" is "Chiefly, and since the 17th c. exclusively, poet[ic]," and it is used as such in the quotation from "A Dream" above, but "Old England" includes another line using "ope" as, presumably, a dialect word ("I would ope me mout' wid wonder at de massive organ soun'").[106] Other examples of elisions that can be used as both dialect and poetic are "'neath" and "'cross," as in the lines, "Which send their search-rays 'neath the time-worn log, and "I scamper quickly 'cross the fire-burnt soil."[107] This indeterminacy recalls that described by James Edward Smethurst in his reading of one of Hughes's poems in *The Negro Mother*, "The Black Clown." He writes that Hughes's use of "the word 'yonder' is both 'poetically' archaic in the context of 'standard' English and colloquial in African-American vernacular English," adding that the word also "appears in the vernacular poem 'Broke' of the same collection."[108] Similarly, Plotkin notes that Hopkins "exploit[ed] the Janus-like properties of a body of words that overlapped the boundary between standard and dialect English."[109] Clearly there is a trend here: perhaps Hopkins, Hughes, and McKay are not peculiar exceptions in this practice. Perhaps this peculiarly deliberate overlap is intrinsic to dialect writing itself.

Hathaway's conclusion that "McKay's linguistic irregularities . . . do not occur in an identifiable system or pattern" and therefore amount to a "subtle invalidation of the vernacular" and "an inconsistent and, in many respects, unconvincing volume of poetry" assumes that McKay's mingling of several registers can only indicate ambivalence.[110] She assumes, in other words, that McKay's chief goal in *Songs of Jamaica* is to be "convincing." It is precisely because of the conspicuousness of the constant shifting and mingling of registers (sometimes, as Hathaway points out, mid-poem) that I contend that *Songs of Jamaica* strains legibility. The book is built upon the alienating effects that this shifting has on all readers.

The alienating experience of reading dialect described by Toolan and Balhorn is, of course, not limited to standard English speakers. However, the standard English speaker has internalized the equivalence between his or her dialect and the written language to such a degree that it seems as if nonstandard dialect speaking is more closely related to dialect writing. In McKay's case, we appear to have his corroboration on this point: "Besides, poems in the dialect were 'so much easier to write than poems in straight English.' McKay did not elaborate on why dialect poems proved easier for him to write."[111] It is fairly easy to conclude that, because McKay speaks in "dialect," he would find it effortless to write dialect. But there are more reasonable ways to read McKay's remark. As we have seen in Jekyll's response to his poetry, McKay found that there was a bias toward dialect in the reception of his work, just as there was a bias toward dialect in the reception of Dunbar's work. It is more likely to be the case that the dialect poems were under less scrutiny. Because of dialect writing's perceived orality, McKay may have found it easier, especially early in his career, to please readers who wanted the exotic and unpolished.

Bernstein's claims that McKay's contribution to the composition of *Songs of Jamaica* is in conflict with Jekyll's do appear, as I have suggested, to be true in terms of the felt opposition between orality and literacy: Jekyll conceived of his apparatus as the "literature" that would make the "oral" verse in the book intelligible. As I mentioned in the previous chapter, Bernstein borrows from Michel de Certeau's concept of "la perruque" (meaning "wig") to view this tension in McKay's use of "pentameter dialect [as] the ruse or wig that allows a running double play of ingratiation and defiance."[112] In a sense, McKay's overturning of Jekyll's "controlling hand," as Bernstein puts it, comes from his replication of the larger-scale shifting between apparatus and text inside the microcosmic space of his poems. McKay uses poetic diction that is designated literate alongside language that is thought of as oral, and he acknowledges no real difference between them. In doing so, he asserts that his contributions to *Songs of Jamaica*, the poems, are not substantively different from Jekyll's framing contribution, rendering the framing structure meaningless.

In using language that can pass for either—and in being equally adept at both—McKay demonstrates his awareness of the unnaturalness of literary dialect and the arbitrary nature of the distinction between it and literary language. For example, McKay claims to have written "Strokes of the Tamarind Switch," another poem written in standard English, in a moment of Wordsworthian spontaneous overflow, which he leaves "rugged and unpolished as [he] wrote it at the moment."[113] These poems serve as counter-attacks to Jekyll's introduction, just as much as "Quashie and Buccra" does, as North points out.[114] The poems that seem most polished are in fact those that come "naturally." And the suggestion is, of course, that conversely those that seem to come naturally in fact were products of much labor. McKay's practice illustrates his belief that neither the "unrefined" literary dialect nor the "refined" poetic diction (to quote Jekyll) is more legible than the other. In his biography of McKay, Wayne Cooper criticizes McKay's "Old England," claiming that it "contained abundant examples of McKay's dialect verse at its worst—painfully forced rhymes, worn poetic clichés ('to sail athwart the ocean an' to hear de billows roar')."[115] But this is the point: McKay infuses dialect with the most conventional poetic diction in order to show how "painfully forced" and overworked dialect can be. "Athwart" and "billows" are as overwrought as "gambol." Both dialect and literary words are chosen by McKay so that he can "make them glow alive by new manipulation," as he writes in his introduction to *Harlem Shadows*.

To call dialect writing "forced," as I assume Cooper means it, amounts to calling it unsuccessful if naturalness is the goal. In fact, Gates writes, after citing a "trite" example of nineteenth-century literary dialect, "The speech sounds forced, of the sort written but never spoken or sung." It is as if Gates forgets that the poem is written. Gates mentions one of the poet's choices—"doin'"—as indicative of a failure to suggest orality. He writes, "If one pronounced 'doing' as 'doin'' is intended to suggest, its spelling would be closer to 'duen.' 'Doin'' is a poor literate translation, meant for the eye of the uninitiate, not meant to suggest a sound."[116] Gates neglects entirely the literate axis of the poem at the expense of the oral.

The divergent modes in Hughes's *The Negro Mother,* a book that prompts readers to respond to it as both an oral and a literate expression of a single writer, together eventually reinforce literacy even as they appear to promote the aural dissemination that can be achieved through recitation. The registers of *Songs of Jamaica,* however—a book in which the apparatus and poem come from different and apparently conflicting sources—shift between the apparatus and poems (as Jekyll insists upon his distance from McKay) but also within the poems themselves. In both cases, however, these apparently simple and minor books promote difficult reading and listening experiences. The strained legibility resulting from McKay's constantly alienating effects essentially levels differences between readers and between types of language. McKay alerts all readers to their distance from various dialects, at various times and places, in his questioning of the concepts of "purity" and "standard language" to which he and his poetry were subject.

Considering that the dialect poets discussed in this book wrote in an environment that was, beginning in the late nineteenth century, filled primarily with advanced alphabetic readers—that is, readers who read nearly automatically—they knew that reading such altered language would challenge their audiences' reading experiences on a very basic level. In *Discourse Networks, 1800/1900,* Frederich A. Kittler discusses how research into aphasia and other language disorders at the turn of the twentieth century helped illuminate understandings of normal reading and speaking processes. He writes of a 1905 physiological study that "reconstructs the path from the speechless patches of light and noise the infant perceives to the ordering of images and speech sounds" and that finally "comes to the conclusion: 'We proceed like poets.'"[117] The creative labor involved in the reading of dialect poetry forged a commonality between dialect poets and their readers that was distinct from the commonality previously supposed, that of rustic familiarity. As I argued in the third chapter of this book, Dunbar turned his subject in "Happy! Happy! Happy!" into a dialect poet. Here I add, in closing, that Dunbar also turns his reader into a dialect poet. Dialect poems worked by turning all of their readers into poets, responsible for actively ordering and piecing together familiar words from unfamiliar bits of written language, as Harper's Aunt Chloe does when she "put[s] the words together / And learn[s] by hook or crook." Rather than operating through the nostalgic myth of residual orality that surrounded the reception of late-nineteenth-century and early-twentieth-century dialect poets, the dialect poem in fact emphasized the role of literacy as equally necessary to its appreciation and popularity.

Conclusion

> I want plane facts, and I want plane words
>   Of the good old-fashioned ways,
> When speech run free as the songs of birds
>   'Way back in the airly days.
> . . .
>   Tell of the things jest as they was—
> They don't need no excuse!—
> Don't tetch 'em up like the poets does,
>   Tel theyr all too fine fer use!
>
> —James Whitcomb Riley, "A Tale of the Airly Days"

> Poetry!—that's the way some chaps puts up an idee,
> But I takes mine 'straight without sugar,' and that's
>   what's the matter with me.
>
> —Bret Harte, "Cicely"

In a publication designed to assist readers with "Riley Day Programs," Indiana Superintendent Charles A. Greathouse called on "the teachers of Indiana" to celebrate Riley's pedagogical impact: "You do well to honor, by appropriate exercises, the man who is the teacher of us all."[1] It is unlikely that Greathouse would have thought of the reading of dialect orthography such as Riley's as a valuable pedagogical experience in and of itself—he was probably thinking of the message of wholesome exemplarity broadcasted in the titles of poems like Riley's "A Life-Lesson"—but his remark points perhaps unwittingly to the ways in which American readers at the turn of the century felt that they *were* instructed by dialect poetry. As Roy Harvey Pearce wrote of turn-of-the-century American poets like

Riley (whom he mentions by name in a "depressing list" that also includes Thomas Bailey Aldrich and Richard Watson Gilder), their "poems are, in the bad sense, exercises in rhetoric."[2] Casting a revisionist eye on the "bad sense" of Riley's rhetoric, however, my aim has not been to defend the aesthetic value of the work of the most popular American dialect poets but to uncover the ways in which the rhetorics of literacy advanced by dialect poetry were especially effective in redirecting the fragile reading processes of the children who constituted a large part of the genre's readership as well as the seemingly established reading practices of advanced readers who found themselves stumbling through the weird spellings they encountered.

Although records of actual literacy rates have been fundamental to my project, the ideology of literacy is what is most relevant to the story of American dialect poetry. As Cathy N. Davidson writes, "literacy itself is never a simple 'rate' but embodies an ideology, a philosophy of education, of who should be educated, at what public cost, and to what end."[3] An unexpectedly useful tool for the nineteenth-century American schoolteacher, dialect poetry addresses these questions both covertly and directly, "educating" its readers in its own systems and frequently thematizing education—specifically literacy acquisition and proper spelling. Because the last decades of the nineteenth century represented a period of dramatic increase in literacy rates, more and more people were responsive to the fact that dialect writing appeared to be, on the page, performing the work it described. In interrupting the reading process and temporarily rebuilding an alternative literacy based upon new and strange orthographies, dialect poetry expressed an ideology of literacy, courting those readers who were familiar with conventional spelling even as it overthrew that spelling and erected a new one in its place. "A work of art," writes Pierre Bourdieu, "has meaning and interest only for someone who possesses the cultural competence, that is, the code, into which it is encoded," and a "beholder who lacks the specific code feels lost in a chaos of sounds and rhythms."[4] It is difficult to imagine a more apt description of what is involved in reading the "chaos of sounds" transliterated by dialect poets, whom Ambrose Bierce disparaged as a "pignoramus crew of malinguists, cacophonologists and apostrophographers."[5] Surprisingly, through a Bourdieuian lens, dialect poetry exemplifies not popular literature but the highbrow and exclusive literature of cultural capital. Celebrating dialect poetry as a kind of classroom misbehavior, then, as does Walter Blair (cited in my first chapter), glosses over its collaborations with general literacy and elite literary culture.

Dialect poetry's ability to force readers' attention to aspects of literacy acquisition and the reading process—the tensions between sounding out and silent reading, the temporal distance between reading and decoding—suggests just how tied it is, in all of its forms, to acts of reading. My attention to form intends to demonstrate that the success of dialect poetry depends upon obstructions on the level of small components of language like phonemes and graphemes; it is a body of writing that necessarily makes reading a laborious activity, as reading in general typically is for the person learning to read. In that labor is the constantly vacillating exclusion and inclusion that defines the dialect poetry reading experience: that is, one moves between being excluded and included as he or she moves through the text.[6] In the work of most of the poets discussed here, this exclusion typically does not occur on a lexical level but a graphic one.

As I have argued throughout this study, all of this labor made dialect poetry reading a difficult experience. Just as the child is first confronted with alien letters that, her teacher tells her, correspond to familiar sounds, the dialect poetry reader must make her way through the labyrinth of a writer's odd and deliberate orthography, nostalgically reliving the early experience of learning to read. To quote Aldon Nielsen:

> It is crucial that we recall that realism of linguistic representation, like social and magical realism in the novel, is a carefully constructed literary style, not a scientific recording of actual speech. It is a fictive orthography adopted for the purpose of conveying an entire literary ideology via style. Even the most lifelike literary representations of colloquial speech only infrequently correspond with exactitude to the recorded utterances of actual speaking subjects.[7]

This opposition between the purported "realism of linguistic representation" in dialect poetry and the artifice of its "constructed literary style" manifested as contradictions in its reception in the late nineteenth and early twentieth centuries. (Nielsen's "infrequently," however, I would replace with "never," unless perhaps the imagined speech is represented using a phonetic alphabet, resulting in writing that is then fairly useless as literary language.) Reactions to dialect poetry's convolutions are in fact comparable to those identified by Dorri Beam in her reading of a type of "highly wrought" fiction by nineteenth-century American women writers: there is a simultaneous appreciation and critical scrutiny of "labor that had become a luxury in its excess, or a surface that had become inappropriately labored," respectively.[8] All of the complex formal mechanics of dialect poetry that I have attempted to identify and illuminate in this book have been obscured by the requisite ease of the subject matter and the pretense of simplicity.

The confusion surrounding the dialect poem's simultaneous graphic difficulty and emotional sincerity also results in some contradictory advice regarding its performance. In *Browning and the Dramatic Monologue*, S. S. Curry, the president of the School of Expression when he published this study in 1908, describes Riley's "homely Hoosier dialect as the clothing of the speaker in most of his monologues," a description that resonates with the fabric metaphor used by Charles Battell Loomis in "The Dialect Store," cited at the start of this book. In his instructions for recitation, Curry advises readers that a "dialect too literally reproduced will be understood with great difficulty, and the reading will cause no enjoyment." "All true art," according to Curry, "is clear; it is not a puzzle" and "must never be labored."[9] What Curry neglects to say here is that, even in performance, in order for a dialect poem not to be a puzzle or a labor for the listener, it must be a puzzle and a labor for the performer.

Authors such as William Dean Howells, as Henry B. Wonham writes, viewed dialect as "a lingua franca for the common man" that was therefore, in theory, "consistent with the official social vision of realism," but, in actuality, dialect "often serves to emphasize the utter strangeness of unassimilable elements."[10] So Riley's speaker, in the poem from which I quote in the epigraph above, can ask for "plane facts" and "plane words," all the while asking for these facts and words in a manner that is anything but plain, and can wish for a time "[w]hen speech run free as the songs of birds," despite the fact that the effort required to voice dialect poetry necessarily impedes smooth recitation. Unlike the "tale" that the speaker desires, Riley's poem is of necessity "tetch[ed] . . . up." Even the word "plain" is misspelled, a homonym providing Riley with a perfectly ironic example of eye dialect.

This study demonstrates how an art form that appears to be most closely linked to the vernacular is in fact preoccupied with investigating its distance from it. As a genre cultivated in order to mimic oral performance and to fashion authentic personalities, dialect poetry lays bare its own construction. Late-nineteenth- and early-twentieth-century American dialect poetry is in essence the mingled product of enduring oral art forms and increased reading and writing practices. And, although the performance of dialect poetry during this period has garnered more scholarly attention than the silent reading of it, the history of dialect poetry's reception proves that readers clearly invited the challenge of printed dialect poetry into their lives, especially in surprising places like elite magazines such as the *Century* or primary school textbooks. In fact, the historical presence of dialect poetry in contexts that are typically associated with silent reading counters the standard view that locates dialect poetry's cultural significance in its performance.

Turning to one of the appendices of Frank Luther Mott's classic *Golden Multitudes: The Story of Best Sellers in the United States* is particularly illuminating in this respect. Sales of books of dialect poetry apparently outstripped sales of books of non-dialect poetry in the late-nineteenth- and early-twentieth-century United States. According to Mott, Riley's *The Old Swimmin' Hole and 'Leven More Poems* is one of a very small number of books of poetry (such as Rudyard Kipling's *Barrack-Room Ballads* and Edgar Guest's *A Heap o' Livin'*, both largely in dialect) that meet his guidelines for "best seller" in the United States from 1870 to 1930, the years covered by *Rhetorics of Literacy*. What did so many readers want from printed dialect poetry and from the private reading of dialect poetry, and why did so many teachers facilitate the sales of dialect poetry books, believing the genre to be wholesome and useful, when they were at the same time so heavily invested in standard orthography? The neglected formal characteristics of dialect poetry allowed the subgenre to be used by authors, readers, editors, and even schoolteachers as a difficult and cultivated form that ironically fostered a novel and experimental sort of literacy through its departures from recognizable forms of written English.

Recontextualizing figures lost to literary history like Harte and Riley within the narratives of the development of American poetry provides us with a new way to understand representations of speech in literature in general, reorienting our approach to such seemingly dissimilar poets as Robert Frost and Charles Olson, poets who were concerned with speech but with whom we do not associate the genre we think of as dialect poetry. This recontextualization can also revise how we think of the literary landscape of earlier American poetry and the twentieth-century history of it—the "continuity of American poetry," to quote Roy Harvey Pearce—that allowed poets like Riley to fall out of the canon. Critics usually elide American poetry of the late nineteenth century, as John Timberman Newcomb has shown, almost as if out of embarrassment. Like Newcomb, I propose "taking seriously the sort of verse we were taught to regard as worthless doggerel." Unlike the prose fiction of the period, Newcomb points out, "verse texts that come across as sentimental in tone, transparent in theme, or conventional in form, are ignored or scorned"; the generic privileging of prose fiction has in fact blinded us to the consequences of this depreciation.[11]

Donald Hall, in his introduction to the *Oxford Book of Children's Verse in America*, presents a narrative that accuses Riley of diverting the stream of American poetry in a manner that destroyed its ability to be simultaneously serious and popular, as it was in Longfellow's day. He associates Riley's embrace of the low-brow with a "considerable decline in literacy from Professor Longfellow"; from Riley, "[t]he path slopes downward through Eugene Field to end in the pages of the *Detroit Free Press* with Edgar A. Guest."[12] And, yet, literacy, I argue here, is what dialect poetry is all about. We have forgotten how writers we think of as modern received the poetry of Harte and Riley as part and parcel of their poetic education. We have forgotten that it was the tremendous success of "Plain Language from Truthful James"—not of the realist Western fiction with which Harte's reputation has become associated—that prompted the *Atlantic Monthly*, needing a "marquee name to shore up subscriptions and raise advertising revenue," to offer him an exclusive contract on June 21, 1870, as contributing editor for the magazine. Harte's travel across the country to assume his new post was greeted with such eagerness that, according to Twain, "one might have supposed he was the Viceroy of India."[13]

Twain's exotic analogy also reminds us of the fact that the story of American dialect poetry is not exclusively American: not only did Harte, Riley, and Dunbar cross the country to present their work, all three also crossed the Atlantic to conduct tours in England. English audiences were interested in the peculiarly American voices, in regional dialects, that they recreated on stage. Following the lead of recent work (including a 2005 special issue of *Victorian Poetry*) on transatlantic Victorianism, emphasizing "the presence of American poetics within Victorian poetics, and of Victorian poetics within American poetics," I believe that, although I focus in this book on American poetry, the cultural impact of dialect poetry should be considered not only transhistorically but also transnationally.[14] Aside from the common ground shared by the American dialect poetries discussed here and British dialect poetries of the same period (like Tennyson's), it is evident that the issue of poetic voice generally and the experiments with the dramatic monologue form among British Victorian poets resonated in the work of late-nineteenth-century American dialect poets. Summarizing Victorianist critic Eric Griffiths's views, Margaret Linley writes that "there is a peculiar specificity to how voice is constituted in acts of reading when that reading is mediated by print. The embodied voice of poetry that is born in the era of the printing press is neither wholly mechanical nor animate but both simultaneously." Dialect poetry is an extreme case that supports this view, as both the animated voice it suspended and the printed features through which a reader must labor are exaggerated. Furthermore, Linley adds that "we might analyze how at the moment when voice would seem to have died onto the page, its spirit returns, as the written sign of voice and in acts of reading aloud, as an organic (though technologically enhanced) prosthesis for the machine-made word."[15] The strange relationship between dialect poetry and the modern sound and visual technologies with which some believed it to be compatible while others perceived it to be dissonant again makes this argument even more strongly; the receptions of the filmic and phonographic representations of Riley heighten and amplify the relationship between his oral and written incarnations. With the work of those critics who "address Victorian poetry as itself a technology" in mind—Victorian poetry on both sides of the Atlantic, I would add—the complexity of dialect poetry's negotiations of voice and print becomes more and more apparent.[16]

I would like to return briefly, in closing, to Loomis's "The Dialect Store," the story that started this book, now retrospectively straightforward and naive in its stitching together of different dialect orthographies after we have explored the various forms of dialect poetry developed by the poets addressed here. When the narrator of "The Dialect Store" finds, at the "Western dialect" counter, that Riley "had just engaged the whole output of the plant," he points not only to the perception of the conventionality of Riley's dialect poetry, but to the enormous demand that takes a factory's output to meet it.[17] As Janice Radway and Perry Frank point out, Riley's "idealizations of farm and country life were enormously popular throughout the country, despite the fact that the peculiar language he employed was nearly incomprehensible to some."[18] Even Henry Van Dyke, one of Riley's admirers, sheepishly writes that he "must confess that [the dialect] sometimes looks a little queer as printed."[19] Why were readers drawn to dialect poetry that was barely legible—essentially, a "difficult" popular poetry, a seeming paradox—and what did that dialect poetry presume to offer them? I propose here that both readers and writers found an edifying pleasure in laboring through that illegibility. Although the late-nineteenth-century craze for dialect poetry has passed, like so much of the nonstandard language that contributed to it, American poets continue to pursue writing that is, as Harryette Mullen describes her dictionary in the poem "Sleeping with the Dictionary," "thick with accented syllables."[20]

notes

Introduction

1. Charles Battell Loomis, "The Dialect Store," *Century* 53.6 (April 1897): 958–59.
2. "This Is Why Not. Literary Man Should Not Write Dialect Verse Because He Can't," *Baltimore American*, 26 June 1909, 11.
3. L. B. Fletcher, "Dialect Spelling," *The Writer* 4 (Feb. 1890): 26.
4. Mrs. George Archibald, "Dialect Spelling," *The Writer* 3 (March 1889): 50.
5. Jennifer DeVere Brody, *Punctuation: Art, Politics, and Play* (Durham: Duke University Press, 2008), 6.
6. Edward Bok to James Whitcomb Riley, 14 March 1890, James Whitcomb Riley Collection, Lilly Library, Indiana University, Bloomington, Indiana.
7. "Literary Notes," *Appleton's Journal*, 31 May 1873, 733.
8. "The Pike Poetry," *The Galaxy* 12 (Nov. 1871): 638.
9. George Merriam Hyde, "A New Crop of Dialect," *The Bookman* 6 (Sept. 1897–Feb. 1898): 56.
10. Ibid.
11. Although David Henkin addresses a period earlier than the one covered by this book, his exploration of the ways in which ephemeral printed texts circulated in the modern city provides a model by which we can understand the consumption of dialect poetry in both public and private arenas a few decades later, when modern advertising methods were even more developed and public print even more prevalent. As Henkin points out, public reading practices have been neglected as a subject of study partly because of "the persistently powerful image of the private reader," who was most often a novel reader. Henkin does not discuss poetry reading practices, but I would argue that poetry reading in the mid- to late nineteenth century happened both publicly *and* privately to an extent far greater than either sign reading on one hand or novel reading on the other, to give two examples. *City Reading: Written Words and Public Spaces in Antebellum New York* (New York: Columbia University Press, 1999), 6.

12. Caroline Levine, "Strategic Formalism: Toward a New Method in Cultural Studies," *Victorian Studies* 48 (2006): 626; Monique Morgan, "Productive Convergences, Producing Converts," *Victorian Poetry* 41 (2003): 502.

13. Qtd. in Virginia Jackson, *Dickinson's Misery: A Theory of Lyric Reading* (Princeton: Princeton University Press, 2005), 56.

14. Susan Stewart, *Crimes of Writing: Problems in the Containment of Representation* (Oxford: Oxford University Press, 1991), 74, 90.

15. Shira Wolosky, "Poetry and Public Discourse, 1820–1910," in *The Cambridge History of American Literature, Volume 4: Nineteenth-Century Poetry, 1800–1910,* ed. Sacvan Bercovitch (Cambridge: Cambridge University Press, 2004), 147, 148.

16. John Shoptaw, "Lyric Cryptography," *Poetics Today* 21 (2000): 239; Garrett Stewart, *Reading Voices: Literature and the Phonotext* (Berkeley: University of California Press, 1990).

17. Sumner Ives points this out in his landmark essay on literary dialect, "A Theory of Literary Dialect," *Tulane Studies in English* 2 (1950): 137–82.

18. Charles Bernstein, "Poetics of the Americas," in *Reading Race in American Poetry: "An Area of Act,"* ed. Aldon Lynn Nielsen (Urbana: University of Illinois Press, 2000), 117–18.

19. Tess Chakkalakal, "To Make an Old Century New," *American Quarterly* 62.4 (2010): 1001.

20. James Weldon Johnson, *The Book of American Negro Poetry* (1931; San Diego: Harcourt Brace Jovanovich, 1983), 41.

21. Henry Louis Gates, Jr., *Figures in Black: Words, Signs, and the "Racial" Self* (New York: Oxford University Press, 1987), 190.

22. "Pike Poetry," 636–37.

23. Ibid., 638.

24. Walter Ong, *Orality and Literacy: The Technologizing of the Word* (London: Methuen, 1982), 115.

25. Philip Collins, "'Agglomerating Dollars with Prodigious Rapidity': British Pioneers on the American Lecture Circuit," in *Victorian Literature and Society: Essays Presented to Richard D. Altick,* ed. James R. Kincaid and Albert J. Kuhn (Columbus: Ohio State University Press, 1983), 7.

26. Ibid., 8.

27. Ong, *Orality,* 115–16.

28. Lee Soltow and Edward Stevens, *The Rise of Literacy and the Common School in the United States: A Socioeconomic Analysis to 1870* (Chicago: University of Chicago Press, 1981), 51.

29. Elizabeth McHenry, *Forgotten Readers: Recovering the Lost History of African American Literary Societies* (Durham: Duke University Press, 2002), 5.

30. Shirley Brice Heath, "Standard English: Biography of a Symbol," in *Standards and Dialects in English,* ed. Timothy Shopen and Joseph M. Williams (Cambridge: Winthrop, 1980), 28.

31. Joan Shelley Rubin, "Making Meaning: Analysis and Affect in the Study and Practice of Reading," in *A History of the Book in America,* vol. 4 (Chapel Hill: University of North Carolina Press, 2008), 518.

32. John Harrington Cox, "The Poem and the Printed Page," *English Journal* 3.7 (Sept. 1914): 405.

33. Lisa Gitelman, *Scripts, Grooves, and Writing Machines: Representing Technology in the Edison Era* (Stanford: Stanford University Press, 2000), 52.

34. What I am calling mechanical complexity corresponds most closely with what George Steiner terms "tactical difficulty" in his essay "On Difficulty," an obscurity that "has its source in the writer's will or in the failure of adequacy between his intention and his performative means." "On Difficulty," in *On Difficulty and Other Essays* (Oxford: Oxford University Press, 1980), 33.

35. Oliver Wendell Holmes, "Notes," *Book News* 13 (Oct. 1894): 53.

36. "The Decay of 'Dialect Poetry,'" *Cincinnati Commercial*, 24 July 1871, 4.

37. James Russell Lowell, "The Five Indispensable Authors (Homer, Dante, Cervantes, Goethe, Shakspere)," *Century* 47 (Dec. 1893): 223.

38. Janice Radway, "The Aesthetic in Mass Culture: Reading the 'Popular' Literary Text," in *The Structure of the Literary Process: Studies Dedicated to the Memory of Felix Vodicka*, ed. Peter Steiner et al. (Amsterdam: Benjamins, 1982), 424–25.

39. William Charvat, *The Profession of Authorship in America, 1800–1870: The Papers of William Charvat*, ed. Matthew J. Bruccoli (Columbus: Ohio State University Press, 1968), 105.

40. Margaret Linley, "Conjuring the Spirit: Victorian Poetry, Culture, and Technology," *Victorian Poetry* 41 (2003): 537.

41. Ivan Kreilkamp, "Victorian Poetry's Modernity," *Victorian Poetry* 41 (2003): 608.

42. Gary Scharnhorst, "Ways That Are Dark: Appropriations of Bret Harte's 'Plain Language from Truthful James,'" *Nineteenth-Century Literature* 51 (1996): 377.

43. James Smethurst, *The African American Roots of Modernism: From Reconstruction to the Harlem Renaissance* (Chapel Hill: University of North Carolina Press, 2011), 26.

44. Bernstein, "Poetics," 125.

45. Bruce Andrews, *Libretto from White Dialect Poetry* (N.p.: /ubu editions, 2006), accessed March 15, 2012, http://www.ubu.com/ubu/unpub/Unpub_002_Andrews_Libretto.pdf; Bruce Andrews, *WhDiP, a sequence* (N.p.: /ubu editions, 2006), accessed March 15, 2012, http://www.ubu.com/ubu/unpub/Unpub_001_Andrews_Whdip.pdf.

46. Frederich A. Kittler, *Discourse Networks, 1800/1900*, trans. Michael Metteer, with Chris Cullens (Stanford: Stanford University Press, 1990), 224–25.

Chapter One

1. Interestingly, Samuel Kirkham's *English Grammar in Familiar Lectures* gives "ort" as a "provincial" pronunciation of "ought" to be avoided, originating in Pennsylvania. Many of Kirkham's Pennsylvanian "improper" pronunciations can be found in Riley's poetry.

2. Dennis E. Baron, *Grammar and Good Taste: Reforming the American Language* (New Haven: Yale University Press, 1982), 91.

3. Brander Matthews, "As to 'American Spelling,'" *Harper's* 85 (July 1892): 284.

4. William Dean Howells, "Mark Twain," *Century* 24 (Sept. 1882): 781.

5. H. L. Mencken, *The American Language: An Inquiry into the Development of English in the United States*, 4th ed. and the two supplements, abridged, with annotations and new material by Raven I. McDavid, Jr. (New York: Knopf, 1974), 493.

6. Mencken would likely find this pairing with Matthews comical; in a letter to Theodore Dreiser, Mencken calls his elder "an old ass." Qtd. in Susanna Ashton, "Authorial Affiliations, or, the Clubbing and Collaborating of Brander Matthews," *symploke* 7.1–2 (1999): 172.

7. Walter Blair, introduction to *The Mirth of a Nation: America's Great Dialect Humor*, ed. Walter Blair and Raven McDavid (Minneapolis: University of Minnesota Press, 1983), xxiii.

8. William Wanless Anderson, "The Craze for Wrong Spelling," *Dial* 19 (1895): 173.

9. Gavin Jones, *Strange Talk: The Politics of Dialect Literature in Gilded Age America* (Berkeley: University of California Press, 1999), 24.

10. In 1892, the former superintendent of Dayton, Ohio, schools (he served from 1874–1884) and friend of Riley's remarked, "Thirty years ago (in those primitive times), spelling was the branch of instruction that received most, and in some schools almost exclusive, attention." W. H. Venable, *John Hancock, PhD* (Cincinnati: C. B. Ruggles & Co., 1892), 145.

11. "Pike Poetry," 635.

12. "The Decay of 'Dialect Poetry,'" 4.

13. T. Edgar Pemberton, *Bret Harte: A Treatise and a Tribute* (London: Greening & Co., Ltd., 1900), 11.

14. "Stories of Famous Poems: Francis Bret Harte," *Charlotte* [NC] *Observer*, 13 Aug. 1911, 2.

15. "Pike Poetry," 635.

16. Ibid.

17. As Gavin Jones writes, "Boston parents became anxious when their children broke out with deep southernisms at the breakfast table—evidence of a secret consumption of dialect stories late at night." *Strange Talk*, 1.

18. P. R. S. [Peter Remsen Strong], "A Recipe for a Poem 'In Dialect,'" in *"Awful," and Other Jingles* (New York: Putnam, 1871).

19. Elizabeth Davey, "Building a Black Audience in the 1930s: Langston Hughes, Poetry Readings, and the Golden Stair Press," in *Print Culture in a Diverse America*, ed. James P. Danky and Wayne A. Wiegand (Champaign: University of Illinois Press, 1998), 230.

20. Richard Grant White, *Every-Day English: A Sequel to "Words and Their Uses"* (Boston: Houghton Mifflin, 1880), 107–8.

21. Cox, "The Poem and the Printed Page," 404–5.

22. Shirley Brice Heath, "Literacy and Language Change," in *Languages and Linguistics: The Interdependence of Theory, Data, and Application*, ed. Deborah Tannen and James E. Alatis, Georgetown University Roundtable on Languages and Linguistics 1985 (Washington, D.C.: Georgetown University Press, 1985), 285. In a history of reading in a small Iowa town during the late nineteenth century, Christine Pawley, too, notes that "oral reading in the schools was giving way to a new emphasis on silent, private reading, focusing on understanding, information, and enjoyment, in contrast to a view of literacy as an aid to rhetoric." These changes were happening even earlier in less rural areas. "What to Read and How to Read: The Social Infrastructure of Young People's Reading, Osage, Iowa," *Library Quarterly* 68 (1998): 280.

23. Nila Banton Smith, *American Reading Instruction* (1934; International Reading Association, 2002), 149–50, 156. It seems more than a little coincidental that the year that saw the publication of *The Waste Land* and *Ulysses* and has long stood chronologically for the ushering in of modernist literature should have also seen a flowering of publications about how to approach texts in a way that excluded oral reading.

24. Lillian Gray, *Teaching Children to Read*, 3rd ed. (New York: Ronald Press, 1963), 50–51; Edmund Burke Huey, *The History and Pedagogy of Reading, with a Review of*

the History of Reading and Writing and of Methods, Texts, and Hygiene in Reading (New York: Macmillan, 1916), 81.

25. Dale D. Johnson and James F. Baumann, "Word Identification," in *Handbook of Reading Research*, vol. 3, ed. P. David Pearson (1984; New York: Lawrence Erlbaum Associates, 2002), 585.

26. A dialect poem published in the *Hartford Courant* teases Riley for this honor. The author worries that, now that Riley will be "doctorin' other fellers' liter'toor," he "may be won't get through / Re'bilitatin' rhymin' stuff that rolls in like the sea / In time to write a word or two for common folks like me."

27. Elizabeth Van Allen, *James Whitcomb Riley: A Life* (Bloomington: Indiana University Press, 1999), 269.

28. Merle Johnson, *You Know These Lines! A Bibliography of the Most Quoted Verses in American Poetry* (New York: G. A. Baker and Company, 1935), v. Although Riley was always treated as a "poet of the people," his reputation suffered during the first half of the twentieth century; he was seen as an overly sentimental, second-rate writer whose humility could not make up for his lack of artistry. In 1913, a reader of the *Nation* complained in a letter to the editor about finding Riley's verse in the magazine— "Doubtless there are many persons who tolerate or even enjoy such barbaric puerilities, but surely few of them are among the regular readers of the *Nation*"—but another reader responded to this letter to defend Riley's appearance in the magazine as a "sane appreciation of a valuable form of literary expression." Burt G. Wilder, "Is 'Hoosier Poetry' Appropriate in the 'Nation'?," *The Nation*, 23 Oct. 1913, 383; Bertrand Shadwell, "Dialect Poetry," *The Nation*, 13 Nov. 1913, 457.

Even as early as 1901, James L. Onderdonk writes that Riley is "in many respects . . . the most artificial of our more conspicuous singers of this realistic era." Riley's work continued to be popular among public readers in the first half of the twentieth century, but Joan Shelley Rubin demonstrates how a newly forming canon was beginning to exclude Riley. In a survey conducted by Rubin, a "respondent who, between 1931 and 1934, had relied on a compilation entitled *One Hundred and One Famous Poems*, was forcibly introduced to categories of taste when a university professor downgraded him for performing a selection from James Whitcomb Riley in a recitation contest." Onderdonk, *History of American Verse, 1610–1897* (Chicago: A. C. McClurg, 1901), 351; Rubin, "'They Flash upon That Inward Eye': Poetry Recitation and American Readers," *Proceedings of the American Antiquarian Society* 106.2 (1996): 283.

This is not to say that the negative assessment of Riley's work was only retrospective. In one of many articles attacking Riley and his fellow dialect poets, Ambrose Bierce writes, "I am something sick of the pignoramus crew of malinguists, cacophonologists and apostropographers who think they get close to nature by depicting the sterile lives and limited emotions of the gawks and sodhoppers that speak only to tangle their tongues." Even if Bierce uses these neologisms to mock "this blessed blatherhood of illiteracy bumpkins," his punning comes very close to the types of punning that are intrinsic to dialect writing. "Prattle," *San Francisco Examiner*, 17 Dec. 1892, 16.

29. Jonathan Culler, "Why Lyric?," *PMLA* 123 (2008): 205.

30. Walter Barnes, *The Children's Poets: Analyses and Appraisals of the Greatest English and American Poets for Children* (New York: World Book Company, 1925), 195.

31. Edgar Dale and Jeanne S. Chall, "The Concept of Readability," *Elementary English* 26 (1949): 23.

32. Frank Luther Mott, *Golden Multitudes: The Story of Best Sellers in the United States* (New York: Macmillan, 1947), 225. In a 1924 history of American literature,

Bruce Weirick writes that Riley wanted his poetry "to be read at country schools, or chautauquas, or sewing circles." It seems likely that his poetry circulated frequently in all of these venues and beyond. *From Whitman to Sandburg in American Poetry: A Critical Survey* (New York: Macmillan, 1924), 50.

33. Lesley Wheeler, *Voicing American Poetry: Sound and Performance from the 1920s to the Present* (Ithaca: Cornell University Press, 2008), 5.

34. Jones, *Strange Talk*, 48.

35. Ibid.

36. Michel de Certeau, *The Practice of Everyday Life* (1974; Berkeley: University of California Press, 1984), 175–76.

37. Ibid., 168.

38. For example, Edith Wyatt writes in 1917, one year after Riley's death, that "[p]eople have always been cutting [Riley's poems] out of newspapers and reciting them at ice cream sociables and church benefits." This quotation demonstrates that the assumption that the literate practice of reading newspapers and the oral practice of poetry recitation would be at odds is antithetical to the phenomenon of dialect poetry, which depends greatly upon both sides of this literary reception at once. *Great Companions* (New York: D. Appleton, 1917), 185.

39. Angela Sorby points out that, in addition to the nostalgic themes presented in Riley's poetry, his rhyme and meter "had in themselves come to constitute the shape of nostalgia." *Schoolroom Poets: Childhood, Performance, and the Place of American Poetry, 1865–1917* (Lebanon: University of New Hampshire Press, 2005), 186.

40. As the 1921 pamphlet *Riley Readings with Living Pictures* suggests, "The name Riley alone is a big drawing card, and people of all classes enjoy an entertainment of this kind." Laura Christine Wegner, *Riley Readings with Living Pictures* (Chicago: T. S. Denison, [c. 1921]), 9.

41. W. D. Howells, "The New Poetry," *The North American Review* 168 (May 1899): 588.

42. Paul H. Gray, "Poet as Entertainer: Will Carleton, James Whitcomb Riley, and the Rise of the Poet-Performer Movement," *Literature in Performance: A Journal of Literary and Performing Art* 5.1 (Nov. 1984): 1.

43. Charles Holstein, Letter to Riley, 29 Dec. 1892, James Whitcomb Riley Collection.

44. Martha Vicinus, *The Industrial Muse: A Study of Nineteenth Century British Working-Class Literature* (New York: Barnes and Noble, 1974), 190.

45. Richard Brodhead, *Cultures of Letters: Scenes of Reading and Writing in Nineteenth-Century America* (Chicago: University of Chicago Press, 1993), 122.

46. Although Alan Trachtenberg includes Riley in a list of authors for whom "the low remained low, subordinated by plot and other devices of social designation to what can be called a discourse of respectability," I question whether the sort of monologic dialect poem Riley typically writes is stratified in the manner he describes. *The Incorporation of America: Culture and Society in the Gilded Age* (1982; New York: Hill and Wang, 2007), 189.

47. Sorby, *Schoolroom Poets*, 105. Harte's "Plain Language from Truthful James" is similarly imitative, appropriating the form of a poem of elite status. He modeled his meter after Algernon Swinburne's *Atalanta in Calydon* because "it whimsically occurred to him that the grand and beautiful sweep of that chorus was just the kind of thing which Truthful James would be the last man in the world to adopt in expressing his views." Pemberton, *Bret Harte*, 74–75.

48. William Carey, Letter to Riley, 20 Aug. 1897, James Whitcomb Riley Collection.
49. Riley, Letter to William Carey, 24 Aug. 1897, James Whitcomb Riley Collection; W. W. Ellsworth, Letter to Riley, 7 Aug. 1897, James Whitcomb Riley Collection.
50. Riley, Letter to William Carey, 26 Aug. 1897, James Whitcomb Riley Collection.
51. Riley, Letter to W. C. Corthill, 12 Dec. 1890, original emphasis, James Whitcomb Riley Collection; William L. Alden, "London Literary Letter," *New York Times*, 23 April 1898, BR266.
52. Riley, *The Rubaiyat of Doc Sifers* (New York: Century Co., 1897), 21.
53. Cawein, Letter to Riley, 9 Aug. 1892, James Whitcomb Riley Collection.
54. Richard Brodhead writes:

> In the years between 1860 and 1900, the *Atlantic Monthly,* the *Century Magazine,* and *Harper's Monthly Magazine* achieved an identification as the three American "quality journals." This means that these three journals produced the same high and distinguished zone in the literary realm that the classical museum or symphony orchestra produced in art or music, a strongly demarcated high-status arena for high-artistic practice. And though actual audiences are notoriously hard to establish there is reason to think that they produced literary writing toward a similarly constituted social public. (*Cultures of Letters,* 124)

55. Although Riley published more poems in the *Century* than in any other magazine, he did not publish much in the *Atlantic Monthly* or in *Harper's Monthly.* As Meredith Nicholson writes, "The only poem he ever contributed to the *Atlantic* was 'Old Glory,' and I recall that he held it for a considerable period, retouching it, and finally reading it at a club dinner to test it thoroughly by his own standards, which were those of the ear as well as the eye. When I asked him why he had not printed it he said he was keeping it 'to boil the dialect out of it.'" Nicholson, *The Man in the Street: Papers on American Topics* (New York: Scribner, 1921), 44–45. Riley's sense of the inappropriateness of his dialect writing in a magazine such as the *Atlantic Monthly* is revealing. In addition, *Harper's Monthly* printed only one poem of Riley's during his lifetime but, according to Anthony J. Russo and Dorothy R. Russo's bibliography, printed dozens of uncollected poems and letters after his death.
56. Mayo Williamson Hazeltine, *Chats about Books: Poets and Novelists* (New York: Scribner's, 1883), 299, 288.
57. Sorby, *Schoolroom Poets,* 100.
58. Lawrence W. Levine, *Highbrow/Lowbrow: The Emergence of Cultural Hierarchy in America* (Cambridge, MA: Harvard University Press, 1988), 233.
59. Charvat, *Profession of Authorship,* 107.
60. Hamlin Garland, "Real Conversations—IV, A Dialogue between James Whitcomb Riley and Hamlin Garland," *McClure's* 2.3 (Feb. 1894): 228. A June 12, 1877, letter from Lee O. Harris compliments Riley on this doggerel, saying, "I did not think that I would ever offer anyone congratulations on an advertizing [*sic*] poem but yours is simply immense—The best thing of the kind I ever saw." From the start of his career, Riley finds for himself a niche between verse and non-verse, being neither. In fact, an early *Scribner's* rejection illustrates this in-betweenness: "Your writings show good poetic feeling but as yet we fear they fall short of literature." Letter to Riley, 22 Jan. 1878, James Whitcomb Riley Collection.
61. Garland, "Real Conversations," 228.
62. Van Allen, *James Whitcomb Riley,* 198, 112.

63. Henry Van Dyke, "James Whitcomb Riley as a Person," *The Book News Monthly* (March 1907): 429.
64. Qtd. in Sorby, *Schoolroom Poets*, 114.
65. Hamlin Garland, *Roadside Meetings* (New York: Macmillan, 1930), 100.
66. Garland, "Real Conversations," 220.
67. Harold K. Bush, "'Absorbing the Character': James Whitcomb Riley and Mark Twain's Theory of Performance," *American Literary Realism* 31.3 (1999): 43.
68. Sorby, *Schoolroom Poets*, 114–15.
69. Wolosky, "Poetry and Public Discourse," 327.
70. Garland, "Real Conversations," 220, 232–33.
71. Hamlin Garland, *Commemorative Tribute to James Whitcomb Riley* (New York: American Academy of Arts and Letters, 1922), 5.
72. Fred C. Kelly, "James Whitcomb Riley's Start," *New York Times*, 21 May 1911, X5.
73. Mabel Potter Daggett, *In Lockerbie Street: A Little Appreciation of James Whitcomb Riley* (New York: B. W. Dodge & Company, 1909), 20, 18.
74. Qtd. in Gary Scharnhorst, *Bret Harte: Opening the American Literary West* (Norman: University of Oklahoma Press, 2000), 96.
75. C. Lewis Hind, *Authors and I* (New York: John Lane Company; London: John Lane, The Bodley Head, 1921), 120, 122.
76. Qtd. in Scharnhorst, *Opening*, 80.
77. Ibid., 97.
78. Garland, "Real Conversations," 220; Daggett, *Lockerbie Street*, 19.
79. Scharnhorst, *Opening*, 101.
80. Roy F. Hudson, "The Contributions of Bret Harte to Western Oratory," *Western American Literature* 2 (1967): 217.
81. This move signified to him that now "he was in his proper sphere among the Brahmin poets." Scharnhorst, *Opening*, 67.
82. Gary Scharnhorst, "'I Do Not Write This in Anger': Bret Harte's Letters to His Sister, 1871–93," *Resources for American Literary Study* 26.2 (2000): 206. In a letter to Bret Harte, Schuyler Colfax, former vice president of the United States, makes a suggestion to Harte that he worries might be "intrusive and unacceptable":

> . . . while very much interested last night in your Lecture & its brilliant passages, I regretted very much & I find the regret shared by our best people, that you had not incorporated into it some of the "dialect" prose & poetry. I can understand very well that you are tired of hearing of the poem which achieved so much celebrity, exactly as [actor Joseph] Jefferson tires of performing Rip Van Winkle, tho' the public insist on it, & continue as enthusiastic about it as ever. (Qtd. in Scharnhorst, "'I Do Not Write This in Anger,'" 207)

Colfax's comparison of Harte's performances to those of an actor must have irritated Harte, considering his desire to *not* inhabit his characters during readings.

83. Van Allen, *James Whitcomb Riley*, 74. Riley, in general, modeled his practice as dialect poet in part after Harte. Meredith Nicholson remembers that Riley "owed much" to Harte, and that "Harte's use of dialect in verse probably strengthened Riley's confidence in the Hoosier speech as a medium when he began to find himself." Harte was also "his expressed favorite writer of fiction." Nicholson, *Man in the Street*, 36; Edward Eitel, "A Close-Up of James Whitcomb Riley," James Whitcomb Riley Collection.

84. Wegner, *Riley Readings*, 13.

85. Alice Moore Dunbar-Nelson, ed., *The Dunbar Speaker and Entertainer* (Naperville: J. L. Nichols & Co., 1920), 14.

86. For example, as Sorby points out, Riley rarely performed the few poems he wrote in "black dialect," perhaps because his performance depended upon a convincing assumption of the total character of the poem's speaker, with more chance of success when the speaker resembles Riley himself (white, male, etc.).

87. Charlotte Canning suggests that the many words used to describe Chautauqua readings "indicate a continuing struggle to avoid any identification with theatre." Philip Collins makes a similar claim, extending it to include public performances of literature in the Victorian era generally, in both England and America: "certainly much of the attraction of readings lay in their being regarded as permissible by the many respectable people who objected to theatres as immoral." Canning, "The Platform Versus the Stage: The Circuit Chautauqua's Antitheatrical Theatre," *Theatre Journal* 50 (1998): 313; Collins, *Reading Aloud: A Victorian Métier* (Lincoln: The Tennyson Society, 1972), 20–22.

88. Alison Byerly, "From Schoolroom to Stage: Reading Aloud and the Domestication of Victorian Theater," in *Culture and Education in Victorian England*, ed. Patrick Scott and Pauline Fletcher (Lewisburg: Bucknell University Press, 1990), 136.

89. Karen Halttunen, *Confidence Men and Painted Women: A Study of Middle-Class Culture in America, 1830–1870* (New Haven: Yale University Press, 1982), 122.

90. Mott, *Golden Multitudes*, 225. Mott classifies Riley's 1883 *The Old Swimmin' Hole and 'Leven More Poems* as a best seller, meaning that it "is believed to have had a total sale equal to one per cent of the population of continental United States . . . for the decade in which it was published," amounting to 500,000 in Riley's case (303).

91. Howells, "The New Poetry," 588. In a review of a collection titled *An American Anthology*, Oscar Lovell Triggs writes, "Recently there have been signs of a shifting emphasis. Longfellow is losing importance, and writers like Riley are gaining. In Longfellow's sense of poetry, Riley has not written poetry so much as in a new and more democratic sense he has depicted life. In some way life has got into a book, but is known like a person. The humanization of poetry may count for more in the twentieth century than Longfellow's poetization of humanity." "A Century of American Poetry," *The Forum* 30 (Jan. 1901): 633. (See also Charvat, quoted above, for his distinction between Longfellow and Riley.)

Countless contemporary reader reviews—or, more accurately, reminiscences—of "Little Orphant Annie" on the website Americanpoems.com testify to the fact that he is still read, particularly among the elderly. These reminiscences frequently mention grandparents' reading the poems aloud, most "by heart," and many recall reading the poem in primary school in the 1940s and '50s. A typical respondent who posted on May 20, 2008, remembers her mother reciting the poem sixty years earlier, "at bedtime and to the accompaniment of a flickering coal oil lamp. . . . [C]ertainly no Hollywood movie could possibly be so entertaining and so touching." Riley's influence also extended to England, where a respondent (posting on September 29, 2005) working in a nursing home found that one of the residents, "a wonderful lady of 95 years[,] recited the first three verses of Little Orphant Annie (word perfect)." "Analysis and Comments on 'Little Orphant Annie' by James Whitcomb Riley," accessed Jan. 1, 2012, http://www.americanpoems.com/poets/James-Whitcomb-Riley/13510/comments.

92. Nellie Frances Milburn, "An Open Letter to James Whitcomb Riley," *The Literary World* 31 (May 1900): 104.

93. Scharnhorst, *Opening*, 52–53.

94. Riley's correspondence with Selig, however, dates back to at least 1910 (when the short film *There Little Girl Don't Cry*, an adaptation of his "A Life Lesson," was produced), and includes a December 21, 1912, letter from W. B. Selig acknowledging the filming of footage of Riley, sent to his home along with a projectionist to assist with his viewing of it.

95. Review of *Little Orphant Annie, Variety,* 6 Dec. 1918, 39.

96. Although a silent film viewing would not have been a silent experience, considering that most were viewed with musical accompaniment, it was still usually a non-verbal experience.

97. Linda Hutcheon, *A Theory of Adaptation* (New York: Routledge, 2006), 4.

98. Kamilla Elliott, *Rethinking the Novel/Film Debate* (Cambridge: Cambridge University Press, 2003), 93, 99.

99. Timothy W. Galow, "Literary Modernism in the Age of Celebrity," *Modernism/Modernity* 17.2 (2010): 313–29.

100. Daggett, *Lockerbie Street*, 13–14. The lines indented in the original text are modeled after the best-known lines of "Little Orphant Annie."

101. Ibid., 16–17.

102. Eitel, "A Close-Up," 10.

103. In a note to the book, editor and illustrator Art Young claims that "[t]he sketches in this volume showing characteristic attitudes of the authors represented are the illustrator's individual impressions from life. They were made by him from pencil sketches drawn while observing the authors read or recite, or from his recollection of the various poses assumed. Some of the original sketches in lead pencil were made at public readings. Others were made in private." "Illustrator's Note," in *Author's Readings* (New York: Frederick A. Stokes Company, 1897), iii.

104. Walter Benjamin, "The Work of Art in the Age of Mechanical Reproduction," in Walter Benjamin, *Illuminations,* ed. Hannah Arendt, trans. Harry Zohn (New York: Schocken, 1968), 238.

105. Elizabeth Van Allen, "The Signifier and the Signified," *Traces of Indiana and Midwestern History* 11.1 (Winter 1999): 29.

106. Benjamin, "The Work of Art," 220; John M. Picker, *Victorian Soundscapes* (Oxford: Oxford University Press, 2003), 123.

107. Jason Camlot, "Early Talking Books: Spoken Recordings and Recitation Anthologies, 1880–1920," *Book History* 6 (2003): 148.

108. "Records Taken of Riley's Voice. Poet Consents After Years to Read Choice Poems for Talking Machine Company. Noted Writer of Verse Hears 'Proofs' of Selections with Manifest Interest," *Indianapolis Star,* 6 July 1912, 1. John M. Picker mentions that the elderly Tennyson's response to this new technology was also marked by amusement and interest: "the new machine so intrigued him that he willingly committed many of his famous works to wax." According to Picker, this desire to record oneself "may seem strikingly modern as an act of mechanical reproduction, yet it was in keeping with the aims of his poetic project: to express the plurality of selves that constitutes the self" (126). Although it may seem odd to compare the two Victorian poets, Riley's poetry, like Tennyson's, depends upon the production of multiple voices necessary to dramatic monologue.

109. Harry O. Sooy, *Memoir of My Career at Victor Talking Machine Company* (1909), 49–51, accessed Jan. 1, 2012, http://www.davidsarnoff.org/sooyh-maintext1909.html. This account differs greatly from that given in a promotional document titled "A Close-Up of James Whitcomb Riley" (presumed to be written by Edward Eitel). Eitel claims that

the supreme annoyance of his life came when he was inveigled into making records of his poems for the Victor people. He had suffered from the stroke that later proved fatal, and it required a lot of persuasion to get him to even consider the attempt. He was unfit to make the trip to Camden, so the operatives, with their paraphranalia [sic], came to him at his home in Indianapolis.

In the first place, he didn't want to do it, and could be most emphatically decided, especially in his later years. He would consent to record only the poems of his own selection, regardless of their length, and he didn't propose to omit any of the verses, even for the convenience of a "talking contraption."

After an endless amount of patience on the part of everybody, a record was completed. "Out to Old Aunt Mary's" was rounded out and everything was fine; but when he had finished the last line, he settled back in his chair, and exclaimed in a grateful tone "I hope that suits you, by Jingo!" Of course this was faithfully recorded and the long, tedious ordeal had to be gone through with once more. (10–11)

110. Camlot, "Early Talking Books," 154.
111. Ibid., 148.
112. Theodore Dreiser, *A Hoosier Holiday* (New York: John Lane Company; London: John Lane, The Bodley Head, 1916), 373.
113. Charles W. Hibbitt, "Poetry and Speech," *Frontier and Midland* 17.3 (Spring 1937): 160.
114. Riley writes, "All day yesterday and today I've been setting up my (not *Gram*-o-phone, but) *Zon*-o-phone, which the Co. says is by no means so complicated. Well, at last, I've mastered it; and with *ten* introductory disks—and *one* from your duplicates, I am now giving a great show, and all we Lockerbie people wish you-all were of our enthusiastic audience. *Your* disk holds favorite, though we have *one* phenomenal one which I'll order duplicate of forwarded your way at once" (emphasis original to letter). Riley, Letter to Joel Chandler Harris, 8 May 1900, James Whitcomb Riley Collection.
115. E. W. Scripture, *Researches in Experimental Phonetics: The Study of Speech Curves* (Washington, D.C.: Carnegie Institution, 1906), 3.
116. William Lyon Phelps, "As I Like It," *Scribner's* 88.5 (Nov. 1930): 547.
117. James Whitcomb Riley, *The Boys of the Old Glee Club* (Indianapolis: Bobbs-Merrill, 1907).
118. Picker, *Victorian Soundscapes*, 123; Ivan Kreilkamp, *Voice and the Victorian Storyteller* (Cambridge: Cambridge University Press, 2005), 185.
119. Review of *The Boys of the Old Glee Club* by James Whitcomb Riley, *The Independent*, 2 April 1908, 756.
120. Minnie Mitchell, *James Whitcomb Riley, as I Knew Him: Real Incidents in the Early Life of America's Beloved Poet* (Greenfield, IN: The Old Swimmin' Hole Press, 1949): 150–51.
121. Ibid., 149–50.
122. Qtd. in Sorby, *Schoolroom Poets*, 99.
123. Riley writes, "I am half sorry that we were not alone yesterday for I could have talked like a phonograph." Letter to Theodore C. Steele, c. 1879, in *Letters*, 22.
124. Camlot, 158, 166.
125. Riley, Letter to the Holsteins, 24 May 1900, James Whitcomb Riley Collection.
126. Kittler, *Discourse Networks*, 236.

127. Qtd. in Picker, *Victorian Soundscapes*, 127.
128. Picker, 123.
129. Camlot, "Early Talking Books," 163–65.
130. Tim Brooks, *Lost Sounds: Blacks and the Birth of the Recording Industry, 1890–1919* (Urbana: University of Illinois Press, 2004), 197, 263.

Chapter Two

1. A famous example is James Joyce's "The Dead"; the name of Joyce's protagonist comes from Harte's *Gabriel Conroy*.
2. Margaret Duckett, "Plain Language from Bret Harte," *Nineteenth-Century Fiction* 11.4 (1957): 241.
3. Jones, *Strange Talk*, 37. One set of Harte's readers that would have recognized the satire were readers of the *Overland Monthly*, the magazine Harte edited and in which the poem appeared. As Tara Penry argues persuasively, the magazine's history of articles on the Chinese in California made the *Overland*'s position clear, such that "established readers could hardly have missed Harte's intended tone" and even "new readers . . . would have found a few clues directing them to a satiric reading of the poem" in the issue's otherwise genteel contents. "The Chinese in Bret Harte's *Overland*: A Context for Truthful James," *American Literary Realism* 43.1 (2010): 74.
4. Jones, *Strange Talk*, 37.
5. Henry B. Wonham, *Playing the Races: Ethnic Caricature and American Literary Realism* (Oxford: Oxford University Press, 2004), 48.
6. "Stories of Famous Poems: Francis Bret Harte," 2.
7. Scharnhorst, *Opening*, 57.
8. Bret Harte, "Plain Language from Truthful James," in *Poems* (Boston: James R. Osgood and Company, 1871), 79–83. Axel Nissen cites one such example: "'We will be ruined by Chinese cheap labor' was in fact a favorite phrase of the boss truckman Dennis Kearney, the 'Sandlots Orator,' when he spoke about the dangers Chinese immigration represented." *Bret Harte: Prince and Pauper* (Jackson: University Press of Mississippi, 2000), 110.
9. The "Bill Nye" of Harte's poem precedes the career of the humorist Bill Nye, who toured with James Whitcomb Riley (the two were compared to Chang and Eng, the Siamese twins, by Mark Twain). David B. Kesterson writes in "The Literary Comedians and the Language of Humor" that "Edgar Wilson Nye capitalizes on the notoriety of Bret Harte's card shark Bill Nye from 'Plain Language from Truthful James,' by adopting the 'Bill' as his first name." "The Literary Comedians and the Language of Humor," *Studies in American Humor*, new series, 1 (1982): 45.
10. Scharnhorst, *Opening*, 55.
11. Bret Harte, "The Rise of the 'Short Story,'" in *The Luck of the Roaring Camp and Other Writings* (New York: Penguin, 2001), 257.
12. John O. Rees, "Some Echoes of English Literature in Frontier Vernacular Humor," *Studies in American Humor*, new series, 1 (1983): 158.
13. Qtd. in Scharnhorst, *Opening*, 48.
14. Ibid., 147.
15. Jones, *Strange Talk*, 43.
16. Edward Eggleston, *The Hoosier School-Master: A Story of Backwoods Life in Indiana* (New York: Macmillan Company, 1928), 7; Mark Twain, *Mark Twain in Eruption*, ed. Bernard DeVoto (New York: Harper and Brothers, 1940), 263.

17. Warren Cheney, "Francis Bret Harte," *Overland Monthly* 1.1 (Jan. 1883): 72. It is worth noting, however, that Cheney's 1883 article appeared in the *Overland Monthly*, a magazine once edited by Harte.

18. Henry Childs Merwin, *The Life of Bret Harte, with Some Account of the California Pioneers* (Detroit: Gale Research Co., 1967), 325–26.

19. George Philip Krapp, *The English Language in America*, vol. 1 (1925; New York: Frederick Ungar Publishing Co., 1960), 244–45.

20. J. C. Heywood, *How They Strike Me, These Authors* (Philadelphia: J. B. Lippincott & Co., 1877), 197–98.

21. Some of the most interesting parodies of "Plain Language from Truthful James" I have come across include one written in German dialect, one attacking the flirtatious "Girl of the Period" in place of the "Heathen Chinee," and a broadside poem titled "The Ho[w]ly Elder" attributed to "Ah Sin-[ner]." All can be found at the American Antiquarian Society. Riley himself published a poem in the *Greenfield Commercial* in the style of Harte's poem, titled "An Unexpected Result," and signed it "Brat Heart." Mitchell, *James Whitcomb Riley*, 134.

22. In *Bret Harte: A Bibliography*, Gary Scharnhorst points out that the attribution of this poem to Harte by its inclusion in a collection of his poetry is disputed by Jacob Blanck, who says that the poem is "almost certainly not by Harte." *Bibliography of American Literature*, 9 vols. (New Haven: Yale University Press, 1955–91): 3: 458.

23. Brodhead, *Cultures of Letters*, 137.

24. Jones, *Strange Talk*, 193.

25. Michael Toolan, "The Significations of Representing Dialect in Writing," *Language and Literature* 1.1 (1992): 42.

26. Michael Kowalewski writes that, in nineteenth-century Western writing, "[w]ith certain groups of people—especially the Chinese and Native Americans, whose members often spoke little English—what was actually available for quotation were pidgin hybrids or 'jargons' that are sometimes made to sound degraded or nonsensical in western texts, whatever the actual complexity of such languages might have been in the context of frontier communication"; however, "[a]s often as not, Chinese and Indian characters in these works appear in degraded silence, with no speech at all." "Quoting the Wicked Wit of the West: Frontier Reportage and Western Vernacular," in *Reading the West: New Essays on the Literature of the American West*, ed. Michael Kowalewski (Cambridge: Cambridge University Press, 1996), 87–88.

27. Bret Harte, "The Latest Chinese Outrage," in *The Poetical Works of Bret Harte* (Boston and New York: Houghton, Mifflin and Company, 1899), 142–45.

28. Scharnhorst says the poem did not "strike a chord with readers; indeed the poem was virtually ignored." *Opening*, 214.

29. "The London Spectator on Bret Harte," *Every Saturday: A Journal of Choice Reading*, 27 May 1871, 486.

30. Osgood qtd. in Scharnhorst, *Opening*, 71, 55. A strange and crudely drawn ephemeral edition of the poem illustrated by H. Palmieri (Philadelphia: Porter Coates, 1871) exhibits the poem's unspoken violence in reverse: Ah Sin is the aggressor, walking into the distance triumphantly in the last illustrated panel, while Truthful James assists a limping, swollen-faced Bill Nye in the foreground. These illustrations apparently led one reviewer to claim that "Ah Sin himself is the narrator" (despite the fact that Harte's text is not altered) and that he "proves how completely 'that truth-telling James' has calumniated him." "Notes on Books and Booksellers," *American Literary Gazette and Publishers' Circular*, 15 April 1871, 250.

31. Jacqueline Romeo, "Irony Lost: Bret Harte's Heathen Chinee and the Populariza-

tion of the Comic Coolie as Trickster in Frontier Melodrama," *Theatre History Studies* 26 (1996): 117–18.

32. "Personal," *Cincinnati Daily Gazette*, 22 April 1871, 2.

33. The illustrations from this edition can be found in Stephen Railton's online archive, "Mark Twain and His Times" at http://etext.virginia.edu/railton/roughingit/map/chiharte.html. In what appears to be another similar "edition" published by the Chicago, Rock Island, and Pacific Railroad and "dedicated to the traveling public," Harte's poem is reprinted along with an anonymous poem titled "An Old-Fashioned Couple." This poem was clearly written for the express purpose of advertising the railroad line's "Palace Cars," which are admired by the poem's eponymous elderly couple for their "silver fixin's" and "paintin's." As they observe the passing landscape on their visit "out West" to see their son John, they decide that "the West has far more charms" than the East, providing a fitting versified prologue to Harte's poem. *The Old-Fashioned Couple and Heathen Chinee*, Chicago: J. J. Spalding & Co., 1873.

34. Yopie Prins, "Robert Browning, Transported by Meter," in *The Traffic in Poems: Nineteenth-Century Poetry and Transatlantic Exchange*, ed. Meredith L. McGill (New Brunswick: Rutgers University Press, 2008), 209.

35. Tom D. Kilton, "The American Railroad as Publisher, Bookseller, and Librarian," *Journal of Library History* 17.1 (1974): 61.

36. Duckett, "Plain Language," 37.

37. Even decades later, the *Columbia* [SC] *State* prints a dedicatory poem that ends with the following quatrain: "He wrote in verse as well as prose, / And be it here confessed— / That many of us know and love / His 'Heathen Chinee' best." "Today in History: Anniversary of the Birth of Bret Harte in 1839," 25 Aug. 1919, 4.

38. Noah Brooks, "Bret Harte: A Biographical and Critical Sketch," *Overland Monthly* 40.3 (Sept. 1902): 206; Fred Lewis Pattee, *A History of American Literature since 1870* (New York: The Century Company, 1915), 398.

39. Pemberton, *Bret Harte*, 73; Taliesin Evans, "History of the 'Heathen Chinee,'" *Overland Monthly* 40.3 (Sept. 1902): 229. In a much reprinted 1910 article, the *New York Times* pointed out that "packs" should most likely read "jacks," but that misprint—"the only instance in literature where a grossly patent error . . . has persisted"—was initially missed by the author:

> . . . the busy Bret Harte let the proofs go down to the printer, and it was not until some time later that he recalled having overlooked an error in it. He hurried down to the press, but already several hundred copies had been struck off and were being distributed about the city to the morning subscribers. Bret Harte, attaching no importance to the fugitive verses, which had merely oozed from his pen the afternoon previous, made no effort at correction then. When, however, the eastern press enthusiastically copied it, and publishers and illustrators rang all manner of comic changes on it, he tried to substitute the correct phrase, but without avail, and 'The Heathen Chinee' has persisted in its original form through numberless editions ever since. ("Bret Harte's 'Heathen Chinee,'" *New York Times*, 13 Nov. 1910, SM5)

A similar story of misprint surrounds Riley's most famous poem. "Little Orphant Annie" was supposed to read "Little Orphant Allie."

40. Garland, "Real Conversations," 233.

41. Walter Barnes writes, "Riley, as all the world knows, is extremely fond of dialect—Hoosier dialect in his verse for grown-ups, child dialect in his verse for growing-

ups. *Little Orphant Annie, The Raggedy Man, The Bumblebee, The Boy Lives on Our Farm, The Squirt-Gun Uncle Maked Me, The Runaway Boy, The Pet Coon*, are all typical child-dialect pieces." Barnes, 185. A glimpse at some of Riley's book titles clearly demonstrates his reliance on this mode: *The Riley Baby Book: Autograph Verses Reproduced in Facsimile, The Book of Joyous Children, Riley Child Rhymes, Rhymes of Childhood, Riley's Child Verse, A Child-World*, etc.

42. James Whitcomb Riley, "Schoolboy Silhouettes—No. 1" (unidentified newspaper clipping), James Whitcomb Riley Collection.

43. For example, *wuz* (perhaps the most commonly used word in eye dialect) seems closer to a phonetic representation than *was* does. Mark Balhorn, "Paper Representations of the Non-Standard Voice," *Visible Language* 32 (1998): 60.

44. Noah Webster, *Dissertations on the English Language* (1789; Menston, England: The Scolar Press Limited, 1967), 397.

45. Charles Read, *Children's Creative Spelling* (London: Routledge and Kegan Paul, 1971), 28.

46. James Whitcomb Riley, "Lisping in Numbers," in *The Complete Poetical Works of James Whitcomb Riley* (Bloomington: Indiana University Press, 1993), 757–78.

47. The British Simplified Spelling Society, for example, published a book in 1911 called *Simplified Spelling: An Appeal to Common Sense*. The rules for using this simplified spelling include, "Drop silent letters when this does not involve a change of pronunciation," such as the *gh* in *bright*, but "[d]o not adopt *brite*, which is contrary to the spelling *ie* suggested for this diphthong in the scheme." It appears that spellings such as "brite" are counterproductive to the simplifying endeavor: "This kind of spelling, by means of a mute *e* following a consonant, is for various reasons unacceptable." *Simplified Spelling: An Appeal to Common Sense* (London: Simplified Spelling Society, 1911), 59, 44.

48. Hibbitt, "Poetry and Speech," 159–60.

49. Dale B. J. Randall, "Dialect in the Verse of 'The Hoosier Poet,'" *American Speech* 35 (1960): 48.

50. As Lee Soltow and Edward Stevens point out, "It was common for both reading and schooling to be used as part of the setting for children's stories or poems, the moral examples contained therein presumably attractive enough to make an impression upon young minds." *The Rise of Literacy,* 64.

51. James Whitcomb Riley, "Almon Keefer," in *A Child-World* (Indianapolis: Bobbs-Merrill, 1896), 51.

52. James Whitcomb Riley, "A Session with Uncle Sidney," in *The Book of Joyous Children* (New York: Charles Scribner's Sons, 1902), 112–15.

53. For Riley's difficulty with spelling, see Richard Crowder, *Those Innocent Years: The Legacy and Inheritance of a Hero of the Victorian Era, James Whitcomb Riley* (Indianapolis: Bobbs-Merrill, 1957), 42.

54. James Whitcomb Riley, "Some Boys," *Century* 41.2 (Dec. 1890): 317.

55. Letter to Benjamin S. Parker, 29 Aug. 1887, qtd. in *Complete Works of James Whitcomb Riley,* vol. 6, 407–8.

56. Letter from Bobbs-Merrill Company to multiple recipients, c. 1915, James Whitcomb Riley Collection.

57. "The Indiana School Journal Teachers' Club—Announcement," James Whitcomb Riley Collection.

58. Bernard Lootens, Letter to Riley, n.d.; Charles Franklin, Letter to Riley, 6 Sept. 1915, James Whitcomb Riley Collection.

59. *St Nicholas,* Letter to Riley, 1 Aug. 1889, James Whitcomb Riley Collection.

60. Riley, Letter to Carey, 27 Aug. 1894, James Whitcomb Riley Collection.
61. Riley, Letter to R. U. Johnson, 14 [?] June 1890, James Whitcomb Riley Collection.
62. Riley, Letter to R. U. Johnson, 15 July 1890, James Whitcomb Riley Collection.
63. *Scribner's* (E. L. Burlingame), Letter to Riley, 6 Jan. 1899, James Whitcomb Riley Collection.
64. Carey, Letter to Riley, 18 July 1895, James Whitcomb Riley Collection.
65. Garland, *Roadside Meetings,* 232.
66. Clara Laughlin thinks Riley's dialect so accurate that future generations may use his notebooks recording dialect speech as valuable resources in studying late nineteenth-century Indiana speech. On the other hand, Fred Lewis Pattee argues that Riley's "dialect does not ring true" and that "Riley must be dismissed as artificial and, on the whole, insincere." Riley's own "Dialect in Literature" defends the use of dialect in literature generally, and Nicholson cites Riley's defense of his own inconsistencies specifically: "He complained to me bitterly of an editor who had directed his attention to apparent inconsistencies in dialect in the proof of a poem. Riley held, and rightly, that the dialect of the Hoosier is not fixed and unalterable, but varies in certain cases, and that words are often pronounced differently in the same sentence." Laughlin, *Reminiscences of James Whitcomb Riley* (New York: Fleming H. Revell Co., 1916), 108; Pattee, *History of American Literature,* 326, 328; Nicholson, *Man in the Street,* 40.
67. Donald M. Scott, "Print and the Public Lecture System, 1840–60," in *Printing and Society in Early America,* ed. William Leonard Joyce et al. (Worcester, MA: American Antiquarian Society, 1983), 280.
68. "Ade's Literary Map of Indiana," *Bellingham* [WA] *Herald,* 17 May 1905, 7.
69. A few of the most interesting turn-of-the-century non-dialect poems about spelling bees I have encountered include Henry H. Johnson's "The Old-Time Spelling-School" (included in *Ballads of the Farm and Home* in 1902), Benjamin F. Taylor's "Going to Spelling School" (originally published in *Scribner's Monthly* in 1874, and in a review said to be "well known all over America"), William Caswell Jones's "The Spelling School" (included in his *Birch-Rod Days, and Other Poems,* published in 1892), Earl Marble's "The Amateur Spelling-Match" (originally published in *Appleton's Journal* in 1877 and reprinted many times in recitation books and anthologies), and Kate Tannatt Woods's "Grandfather Grey" (in *Grandfather Grey,* published in 1892). A *Time* magazine article from February 19, 1940, cites a group of poems titled "Lincoln Lyrics," by Edwin Markham of "The Man with the Hoe" fame, written in 1925 but "never before published or broadcast" until the Staten Island Chamber of Commerce played a recording of them on the radio in honor of Lincoln's birthday. One of them depicts a spelling bee in which Abraham Lincoln allows his sweetheart to beat him. Coincidentally, young Lincoln "stands pat on . . . Phthisic" ("Radio: Spelldown," 47).

In addition, the June 1898 issue of *Primary Education* includes a much-cited poem titled "The Spelling Match." Because the poem includes misspelled words in its narrative, the editor's note asks, "Is it pedagogically wrong to give these verses to the children?" Another educational journal, an 1896 issue of *American Annals of the Deaf,* found the poem useful in combating bad spelling, as "after the first couplet, the class comprehended the 'joke,' and was then interested in watching for the mistake in each succeeding stanza." *Primary Education* 6 (June 1898): 239; *American Annals of the Deaf* 41 (1896): 187–88.
70. Bret Harte, "The Spelling Bee at Angel's (Reported by Truthful James)," *Scribner's* 17.1 (Nov. 1879): 38–40.
71. In fact, Seth Lerer writes, "But if there is one word that emblematizes region, dia-

lect and distance in this passage it is *phthisic.* . . . By the mid-nineteenth century in England, the word seems to have evaporated, but in regional American, it flourished." Lerer cites the *Dictionary of American Regional English* entry, which explains that the word's "peculiar orthography made it a favorite in old-time spelling bees." That "phthisic," as Lerer points out, "makes us palpably aware of speech as a physical activity—and, as a consequence, of dialect itself as something laborious for the uninitiated to pronounce," makes it especially suitable, I argue, for both the public and social environment of the spelling bee and the alienating and difficult experience of dialect poetry reading. *Inventing English: A Portable History of the Language* (New York: Columbia University Press, 2007), 201.

72. The title of Wister's book lampoons the first line of Isaac Watts's poem "Against Idleness and Mischief": "How doth the little busy bee." The poem was printed in *Divine Songs Attempted in Easy Language for Children* in 1715, and was a popular recitation piece and well-known poem frequently used in spellers.

73. Owen Wister, *How Doth the Simple Spelling Bee* (New York: Macmillan, 1907), 61.

74. Ibid., 62. Wister also responds to this argument in a *New York Times* piece, in which he writes, "It is difficult for school-children. Here is truly a solemn indictment. Can we keep our faces straight? This difficulty does not somehow seem to have prevented various children all along through the years from growing up and writing Hamlet and Ivanhoe and Vanity Fair and Robinson Crusoe and The Scarlet Letter—in short has not prevented English from producing the greatest Literature the world has ever seen, and also the widest number of readers of this Literature." As far as foreigners are concerned, he sarcastically exclaims, "Poor dears! So difficult that English has steadily spread through every nation, and is now the dominant language of the civilized world, and growing more so every day." "What Is True Spelling? One of the Foremost of our Younger Writers Does Not Think It Is the Kind Recommended by the Simplified Spelling Board," *New York Times,* 5 Oct. 1906, BR614.

75. Webster, *Dissertations,* 394–95.

76. A word derived from the hook hanging above the hearth upon which pots were hung, a "pot-hook" is a rudimentary effect of penmanship; young students who couldn't write properly would produce letters that resembled pot-hooks.

77. David Simpson, *The Politics of American English, 1776–1850* (New York: Oxford University Press, 1986), 143.

78. Allen Walker Read, "The Spelling Bee: A Linguistic Institution of the American Folk," *PMLA* 56 (1941): 504.

79. Eggleston, *Hoosier School-Master,* 79.

80. Webster, *Dissertations,* 108–9.

81. J. E. Worcester, *A Pronouncing Spelling-Book of the English Language* (Boston: William Ware and Company, 1879), 9.

82. Suzanne de Castell and Allan Luke, "Models of Literacy in North American Schools: Social and Historical Conditions and Consequences," in *Literacy, Society, and Schooling: A Reader,* ed. Suzanne de Castell, Allan Luke, and Kieran Egan (Cambridge: Cambridge University Press, 1986), 94.

83. As Charles Carpenter writes, "Not so much importance is attached to the ability to spell correctly at present as there was in the nineteenth century. It has been pointed out many times that spelling was over valued at the expense of other studies during the nineteenth century, and that this criticism is justified cannot be denied." *History of American Schoolbooks* (Philadelphia: University of Pennsylvania Press, 1963), 158.

84. Eggleston, *Hoosier School-Master,* 54, 79.

85. "Spelling," *Littell's Living Age,* 19 Feb. 1876, 510–11.
86. White, *Every-Day English,* 100.
87. Qtd. in Read, "The Spelling Bee," 500. Although the term "spelling bee" was preceded by "spelling-school," "spelling-match" and related terms as early as the late eighteenth century, "spelling bee" appears to have emerged in the nineteenth century, according to the *Oxford English Dictionary,* and appears to be of American origin. Read writes, "Sir Charles Reed, chairman of the London School Board, visited America . . . , and reported that the spelling bees had 'done a great deal to improve the popular knowledge of English.' . . . They reached England in the winter season of 1875–6, attracting much attention, but they soon died down there" (508–9). In the United States, however, spelling bees have been popular, on and off, for two centuries.
88. Shirley Brice Heath, "Toward an Ethnohistory of Writing in American Education," in *Writing: The Nature, Development and Teaching of Written Communication, Vol. 1: Variation in Writing: Functional and Linguistic-Cultural Differences,* ed. Marcia Farr Whiteman (Hillsdale, NJ: Lawrence Erlbaum Associates, 1981), 35.
89. Venable, *John Hancock,* 145.
90. Eggleston, *The Hoosier School-Master,* 53.
91. Joaquin Miller, "The Slump in Poetry, Further Discussed by the Poets," *Critic* 46 (April 1905): 350.
92. Mitchell, *James Whitcomb Riley,* 74.

Chapter Three

1. Paul Laurence Dunbar, "Welcome Address to the Western Association of Writers," in *The Collected Poetry of Paul Laurence Dunbar,* ed. Joanne M. Braxton (Charlottesville: University of Virginia Press, 1993), 307.
2. In 1900, an article from the *Augusta Democrat* declared that "[n]either from the picturesque South or the cultured North come specimens of negro talent, but from the vigorous hurrying West," and cited Dunbar as one example. Untitled, *Augusta* [GA] *Democrat,* 14 Feb. 1900 [?], n.p., The Paul Laurence Dunbar Collection, Ohio Historical Society, Dayton, reel 5.
3. It is worth noting that the subtitle of Dunbar's poem "James Whitcomb Riley" is "From a Westerner's Point of View." Although the poem's speaker is the said "Westerner," speaking in Hoosier dialect, the "Westerner's Point of View" is also that of Dunbar himself, who shares with the poem's speaker a passionate admiration for Riley's verse.
4. Jay Martin and Gossie H. Hudson, eds., *The Paul Laurence Dunbar Reader* (New York: Dodd, Mead and Co., 1975), 410.
5. "The Colored Poet Paul Laurence Dunbar in the City on His Way East," *Indianapolis News,* 26 Oct. 1900, n.p., The Paul Laurence Dunbar Collection, Ohio Historical Society, Dayton, reel 5.
6. James Whitcomb Riley, *The Letters of James Whitcomb Riley,* ed. William Lyon Phelps (Indianapolis: Bobbs-Merrill, 1930), 168.
7. Paul M. Pearson writes that Dunbar's "books have always sold well; better, indeed, than any books of recent verse except those of Riley and of Field," a fact cited by many critics of the period. *Paul Laurence Dunbar: A Tribute* (n.p: n.p., [c. 1906]), 8.
8. Consider, for example, Walter C. Bronson's *A Short History of American Literature, Designed Primarily for Use in Schools and Colleges* (Boston: D. C. Heath & Co.,

1900), which lists Dunbar alongside Joel Chandler Harris and Thomas Nelson Page as a writer of "literature which has sprung up in that region," heralding a "literary New South" (287).

9. For instance, Gavin Jones writes that Dunbar's "We Wear the Mask" is an example of "his exploration of black vernacular masking" and that "[t]he subtle mouthing in Dunbar's poem clearly refers to the black rhetorical masking which . . . maintains subversive meaning under conventional or nonsensical forms." (See also Henry Louis Gates's discussion of Dunbar in *Figures in Black: Words, Signs, and the "Racial" Self.*) The centrality of Dunbar's "We Wear the Mask" to his oeuvre prompts readers of Dunbar to call upon the mask metaphor in describing his general poetics, with the mask standing for his inauthentic dialect orthography. In attempting to subvert readings of Dunbar's poetry as simply reactionary, Jones writes that "there is much that is seemingly inauthentic in Dunbar's representation of dialect, especially his use of conventional dialect spelling and of a demeaning vocabulary of racist clichés. Yet there is also a politically subtle use of black vernacular techniques *beneath this orthographic mask.*" *Strange Talk,* 189–90, 207, emphasis added.

10. Smethurst, *The African American Roots of Modernism,* 33.

11. Gene Andrew Jarrett, *Deans and Truants: Race and Realism in African American Literature* (Philadelphia: University of Pennsylvania Press, 2007), 37; Wonham, *Playing the Races,* 8.

12. Jarrett, *Deans and Truants,* 32.

13. Edward H. Lawson writes in 1906 that "there will be no such southern Negro speech" in fifty years, and "if this . . . dialect is to become a dead language, may God bless Paul Dunbar for having saved it to us in his immortal lyrics!" Over a decade later, *Half Century Magazine* writes that Dunbar's poetry "will preserve . . . the optimism of the colored people while at the same time it keeps . . . the odd phrases of a by-gone day." Lawson, "Paul Laurence Dunbar," *Alexander's Magazine* (March 1906): 49; qtd. in E. W. Metcalf, *Paul Laurence Dunbar: A Bibliography* (Metuchen, NJ: Scarecrow Press, 1975), 116. As Michael North points out, the myth of the "disappearing Negro" was the "central trope of the movement." He argues:

> It functioned as wish fulfillment, revealing the barely submerged hope that the freed slaves would simply die off. It served as a metaphor of the temporal reversal of the post-Reconstruction period, taking readers imaginatively back in time as the South was being taken politically back in time. And it fed nostalgia for a time when racial relationships had been simple and happy, as least for whites, suggesting that they might be simple and happy again if southern whites were simply left alone to resolve things themselves. (*The Dialect of Modernism: Race, Language, and Twentieth-Century Literature* [New York: Oxford University Press, 1994], 22–23)

14. Untitled, *Atlanta Sunny South,* 4 May 1901, n.p., The Paul Laurence Dunbar Collection, Ohio Historical Society, Dayton, reel 4.

15. See J. Martin Favor's *Authentic Blackness: The Folk in the New Negro Renaissance* (Durham: Duke University Press, 1999).

16. Peter Revell, *Paul Laurence Dunbar* (Boston: Twayne Publishers, 1979), 63.

17. Richard La Galienne, "Paul Laurence Dunbar: Diversity of Talent and Genuine Inspiration in the Poetry of One of the Leading Singers of His Race," *New York Times Magazine,* 18 Jan. 1914, 17.

18. One of many articles mentioning Riley's influence was written by the African American poet (and Riley protégé) James David Corrothers, who writes that "[i]t is probable . . . that Dunbar used Riley's style as the model for his earlier efforts, for the delightful spirit of the author of 'When the Frost is on the Pumpkin' breathes through many of the quaint negro melodies of the colored man, and it is quite evident that no one enjoys the fact more thoroughly than does the good Hoosier poet himself." "An Afro-American Poet," *Chicago Journal* [?], n.d., n.p., The Paul Laurence Dunbar Collection, Ohio Historical Society, Dayton, reel 4.

19. Of the poem "Speakin' o' Christmas," Revell writes, "To read this poem alone is to realize how thoroughly Dunbar had absorbed Riley's style and sentiment. It is not always appreciated how much some of Dunbar's more popular pieces owe to this source" (81).

20. Dunbar's perceived lack of authenticity in some of his poetry and fiction leads Jarrett to call him a writer of "anomalous" texts that "unsettle[d] the models of racial realism" forwarded by the "deans" of the African American literary tradition. Jarrett, *Deans and Truants*, 2.

21. Carrie Tirado Bramen, *The Uses of Variety: Modern Americanism and the Quest for National Distinctiveness* (Cambridge, MA: Harvard University Press, 2000), 119.

22. W. D. Howells, introduction to *Lyrics of Lowly Life* by Paul Laurence Dunbar (New York: Dodd, Mead, 1896), xvi. *The Bookman* claims that the dialect pieces show "how clever and original [Dunbar] can be when he is thoroughly spontaneous and natural" and "how comparatively feeble and ineffective he will always show himself when he is merely imitating the Caucasian." Dialect writing is said to be, in the *Critic*, "the best way the Negro can express himself" and, in a *New York Times* review, "the natural expression of the Negro race in its least exalted aspects." H. T. Peck, "An Afro-American Poet," *The Bookman* 4.6 (Feb. 1897): 568; qtd. in Metcalf, *Paul Laurence Dunbar*, 148; Review of *Li'l Gal* by Paul Laurence Dunbar, *New York Times,* 26 Nov. 1904, 817.

23. The *Colored American Magazine* says Dunbar's dialect poetry is best; the *Southern Workman,* too, prefers dialect. Qtd. in Metcalf, *Paul Laurence Dunbar,* 110, 114. The *AME Church Review,* though, is an exception, writing of the dialect poems: "We prefer to let these things go for the titillation they will occasion among folk-lore fanciers and soda-fountain drinkers. . . . Editors with the commercial side well developed will besiege him for a copy in a 'minor' view, but we shall wait." H. T. Kealing, review of *Majors and Minors* by Paul Laurence Dunbar, *AME Church Review* 13 (Oct. 1896): 256–59.

24. Dickson D. Bruce, Jr., *Black American Writing from the Nadir: The Evolution of a Literary Tradition, 1877–1915* (Baton Rouge: Louisiana University Press, 1989), 99, 102. J. Saunders Redding agrees that dialect writing "was not altogether a failure in appealing to the black [audience]," and attributes its interest to "the heaven-sent capacity for recognizing and finding amusing the limitations dialect suggested. This audience's amusement derived from its knowledge that whites were incapable of perceiving the essence and the spirit which underlay the dialect. It was in-house amusement, coterie humor, nurtured by an ironic perception." *A Scholar's Conscience: Selected Writings of J. Saunders Redding, 1942–1977* (Lexington: University Press of Kentucky, 1992), 205–6.

25. Lorenzo Thomas, *Extraordinary Measures: Afrocentric Modernism and Twentieth-Century American Poetry* (Tuscaloosa: University of Alabama Press, 2000), 193.

26. He wrote in a letter to Helen Douglass, Frederick Douglass's widow, that he saw his poetry as an attempt to "differentiate dialect as a philological branch from the burlesque of Negro minstrelsy." Letter to Helen Douglass, 22 Oct. 1896, The Paul Laurence

Dunbar Collection, Ohio Historical Society, Dayton, reel 1. However, as Bruce points out, for Dunbar's dialect poetry, "a key source undoubtedly was the plantation tradition itself" (58).

27. Jarrett, *Deans and Truants*, 41.

28. Langston Hughes writes that "[t]he quaint charm and humor of Dunbar's dialect verse brought to him, in his day, largely the same kind of encouragement one would give a sideshow freak (A colored man writing poetry! How odd!) or a clown (How amusing!)." Dunbar himself expressed concern that about this, writing, "I hope there is something worthy in my writings and not merely the novelty of a black face associated with the power to rhyme that has attracted attention." "The Negro Artist and the Racial Mountain," in *Within the Circle: An Anthology of African American Literary Criticism from the Harlem Renaissance to the Present*, ed. Angelyn Mitchell (Durham: Duke University Press, 1994), 57; Martin and Hudson, *Dunbar Reader*, 412.

29. As Gavin Jones points out, "blacks were never so free to impersonate other ethnic groups as were, say, Jewish or Irish Americans." *Strange Talk*, 196.

30. "Paul Dunbar Heard," *Toledo Bee*, n.d., n.p., The Paul Laurence Dunbar Collection, Ohio Historical Society, Dayton, reel 4.

31. Jones, *Strange Talk*, 182. Riley once wrote to an aspiring writer, Lucy S. Furman, that she should "[i]n dialect be as conscientious as in your purest English—seeing to it always, with most vigilant minuteness, that your unlettered characters are themselves in thought, word and deed. . . . The work must appear positively veracious." *Letters*, 178.

32. J. Saunders Redding, *To Make A Poet Black* (Chapel Hill: University of North Carolina Press, 1939), 52, 63.

33. Bruce, *Black American Writing*, 61–62.

34. Revell, *Paul Laurence Dunbar*, 82.

35. Ibid., 56–57.

36. Bruce, *Black American Writing*, 106–7.

37. The "pure African blood" of some writers was often emphasized (as it was in McKay's case, discussed in this book's final chapter) in order to disprove arguments that their talents were somehow attributable to their white ancestry.

38. W. D. Howells, review of *Majors and Minors* by Paul Laurence Dunbar, *Harper's Weekly*, 27 June 1896, 630.

39. Alice Dunbar-Nelson, "The Poet and His Song," *AME Church Review* 31 (Oct. 1914): 124.

40. James Weldon Johnson, *Along This Way: The Autobiography of James Weldon Johnson* (1933; New York: Penguin, 1990), 160.

41. Pearson, *Tribute*, 8.

42. His famous poems "received the heartiest applause during readings, while those 'of deeper note' were accorded only polite, condescending recognition." Addison Gayle, *Oak and Ivy: A Biography of Paul Laurence Dunbar* (Garden City, NY: Doubleday, 1971), 43.

43. Daniel Borus, *Writing Realism: Howells, James, and Norris in the Mass Market* (Chapel Hill: University of North Carolina Press, 1989), 108.

44. After gaining the hearing, Dunbar wrote to James Weldon Johnson, "now they don't want me to write anything but dialect." Johnson describes the predicament of the African American dialect poet at the turn of the century as follows:

> I could see that the poet writing in the conventionalized dialect no matter how sincere he might be, was dominated by his audience; that his audi-

ence was a section of the white American reading public; that when he wrote he was expressing what often bore little relation, sometimes no relation at all, to actual Negro life; that he was really expressing only certain conceptions about Negro life that his audience was willing to accept and ready to enjoy; that in fact, he wrote mainly for the delectation of an audience that was an outside group. And I could discern that it was on this line that the psychological attitude of the poets writing in the dialect and that of the folk artists faced in different directions: because the latter, although working in the dialect, sought only to express themselves, and to their *own group*. I have frequently speculated upon what Dunbar might have done with Negro dialect if it had come to him fresh and plastic. (*Along This Way*, 159–60)

45. Following one of Dunbar's readings, one reporter wrote, "He certainly has the same dramatic perception, graceful delivery and sympathetic voice which add so much to the readings of the Hoosier poet." "Paul Dunbar's Reading," *Toledo Blade*, 10 Dec. 1898, n.p., The Paul Laurence Dunbar Collection, Ohio Historical Society, Dayton, reel 4.

46. I am excluding, of course, the lecture circuit, especially that associated with the abolitionist movement, with renowned lecturers such as Frederick Douglass, because the generic difference (entertaining versus didactic) and difference in intended audience are so significant. As Gene Andrew Jarrett writes, "More than any other writer during the American realism movement . . . , Dunbar negotiated, exploited, and suffered from the ideological force of minstrelsy." *Deans and Truants*, 36.

47. Johnson, *Along This Way*, 162. It is worth noting that Dunbar's cakewalk performance to Rosamond Johnson's adaptation of his poem comes three years after Dunbar's collaboration with Will Marion Cook on *Clorindy, or the Origin of the Cakewalk*.

48. Virginia Cunningham, *Paul Laurence Dunbar and His Song* (New York: Dodd, Mead, 1948), 219.

49. Pearson, *Tribute*, 8.

50. Benjamin Brawley, "Dunbar Thirty Years After," *Southern Workman* 59 (April 1930): 190.

51. Johnson, *You Know These Lines!*, v.

52. Thomas D. Pawley argues that "Dunbar had an inherent sense of the dramatic," claiming that "[t]he fact that so many of his poems are still in the repertoire of dramatic readers would seem to support this assessment." "Dunbar as Playwright," *Black World* 24.6 (1975): 71. And, as Jay Martin and Gossie H. Hudson write, "Though not known literally as a dramatist, Dunbar, in fact, was engaged in dramatic writing during his whole career, and the influence of his dramatic work upon his poetry is evident." *Dunbar Reader*, 265.

53. The last poem mentioned by Gates, "Sympathy," is non-dialect, but if inclusion in anthologies is any indication, this poem does not appear to have been popular until the periods of the Harlem Renaissance and especially the Black Arts Movement, when its message was more consistent with the valued literature of the periods. Relatively unpopular in anthologies prior to the Black Arts Movement, "Sympathy" appears in nearly half of the anthologies published after 1967 including more than one poem by Dunbar (according to E. W. Metcalf's *Paul Laurence Dunbar: A Bibliography*).

54. Henry Louis Gates, foreword to *In His Own Voice: The Dramatic and Other Uncollected Works of Paul Laurence Dunbar,* ed. Herbert Woodward Martin and Ronald Primeau (Athens: Ohio University Press, 2002), xi. In the conventional sense of the

word, too, Dunbar's black Southern dialect poems were "anthologized" as frequently as, if not more frequently than, his poems in standard English; his other dialect poems were generally unrepresented. According to Keneth Kinnamon's survey of selected popular anthologies published before 1968, seven of the twenty-nine include Dunbar, and the majority are his poems in dialect. Despite the consensus that there is a greater disparity in quality between Riley's non-dialect and dialect verse—with the former generally inferior in quality to the latter—than there is between the two modes in Dunbar's work, Dunbar's dialect poetry is given disproportionate weight. More recent generations "anthologize" (to use Gates's term) Dunbar's standard English poems more frequently than did earlier generations educated in the 1910s, 1920s, and 1930s. From the peak of his popularity to the 1940s, Dunbar's presence in anthologies diminished until the 1950s, when "Dunbar had faded from the memories of anthologists." Social changes of the post-Civil Rights Era and the Black Arts Movement reasserted the importance of the African American literary tradition, however equivocal the reception and appraisal of Dunbar's dialect. The tendency to favor the non-dialect pieces continues among critics of African American literature even today: the *Norton Anthology of African American Literature* includes twenty pieces by Dunbar, but only six feature dialect. And, in fact, this selection more accurately reflects the distribution of Dunbar's literary output: less than half of Dunbar's poetry is in dialect. "Three Black Writers and the Anthologized Canon," in *American Realism and the Canon*, ed. Tom Quirk and Gary Scharnhorst (Newark: University of Delaware Press, 1994), 143–53.

The partiality for Dunbar's non-dialect verse among many contemporary critics and anthologists of African American literature might profitably be traced back to James Weldon Johnson's resistance to Dunbar's representations of speech as "mere mutilation[s]." Instead, Johnson identifies Langston Hughes and Sterling Brown as the leading practitioners of a successful dialect poetry: their language "is not the dialect of the comic minstrel tradition; it is the common, racy, living, authentic speech of the Negro in certain phases of real life." Authenticity and sincerity—Johnson praises Brown's sincerity, claiming that there isn't a "false note" in his poetry—continue to be emphasized in evaluations of dialect writing. *Book,* 41, 4, 247.

55. Claude McKay uses the epistolary dialect form perhaps most notably in "School-Teacher Nell's Lub-Letter" and "Nellie White (An Answer to the Foregoing)," published in *Songs of Jamaica,* and Hughes in "Letter from Spain" and "Postcard from Spain."

56. Dunbar's epistolary dialect poems differ in this way from, for example, those by Robert Burns. Unlike Burns, whose poems function as letters, Dunbar assumes characters in his epistolary dialect poems.

57. The private exchange I am describing is an idealized one, and one that did not always apply in nineteenth-century America, when many letter recipients were unable to read the letters they received. Although the intermediation of a third party was often necessary, Dunbar depicts the presence of these third parties as a dramatic intrusion into the idealized space of private communication. In "A Love Letter," an illiterate speaker has a letter from his beloved recited to him, but the literate courtship ritual must end there, because "dey's t'ings dat I's a-t'inkin' date is only fu' huh eahs." Letters in Dunbar's poems are often kept between two individuals even if one of them cannot read. In "A Letter," for example, the letter writer adds a postscript telling his beloved Lucy, "Ef you cain't mek out dis letter, lay it by erpon de she'f / An' when I git home, I'll read it, darlin,' to you my own se'f."

58. These poems were unpublished in book form until 2002, when they were included in *In His Own Voice.*

59. Paul Laurence Dunbar, "Happy! Happy! Happy!," in *In His Own Voice,* 266.
60. These commas are not found in the manuscript, but they occur in the typescript.
61. Halttunen, *Confidence Men,* 119.
62. Eliza Leslie, *Miss Leslie's Behaviour Book: A Guide and Manual for Ladies* (Philadelphia: T. B. Peterson & Brothers, 1859), 166.
63. "Pleasure," along with the words and phrases related to it in this poem, provides us with a way of reading Julius's supposed misunderstanding. If his being *"non grata"* is the result of Mandy's "[h]aving mounted in position," his response to her letter—he is "fill[ed] . . . / Wid de sugar-drip of pleasure"—could reflect sexual desire, as being *"non grata"* is interpreted by him as a necessarily pleasurable or pleased state. In fact, *"grata,"* etymologically, points to "pleasure," meaning that Mandy means to offer him something like unpleasure.
64. For example, Gavin Jones writes that, in the poem "Appreciation," Dunbar "places tremendous emphasis on the conventional status of language by writing in an indeterminate dialect." *Strange Talk,* 197.
65. All citations to this collection refer to a microfilm copy of the Dunbar Collection.
66. This poem should not be confused with Dunbar's published poem also titled "A Letter."
67. The lines cited above come from one typescript of the poem found in the Ohio Historical Society microfilm of the Paul Laurence Dunbar Collection. Three discrete versions of the poem—two typed, one handwritten (incomplete)—reside there, and the version in *In His Own Voice* appears to have been reproduced from one of the typescripts. There are several inconsistencies between the three versions; however, there are errors printed in *In His Own Voice* that are not supported by any of the Ohio Historical Society copies: there should be a stanza break between lines 24 and 25, "tings" in line 10 should read "t'ings," "give" in line 19 should read "gin" [given], "behind" in line 32 should read "behin'," etc.
68. Dunbar, "Goin' Back," in *Collected Poetry of Paul Laurence Dunbar,* 316–17.
69. This is an estimate; Dunbar's poem is undated.
70. North, *Dialect of Modernism,* 112.
71. Jones, *Strange Talk,* 195.
72. Review of *Li'l Gal,* 817.
73. To be sure, both possibilities result in awkward lines, but these usages are not unprecedented. Poet Eliza Ann Horton uses "full well" in this manner in "Life's Web" ("The weaving is full well done"). The sense of "for well" that I suggest here is, I believe, supported by the availability of the phrase "for well and good," a phrase that implies interchangeability between the components "for well" and "for good"; a contemporary use of this common phrase can be found, for example, in a novel by Charles Felton Pidgin ("she should leave town for well and good"). Horton, *The Poems of Annie Hawthorne,* ed. E. Jay Hanford (New York: The Grafton Press, 1910), 114; Pidgin, *Quincy Adams Sawyer and Mason's Corner Folks, A Novel: A Picture of New England Home Life* (Boston: C. M. Clark Publishing Co., 1900), 330.
74. Mark Twain famously claimed to have been the first author to submit a typescript of a novel to his publisher, but he dictated it.
75. In response to a questionnaire asking "How does the verse-form come to you?" among other questions, Riley says that his poem "The Cost of a Song" came to him first as a couplet of lines that "were to [him] a kind of music that led to other music, and allowing the second feeling to express itself, I began striking the words on the typewriter

'over and over and over.'" Being only a catalyst, the initial inspirational "music" did not end up in the final poem, but the words "over and over and over," typed by a seemingly entranced Riley, end up as the poem's opening and repeat throughout the poem. Although the first music comes to the poet through a typical experience of poetic inspiration, the second music comes as an experience of poetic inspiration facilitated by new technology. J. E. Wallace Wallin, "Researches on the Rhythm of Speech," *Studies from the Yale Psychological Laboratory,* ed. E. W. Scripture, vol. 9 (New Haven: Yale University, 1901), 139.

76. Davis W. Clark, *Paul Laurence Dunbar Laurel-Decked* (Dayton: Paul Laurence Dunbar Scholarship Fund, 1909), 7.

77. Charles Olson, "Projective Verse," in *The New American Poetry, 1945–1960,* ed. Donald Allen (1960; Berkeley: University of California Press, 1999), 393.

78. Bruce, *Black American Writing,* 66.

79. Paul Laurence Dunbar, "Negro Society in Washington," *Saturday Evening Post,* 14 Dec. 1901, 9.

80. Dunbar, "The Tuskegee Meeting," in *In His Own Voice,* 187.

81. Martin and Hudson, *Dunbar Reader,* 453.

82. Robert Stepto, "Distrust of the Reader in Afro-American Narratives," in *Reconstructing American Literary History,* ed. Sacvan Bercovitch, Harvard English Studies 13 (Cambridge, MA: Harvard University Press, 1986), 300.

83. Although the writer of the article is often racist and conservative in his suggestions, most of the respondents are extremely reactionary in their derision of the project of African American education. Typical responses include, "When left to an exclusive association with his own people, there is a powerful inclination on the part of the Southern negro to revert to all of the distinctive features of his African ancestors," with the respondent suggesting that the assumption of African "features" would represent a regression equivalent to devolution, and "One of the discouraging features in the character of the young Southern negro is that apparently he has inherited but a small share of the steadiness and industry which were acquired under compulsion by his fathers," with the respondent essentially forwarding the familiar argument that blacks were better off as slaves. W. T. Harris, "The Education of the Negro," *Atlantic Monthly* 69 (June 1892): 723, 725.

84. Lida Keck Wiggins, *The Life and Works of Paul Laurence Dunbar: Containing His Complete Poetical Works, His Best Short Stories, Numerous Anecdotes and a Complete Biography of the Famous Poet* (Naperville, IL: J. L. Nichols and Company, [c. 1907]), 113.

85. Cunningham, *Paul Laurence Dunbar and His Song,* 245.

86. Brawley, "Dunbar Thirty Years After," 189.

87. Paul Laurence Dunbar, "Negro Life in Washington," *Harper's Weekly,* 13 Jan. 1900, 32.

88. Dunbar writes, "I believe I know my own people pretty thoroughly. I know them in all classes, the high and the low, and I have yet to see any young man or young woman who had the spirit of work in them before, driven from labor by a college education." "Is Higher Education for the Negro Hopeless?," *Philadelphia Times,* 10 June 1900, n.p., The Paul Laurence Dunbar Collection, Ohio Historical Society, Dayton.

89. Howells, review, 630.

90. Emeka Okeke-Ezigbo, "Paul Laurence Dunbar: Straightening the Record," *CLA Journal* 24 (1981): 492.

91. Ibid., 481.

92. Jean Wagner, *Black Poets of the United States: From Paul Laurence Dunbar to Langston Hughes* (Urbana: University of Illinois Press, 1973), 110.

93. Charles T. Davis, *Black Is the Color of the Cosmos: Essays on Afro-American Literature and Culture, 1942–1981* (New York: Garland Publishing, Inc., 1982), 121. Burton Raffel argues that "Riley was a driven man, and what drove him was the same pair of American gods that impelled most of his countrymen in his own lifetime and impel them still: money and success." As Okeke-Ezigbo suggests, "Dunbar apparently learned from Riley, or shared with him, the tendency to hanker after public approval." Raffel, *Politicians, Poets, and Con Men: Emotional History in Late Victorian America* (Hamden, CT: Archon, 1986), 137; Okeke-Ezigbo, "Paul Laurence Dunbar," 483.

94. Joan R. Sherman, *Invisible Poets: Afro-Americans of the Nineteenth Century* (Urbana: University of Illinois, 1989), 166. In addition, Cotter wrote a poem titled "On Hearing James W. Riley Read (from a Kentucky Standpoint)," which appears in Joan R. Sherman's anthology of nineteenth-century African American poetry. Its first stanza describes an emotional reaction to a performance by Riley:

> To tell the truth, each piece he read
> Set up a jingle in my head
> That bumped and thumped and roared about,
> Then on a sudden just crept out,
> Gently and slowly at the start,
> Then made a bee-line for my heart.
> (Joan R. Sherman, ed., *African-American Poetry of the Nineteenth Century: An Anthology.* [Urbana: University of Illinois Press, 1992], 330–31)

95. A fragment titled "Farmer Spittle's Spellin' Bee" can be found in the Dunbar Collection. It is unclear whether this was an early draft of "The Spellin' Bee" or a new poem, but the fragment as it stands shares little with "The Spellin' Bee."

96. Revell, *Paul Laurence Dunbar*, 81.

97. Dunbar, "The Spellin'-Bee," in *The Collected Poetry of Paul Laurence Dunbar*, 42–45.

98. Read, "The Spelling Bee," 500–501.

99. George Bernard Shaw, *Pygmalion: A Romance in Five Acts* (1913; London: Penguin, 1957), 131.

100. J. E. Carpenter, *The Popular Elocutionist and Reader* (London: Frederick Warne and Company, 1894), 7.

Chapter Four

1. Dunbar's first two collections, *Oak and Ivy* (1892) and *Majors and Minors* (1896), were self-published.

2. Paul Laurence Dunbar, "The Poet and His Song," *Current Literature* 21 (Feb. 1897): 102.

3. A. Robert Lee, "The Fiction of Paul Laurence Dunbar," *Negro American Literature Forum* 8 (1928): 166.

4. To cite metaphors by just two nineteenth-century predecessors with which Dunbar likely would have been familiar, John Keats's "When I Have Fears" describes books

containing "like rich garners the full-ripen'd grain" and Henry David Thoreau, similarly, writes, "Instead of cultivating the earth for wheat and potatoes, [authors] cultivate literature, and fill a place in the Republic of Letters." Keats, *Complete Poems* (Cambridge, MA: Harvard University Press, 1982), 166; Thoreau, *A Week on the Concord and Merrimack Rivers* (Boston: Osgood, 1873), 104.

   5. Martin and Hudson, *Dunbar Reader*, 431. Dunbar also uses "cultivation" in a letter to Dr. James Newton Matthews in a manner that falls somewhere between the second and third senses: "If there is anything in me, the fact that you have taken such pains to help me, and that others are interested in my career will spur me on to its highest cultivation" (415).

   6. Shelley Fisher Fishkin, "Race and the Politics of Memory: Mark Twain and Paul Laurence Dunbar," *Journal of American Studies* 40 (2006): 299.

   7. For example, J. A. Macon published 36 pieces, most in dialect, between 1881 and 1892, according to Cornell University's *Making of America* database, http://cdl.library.cornell.edu/moa/. Macon's perspective, Jean Wagner claims, is "that of a collector whose good faith is unquestionable." Wagner, *Black Poets of the United States*, 65.

   8. African American writers James Corrothers and James Weldon Johnson would follow him just a few years later with *Century* publications of their own, influenced by Dunbar.

   9. Jarrett and Morgan, *The Complete Stories of Paul Laurence Dunbar* (Athens: Ohio University Press, 2005), xxxvi.

   10. Michael Cohen, "Paul Laurence Dunbar and the Genres of Dialect," *African American Review* 41 (2007): 252.

   11. Brander Matthews, "On Working Too Much and Working Too Fast," in *The Tocsin of Revolt and Other Essays* (New York: Scribner's, 1922), 212.

   12. Edward Bok, *The Americanization of Edward Bok: The Autobiography of a Dutch Boy Fifty Years After* (1920; New York: Scribner's, 1921), 114.

   13. De Certeau, *Practice of Everyday Life*, 174.

   14. This advertisement can be found in the Paul Laurence Dunbar Collection, Ohio Historical Society, Dayton, reel 3.

   15. Martin and Hudson, *Dunbar Reader*, 424.

   16. Martin and Hudson, *Dunbar Reader*, 416; Edward Bok, "The Modern Literary King," *Forum* 20 (Nov. 1895): 335.

   17. Martin and Hudson, *Dunbar Reader*, 442. The slang sense of "hustle," to mean "To sell or serve (goods, etc.), esp. in an aggressive, pushing manner" (OED) was current in 1897.

   18. Rebekah Baldwin, "An Unpublished Letter Written to Paul Laurence Dunbar, 1894," ed. Gossie Harold Hudson, *Journal of Negro History* 55 (1970): 217.

   19. The irony, of course, is that if Riley didn't "rhyme / for money," no one did; he was the best-selling poet of the era and, in a single year (1903), made $23,000 in royalties from his poetry. Charvat, *Profession of Authorship*, 106.

   20. Dunbar, "James Whitcomb Riley," in *The Collected Poetry of Paul Laurence Dunbar*, 287.

   21. Martin and Hudson, *Dunbar Reader*, 415. The phrase "on flow'ry beds of ease" comes from an eighteenth-century hymn by Isaac Watts titled "Am I a Soldier of the Cross?" The verse reads, "Must I be carried to the skies / On flowery beds of ease, / While others fought to win the prize, / And sailed through bloody seas?" In other words, suffering through this world and laboring—to "bear the toil" and "endure the pain,"

as the hymn continues—is noble and will be rewarded. It's a sentiment expressed frequently in Dunbar's poems (for example, in "Not They Who Soar" and "Keep a-Pluggin' Away"): the value of steadfastness and of struggle.

22. Paul Laurence Dunbar, "The Dilettante," *Century* 50.3 (July 1895): 480.

23. Lawrence Buell, *New England Literary Culture: From Revolution through Renaissance* (New York: Cambridge University Press, 1986), 58.

24. Rolf Engelsing popularized the terms "intensive reading" and "extensive reading." The former, as Cathy N. Davidson defines it, refers to "rereading over the course of a lifetime the same few precious books and incorporating those books into life's most intimate and portentous activities"; the latter describes "rapidly consuming more and more books while placing increasingly less significance" on the reading material. "Towards a History of Books and Readers," *American Quarterly* 40 (1988): 12.

25. In fact, Riley-as-excavator may have inspired one of the iterations of the "humble little motto" driving Dunbar's "Keep a-Pluggin' Away": "Delve away beneath the surface, / There is treasure farther down." *Collected Poetry of Paul Laurence Dunbar*, 46.

26. Charles S. Johnson, "The Rise of the Negro Magazine," *The Journal of Negro History* 13.1 (Jan. 1928): 21. This article was adapted from a speech delivered in October 1927. The article appears only two months before Johnson, one of the fathers of the Harlem Renaissance, would resign as editor of *Opportunity*, one of the formative magazines of that movement.

27. Raymond Williams, *Keywords: A Vocabulary of Culture and Society* (New York: Oxford University Press, 1983), 87, 88, 92.

28. Ellery Sedgwick, "Magazines and the Profession of Authorship in the United States, 1840–1900," *Papers of the Bibliographical Society of America* 94 (2000), 422; Roger Burlingame, *Of Making Many Books: A Hundred Years of Reading, Writing and Publishing* (New York: Scribner's, 1946), 249. David Perkins differs from most literary historians in his argument that short lyric poems, for which writers were paid, on average, "five to twelve dollars" were not an insignificant source of income. He cites the example of Madison Cawein, who claimed "that his returns from 'magazine verse from the year 1900 were about $100 per month,' at a time when the salary of university professors was likely to be $1500 to $2000 per year." But, compare, for example, William Dean Howells's earnings from prose: "Gilder and Howells concurred that a story for the *Century* would sell at . . . $2,250 for thirty pages" or seventy-five dollars per page. To be sure, Howells was not typical, but neither was Cawein. Perkins, *A History of Modern Poetry, Volume One: From the 1890s to the High Modernist Mode* (1976; Cambridge, MA: Harvard University Press, 2006), 98; John W. Crowley, *The Dean of American Letters: The Late Career of William Dean Howells* (Amherst: University of Massachusetts Press, 1999), 34.

29. This letter is included in the Paul Laurence Dunbar Collection, 1892–1902, Schomburg Center for Research in Black Culture, New York Public Library.

30. Henry Collins Brown, *In the Golden Nineties* (Hastings-on-Hudson: Valentine's Manual, 1928), 233; Earnest Elmo Calkins, "The Hazen Era," *Advertising & Selling* 37 (May 1944): 42.

31. William Webster Ellsworth, *A Golden Age of Authors: A Publisher's Recollection* (Boston: Houghton Mifflin, 1919), 12.

32. Dunbar, "Of Negro Journals," The Paul Laurence Dunbar Collection, Ohio Historical Society, Dayton, reel 4.

33. Bok, *Americanization*, 153.

34. "The Lounger," *Critic*, 7 June 1890, 286.

35. Bok, "The Modern Literary King," 334, 340.

36. Susanna Ashton, "Authorial Affiliations, or, the Clubbing and Collaborating of Brander Matthews," *symploke* 7 (1999): 165–66; Brander Matthews, "Literature as a Profession," in *The Historical Novel and Other Essays* (New York: Scribner's, 1901), 198.

37. Bok, *Americanization*, 295.

38. W. D. Howells, "The Man of Letters as a Man of Business," *Scribner's* 14 (Oct. 1893): 432.

39. During the antebellum period, "no American poet, not even Longfellow, was able to live comfortably or with any sense of security on his income from verse." Charvat, *Profession of Authorship*, 106.

40. Howells, "The Man of Letters," 445.

41. Charvat, *Profession of Authorship*, 133.

42. Matthew Gartner's essay revolves specifically around artisanal work (the labor of "master craftsmen") as it is presented in Longfellow's poetry. "Becoming Longfellow: Work, Manhood, and Poetry," *American Literature* 72 (2000): 63.

43. Ibid., 61–62.

44. W. D. Howells, "Editor's Study," *Harper's New Monthly Magazine* 83 (Nov. 1891): 966.

45. Martin and Hudson, *Dunbar Reader,* 430–31.

46. Ibid., 410.

47. Kevin K. Gaines, *Uplifting the Race: Black Leadership, Politics, and Culture in the Twentieth Century* (Chapel Hill: University of North Carolina Press, 1996), 184.

48. As Howells writes, "our literature has always been distinguished by two tendencies, apparently opposite, but probably parallel: one a tendency toward an elegance refined and polished, both in thought and phrase, almost to tenuity; the other a tendency to grotesqueness, wild and extravagant, to the point of anarchy." "Editor's Study," 964.

49. Johnson, *Book,* 35–36.

50. Martin and Hudson, *Dunbar Reader,* 428.

51. See, for example, Ellen Gruber Garvey's *The Adman in the Parlor: Magazines and the Gendering of Consumer Culture, 1880s to 1910s* (New York: Oxford University Press, 1996).

52. My observations here do not take Dunbar's prose fiction and nonfiction into account, for which he appears to have had a different marketing strategy. In letters written to his literary agent, Paul Revere Reynolds, Dunbar complains of his failure to get the *Century* interested in his fiction. On September 15, 1900, he writes, "I have so often tried them with my stories but I can only get them to handle verse," and, on December 20, 1900, "Mr. [Robert Underwood] Johnson took three poems and as usual sent the stories back." (This letter is included in the Paul Laurence Dunbar Collection, 1892–1902, Schomburg Center for Research in Black Culture, New York Public Library.)

Dunbar published much of his prose fiction in *Lippincott's,* and his relationship with this magazine may explain why they also published fourteen of his poems between 1900 and 1905, putting the magazine second only to the *Century* in number of Dunbar's poems published; conversely, Dunbar was "one of *Lippincott's* chief poets." Although *Lippincott's* is usually not counted among the "elite" magazines with high subscription rates, it cost twenty cents—twice as much as *Munsey's*—and was the "only [magazine] of high grade that Philadelphia could boast" (even though "it was on the decline" by the 1880s). In addition, Jarrett and Morgan speculate that, "in the last few years before his death, the magazine . . . represented one of the few and last places where he could write on his own terms." Mott, *Golden Multitudes,* 400, 87; Jarrett and Morgan, *Complete Stories,* xxxviii.

53. Burlingame, *Of Making Many Books,* 217.

54. Paul Laurence Dunbar, "Early Struggles of a Negro Poet," *Argus* [Albany, NY], 9 March 1902, The Paul Laurence Dunbar Collection, Ohio Historical Society, Dayton, reel 4; Benjamin Brawley, *Paul Laurence Dunbar: Poet of His People* (Port Washington, NY: Kennikat Press, 1967), 21; Cunningham, *Paul Laurence Dunbar and His Song,* 56.

55. Janet Gabler-Hover, "The North–South Reconciliation Theme and the 'Shadow of the Negro' in *Century Illustrated Magazine,*" in *Periodical Literature in Nineteenth-Century America,* ed. Kenneth M. Price and Susan Belasco Smith (Charlottesville: University of Virginia Press, 1995), 240.

56. Reynolds J. Scott-Childress, "Paul Laurence Dunbar and the Project of Cultural Reconstruction," *African American Review* 41 (2007): 368.

57. Cunningham, *Paul Laurence Dunbar and His Song,* 207.

58. Arthur John, *The Best Years of the Century: Richard Watson Gilder, Scribner's Monthly, and the Century Magazine, 1870–1909* (Urbana: University of Illinois Press, 1981), 137, 256.

59. Brawley, *Paul Laurence Dunbar,* 55; Cunningham, *Paul Laurence Dunbar and His Song,* 57.

60. R. U. Johnson, Letter to Dunbar, 8 Dec. 1894, The Paul Laurence Dunbar Collection, Ohio Historical Society, Dayton, reel 1.

61. His references included Brigadier Major-General Thomas J. Wood, James Whitcomb Riley, and James Newton Matthews. Cunningham, *Paul Laurence Dunbar and His Song,* 118.

62. [Frank H. Scott], "The Modern Magazine," *Critic,* 26 May 1894, 364. This article consisted of a transcript of an address delivered by Scott earlier that month.

63. The magazine "received 1,700 manuscripts in 1873, 2,000 in 1874, 2,400 in 1875, and 3,200 in 1876." Matthew Schneirov, *The Dream of a New Social Order: Popular Magazines in America, 1893–1914* (New York: Columbia University Press, 1994), 66.

64. Perkins, *History of Modern Poetry,* 99. Early in his career, Dunbar lamented the fact that it was "so hard to get a hearing for a new voice in the literary world." Martin and Hudson, *Dunbar Reader,* 417.

65. Martin and Hudson, *Dunbar Reader,* 428.

66. Gayle, *Oak and Ivy,* 37.

67. John compares the *Century*'s "In Lighter Vein" department to *Harper's* "The Editor's Drawer," calling the former "[m]ore elastic in content," allowing it to serve "as a vehicle for early experiments in dialect verse and story." *Best Years of the Century,* 257, 20.

68. Garland, *Roadside Meetings,* 182–83.

69. Mott, *Golden Multitudes,* 30.

70. Frank Presbrey, *The History and Development of Advertising* (Garden City, NY: Doubleday, 1929), 381.

71. Culler, "Why Lyric?," 205.

72. Janice Radway, "Learned and Literary Print Cultures in an Age of Professionalization and Diversification," in *A History of the Book in America, Vol. 4: Print in Motion: The Expansion of Publishing and Reading in the United States, 1880–1940* (Chapel Hill: University of North Carolina Press, 2009), 212–13.

73. Garvey, *Ad Man in the Parlor,* 76.

74. Antony Easthope, *Poetry as Discourse* (London: Methuen and Co., 1983), 65.

75. I base the likelihood of Dunbar's having read this issue (May 1882) on the fact that a volume of the *Century* dated only one year later (November 1883–April 1884) is collected among Dunbar's possessions at the Paul Laurence Dunbar House.

76. Martin and Hudson, *Dunbar Reader*, 444.

77. Ibid.

78. I use the term "lowly" as Dunbar uses it in the title of his poetry collection, *Lyrics of Lowly Life*.

79. Dickson D. Bruce articulates the charges of many critics in his claim that "despite Dunbar's professed interest in folk life, the folk Negroes whose lives his dialect poems evoked were not the black people he most admired," pointing to Dunbar's 1901 essay "Negro Society in Washington" in which Dunbar "praised the black elite's distinctive love of pleasure" (9).

80. Dunbar, "Negro Society in Washington," 9.

81. Martin and Hudson, *Dunbar Reader*, 437.

82. A *Boston Herald* review cited on a poster advertising an 1899 reading in Albany called Dunbar "a cultivated young man" who reads with "cultivated expression." (This advertisement is included in the Paul Laurence Dunbar Collection, 1892–1902, at the Schomburg Center for Research in Black Culture, New York Public Library.)

83. "Like Return of a Hero Was Visit of Paul Laurence Dunbar, the Colored Poet, to the N.C.R. Works Where a Few Years Ago He Was Employed on the Force of Janitors—An Enthusiastic Reception Accorded Him by the Employees," *Dayton Evening News*, 7 Jan. 1904, n.p. Thank you to NCR archivist Jeff Opt for this transcription.

84. The third line of this stanza, as printed in *Majors and Minors*, reads "Mockin' bird was singin, fine," but I am assuming that the comma following "singin" is a typographical error and should be an apostrophe.

85. Dunbar's later poems do not show this degree of variation.

86. Paul Laurence Dunbar, undated letter to the editor, The Century Company Records, 1870–1924, New York Public Library.

87. Hamlin Garland, *A Son of the Middle Border* (New York: Macmillan, 1923), 412.

Chapter Five

1. However, it appears to have been fairly common—judging from collections reprinted as part of the *Schomburg Library of Nineteenth-Century Black Women Writers* series and the *African-American Women Writers, 1910–1940* series (both edited by Henry Louis Gates, Jr.)—for women poets of the late nineteenth and early twentieth centuries to include one or two dialect poems in a collection otherwise comprised of standard English poems.

2. Caroline Gebhard, "Inventing a 'Negro Literature': Race, Dialect, and Gender in the Early Work of Paul Laurence Dunbar, James Weldon Johnson, and Alice Dunbar-Nelson," in *Post-Bellum, Pre-Harlem: African American Literature and Culture, 1877–1919*, ed. Barbara McCaskill and Caroline Gebhard (New York: New York University Press, 2006), 172.

3. Martin and Hudson, *Dunbar Reader*, 428. Moore wrote to Dunbar with the following response: "I frankly believe in everyone following his best. If it is so that one has a special aptitude for dialect work, why it is only right that dialect work should be made

a specialty. But if one should be like me—absolutely devoid of the ability to manage dialect—I don't see the necessity of cramming and forcing oneself into that plane because one is a Negro or a Southerner." Pamela Newkirk, ed., *Letters from Black America* (New York: Farrar, Straus, and Giroux, 2009), 272. She apparently observed a difference between the type of Southern dialect represented in Dunbar's and others' poetry, and the Creole dialect she used occasionally in her prose fiction.

4. Susan Zlotnick, "'A Thousand Times I'd Be a Factory Girl': Dialect, Domesticity, and Working-Class Women's Poetry in Victorian Britain," *Victorian Studies* 35.1 (1991): 9.

5. An interesting example of an often-anthologized dialect poem by a woman who fits neither category (neither black bourgeois nor white working-class) is "How Persimmons Took Cah ob der Baby" by Lizzie W. Champney, published originally in *St. Nicholas*. But, as Janet Gray writes, "[d]ialect fades in and out of the narrative, sometimes appearing in quotes, as if to signify that the narrator merely imitates colloquial speech to enliven the poem's diction." Although Champney's social status would have allowed her more liberty to write in dialect without consequence, she still avoided writing a monologic dialect poem. *Race and Time: American Women's Poetics from Antislavery to Racial Modernity* (Iowa City: University of Iowa Press, 2004), 223.

6. Harper had a significant audience, but Johnson was probably "a coterie poet, producing entertaining verse . . . for her own crowd." The Stone Printing and Manufacturing Company of Roanoke, Virginia, which printed her second book, was "the largest and most modern printing establishment in the South," having "developed a broad niche market in the production of high quality, short-run publications for private clients and well-established publishers." Paula Bernat Bennett, "Rewriting Dunbar: Realism, Black Women Poets, and the Genteel," in *Post-Bellum, Pre-Harlem*, 151; Rand Dotson, *Roanoke, Virginia, 1882–1912: Magic City of the New South* (Knoxville: University of Tennessee Press, 2007), 178, 182.

7. Elizabeth McHenry, "Toward a History of Access: The Case of Mary Church Terrell," *American Literary History* 19.2 (2007): 383.

8. Ibid., 382.

9. McHenry writes, "Given their attention to texts associated with the genteel tradition, the extent to which [they] embraced Dunbar's so-called dialect poems is also striking. Praising these poems in particular as 'remarkable . . . masterpieces of their kind,' the editors of the *Women's Era* reprinted Dunbar's 'When De Co'n Pone's Hot' in the fall of 1896." *Forgotten Readers*, 234.

10. "Miss Lois C. Simmons Entertains," *Chicago Defender*, 3 Jan. 1914, 6.

11. Howells, "The Man of Letters," 438.

12. In *Golden Multitudes: The Story of Best Sellers in the United States*, Mott lists several books by dialect writers that according to his formula qualify as best sellers between 1870 and 1900, including Bret Harte's *The Luck of Roaring Camp and Other Stories*; Edward Eggleston's *The Hoosier School-Master*; Mark Twain's *Tom Sawyer, Life on the Mississippi* and *Huckleberry Finn*; Joel Chandler Harris's *Uncle Remus*; James Whitcomb Riley's *The Old Swimmin' Hole and 'Leven More Poems*; Opie Read's *The Jucklins*; and Edward Noyes Westcott's *David Harum*. With the exception of books by children's authors (Louisa May Alcott's *Little Men*, John Habberton's *Helen's Babies*, Margaret Sidney's *Five Little Peppers and How They Grew*, and Frances Hodgson Burnett's *Little Lord Fauntleroy*), an author of detective fiction (Anna Katharine Green's *The Leavenworth Case*), and a Christian author (Edward Payson Roe's *Barriers Burned*

Away and *Opening a Chestnut Burr*), these books account for most of the fictional books by American authors on the list. The others are Lew Wallace's *Ben Hur,* Paul Leicester Ford's *Janice Meredith,* Edward Bellamy's *Looking Backward,* Archibald Clavering Gunter's *Mr. Barnes of New York,* and Stephen Crane's *The Red Badge of Courage.*

13. Martyn Lyons, "New Readers in the Nineteenth Century: Women, Children, Workers," in *A History of Reading in the West,* ed. Guglielmo Cavallo and Roger Chartier (Amherst: University of Massachusetts Press, 1999), 323–24.

14. Melba Joyce Boyd, *Discarded Legacy: Politics and Poetics in the Life of Frances E. W. Harper, 1825–1911* (Detroit: Wayne State University Press, 1994), 150.

15. Ibid., 151, 150.

16. Redding, *To Make a Poet Black,* 42–43.

17. Elizabeth A. Petrino, "'We Are Rising as a People': Frances Harper's Radical Views on Class and Racial Equality in *Sketches of Southern Life,*" *American Transcendental Quarterly* 19.2 (2005): 140.

18. Boyd, *Discarded Legacy,* 150.

19. Gloria T. Hull, "Rewriting Afro-American Literature: A Case for Black Women Writers," in *Politics of Education: Essays from* Radical Teacher, ed. Susan Gushee O'Malley et al. (Albany: State University of New York Press, 1990), 101.

20. Paul Lauter, *Canons and Contexts* (Oxford: Oxford University Press, 1991), 119.

21. Boyd, *Discarded Legacy,* 155. Although, as James Christmann argues, Harper generally "privileges 'standard' speakers" of the younger, bourgeois generation in *Iola Leroy,* the fact that she also dedicates a series of poems to representing the dialect voice of an older-generation character proves her commitment to the population Aunt Chloe represents and her belief that non-dialect speakers are not necessarily the group that stands for the promising future of the race. "Raising Voices, Lifting Shadows: Competing Voice-Paradigms in Frances E. W. Harper's *Iola Leroy,*" *African American Review* 34.1 (March 2000): 10.

22. Frances E. Watkins Harper, "Learning to Read," in *Sketches of Southern Life* (Philadelphia: Ferguson Bros. & Co., 1891), 17–19.

23. Frederich A. Kittler, *Gramophone, Film, Typewriter* (Stanford: Stanford University Press, 1999), 7.

24. Patricia Bizzell, "'Stolen' Literacies in *Iola Leroy,*" in *Popular Literacy: Studies in Cultural Practices and Poetics,* ed. John Trimbur (Pittsburgh: University of Pittsburgh Press, 2001), 144.

25. De Certeau, *Practice of Everyday Life,* 25–28, qtd. in Bernstein, "Poetics," 120.

26. Bernstein, "Poetics," 120.

27. Heather Andrea Williams, *Self-Taught: African American Education in Slavery and Freedom* (Chapel Hill: University of North Carolina Press, 2005), 20.

28. Harper, *Iola Leroy, or Shadows Uplifted,* ed. Frances Smith Foster (Oxford: Oxford University Press, 1988), 44–45.

29. Boyd, *Discarded Legacy,* 164.

30. Janet Cornelius writes, "Historians of education have drawn a distinction between 'Bible Literacy,' whose prime motive was the conservation of piety, and 'liberating literacy,' which facilitates diversity and mobility. The majority of owners who taught slaves were concerned with Bible literacy, and connected their instruction with Christian worship and catechization. The traditional nature of this teaching is shown by the number of slaveowners who gave slaves religion-associated instruction in reading but not in writing, a practice which recalled the early Protestant insistence that even the poor and

powerless should be able to read the word of God for themselves, but that teaching them to write would threaten the social order." "'We Slipped and Learned to Read': Slave Accounts of the Literacy Process, 1830–1865," *Phylon* 44.3 (1983): 171.

31. See Henry Louis Gates's *The Signifying Monkey: A Theory of Afro-American Literary Criticism* (Oxford: Oxford University Press, 1988).

32. Paula Bernat Bennett, *Poets in the Public Sphere: The Emancipatory Project of American Women's Poetry, 1800–1900* (Princeton: Princeton University Press, 2003), 90.

33. P. Gabrielle Forman points out that Harper's essays, however, such as "Women's Political Future," often reject "fixed theories of literacy as an absolute good." "'Reading Aright': White Slavery, Black Referents, and the Strategy of Histotextuality in *Iola Leroy*," *Yale Journal of Criticism* 10.2 (1997): 333.

34. See, for example, Boyd's *Discarded Legacy*, Gray's *Race and Time* (both cited in full above), and Frances Smith Foster's *A Brighter Coming Day: A Frances Ellen Watkins Harper Reader* (New York: The Feminist Press at the City University of New York, 1990).

35. Christmann, "Raising Voices," 13.

36. Harper, *Iola Leroy*, 276.

37. Ibid., 9.

38. Ibid., 22.

39. The desire to keep literacy from slaves is similarly put in moral terms as contrary to "goodness" in Douglass's *Narrative*. After being taught to read by Mrs. Auld, Douglass finds his progress obstructed by her husband, who insisted that literacy was not "good" for slaves: "it could do him no good, but a great deal of harm. It would make him discontented and unhappy." Recognizing Mr. Auld's lack of goodness, Douglass decides to operate according to the reverse of his moral compass, deciding "[t]hat which to him was a great evil, to be carefully shunned, was to me a great good, to be diligently sought." *Narrative of the Life of Frederick Douglass, an American Slave*, ed. Deborah E. McDowell (Oxford: Oxford University Press, 1999), 39.

40. Harper, *Iola Leroy*, 146.

41. Foster, *Brighter Coming Day*, 126.

42. Gray, *Race and Time*, 141.

43. Foster, *Brighter Coming Day*, 126–27.

44. Ibid., 11.

45. Mary Loeffelholz, *From School to Salon: Reading Nineteenth-Century American Women's Poetry* (Princeton: Princeton University Press, 2004), 97.

46. Carla L. Peterson, *"Doers of the Word": African-American Women Speakers & Writers in the North (1830–1880)* (Oxford: Oxford University Press, 1995), 22.

47. Foster, *Brighter Coming Day*, 15; "The Woman Suffragists," *Lancaster Daily Intelligencer*, 22 Feb. 1890, 6.

48. "Council of Women. The Varied Subjects of Interest Discussed in Washington. Complimenting President Willard," *Baltimore Sun*, 25 Feb. 1891, 3.

49. Peterson, *"Doers of the Word,"* 22.

50. Michael Bennett, "Frances Ellen Watkins Sings the Body Electric," in *Recovering the Black Female Body: Self-Representations by African American Women*, ed. Michael Bennett and Vanessa D. Dickerson (New Brunswick: Rutgers University Press, 2001), 20.

51. Frances E. W. Harper, "Free Labor," in *Complete Poems of Frances E. W. Harper*, ed. Maryemma Graham (Oxford: Oxford University Press, 1988), 25.

52. "Pulpit and Platform," [Chicago] *Daily Inter Ocean*, 9 May 1888, 6.

53. Richard J. Powell, "Sartor Africanus," in *Dandies: Fashion and Finesse in Art and Culture*, ed. Susan Fillin-Yeh (New York: New York University Press, 2001), 222.

54. Boyd, *Discarded Legacy,* 150–51.

55. Clara Ann Thompson, "Uncle Rube to the Young People," in *Songs from the Wayside* (Rossmoyne, OH: n.p., 1908), in *Collected Black Women's Poetry,* vol. 2, ed. Joan R. Sherman (Oxford: Oxford University Press, 1998), 52.

56. Siobhan B. Somerville, "'The Prettiest Specimen of Boyhood': Cross-Gender and Racial Disguise in Pauline E. Hopkins's *Winona*," in *Skin Deep, Spirit Strong: The Black Female Body in American Culture,* ed. Kimberly Wallace-Sanders (Ann Arbor: University of Michigan Press, 2002), 201–2.

57. Tavia Nyong'o, "Hiawatha's Black Atlantic Itineraries," in *Traffic in Poems: Nineteenth-Century Poetry and Transatlantic Exchange,* ed. Meredith L. McGill (New Brunswick: Rutgers University Press, 2008), 93–94.

58. The poem is included in *From My People: 400 Years of African American Folklore* and *Honey, Hush!: An Anthology of African-American Women's Humor* (both edited by Daryl C. Dance).

59. Ajuan Maria Mance, *Inventing Black Women: African American Women Poets and Self-Representation, 1877–2000* (Knoxville: University of Tennessee Press, 2007), 35.

60. Ibid.

61. Maggie Pogue Johnson, "What's Mo' Temptin' to the Palate," in *Virginia Dreams: Lyrics for the Idle Hour. Tales of the Time Told in Rhyme* (N.p.: John M. Leonard, 1910), in *Collected Black Women's Poetry,* vol. 4, ed. Joan R. Sherman (Oxford: Oxford University Press, 1988), 29–30.

62. As Zlotnick writes regarding nineteenth-century English working-class men—a claim that I would argue could obtain for African American working-class men in the postbellum South—the domestic sphere held a false nostalgic appeal in the face of the increasing difficulties of the social world outside the home and was "imaginatively transformed into a paradise for husbands." She claims that "it is not surprising that working men would wish to seek refuge from the workaday world of the factories, even if that refuge took the form of poetic fantasies." "'A Thousand Times I'd Be a Factory Girl,'" 10, 11.

63. Maggie Pogue Johnson, "The Drunkard's Dream," in *Six Poets of Racial Uplift: Effie T. Battle, Gertrude Arquene Fisher, Myra Viola Wilds, and Others,* intro. by Gayle Pemberton (New York: G. K. Hall & Co., 1996), 310. Compare "The Drunkard's Child," one of Harper's temperance poems, in which the father's reform comes tragically too late; it is only when he visits his son's deathbed that the child's "smile reached to his callous heart" and he feels "guilt, remorse and shame."

64. Waltye Rasulala (Johnson's granddaughter), in discussion with and e-mail message to the author, 28 Aug. 2011 and 18 Aug. 2011.

65. Johnson dedicates one of her poems ("Poet of Our Race") to Dunbar, and many of her poems, both dialect and standard English, are modeled after his ("Meal Time," for example, is a near copy of his "In the Morning," with "Liza!" replacing "'Lias!").

66. Johnson, "Krismas Dinner," in *Virginia Dreams,* 12–14.

67. Johnson, "De Men Folks ob Today," in *Virginia Dreams,* 44.

68. As Paula Bernat Bennett observes, Johnson's speakers are often "curious about new fashions for women and men, but slyly mocking of them as well." "Rewriting Dunbar," 152.

69. Johnson, "De Wintah Styles," in *Virginia Dreams*, 40–41.
70. Although frock-coats were occasionally abbreviated as "frocks," the term "frock" most frequently referred to women's dresses (and sometimes to monk's attire, men's military uniforms, loose tunics, and children's clothes).
71. Johnson, "I Wish I Was a Grown Up Man," in *Virginia Dreams*, 7.
72. Waltye Rasulala, in discussion with the author, 28 Aug. 2011.
73. Johnson, "Aunt Cloe's Trip to See Miss Lisa Kyle," in *Six Poets of Racial Uplift*, 316–23.
74. Harryette Mullen, "Off the Top," in *Trimmings* (New York: Tender Buttons, 1991), n.p.
75. Bruce, *Black American Writing*, 194.
76. Christmann, "Raising Voices," 6.
77. Deborah E. McDowell, *"The Changing Same": Black Women's Literature, Criticism, and Theory* (Bloomington: Indiana University Press, 1995), 40.
78. A similar preface introduces an 1887 book of poetry titled *Amusement of Idle Hours*, whose author, S. Attwood Butterfield, only "compl[ies] with the request of a few friends . . . but if what I have written here shall cause one human being to be better or happier I will feel myself rewarded for my labor, which has been resorted to only as a favorite amusement for idle hours." *Amusement of Idle Hours* (Indianapolis: C. S. Butterfield, 1887), n.p.
79. Compare Myra Viola Wilds's *Thoughts of Idle Hours* (1915), or C. Augustus Haviland's *A Lawyer's Idle Hours* (1902), or even Byron's 1807 collection of juvenilia *Hours of Idleness*. The subtle change of preposition in Johnson's titles allows her to imagine a shared moment of leisure between author and reader, rather than pointing only to the verse as the product of the author's idleness.
80. Frank Lincoln Mather, ed., *Who's Who of the Colored Race: A General Biographical Dictionary of Men and Women of African Descent*, vol. 1 (Chicago: n.p., 1915), 157.
81. This information comes from Rita B. Dandridge's review of *Black Female Playwrights: An Anthology of Plays before 1950* in MELUS 19 (1994): 142; and from Waltye Rasulala, in discussion with the author, 28 Aug. 2011.
82. For open-armed images of the *alma mater*, see, for example, the statues at the University of Havana, Columbia University, and the University of Illinois at Urbana-Champaign.
83. Johnson, "The Negro Has a Chance" and "The V.N. and C.I.," in *Virginia Dreams*, 15, 8.
84. This is not to say that Johnson and other female dialect poets who valorize "great men" do not also express feminist ideals in their poetry. Johnson's "What Task Must the Woman Fulfill" demonstrates her commitment to the pursuit of woman's rights and equality: "Yea! woman in by-gone years, / Thou wert not recognized."
85. Johnson, "James Hugo Johnston," in *Virginia Dreams*, 55.
86. G. F. Richings, *Evidences of Progress among Colored People* (Philadelphia: Geo. S. Ferguson Co., 1905), 463.
87. Booker T. Washington, *Up from Slavery*, ed. William L. Andrews (Oxford: Oxford University Press, 2008), 32.
88. Dunbar, "Representative American Negroes," in *Dunbar Reader*, 51, 55. In an essay about schoolteachers in *Iola Leroy* and Charles Chesnutt's *Mandy Oxendine*, Cassandra Jackson presents a historical view that corresponds with Dunbar's perspective: "Because black educators were hailed as leaders, to be a black teacher was more than a profession. It was to be a representative, a litmus test for the future of the race. Even

outside black communities, black teachers were often viewed as specimens to gauge the potential of black Americans." "'I Will Gladly Share with Them My Richer Heritage': Schoolteachers in Frances E. W. Harper's *Iola Leroy* and Charles Chesnutt's *Mandy Oxendine*," *African American Review* 37.4 (2003): 555.

89. Kenneth Warren, panel titled "Paul Laurence Dunbar: The Racial Politics of the Nadir," accessed Jan. 1, 2012, http://www.youtube.com/watch?v=07Y01f1NcSQ.

90. Identifying as a "schoolmaster" was apparently acceptable to Longfellow, as it was "a role that could set up no social barrier between him and the common reader." Charvat, *Profession of Authorship*, 129.

91. Johnson, "To Professor Byrd Prillerman," in *Virginia Dreams*, 52–53.

92. Johnson, "Poet of Our Race," in *Virginia Dreams*, 51. Although most popular in the mid nineteenth century, the language of flowers was still culturally resonant decades later when Johnson was writing. For example, Henry Davenport Northrop's *The College of Life, or Practical Self-Educator: A Manual of Self-Improvement for the Colored Race*, published in 1896, contains a chapter titled "The Language and Sentiment of Flowers," which serves as a brief floral dictionary.

93. Along with Dunbar, Washington is featured in several of Johnson's poems, such as "The Lad without a Name," included in her 1915 *Thoughts for Idle Hours*. She claims in a note appended to the poem as it appears in her later *Fallen Blossoms* that it consists of "facts put to poetry after reading his life story," such as the erroneous "fact" that "[h]is mother called him Booker / Just because of books he's fond." Johnson also wrote an elegy for Washington, titled "Tuskegee's Sorrow." In *Six Poets of Racial Uplift*, 352–55.

94. Johnson, "To See Ol' Booker T.," in *Virginia Dreams*, 34–36.

Chapter Six

1. Bernstein, "Poetics," 120.

2. Gavin Jones also discusses Hughes's work as a "continuation of work already begun by Dunbar," but his claim depends instead upon their shared "oscillation between vernacular and 'standard' English." *Strange Talk*, 186.

3. Arnold Rampersad, along with many other scholars, has emphasized the influence of Whitman upon Hughes, calling Hughes "a spiritual and poetic child of the good grey poet," and pointing to such poems as Hughes's "I, Too, Sing America" as evidence of this influence. *The Life of Langston Hughes, Vol. 1, 1902–1941: "I, Too, Sing America"* (Oxford: Oxford University Press, 2002), 28, 95.

4. See, for example, Whitman's "Slang in America" and *An American Primer* for his views on the peculiarity of American English and its use in poetry. In 1894, Hamlin Garland writes that Whitman and Riley represent two phases of what he identifies as a "veritist" (because of the "indiscriminate" use of the label "realist" among his contemporaries) school of poetry, one that is "a closer approach to the passionate speech of modern men." "Productive Conditions of American Literature," *Forum* 17 (Aug. 1894): 690, 697.

5. Okeke-Ezigbo argues that "Dunbar probably inherited his dislike of Whitman from Riley, who, hating 'free verse with uncompromising ardor,' declared that Whitman's poetry 'has positively refused, and still refuses, my applause.' Riley cherished poetry of *heart* appeal, and discredited Whitman for being 'more of a poet at soul than at heart.'" Dunbar's dislike for Whitman is featured in Ishmael Reed's poem "Paul Laurence Dunbar in the Tenderloin." "Paul Laurence Dunbar," 483.

6. Johnson, *Along This Way*, 159.

7. Ibid., 161.

8. Alain Locke, review of *The Weary Blues* by Langston Hughes, in *Critical Essays on Langston Hughes*, ed. Edward J. Mullen (Boston: G. K. Hall and Company, 1986), 44.

9. One year after the publication of the review cited above, in a pamphlet titled *Four Negro Poets,* Alain Locke calls Hughes the "Dunbar of his generation," thereby undermining his previous claim that Hughes is doing the work that Dunbar could not. Locke, ed., *Four Negro Poets,* The Pamphlet Poets Series (New York: Simon and Schuster, 1927), 6.

10. Kenneth Fearing, "Limiting Devices," *The New Masses* (Sept. 1927): 29.

11. Charvat, *Profession of Authorship,* 109–10.

12. Langston Hughes, "The Negro Artist and the Racial Mountain," in *Within the Circle,* 56.

13. Emily Bernard, ed., *Remember Me to Harlem: The Letters of Langston Hughes and Carl Van Vechten* (New York: Vintage, 2001), 36.

14. Michael Fultz, "'The Morning Cometh': African-American Periodicals, Education, and the Black Middle Class, 1900–1930," in *Print Culture in a Diverse America,* ed. James P. Danky and Wayne A. Wiegand (Urbana: University of Illinois Press, 1998), 140.

15. Sterling Brown, "Our Literary Audience," in *Within the Circle,* 70.

16. Henry Louis Gates, preface to *Langston Hughes: Critical Perspectives Past and Present,* ed. Henry Louis Gates, Jr., and K. A. Appiah (New York: Amistad, 1993), xi.

17. Langston Hughes, "Our Wonderful Society: Washington," *Opportunity* 5.8 (Aug. 1927): 226.

18. Raymond Wolters describes student reaction to the anachronism of the moral values enforced in historically black colleges and universities of the 1920s:

> Black students naturally objected to regimentation on the campus, but the discipline was tolerable in the late nineteenth century when it was thought to be prompted by Christian piety and was applied to white students as well as blacks. Yet the tradition of piety remained in force at the black schools long after the leading white colleges had deemphasized their concern for moral uplift and had begun to stress secular scholarship. Thus many blacks suspected that the extraordinarily strict regulations still in force in their schools during the 1920s were prompted by a racist belief that Negroes were particularly sensuous beings who could not discipline themselves and were not prepared to exercise free will. (*The New Negro on Campus: Black College Rebellions of the 1920s* [Princeton: Princeton University Press, 1975], 13)

Apparently, Hughes's views reflected those of many students at historically black colleges and universities during this period.

19. Langston Hughes, "Cowards from the Colleges," *Crisis* 41.8 (Aug. 1934): 226–28.

20. Ibid., 228.

21. Qtd. in Steven C. Tracy, *Langston Hughes & The Blues* (Urbana: University of Illinois Press, 1988), 44.

22. Babette Deutsch, "Four Poets," *The Bookman* 65 (Apr. 1927): 221.

23. See, for example, R. Baxter Miller's "Framing and Framed Languages in Hughes's *Ask Your Mama: 12 Moods for Jazz,*" *MELUS* 17.4 (1991–92): 3–13.

24. Countee Cullen, review of *The Weary Blues* by Langston Hughes, in *Langston Hughes: Critical Perspectives Past and Present*, 4.

25. Langston Hughes, "The Cat and the Saxophone (2 A.M.)," in *The Collected Poems of Langston Hughes*, ed. Arnold Rampersad (New York: Vintage, 1994), 89.

26. Bernard, *Remember Me to Harlem*, 26.

27. In the review mentioned above, grouping Hughes with Pound, Ransom, and Van Doren, Deutsch claims that "[t]he dialect pieces fairly sing themselves when read aloud, and the others show craftsmanship of a high order." She does not associate craftsmanship with the dialect poems. "Four Poets," 221.

28. Ong, *Orality*, 150.

29. Bernard, *Remember Me to Harlem*, 36.

30. Langston Hughes, promotional letter, 13 Oct. 1931, in *The Prentiss Taylor Papers, 1885–1991*, Smithsonian *Archives of American Art*, Series 10, reel 5921, frame 714, accessed Jan. 1, 2012, http://www.aaa.si.edu/collectionsonline/taylpren/container258041.htm.

31. Gerard Genette, *Paratexts: Thresholds of Interpretation* (Cambridge: Cambridge University Press, 1997), 334.

32. Langston Hughes, "The Big-Timer," in *The Negro Mother and Other Dramatic Recitations* (New York: Golden Stair Press, 1931), 14.

33. Kittler, *Discourse Networks*, 6.

34. Bruce Kellner, "Working Friendship: A Harlem Renaissance Footnote," in *The Lithographs of Prentiss Taylor: A Catalogue Raisonné*, ed. Ingrid Rose and Roderick S. Quiroz (Bronx, NY: Fordham University Press, 1996), 13.

35. Edward Burns, ed., *The Letters of Gertrude Stein and Carl Van Vechten, Vol. 1: 1913–1935* (New York: Columbia University Press, 1986), 246.

36. Davey, "Building a Black Audience," 224.

37. Hughes states that "because it was depression times—even a dollar was a lot to some people—I prepared a smaller booklet of some of my newer poems to sell for a quarter." *I Wonder as I Wander: An Autobiographical Journey* (New York: Hill and Wang, 1956), 47.

38. Rampersad, *Life of Langston Hughes 1*, 222.

39. Rampersad calls the offensive title of *Fine Clothes to the Jew*, a title suggested by Carl Van Vechten and taken from the title of one of Hughes's poems, "unfortunate," saying that "no one alerted Hughes to the effect his title would have on sales, which proved to be the opposite to the result of Van Vechten's own crudeness" in the title of his *Nigger Heaven*. *Fine Clothes to the Jew* preceded the publication of *The Negro Mother* by only four years, when the disappointing sales and reception of the former must have been a factor in the presentation of the latter. Bruce Kellner, however, believes that "the possibility of actually realizing some income on [*The Negro Mother*] must have come as a shock, especially when a fourth printing seemed inevitable because of the tour," because, Kellner claims, "[n]either Hughes nor [illustrator Prentiss] Taylor had ever thought of *The Negro Mother* as a commercial venture." Rampersad, *Life of Langston Hughes 1*, 138; Kellner, "Working Friendship," 13–14.

40. I am assuming here that most people buying *The Negro Mother* would do so in order to read it, but I am grateful to Arlene Keizer for pointing out motivations for purchasing the book that I had overlooked: the book could have value as an object for nonreading purposes (for example, to appreciate the illustrations, which take up as much space in *The Negro Mother* as the text). As Leah Price points out, "literary critics tend to act as if reading were the only legitimate use of books. They forget that the book can take

on a ritual function (even, or especially, for nonliterates)." I would add that racial pride and historical importance might also drive people to purchase a book as an artifact or souvenir during one of Hughes's readings. "Reading: The State of the Discipline," *Book History* 7 (2004): 305.

41. Hughes, *I Wonder as I Wander,* 48; Rampersad, *Life of Langston Hughes 1,* 222.

42. Hughes, *I Wonder as I Wander,* 47.

43. McHenry writes, "Much has been written about the absence of literacy skills among African Americans.... [T]he singular identification of African American culture as 'oral in nature' has helped to push aside facts surrounding other language uses—especially those related to reading and writing." *Forgotten Readers,* 4–5.

44. Elizabeth McHenry and Shirley Brice Heath, "The Literate and the Literary: African-American Readers as Writers, 1830–1940," *Written Communication* 11.4 (1994): 429.

45. Carl F. Kaestle et al., *Literacy in the United States: Readers and Reading since 1880* (New Haven: Yale University Press, 1991), 25.

46. Penelope L. Bullock, *The Afro-American Periodical Press, 1838–1909* (Baton Rouge: Louisiana State University Press, 1981), 9.

47. Davey, "Building a Black Audience," 226.

48. Henry Allen Bullock, *A History of Negro Education in the South: From 1619 to the Present* (Cambridge, MA: Harvard University Press, 1967), 173.

49. Hughes, *I Wonder as I Wander,* 55.

50. Hughes, *Shakespeare in Harlem* (New York: Knopf, 1942), n.p.

51. Davey, "Building a Black Audience," 233–34.

52. Hughes, *I Wonder as I Wander,* 50.

53. Hughes, "The Negro Mother," in *The Negro Mother and Other Dramatic Recitations,* 17.

54. Genette, *Paratexts,* 269.

55. The speaker's sentiment echoes that of W. E. B. Du Bois in a piece appearing in the *Crisis:* "We return from the slavery of uniform which the world's madness demanded us to don to the freedom of civil garb. We stand again to look America squarely in the face and call a spade a spade. We sing: this country of ours, despite all its better souls have done and dreamed, is still a shameful land." "Returning Soldiers," *Crisis* 18.1 (May 1919): 14.

56. Hughes, "The Colored Soldier," in *The Negro Mother and Other Dramatic Recitations,* 1–3.

57. The Hughes poem that resembles those of *The Negro Mother* most closely visually, at first glance, is *Ask Your Mama.* The notes alongside this text, unlike those to *The Negro Mother,* give precise instructions for musical accompaniment; they rarely stray into the kind of interdependent parallel narratives that I find in "The Colored Soldier" and "The Big-Timer." R. Baxter Miller writes that "[t]hough the verbal script (the framed language at the center of the page) discloses the voice of the personal narrator who retells history, the musical marginalia (the outer frames) provide the sonorous *complement* of a communal narrative" (emphasis added). There is no information, in other words, in the marginalia that is not intended to support the main text (in this case, musically). However, what would be closer to the equivalent of the notes to the *Negro Mother* are the "Liner Notes" to *Ask Your Mama,* appended to the text. In a challenge to Arnold Rampersad's claim that the "Liner Notes" are "a literal explanation of the poems they refer to," Meta DuEwa Jones writes that "[t]hey resist paraphraseable or explanatory statement and implicitly challenge the mainstream aesthetic notion that the poem must describe,

narrate, or explain. Thus, the note for the poem 'Bird in Orbit' contains sentences that are syntactically logical but are *not* simple declarative statements." They, therefore, like the notes to *The Negro Mother,* produce related but ultimately distinct narratives; they are parallel poems. Miller, "Framing and Framed Languages," 3; Jones, "Listening to What the Ear Demands: Langston Hughes and His Critics," *Callaloo* 25.4 (2002): 1149.

58. "The Colored Soldier" is almost completely in standard English: the only dialect word is "'cause," a clipping that is highly readable. "Broke" and "The Big-Timer" are in dialect; "The Black Clown," "The Negro Mother," and "Dark Youth of the U.S.A." are not in dialect. As James Edward Smethurst points out, the title poem employs "a 'high' literary diction, despite the fact that the poem's speaker is explicitly the ur-mother of the African-American folk whom one would expect to speak in some representation of African-American vernacular after the fashion of the speaker in Hughes's 'Mother to Son.'" *The New Red Negro: The Literary Left and African American Poetry, 1930–1946* (Oxford: Oxford University Press, 1999), 95.

59. Cary Nelson, *Revolutionary Memory: Recovering the Poetry of the American Left* (London: Routledge, 2001), 202.

60. Byerly, "From Schoolroom to Stage," 139.

61. See Byerly's "From Schoolroom to Stage," Collins's "'Agglomerating Dollars" (both cited in full above), and Mark Morrisson's *The Public Face of Modernism: Little Magazines, Audiences, and Reception, 1905–1920* (Madison: University of Wisconsin Press, 2001).

62. Hughes, "The Negro Mother," "The Black Clown," and "Dark Youth of the U.S.A," in *The Negro Mother and Other Dramatic Recitations,* 16–18, 8–11, 19–20.

63. Stanley Schatt, "Langston Hughes: The Minstrel as Artificer," *Journal of Modern Literature* 4 (1974): 115.

64. Steven C. Tracy, for example, quotes Phyllis Brooks Bartlett's 1951 *Poems in Process,* in which she writes that Hughes rarely revises: "The only problem that puzzles him is the arrangement of the lines—where to break them so that their appearance on the page will indicate to the reader how they should be read." What is interesting about Bartlett's observation is that the only revision she finds points to the text's orality, to her own preconceived notion of Hughes's concern about scoring the text. In any case, Tracy disagrees: "Hughes employed revisions to help smooth out dialect, paying close attention to words and punctuation and altering structure for literary purposes" (244–45).

65. Carl Van Vechten, introduction to *The Weary Blues* by Langston Hughes (1926; New York: Knopf, 1947), 13.

66. Jesse S. Crisler, Robert C. Leitz, III, and Joseph R. McElrath, Jr., eds., *An Exemplary Citizen: Letters of Charles W. Chesnutt, 1906–1932* (Stanford: Stanford University Press, 2002), 292.

67. Fowler D. Brooks, *The Applied Psychology of Reading: With Exercises and Directions for Improving Silent and Oral Reading* (New York: D. Appleton, 1926), 132, 54.

68. Herbert G. Lull and H. B. Wilson, *The Redirection of High-School Instruction* (Philadelphia, London, Chicago: J. B. Lippincott Company, 1921), 39.

69. Walter Jekyll, preface to *Songs of Jamaica* by Claude McKay (1912; Miami: Mnemosyne Publishing, 1969), 9.

70. Claude McKay, "Boyhood in Jamaica," *Phylon* 14 (1953): 142.

71. North, *Dialect of Modernism,* 100, 103. Wayne Cooper notes that, "[i]n a recording made near the end of his life, he still retained, after an absence of more than thirty years, the 'quaint' accent of a Jamaican hill countryman." *Claude McKay: Rebel*

Sojourner in the Harlem Renaissance (Baton Rouge: Louisiana State University Press, 1987), 27.

72. Heather Hathaway, *Caribbean Waves: Relocating Claude McKay and Paule Marshall* (Bloomington: Indiana University Press, 1999), 35.

73. Bernstein, "Poetics," 120.

74. Max Eastman, introduction to *Harlem Shadows: The Poems of Claude McKay* by Claude McKay (New York: Harcourt, Brace and Company, 1922), ix.

75. Jekyll, preface, 5.

76. North, *Dialect of Modernism*, 19.

77. Jekyll, preface, 7.

78. Michael North points out (citing Tony Crowley's *Standard English and the Politics of Language*) that alongside arguments that dialectal differences were compromising and tainting the "purity" of the language were arguments that "[d]ialect . . . was 'purer' than the standard written language because it was less affected by printing, education, and 'elocution masters'" (19).

79. North, *Dialect of Modernism*, 106.

80. Bernstein, "Poetics," 120.

81. McKay, "Heartless Rhoda," in *Songs of Jamaica*, 94.

82. Jekyll, preface, 14.

83. Robert Stepto, *From Behind the Veil: A Study of Afro-American Narrative* (Urbana: University of Illinois Press, 1979), 10.

84. Claude McKay, "Author's Word," in *Harlem Shadows*, xix.

85. Claude McKay, *Banana Bottom* (New York: Harper & Row, 1933), 140.

86. Claude McKay, *A Long Way from Home* (New York: Arno Press and the New York Times, 1969), 12–13.

87. Ibid., 13, 66.

88. Hathaway, *Caribbean Waves*, 35.

89. Toolan, "Significations," 34.

90. Balhorn, "Paper Representations," 68–69.

91. Bernstein, "Poetics," 125.

92. Lee M. Jenkins, *The Language of Caribbean Poetry: Boundaries of Expression* (Gainesville. University Press of Florida, 2004), 23.

93. "This Is Why Not," 11.

94. McKay, "To E.M.E.," in *Songs of Jamaica*, 51.

95. Donald Wesling, *Bakhtin and the Social Moorings of Poetry* (Lewisburg, PA: Bucknell University Press, 2003), 64.

96. Claude McKay, "Author's Word," in *Harlem Shadows*, xxi.

97. Ezra Pound, "A Few Don'ts by an Imagiste," *Poetry* 1.6 (March 1913): 201.

98. McKay, "A Dream," in *Songs of Jamaica*, 98.

99. For example, in "Standard Language and Poetic Language," Jan Mukarovsky asserts that "the theory of poetic language is primarily interested in the *differences* between the standard and poetic language" (emphasis added). Paul Kiparsky, also, reveals his assumptions about the distinctiveness of literary language in a critical response to Stanley Fish's essay, "How Ordinary is Ordinary Language?" Kiparsky claims that one of the qualities that distinguishes literary language from ordinary is ambiguity: if an ordinary sentence "happens to have several meanings, only one is relevant, and as part of interpreting the sentence one must find the intended meaning. In poetry, however, ambiguity is a constitutive element, and all meanings of an ambiguous expression become relevant to its interpretation." Both Mukarovsky and Kiparsky assume that poetic language is at one end of a continuum, with ordinary and prosaic language on the other.

Mukarovsky, in fact, uses dialect writing as a parallel to poetic language, in its ability to define itself against the standard, but never really equates them. He proposes, "Let us, for instance, visualize a work in which . . . distortion is carried out by the interpenetration of dialect speech with the standard; it is clear, then, that it is not the standard which is perceived as a distortion of the dialect, but the dialect as a distortion of the standard. . . . The violation of the norm of the standard, its systematic violation, is what makes possible the poetic utilization of language; without this possibility there would be no poetry." Mukarovsky, "Standard Language and Poetic Language," in *A Prague School Reader on Esthetics, Literary Structure, and Style*, selected and translated by Paul L. Garvin (Washington, D.C.: Georgetown University Press, 1964), 17–18; Kiparsky, Commentary, *New Literary History* 5 (1973): 181.

100. Stanley Fish, "How Ordinary Is Ordinary Language?," *New Literary History* 5 (1973): 45.

101. Cary H. Plotkin, *The Tenth Muse: Victorian Philology and the Genesis of the Poetic Language of Gerard Manley Hopkins* (Carbondale: Southern Illinois University Press, 1989), 87.

102. As E. A. Levenston points out, elisions like "o'er" are "common from the Augustan to the Victorian age, but did not survive the First World War." McKay is the exception that proves this rule. *The Stuff of Literature: Physical Aspects of Texts and Their Relation to Literary Meaning* (Albany: State University of New York Press, 1992), 37.

103. Otto Jesperson, *Growth and Structure of the English Language* (1905; Leipzig: B. G. Teubner, 1912), 230–31.

104. Daniel T. McGee, "Dada Da Da: Sounding the Jew in Modernism," *ELH* 68 (2001): 508.

105. Hathaway, *Caribbean Waves*, 35–36.
106. McKay, "Old England," in *Songs of Jamaica*, 64.
107. McKay, "A Dream," in *Songs of Jamaica*, 96–97.
108. Smethurst, *The New Red Negro*, 96.
109. Plotkin, *Tenth Muse*, 88.
110. Hathaway, *Caribbean Waves*, 37.
111. Cooper, *Claude McKay*, 27.
112. Bernstein, "Poetics," 120.
113. McKay, "Strokes of the Tamarind Switch," in *Songs of Jamaica*, 113.

114. North writes that "the notes . . . expose, by their very existence, a metatextual situation that their content tries to obscure. The Buccra to whom Quashie addresses his warning is also the white reader unfamiliar with black Jamaican life. As the first poem in the collection, 'Quashie to Buccra' assumes the traditional role of addressing itself to the reader, in this case warning the white reader in particular against a superficial reading of what's to follow" (*Dialect of Modernism*, 106).

115. Cooper, *Claude McKay*, 37.
116. Gates, *Figures in Black*, 188.
117. Kittler, *Discourse Networks*, 219.

Conclusion

1. Charles A. Greathouse, *Suggestions and Materials. Riley Day Programs* (Indianapolis: n.p., 1915), 5.

2. Roy Harvey Pearce, *The Continuity of American Poetry* (Princeton: Princeton University Press, 1961), 255–56.

3. Davidson, "Towards a History of Books and Readers," 10.

4. Pierre Bourdieu, *Distinction: A Social Critique of the Judgement of Taste,* trans. Richard Nice (Cambridge, MA: Harvard University Press, 1984), 2.

5. Ambrose Bierce, "Prattle," *San Francisco Examiner,* 17 Dec. 1892, 16.

6. Harryette Mullen describes a similar reader response in a different context in "Imagining the Unimagined Reader: Writing to the Unborn and Including the Excluded," *boundary2* 26.1 (1999): 198–203.

7. Aldon Lynn Nielsen, *Black Chant: Languages of African-American Postmodernism* (Cambridge: Cambridge University Press, 1997), 9.

8. Dorri Beam, *Style, Gender, and Fantasy in Nineteenth-Century American Women's Writing* (Cambridge: Cambridge University Press, 2010), 2.

9. S. S. Curry, *Browning and the Dramatic Monologue: Nature and Interpretation of an Overlooked Form of Literature* (Boston: Expression Company, 1908), 225, 227.

10. Wonham, *Playing the Races,* 46.

11. John Timberman Newcomb, *Would Poetry Disappear? American Verse and the Crisis of Modernity* (Columbus: Ohio State University Press, 2004), xxv, xix.

12. Donald Hall, introduction to *The Oxford Book of Children's Verse in America,* ed. Donald Hall (Oxford: Oxford University Press, 1985), xxxv.

13. Scharnhorst, *Opening,* 60, 68, 63.

14. Virginia Jackson, "American Victorian Poetry: The Transatlantic Poetic," *Victorian Poetry* 43 (2005): 159.

15. Linley, "Conjuring the Spirit," 539.

16. Ibid., 537.

17. Loomis, "The Dialect Store," 959.

18. Janice Radway and Perry Frank, "Verse and Popular Poetry," in *Handbook of American Popular Literature,* ed. M. Thomas Inge (New York: Greenwood Press, 1988), 305–6, 299–322.

19. Van Dyke, "James Whitcomb Riley as a Person," 430.

20. Harryette Mullen, "Sleeping with the Dictionary," in *Sleeping with the Dictionary* (Berkeley: University of California Press, 2002), 67.

bibliography

Archives

James Whitcomb Riley Collection, Lilly Library, Indiana University, Bloomington, Indiana.
Paul Laurence Dunbar Collection, 1892–1902, Microfilm Collection, Schomburg Center for Research in Black Culture, New York Public Library.
The Paul Laurence Dunbar Collection, Microfilm Collection, Ohio Historical Society, Dayton.

Secondary Sources

"Ade's Literary map of Indiana." *Bellingham* [WA] *Herald*, 17 May 1905, 7.
"Ah Sin's Reply to Truthful James." *Chicago Tribune*, 22 Jan. 1871, 5.
Alden, William L. "London Literary Letter." *New York Times*, 23 Apr. 1898, BR266.
"Analysis and Comments on 'Little Orphant Annie' by James Whitcomb Riley." Accessed Jan. 1, 2012. http://www.americanpoems.com/poets/James-Whitcomb-Riley/13510/comments.
Anderson, William W. "The Craze for Wrong Spelling." *Dial* 19 (1895): 173.
Andrews, Bruce. *Libretto from White Dialect Poetry*. N.p.: /ubu editions, 2006. Accessed March 15, 2012. http://www.ubu.com/ubu/unpub/Unpub_002_Andrews_Libretto.pdf.
———. *WhDiP, a sequence*. N.p.: /ubu editions, 2006. Accessed March 15, 2012. http://www.ubu.com/ubu/unpub/Unpub_001_Andrews_Whdip.pdf.
Archibald, Mrs. George. "Dialect Spelling." *The Writer* 3 (March 1889): 49–50.
Ashton, Susanna. "Authorial Affiliations, or, the Clubbing and Collaborating of Brander Matthews." *symplokē* 7.1–2 (1999): 165–87.
Baldwin, Rebekah. "An Unpublished Letter Written to Paul Laurence Dunbar, 1894." Ed. Gossie Harold Hudson. *Journal of Negro History* 55 (1970): 215–17.

Balhorn, Mark. "Paper Representations of the Non-Standard Voice." *Visible Language* 32 (1998): 56–74.
Barnes, Walter. *The Children's Poets: Analyses and Appraisals of the Greatest English and American Poets for Children*. New York: World Book Company, 1925.
Baron, Dennis E. *Grammar and Good Taste: Reforming the American Language*. New Haven: Yale University Press, 1982.
Beam, Dorri. *Style, Gender, and Fantasy in Nineteenth-Century American Women's Writing*. Cambridge: Cambridge University Press, 2010.
Benjamin, Walter. "The Work of Art in the Age of Mechanical Reproduction." In Walter Benjamin, *Illuminations*, ed. Hannah Arendt, trans. Harry Zohn, 217–51. New York: Schocken, 1968.
Bennett, Michael. "Frances Ellen Watkins Sings the Body Electric." In *Recovering the Black Female Body: Self-Representations by African American Women*, ed. Michael Bennett and Vanessa D. Dickerson, 19–40. New Brunswick: Rutgers University Press, 2001.
Bennett, Paula Bernat. *Poets in the Public Sphere: The Emancipatory Project of American Women's Poetry, 1800–1900*. Princeton: Princeton University Press, 2003.
———. "Rewriting Dunbar: Realism, Black Women Poets, and the Genteel." In *Post-Bellum, Pre-Harlem: African American Literature and Culture, 1877–1919*, ed. Barbara McCaskill and Caroline Gebhard, 146–61. New York: New York University Press, 2006.
Bernard, Emily, ed. *Remember Me to Harlem: The Letters of Langston Hughes and Carl Van Vechten*. New York: Vintage, 2001.
Bernstein, Charles. "Poetics of the Americas." In *Reading Race in American Poetry: "An Area of Act,"* ed. Aldon Lynn Nielsen, 107–32. Urbana: University of Illinois Press, 2000.
Bierce, Ambrose. "Prattle." *San Francisco Examiner*, 17 Dec. 1892, 16.
Bizzell, Patricia. "'Stolen' Literacies in *Iola Leroy*." In *Popular Literacy: Studies in Cultural Practices and Poetics*, ed. John Trimbur, 143–50. Pittsburgh: University of Pittsburgh Press, 2001.
Blair, Walter. Introduction to *The Mirth of a Nation: America's Great Dialect Humor*, ed. Walter Blair and Raven McDavid, ix–xxvii. Minneapolis: University of Minnesota Press, 1983.
Blanck, Jacob. *Bibliography of American Literature*. 9 vols. New Haven: Yale University Press, 1955–91.
Bok, Edward. *The Americanization of Edward Bok: The Autobiography of a Dutch Boy Fifty Years After*. 1920; New York: Scribner's, 1921.
———. "The Modern Literary King." *Forum* 20 (Nov. 1895): 334–43.
Borus, Daniel. *Writing Realism: Howells, James, and Norris in the Mass Market*. Chapel Hill: University of North Carolina Press, 1989.
Bourdieu, Pierre. *Distinction: A Social Critique of the Judgement of Taste*, trans. Richard Nice. Cambridge, MA: Harvard University Press, 1984.
Boyd, Melba Joyce. *Discarded Legacy: Politics and Poetics in the Life of Frances E. W. Harper, 1825–1911*. Detroit: Wayne State University Press, 1994.
Bramen, Carrie Tirado. *The Uses of Variety: Modern Americanism and the Quest for National Distinctiveness*. Cambridge, MA: Harvard University Press, 2000.
Brawley, Benjamin. "Dunbar Thirty Years After." *Southern Workman* 59 (Apr. 1930): 189–91.
———. *Paul Laurence Dunbar: Poet of His People*. Port Washington, NY: Kennikat Press, 1967.

"Bret Harte's 'Heathen Chinee.'" *New York Times,* 13 Nov. 1910, SM5.
Brodhead, Richard H. *Cultures of Letters: Scenes of Reading and Writing in Nineteenth-Century America.* Chicago: University of Chicago Press, 1993.
Brody, Jennifer DeVere. *Punctuation: Art, Politics, and Play.* Durham: Duke University Press, 2008.
Bronson, Walter C. *A Short History of American Literature, Designed Primarily for Use in Schools and Colleges.* Boston: D. C. Heath & Co., 1900.
Brooks, Fowler D. *The Applied Psychology of Reading: With Exercises and Directions for Improving Silent and Oral Reading.* New York: D. Appleton, 1926.
Brooks, Noah. "Bret Harte: A Biographical and Critical Sketch." *Overland Monthly* 40.3 (Sept. 1902): 201–7.
Brooks, Tim. *Lost Sounds: Blacks and the Birth of the Recording Industry, 1890–1919.* Urbana: University of Illinois Press, 2004.
Brown, Henry Collins. *In the Golden Nineties.* Hastings-on Hudson: Valentine's Manual, 1928.
Brown, Sterling. "Our Literary Audience." In *Within the Circle: An Anthology of African American Literary Criticism from the Harlem Renaissance to the Present,* ed. Angelyn Mitchell, 69–78. Durham: Duke University Press, 1994.
Bruce, Dickson D. Jr. *Black American Writing from the Nadir: The Evolution of a Literary Tradition, 1877–1915.* Baton Rouge: Louisiana University Press, 1989.
Buell, Lawrence. *New England Literary Culture: From Revolution through Renaissance.* New York: Cambridge University Press, 1986.
Bullock, Henry Allen. *A History of Negro Education in the South: From 1619 to the Present.* Cambridge, MA: Harvard University Press, 1967.
Bullock, Penelope L. *The Afro-American Periodical Press, 1838–1909.* Baton Rouge: Louisiana State University Press, 1981.
Burlingame, Roger. *Of Making Many Books: A Hundred Years of Reading, Writing and Publishing.* New York: Scribner's, 1946.
Burns, Edward, ed. *The Letters of Gertrude Stein and Carl Van Vechten, Vol. 1: 1913–1935.* New York: Columbia University Press, 1986.
Bush, Harold K. "'Absorbing the Character': James Whitcomb Riley and Mark Twain's Theory of Performance." *American Literary Realism* 31.3 (1999): 31–47.
Butterfield, S. Attwood, M.D. *Amusement of Idle Hours.* Indianapolis: C. S. Butterfield, 1887.
Byerly, Alison. "From Schoolroom to Stage: Reading Aloud and the Domestication of Victorian Theater." In *Culture and Education in Victorian England,* ed. Patrick Scott and Pauline Fletcher, 125–41. Lewisburg: Bucknell University Press, 1990.
Calkins, Earnest Elmo. "The Hazen Era." *Advertising & Selling* 37 (May 1944): 42, 80.
Camlot, Jason. "Early Talking Books: Spoken Recordings and Recitation Anthologies, 1880–1920." *Book History* 6 (2003): 147–73.
Canning, Charlotte. "The Platform Versus the Stage: The Circuit Chautauqua's Antitheatrical Theatre." *Theatre Journal* 50 (1998): 303–18.
Carpenter, Charles. *History of American Schoolbooks.* Philadelphia: University of Pennsylvania Press, 1963.
Carpenter, J. E. *The Popular Elocutionist and Reader.* London: Frederick Warne and Company, 1894.
Certeau, Michel de. *The Practice of Everyday Life.* 1974; Berkeley: University of California Press, 1984.
Chakkalakal, Tess. "To Make an Old Century New." *American Quarterly* 62.4 (Dec. 2010): 1001–12.

Charvat, William. *The Profession of Authorship in America, 1800–1870: The Papers of William Charvat*. Ed. Matthew J. Bruccoli. Columbus: Ohio State University Press, 1968.
Cheney, Warren. "Francis Bret Harte." *Overland Monthly* 1.1 (Jan. 1883): 68–81.
Chesnutt, Charles. *An Exemplary Citizen: Letters of Charles W. Chesnutt, 1906–1932*. Ed. Jesse S. Crisler, Robert C. Leitz, III, and Joseph R. McElrath, Jr. Stanford: Stanford University Press, 2002.
Christmann, James. "Raising Voices, Lifting Shadows: Competing Voice-Paradigms in Frances E. W. Harper's *Iola Leroy*." *African American Review* 34.1 (March 2000): 5–18.
Clark, Davis W. *Paul Laurence Dunbar Laurel-Decked*. Dayton: Paul Laurence Dunbar Scholarship Fund, 1909.
Cmiel, Kenneth. "'A Broad Fluid Language of Democracy': Discovering the American Idiom." *Journal of American History* 79 (1992): 913–36.
Cohen, Michael. "Paul Laurence Dunbar and the Genres of Dialect." *African American Review* 41 (2007): 247–57.
Collins, Philip. "'Agglomerating Dollars with Prodigious Rapidity': British Pioneers on the American Lecture Circuit." In *Victorian Literature and Society: Essays Presented to Richard D. Altick*, ed. James R. Kincaid and Albert J. Kuhn, 3–29. Columbus: Ohio State University Press, 1983.
———. *Reading Aloud: A Victorian Métier*. Lincoln: The Tennyson Society, 1972.
Cooper, Wayne. *Claude McKay: Rebel Sojourner in the Harlem Renaissance*. Baton Rouge: Louisiana State University Press, 1987.
Cornelius, Janet. "'We Slipped and Learned to Read': Slave Accounts of the Literacy Process, 1830–1865." *Phylon* 44.3 (1983): 171–86.
"Council of Women. The Varied Subjects of Interest Discussed in Washington. Complimenting President Willard." *Baltimore Sun,* 25 Feb. 1891, 3.
Cox, John Harrington. "The Poem and the Printed Page." *English Journal* 3.7 (Sept. 1914): 399–407.
Crowder, Richard. *Those Innocent Years: The Legacy and Inheritance of a Hero of the Victorian Era, James Whitcomb Riley*. Indianapolis: Bobbs-Merrill, 1957.
Crowley, John W. *The Dean of American Letters: The Late Career of William Dean Howells*. Amherst: University of Massachusetts Press, 1999.
Cullen, Countee. Review of *The Weary Blues* by Langston Hughes. In *Langston Hughes: Critical Perspectives Past and Present*. Ed. Henry Louis Gates, Jr., and K. A. Appiah, 4. New York: Amistad, 1993.
Culler, Jonathan. "Why Lyric?" *PMLA* 123 (2008): 201–6.
Cunningham, Virginia. *Paul Laurence Dunbar and His Song*. New York: Dodd, Mead, 1948.
Curry, S. S. *Browning and the Dramatic Monologue: Nature and Interpretation of an Overlooked Form of Literature*. Boston: Expression Company, 1908.
Daggett, Mabel Potter. *In Lockerbie Street: A Little Appreciation of James Whitcomb Riley*. New York: B. W. Dodge & Company, 1909.
Dale, Edgar, and Jeanne Chall. "The Concept of Readability." *Elementary English* 26 (1949): 19–26.
Dandridge, Rita B. Review of *Black Female Playwrights: An Anthology of Plays before 1950*. *MELUS* 19 (1994): 141–43.
Davey, Elizabeth. "Building a Black Audience in the 1930s: Langston Hughes, Poetry Readings, and the Golden Stair Press." In *Print Culture in a Diverse America*, ed.

James P. Danky and Wayne A. Wiegand, 223–43. Champaign: University of Illinois Press, 1998.

Davidson, Cathy N. "Towards a History of Books and Readers." *American Quarterly* 40 (1988): 7–17.

Davis, Charles T. *Black Is the Color of the Cosmos: Essays on Afro-American Literature and Culture, 1942–1981.* New York: Garland Publishing, Inc., 1982.

de Castell, Suzanne, and Allan Luke. "Models of Literacy in North American Schools: Social and Historical Conditions and Consequences." In *Literacy, Society, and Schooling: A Reader,* ed. Suzanne de Castell, Allan Luke, and Kieran Egan, 87–109. Cambridge: Cambridge University Press, 1986.

"The Decay of 'Dialect Poetry.'" *Cincinnati Commercial,* 24 July 1871, 4.

Deutsch, Babette. "Four Poets." *The Bookman* 65 (Apr. 1927): 220–21.

Dotson, Rand. *Roanoke, Virginia, 1882–1912: Magic City of the New South.* Knoxville: University of Tennessee Press, 2007.

Douglass, Frederick. *Narrative of the Life of Frederick Douglass, an American Slave.* Ed. Deborah E. McDowell. Oxford: Oxford University Press, 1999.

Dreiser, Theodore. *A Hoosier Holiday.* New York: John Lane Company; London: John Lane, The Bodley Head, 1916.

Du Bois, W. E. B. "Returning Soldiers." *Crisis* 18.1 (May 1919): 13–14.

Duckett, Margaret. "Plain Language from Bret Harte." *Nineteenth-Century Fiction* 11.4 (1957): 241–60.

Dunbar, Paul Laurence. *The Collected Poetry of Paul Laurence Dunbar.* Ed. Joanne M. Braxton. Charlottesville: University of Virginia, 1993.

———. *The Complete Stories of Paul Laurence Dunbar.* Ed. Gene Andrew Jarrett and Thomas Lewis Morgan. Athens: Ohio University Press, 2005.

———. "The Dilettante." *Century* 50.3 (July 1895): 480.

———. *In His Own Voice: The Dramatic and Other Uncollected Works of Paul Laurence Dunbar.* Ed. Herbert Woodward Martin and Ronald Primeau. Athens: Ohio University Press, 2002.

———. "Negro Life in Washington." *Harper's Weekly,* 13 Jan. 1900, 32.

———. "Negro Society in Washington." *Saturday Evening Post,* 14 Dec. 1901, 9.

———. *The Paul Laurence Dunbar Reader.* Ed. Jay Martin and Gossie H. Hudson. New York: Dodd, Mead and Co., 1975.

———. "The Poet and His Song." *Current Literature* 21 (Feb. 1897): 102.

Dunbar-Nelson, Alice Moore, ed., *The Dunbar Speaker and Entertainer.* Naperville: J. L. Nichols & Co., 1920.

———. "The Poet and His Song." *AME Church Review* 31 (Oct. 1914): 121–35.

Easthope, Antony. *Poetry as Discourse.* London: Methuen and Co., 1983.

Eastman, Max. Introduction to *Harlem Shadows: The Poems of Claude McKay* by Claude McKay, ix–xviii. New York: Harcourt, Brace and Company, 1922.

Eggleston, Edward. *The Hoosier School-Master: A Story of Backwoods Life in Indiana.* New York: Macmillan Company, 1928.

Elliott, Kamilla. *Rethinking the Novel/Film Debate.* Cambridge: Cambridge University Press, 2003.

Ellsworth, William Webster. *A Golden Age of Authors: A Publisher's Recollection.* Boston: Houghton Mifflin, 1919.

Evans, Taliesin. "History of the 'Heathen Chinee.'" *Overland Monthly* 40.3 (Sept. 1902): 229.

Fearing, Kenneth. "Limiting Devices." *The New Masses* (Sept. 1927): 29.

Fish, Stanley. "How Ordinary Is Ordinary Language?" *New Literary History* 5 (1973): 41–54.

Fishkin, Shelley Fisher. "Race and the Politics of Memory: Mark Twain and Paul Laurence Dunbar." *Journal of American Studies* 40 (2006): 283–309.

Fletcher, L. B. "Dialect Spelling." *The Writer* 4 (Feb. 1890): 26–27.

Forman, P. Gabrielle. "'Reading Aright': White Slavery, Black Referents, and the Strategy of Histotextuality in *Iola Leroy*." *Yale Journal of Criticism* 10.2 (1997): 327–54.

Foster, Frances Smith. *A Brighter Coming Day: A Frances Ellen Watkins Harper Reader.* New York: The Feminist Press at the City University of New York, 1990.

Fultz, Michael. "'The Morning Cometh': African-American Periodicals, Education, and the Black Middle Class, 1900–1930." In *Print Culture in a Diverse America*, ed. James P. Danky and Wayne A. Wiegand, 129–48. Urbana: University of Illinois Press, 1998.

Gabler-Hover, Janet. "The North–South Reconciliation Theme and the 'Shadow of the Negro' in *Century Illustrated Magazine*." In *Periodical Literature in Nineteenth-Century America*, ed. Kenneth M. Price and Susan Belasco Smith, 239–56. Charlottesville: University of Virginia Press, 1995.

Gaines, Kevin K. *Uplifting the Race: Black Leadership, Politics, and Culture in the Twentieth Century.* Chapel Hill: University of North Carolina Press, 1996.

Galow, Timothy W. "Literary Modernism in the Age of Celebrity." *Modernism/Modernity* 17.2 (2010): 313–29.

Garland, Hamlin. *Commemorative Tribute to James Whitcomb Riley.* New York: American Academy of Arts and Letters, 1922.

———. "Productive Conditions of American Literature." *Forum* 17 (Aug. 1894): 690–98.

———. "Real Conversations—IV, A Dialogue between James Whitcomb Riley and Hamlin Garland." *McClure's* 2.3 (Feb. 1894): 219–34.

———. *Roadside Meetings.* New York: Macmillan, 1930.

———. *A Son of the Middle Border.* New York: Macmillan, 1923.

Gartner, Matthew. "Becoming Longfellow: Work, Manhood, and Poetry." *American Literature* 72 (2000): 59–86.

Garvey, Ellen Gruber. *The Adman in the Parlor: Magazines and the Gendering of Consumer Culture, 1880s to 1910s.* New York: Oxford University Press, 1996.

Gates, Henry Louis, Jr. *Figures in Black: Words, Signs, and the "Racial" Self.* New York: Oxford, 1987.

———. Foreword to *In His Own Voice: The Dramatic and Other Uncollected Works of Paul Laurence Dunbar*, ed. Herbert Woodward Martin and Ronald Primeau, xi–xiv. Athens: Ohio University Press, 2002.

———. Preface to *Langston Hughes: Critical Perspectives Past and Present*, ed. Henry Louis Gates, Jr., and K. A. Appiah, ix–xii. New York: Amistad, 1993.

Gayle, Addison. *Oak and Ivy: A Biography of Paul Laurence Dunbar.* Garden City, NY: Doubleday, 1971.

Gebhard, Caroline. "Inventing a 'Negro Literature': Race, Dialect, and Gender in the Early Work of Paul Laurence Dunbar, James Weldon Johnson, and Alice Dunbar-Nelson." In *Post-Bellum, Pre-Harlem: African American Literature and Culture, 1877–1919*, ed. Barbara McCaskill and Caroline Gebhard, 162–78. New York: New York University Press, 2006.

Genette, Gerard. *Paratexts: Thresholds of Interpretation.* Cambridge: Cambridge University Press, 1997.

[Gilder, Jeanette.] "The Lounger." *Critic: A Weekly Review of Literature and the Arts*, 7 June 1890, 286.

Gitelman, Lisa. *Scripts, Grooves, and Writing Machines: Representing Technology in the Edison Era*. Stanford: Stanford University Press, 2000.
Gray, Janet. *Race and Time: American Women's Poetics from Antislavery to Racial Modernity*. Iowa City: University of Iowa Press, 2004.
Gray, Lillian. *Teaching Children to Read*, 3rd ed. New York: Ronald Press, 1963.
Gray, Paul H. "Poet as Entertainer: Will Carleton, James Whitcomb Riley, and the Rise of the Poet-Performer Movement." *Literature in Performance: A Journal of Literary and Performing Art* 5.1 (Nov. 1984): 1–12.
Greathouse, Charles A. *Suggestions and Materials. Riley Day Programs*. Indianapolis: n.p., 1915.
Hall, Donald. Introduction to *The Oxford Book of Children's Verse in America*, ed. Donald Hall, xxiii–xxxviii. Oxford: Oxford University Press, 1985.
Halttunen, Karen. *Confidence Men and Painted Women: A Study of Middle-Class Culture in America, 1830–1870*. New Haven: Yale University Press, 1982.
Harper, Frances E. W. *Complete Poems of Frances E. W. Harper*. Ed. Maryemma Graham. Oxford: Oxford University Press, 1988.
———. *Iola Leroy, or Shadows Uplifted*. Ed. Frances Smith Foster. Oxford: Oxford University Press, 1988.
———. *Sketches of Southern Life*. Philadelphia: Ferguson Bros. & Co., 1891.
Harris, W. T. "The Education of the Negro." *Atlantic Monthly* 69 (June 1892): 721–36.
Harte, Francis Bret. *Facsimile of the Original Manuscript of the Heathen Chinee, as Written for the Overland Monthly*. San Francisco: J. H. Carmany, 1871.
———. *The Luck of the Roaring Camp and Other Writings*. New York: Penguin, 2001.
———. *Poems*. Boston: James R. Osgood and Company, 1871.
———. *The Poetical Works of Bret Harte*. Boston and New York: Houghton, Mifflin and Company, 1899.
———. "The Spelling Bee at Angel's (Reported by Truthful James)." *Scribner's* 17.1 (Nov. 1879): 38–40.
Hathaway, Heather. *Caribbean Waves: Relocating Claude McKay and Paule Marshall*. Bloomington: Indiana University Press, 1999.
Hazeltine, Mayo Williamson. *Chats about Books: Poets and Novelists*. New York: Scribner's, 1883.
Heath, Shirley Brice. "Literacy and Language Change." In *Languages and Linguistics: The Interdependence of Theory, Data, and Application*, ed. Deborah Tannen and James E. Alatis, Georgetown University Roundtable on Languages and Linguistics 1985, 282–93. Washington, D.C.: Georgetown University Press, 1985.
———. "Standard English: Biography of a Symbol." In *Standards and Dialects in English*, ed. Timothy Shopen and Joseph M. Williams, 3–32. Cambridge: Winthrop, 1980.
———. "Toward an Ethnohistory of Writing in American Education." In *Writing: The Nature, Development and Teaching of Written Communication, Vol. 1: Variation in Writing: Functional and Linguistic-Cultural Differences*, ed. Marcia Farr Whiteman, 25–46. Hillsdale, NJ: Lawrence Erlbaum Associates, 1981.
Henkin, David. *City Reading: Written Words and Public Spaces in Antebellum New York*. New York: Columbia University Press, 1999.
Heywood, J. C. *How They Strike Me, These Authors*. Philadelphia: J. B. Lippincott & Co., 1877.
Hibbitt, George W. "Poetry and Speech." *Frontier and Midland* 17.3 (Spring 1937): 160.
Hind, C. Lewis. *Authors and I*. New York: John Lane Company; London: John Lane, The Bodley Head, 1921.

Holmes, Oliver Wendell. "Notes." *Book News* 13 (Oct. 1894): 53.
Horton, Eliza Ann. *The Poems of Annie Hawthorne*. Ed. E. Jay Hanford. New York: The Grafton Press, 1910.
Howells, William Dean. "Editor's Study." *Harper's New Monthly Magazine* 83 (Nov. 1891): 964–68.
———. Introduction to *Lyrics of Lowly Life* by Paul Laurence Dunbar, xiii–xx. New York: Dodd, Mead, 1896.
———. "The Man of Letters as a Man of Business." *Scribner's* 14 (Oct. 1893): 432.
———. "Mark Twain." *Century* 24 (Sept. 1882): 780–83.
———. "The New Poetry." *The North American Review* 168 (May 1899): 581–93.
———. Review of *Majors and Minors* by Paul Laurence Dunbar. *Harper's Weekly*, 27 June 1896, 630.
Hudson, Roy F. "The Contributions of Bret Harte to Western Oratory." *Western American Literature* 2 (1967): 213–22.
Huey, Edmund Burke. *The History and Pedagogy of Reading, with a Review of the History of Reading and Writing and of Methods, Texts, and Hygiene in Reading*. New York: Macmillan, 1916.
Hughes, Langston. *The Collected Poems of Langston Hughes*. Ed. Arnold Rampersad. New York: Vintage, 1994.
———. "Cowards from the Colleges." *Crisis* 41.8 (Aug. 1934): 226–28.
———. *I Wonder as I Wander: An Autobiographical Journey*. New York: Hill and Wang, 1956.
———. "The Negro Artist and the Racial Mountain." In *Within the Circle: An Anthology of African American Literary Criticism from the Harlem Renaissance to the Present*, ed. Angelyn Mitchell, 55–59. Durham: Duke University Press, 1994.
———. *The Negro Mother and Other Dramatic Recitations*. New York: Golden Stair Press, 1931.
———. "Our Wonderful Society: Washington." *Opportunity* 5.8 (Aug. 1927): 226–27.
———. Promotional Letter, 13 Oct. 1931. In The Prentiss Taylor Papers, 1885–1991, Smithsonian *Archives of American Art,* Series 10, reel 5921, frame 714. Accessed Jan. 1, 2012. http://www.aaa.si.edu/collectionsonline/taylpren/container258041.htm.
———. *Shakespeare in Harlem*. New York: Knopf, 1942.
Hull, Gloria. "Rewriting Afro-American Literature: A Case for Black Women Writers." In *Politics of Education: Essays from Radical Teacher*, ed. Susan Gushee O'Malley et al., 99–109. Albany: State University of New York Press, 1990.
Hutcheon, Linda. *A Theory of Adaptation*. New York: Routledge, 2006.
Hyde, George Merriam. "A New Crop of Dialect." *The Bookman* 6 (Sept. 1897–Feb. 1898): 56–57.
Ives, Sumner. "A Theory of Literary Dialect." *Tulane Studies in English* 2 (1950): 137–82.
Jackson, Cassandra. "'I Will Gladly Share with Them My Richer Heritage': Schoolteachers in Frances E. W. Harper's *Iola Leroy* and Charles Chesnutt's *Mandy Oxendine*." *African American Review* 37.4 (2003): 553–68.
Jackson, Virginia. "American Victorian Poetry: The Transatlantic Poetic." *Victorian Poetry* 43 (2005): 157–64.
———. *Dickinson's Misery: A Theory of Lyric Reading*. Princeton: Princeton University Press, 2005.
Jarrett, Gene Andrew. *Deans and Truants: Race and Realism in African-American Literature*. Philadelphia: University of Pennsylvania Press, 2007.

Jekyll, Walter. Preface to *Songs of Jamaica* by Claude McKay, 5–9. 1912; Miami: Mnemosyne Publishing, 1969.
Jenkins, Lee. *The Language of Caribbean Poetry: Boundaries of Expression.* Gainesville: University Press of Florida, 2004.
Jesperson, Otto. *Growth and Structure of the English Language.* 1905; Leipzig: B. G. Teubner, 1912.
John, Arthur. *The Best Years of the Century: Richard Watson Gilder, Scribner's Monthly, and the Century Magazine, 1870–1909.* Urbana: University of Illinois Press, 1981.
Johnson, Charles S. "The Rise of the Negro Magazine." *The Journal of Negro History* 13.1 (Jan. 1928): 7–21.
Johnson, Dale D., and James F. Baumann. "Word Identification." In *Handbook of Reading Research,* vol. 3, ed. P. David Pearson, 583–608. 1984; New York: Lawrence Erlbaum Associates, 2002.
Johnson, James Weldon. *Along This Way: The Autobiography of James Weldon Johnson.* 1933; New York: Penguin, 1990.
———. *The Book of American Negro Poetry.* 1931; San Diego: Harcourt Brace Jovanovich, 1983.
Johnson, Maggie Pogue. *Six Poets of Racial Uplift: Effie T. Battle, Gertrude Arquene Fisher, Myra Viola Wilds, and Others.* Introduction by Gayle Pemberton. New York: G. K. Hall & Co., 1996.
———. *Virginia Dreams: Lyrics for the Idle Hour. Tales of the Time Told in Rhyme* (N.p.: John M. Leonard, 1910). In *Collected Black Women's Poetry,* vol. 4, ed. Joan R. Sherman. Oxford: Oxford University Press, 1988.
Johnson, Merle. *You Know These Lines! A Bibliography of the Most Quoted Verses in American Poetry.* New York: G. A. Baker and Company, 1935.
Jones, Gavin. *Strange Talk: The Politics of Dialect Literature in Gilded Age America.* Berkeley: University of California Press, 1999.
Jones, Meta DuEwa. "Listening to What the Ear Demands: Langston Hughes and His Critics." *Callaloo* 25.4 (2002): 1145–75.
Kaestle, Carl F., et al. *Literacy in the United States: Readers and Reading since 1880.* New Haven: Yale University Press, 1991.
Kealing, H. T. Review of *Majors and Minors* by Paul Laurence Dunbar. *AME Church Review* 13 (Oct. 1896): 256–59.
Keats, John. *Complete Poems.* Cambridge, MA: Harvard University Press, 1982.
Kellner, Bruce. "Working Friendship: A Harlem Renaissance Footnote." In *The Lithographs of Prentiss Taylor: A Catalogue Raisonné,* ed. Ingrid Rose and Roderick S. Quiroz, 11–18. Bronx, NY: Fordham University Press, 1996.
Kelly, Fred C. "James Whitcomb Riley's Start." *New York Times,* 21 May 1911, X5.
Kesterson, David B. "The Literary Comedians and the Language of Humor." *Studies in American Humor,* new series, 1 (1982): 44–51.
Kilton, Tom. "The American Railroad as Publisher, Bookseller, and Librarian." *Journal of Library History* 17.1 (1974): 39–64.
Kinnamon, Keneth. "Three Black Writers and the Anthologized Canon." In *American Realism and the Canon,* ed. Tom Quirk and Gary Scharnhorst, 143–53. Newark: University of Delaware Press, 1994.
Kiparsky, Paul. Commentary. *New Literary History* 5 (1973): 177–85.
Kittler, Frederich A. *Discourse Networks, 1800/1900.* Trans. Michael Metteer, with Chris Cullens. Stanford: Stanford University Press, 1990.
———. *Gramophone, Film, Typewriter.* Stanford: Stanford University Press, 1999.

Kowalewski, Michael. "Quoting the Wicked Wit of the West: Frontier Reportage and Western Vernacular." In *Reading the West: New Essays on the Literature of the American West*, ed. Michael Kowalewski, 82–98. Cambridge: Cambridge University Press, 1996.

Krapp, George Philip. *The English Language in America*. New York: The Century Company, 1925.

Kreilkamp, Ivan. "Victorian Poetry's Modernity." *Victorian Poetry* 41 (2003): 603–11.

———. *Voice and the Victorian Storyteller*. Cambridge: Cambridge University Press, 2005.

La Galienne, Richard. "Paul Laurence Dunbar: Diversity of Talent and Genuine Inspiration in the Poetry of One of the Leading Singers of His Race." *New York Times Magazine*, 18 Jan. 1914, 17.

Laughlin, Clara. *Reminiscences of James Whitcomb Riley*. New York: Fleming H. Revell Co., 1916.

Lauter, Paul. *Canons and Contexts*. Oxford: Oxford University Press, 1991.

Lawson, Edward H. "Paul Laurence Dunbar." *Alexander's Magazine* (March 1906): 47–50.

Lee, A. Robert. "The Fiction of Paul Laurence Dunbar." *Negro American Literature Forum* 8 (1928): 166–72.

Lerer, Seth. *Inventing English: A Portable History of the Language*. New York: Columbia University Press, 2007.

Leslie, Eliza. *Miss Leslie's Behaviour Book: A Guide and Manual for Ladies*. Philadelphia: T. B. Peterson & Brothers, 1859.

Levenston, E. A. *The Stuff of Literature: Physical Aspects of Texts and Their Relation to Literary Meaning*. Albany: State University of New York Press, 1992.

Levine, Caroline. "Strategic Formalism: Toward a New Method in Cultural Studies." *Victorian Studies* 48.4 (2006): 625–57.

Levine, Lawrence W. *Highbrow/Lowbrow: The Emergence of Cultural Hierarchy in America*. Cambridge, MA: Harvard University Press, 1988.

"Like Return of a Hero Was Visit of Paul Laurence Dunbar, the Colored Poet, to the N.C.R. Works Where a Few Years Ago He Was Employed on the Force of Janitors—An Enthusiastic Reception Accorded Him by the Employees." *Dayton Evening News*, 7 Jan. 1904, n.p.

Linley, Margaret. "Conjuring the Spirit: Victorian Poetry, Culture, and Technology." *Victorian Poetry* 41 (2003): 536–44.

"Literary Notes." *Appleton's Journal*, 31 May 1873, 732–33.

Locke, Alain, ed. *Four Negro Poets*. The Pamphlet Poets Series. New York: Simon and Schuster, 1927.

———. Review of *The Weary Blues* by Langston Hughes. In *Critical Essays on Langston Hughes*, ed. Edward J. Mullen, 44–46. Boston: G. K. Hall and Company, 1986.

Loeffelholz, Mary. *From School to Salon: Reading Nineteenth-Century American Women's Poetry*. Princeton: Princeton University Press, 2004.

"The London Spectator on Bret Harte." *Every Saturday: A Journal of Choice Reading*, 27 May 1871, 486–87.

Loomis, Charles Battell. "The Dialect Store." *Century* 53.6 (Apr. 1897): 958–59.

Lowell, James Russell. "The Five Indispensable Authors (Homer, Dante, Cervantes, Goethe, Shakspere)." *Century* 47 (Dec. 1893): 223–24.

Lull, Herbert G., and H. B. Wilson. *The Redirection of High-School Instruction*. Philadelphia, London, Chicago: J. B. Lippincott Company, 1921.

Lyons, Martyn. "New Readers in the Nineteenth Century: Women, Children, Workers." In *A History of Reading in the West*, ed. Guglielmo Cavallo and Roger Chartier, 313–44. Amherst: University of Massachusetts Press, 1999.

Mance, Ajuan Maria. *Inventing Black Women: African American Women Poets and Self-Representation, 1877–2000*. Knoxville: University of Tennessee Press, 2007.

Mather, Frank Lincoln, ed. *Who's Who of the Colored Race: A General Biographical Dictionary of Men and Women of African Descent*, vol. 1. Chicago, 1915.

Matthews, Brander. "As to 'American Spelling.'" *Harper's* 85 (July 1892): 284.

———. "Literature as a Profession." In *The Historical Novel and Other Essays*, 193–213. New York: Scribner's, 1901.

———. "On Working Too Much and Working Too Fast." In *The Tocsin of Revolt and Other Essays*, 205–15. New York: Scribner's, 1922.

McDowell, Deborah E. *"The Changing Same": Black Women's Literature, Criticism, and Theory*. Bloomington: Indiana University Press, 1995.

McGee, Daniel. "Dada Da Da: Sounding the Jew in Modernism." *ELH* 68 (2001): 501–27.

McHenry, Elizabeth. *Forgotten Readers: Recovering the Lost History of African American Literary Societies*. Durham: Duke University Press, 2002.

———. "Toward a History of Access: The Case of Mary Church Terrell." *American Literary History* 19.2 (2007): 381–401.

McHenry, Elizabeth, and Shirley Brice Heath. "The Literate and the Literary: African-American Readers as Writers, 1830–1940." *Written Communication* 11.4 (1994): 419–44.

McKay, Claude. *A Long Way from Home*. New York: Arno Press and the New York Times, 1969.

———. *Banana Bottom*. New York: Harper & Row, 1933.

———. "Boyhood in Jamaica," *Phylon* 14 (1953): 134–45.

———. *Harlem Shadows: The Poems of Claude McKay*. New York: Harcourt, Brace and Company, 1922.

———. *Songs of Jamaica*. 1912; Miami: Mnemosyne Publishing, 1969.

Mencken, H. L. *The American Language: An Inquiry into the Development of English in the United States*, 4th ed. and the two supplements, abridged, with annotations and new material by Raven I. McDavid, Jr. 1921; New York: Knopf, 1974.

———. Foreword. *You Know These Lines!: A Bibliography of the Most Quoted Verses in American Poetry*, by Merle Johnson. New York: G. A. Baker and Company, 1935. ix–xi.

Merwin, Henry Childs. *The Life of Bret Harte, with Some Account of the California Pioneers*. Detroit: Gale Research Co., 1967.

Metcalf, E. W. *Paul Laurence Dunbar: A Bibliography*. Metuchen, NJ: Scarecrow Press, 1975.

Milburn, Nellie Francis. "An Open Letter to James Whitcomb Riley." *The Literary World* 31 (May 1990): 104.

Miller, Joaquin. "The Slump in Poetry." *The Critic* (Apr. 1905): 350.

Miller, R. Baxter. "Framing and Framed Languages in Hughes's *Ask Your Mama: 12 Moods for Jazz*." *MELUS* 17.4 (1991–92): 3–13.

"Miss Lois C. Simmons Entertains." *Chicago Defender*, 3 Jan. 1914, 6.

Mitchell, Minnie. *James Whitcomb Riley, as I Knew Him: Real Incidents in the Early Life of America's Beloved Poet*. Greenfield, IN: The Old Swimmin' Hole Press, 1949.

Morgan, Monique. "Productive Convergences, Producing Converts." *Victorian Poetry* 41 (2003): 500–504.
Morrisson, Mark. *The Public Face of Modernism: Little Magazines, Audiences, and Reception, 1905–1920.* Madison: University of Wisconsin Press, 2001.
Mott, Frank Luther. *Golden Multitudes: The Story of Best Sellers in the United States.* New York: Macmillan, 1947.
Mukarovsky, Jan. "Standard Language and Poetic Language." In *A Prague School Reader on Esthetics, Literary Structure, and Style,* selected and translated by Paul L. Garvin, 17–30. Washington, D.C.: Georgetown University Press, 1964.
Mullen, Harryette. "Off the Top." In *Trimmings,* n.p. New York: Tender Buttons, 1991.
———. "Sleeping with the Dictionary." In *Sleeping with the Dictionary,* 67. Berkeley: University of California Press, 2002.
Nelson, Cary. *Revolutionary Memory: Recovering the Poetry of the American Left.* London: Routledge, 2001.
Newcomb, John Timberman. *Would Poetry Disappear? American Verse and the Crisis of Modernity.* Columbus: Ohio State University Press, 2004.
Newkirk, Pamela, ed. *Letters from Black America.* New York: Farrar, Straus, and Giroux, 2009.
Nicholson, Meredith. *The Man in the Street: Papers on American Topics.* New York: Scribner, 1921.
Nielsen, Aldon Lynn. *Black Chant: Languages of African-American Postmodernism.* Cambridge: Cambridge University Press, 1997.
Nissen, Axel. *Bret Harte: Prince and Pauper.* Jackson: University Press of Mississippi, 2000.
North, Michael. *The Dialect of Modernism: Race, Language, and Twentieth-Century Literature.* New York: Oxford University Press, 1994.
Northrop, Henry Davenport. *The College of Life, or Practical Self-Educator: A Manual of Self-Improvement for the Colored Race.* [Denver, CO]: Western Book Co., 1896.
"Notes on Books and Booksellers." *American Literary Gazette and Publishers' Circular,* 15 Apr 1871, 250–54.
Nyong'o, Tavia. "Hiawatha's Black Atlantic Itineraries." In *The Traffic in Poems: Nineteenth-Century Poetry and Transatlantic Exchange,* ed. Meredith L. McGill, 81–96. New Brunswick: Rutgers University Press, 2008.
Okeke-Ezigbo, Emeka. "Paul Laurence Dunbar: Straightening the Record." *CLA Journal* 24 (1981): 481–96.
The Old-Fashioned Couple and Heathen Chinee. Chicago: J. J. Spalding & Co., 1873.
Olson, Charles. "Projective Verse." In *The New American Poetry, 1945–1960,* ed. Donald Allen, 386–97. 1960; Berkeley: University of California Press, 1999.
Onderdonk, James L. *History of American Verse, 1610–1897.* Chicago: A. C. McClurg, 1901.
Ong, Walter. *Orality and Literacy: The Technologizing of the Word.* London: Methuen, 1982.
"Paragraphs—II." *American Annals of the Deaf* 41 (1896): 184–89.
Pattee, Fred Lewis. *A History of American Literature since 1870.* New York: The Century Company, 1915.
Pawley, Christine. "What to Read and How to Read: The Social Infrastructure of Young People's Reading, Osage, Iowa." *Library Quarterly* 68 (1998): 276–97.
Pawley, Thomas D. "Dunbar as Playwright." *Black World* 24.6 (1975): 70–79.
Pearce, Roy Harvey. *The Continuity of American Poetry.* Princeton: Princeton University Press, 1961.

Pearson, Paul M. *Paul Laurence Dunbar: A Tribute.* N.p: n.p., [c. 1906].
Peck, H. T. "An Afro-American Poet." *The Bookman* 4.6 (Feb. 1897): 568.
Pemberton, T. Edgar. *Bret Harte: A Treatise and a Tribute.* London: Greening & Co., Ltd., 1900.
Perkins, David. *A History of Modern Poetry, Volume One: From the 1890s to the High Modernist Mode.* 1976; Cambridge, MA: Harvard University Press, 2006.
"Personal." *Cincinnati Daily Gazette,* 22 Apr. 1871, 2.
Peterson, Carla L. *"Doers of the Word": African-American Women Speakers & Writers in the North (1830–1880).* Oxford: Oxford University Press, 1995.
Petrino, Elizabeth A. "'We Are Rising as a People': Frances Harper's Radical Views on Class and Racial Equality in *Sketches of Southern Life.*" *American Transcendental Quarterly* 19.2 (2005): 133–53.
Phelps, William Lyon. "As I Like It." *Scribner's* 88.5 (Nov. 1930): 547.
Picker, John M. *Victorian Soundscapes.* Oxford: Oxford University Press, 2003.
Pidgin, Charles Felton. *Quincy Adams Sawyer and Mason's Corner Folks, A Novel: A Picture of New England Home Life.* Boston: C. M. Clark Publishing Co., 1900.
"The Pike Poetry." *The Galaxy* 12.5 (Nov. 1871): 635–42.
Plotkin, Cary. *The Tenth Muse: Victorian Philology and the Genesis of the Poetic Language of Gerard Manley Hopkins.* Carbondale: Southern Illinois University Press, 1989.
Pound, Ezra. "A Few Don'ts by an Imagiste." *Poetry* 1.6 (March 1913): 200–206.
Powell, Richard J. "Sartor Africanus." In *Dandies: Fashion and Finesse in Art and Culture,* ed. Susan Fillin-Yeh, 217–42. New York: New York University Press, 2001.
Presbrey, Frank. *The History and Development of Advertising.* Garden City, NY: Doubleday, 1929.
Price, Leah. "Reading: The State of the Discipline." *Book History* 7 (2004): 303–20.
Prins, Yopie. "Robert Browning, Transported by Meter." In *The Traffic in Poems: Nineteenth-Century Poetry and Transatlantic Exchange,* ed. Meredith L. McGill, 205–30. New Brunswick: Rutgers University Press, 2008.
"Pulpit and Platform." [Chicago] *Daily Inter Ocean,* 9 May 1888, 6.
Radway, Janice. "The Aesthetic in Mass Culture: Reading the 'Popular' Literary Text." In *The Structure of the Literary Process: Studies Dedicated to the Memory of Felix Vodicka,* ed. Peter Steiner et al., 397–429. Amsterdam: Benjamins, 1982.
———. "Learned and Literary Print Cultures in an Age of Professionalization and Diversification." In *A History of the Book in America, Vol. 4: Print in Motion: The Expansion of Publishing and Reading in the United States, 1880–1940,* 197–233. Chapel Hill: University of North Carolina Press, 2009.
Radway, Janice, and Perry Frank. "Verse and Popular Poetry." In *Handbook of American Popular Literature,* ed. M. Thomas Inge, 299–322. New York: Greenwood Press, 1988.
Raffel, Burton. *Politicians, Poets, and Con Men: Emotional History in Late Victorian America.* Hamden, CT: Archon, 1986.
Railton, Stephen. "'Plain Language from Truthful James, by Bret Harte.'" *Mark Twain in His Times,* Special Collections, University of Virginia. Accessed Jan. 1, 2012. http://etext.lib.virginia.edu/railton/roughingit/map/chiharte.html.
Rampersad, Arnold. *The Life of Langston Hughes, Vol. 1, 1902–1941: "I, Too, Sing America."* Oxford: Oxford University Press, 2002.
Randall, Dale B. J. "Dialect in the Verse of 'The Hoosier Poet.'" *American Speech* 35 (1960): 36–50.
Read, Allen Walker. "The Spelling Bee: A Linguistic Institution of the American Folk." *PMLA* 56 (1941): 495–512.

Read, Charles. *Children's Creative Spelling*. London: Routledge and Kegan Paul, 1971.

"Records Taken of Riley's Voice. Poet Consents after Years to Read Choice Poems for Talking Machine Company. Noted Writer of Verse Hears 'Proofs' of Selections with Manifest Interest." *Indianapolis Star*, 6 July 1912, 1.

Redding, J. Saunders. *A Scholar's Conscience: Selected Writings of J. Saunders Redding, 1942–1977*. Lexington: University Press of Kentucky, 1992.

———. *To Make a Poet Black*. Chapel Hill: University of North Carolina Press, 1939.

Rees, John O. "Some Echoes of English Literature in Frontier Vernacular Humor." *Studies in American Humor*, new series, 1 (1983): 153–62.

Revell, Peter. *Paul Laurence Dunbar*. Boston: Twayne Publishers, 1979.

Review of *The Boys of the Old Glee Club* by James Whitcomb Riley. *The Independent*, 2 Apr. 1908, 756.

Review of *Li'l Gal* by Paul Laurence Dunbar. *New York Times*, 26 Nov. 1904: 817.

Review of *Little Orphant Annie*. *Variety*, 6 Dec. 1918, 39.

Richings, G. F. *Evidences of Progress among Colored People*. Philadelphia: Geo. S. Ferguson Co., 1905.

Riley, James Whitcomb. *The Book of Joyous Children*. New York: Charles Scribner's Sons, 1902.

———. *The Boys of the Old Glee Club*. Indianapolis: Bobbs-Merrill, 1907.

———. *A Child-World*. Indianapolis: Bobbs-Merrill, 1896.

———. *The Complete Poetical Works of James Whitcomb Riley*. Bloomington: Indiana University Press, 1993.

———. *The Complete Works of James Whitcomb Riley*. 10 vols. New York and London: Harper & Brothers, 1916.

———. *The Letters of James Whitcomb Riley*. Ed. William Lyon Phelps. Indianapolis: Bobbs-Merrill, 1930.

———. *The Rubaiyat of Doc Sifers*. New York: Century Co., 1897.

———. "Some Boys." *Century* 41.2 (Dec. 1890): 317–19.

Romeo, Jacqueline. "Irony Lost: Bret Harte's Heathen Chinee and the Popularization of the Comic Coolie as Trickster in Frontier Melodrama." *Theatre History Studies* 26 (1996): 108–36.

Rubin, Joan Shelley. "Making Meaning: Analysis and Affect in the Study and Practice of Reading." In *A History of the Book in America*, vol. 4, 511–27. Chapel Hill: University of North Carolina, 2008.

———. "'They Flash upon That Inward Eye': Poetry Recitation and American Readers." *Proceedings of the American Antiquarian Society* 106.2 (1996): 273–300.

Russo, Anthony J., and Dorothy R. Russo. *A Bibliography of James Whitcomb Riley*. Indianapolis: Indiana Historical Society, 1944.

Scharnhorst, Gary. *Bret Harte: Opening the American Literary West*. Norman: University of Oklahoma Press, 2000.

———. "'I Do Not Write This in Anger': Bret Harte's Letters to His Sister, 1871–93." *Resources for American Literary Study* 26.2 (2000): 200–222.

———. "Ways That Are Dark: Appropriations of Bret Harte's 'Plain Language from Truthful James.'" *Nineteenth-Century Literature* 51 (1996): 377–99.

Schatt, Stanley. "Langston Hughes: The Minstrel as Artificer." *Journal of Modern Literature* 4 (1974): 115–20.

Schneirov, Matthew. *The Dream of a New Social Order: Popular Magazines in America, 1893–1914*. New York: Columbia University Press, 1994.

Scott, Donald M. "Print and the Public Lecture System, 1840–60." In *Printing and Soci-

ety in Early America, ed. William Leonard Joyce et al., 278–99. Worcester, MA: American Antiquarian Society, 1983.
[Scott, Frank H.] "The Modern Magazine." *The Critic*, 26 May 1894, 364–66.
Scott-Childress, Reynolds J. "Paul Laurence Dunbar and the Project of Cultural Reconstruction." *African American Review* 41 (2007): 367–75.
Scripture, Edward Wheeler. *Researches in Experimental Phonetics: The Study of Speech Curves*. Washington, D.C.: Carnegie Institution, 1906.
Sedgwick, Ellery. "Magazines and the Profession of Authorship in the United States, 1840–1900." *Papers of the Bibliographical Society of America* 94 (2000), 399–425.
Shaw, George Bernard. *Pygmalion: A Romance in Five Acts*. 1913; London: Penguin, 1957.
Sherman, Joan R., ed. *African-American Poetry of the Nineteenth Century: An Anthology*. Urbana: University of Illinois Press, 1992.
———. *Invisible Poets: Afro-Americans of the Nineteenth Century*. Urbana: University of Illinois, 1989.
Shoptaw, John. "Lyric Cryptography." *Poetics Today* 21 (2000): 221–62.
Simplified Spelling: An Appeal to Common Sense. London: Simplified Spelling Society, 1911.
Simpson, David. *The Politics of American English, 1776–1850*. New York: Oxford University Press, 1986.
Smethurst, James Edward. *The African American Roots of Modernism: From Reconstruction to the Harlem Renaissance*. Chapel Hill: University of North Carolina Press, 2011.
———. *The New Red Negro: The Literary Left and African American Poetry, 1930–1946*. Oxford: Oxford University Press, 1999.
Smith, Nila Banton. *American Reading Instruction*. 1934; International Reading Association, 2002.
Soltow, Lee, and Edward Stevens. *The Rise of Literacy and the Common School in the United States: A Socioeconomic Analysis to 1870*. Chicago: University of Chicago Press, 1981.
Somerville, Siobhan B. "'The Prettiest Specimen of Boyhood': Cross-Gender and Racial Disguise in Pauline E. Hopkins's *Winona*." In *Skin Deep, Spirit Strong: The Black Female Body in American Culture*, ed. Kimberly Wallace-Sanders, 201–17. Ann Arbor: University of Michigan Press, 2002.
Sooy, Harry O. *Memoir of My Career at Victor Talking Machine Company* (1909), 49–51. Accessed Jan. 1, 2012. http://www.davidsarnoff.org/sooyh-maintext1909.html.
Sorby, Angela. *Schoolroom Poets: Childhood, Performance, and the Place of American Poetry, 1865–1917*. Lebanon: University of New Hampshire Press, 2005.
"Spelling." *Littell's Living Age*, 19 Feb. 1876, 509–11.
"The Spelling Match." *Primary Education* 6 (June 1898): 239.
Steiner, George. *On Difficulty and Other Essays*. Oxford: Oxford University Press, 1980.
Stepto, Robert. "Distrust of the Reader in Afro-American Narratives." In *Reconstructing American Literary History*, ed. Sacvan Bercovitch, Harvard English Studies 13, 300–22. Cambridge, MA: Harvard University Press, 1986.
———. *From Behind the Veil: A Study of Afro-American Narrative*. Urbana: University of Illinois Press, 1979.
Stewart, Garrett. *Reading Voices: Literature and the Phonotext*. Berkeley: University of California Press, 1990.

Stewart, Susan. *Crimes of Writing: Problems in the Containment of Representation.* Oxford: Oxford University Press, 1991.
"Stories of Famous Poems: Francis Bret Harte." *Charlotte* [NC] *Observer,* 13 Aug. 1911, 2.
[Strong, Peter Remsen]. "A Recipe for a Poem 'In Dialect.'" In *"Awful," and Other Jingles,* 14–17. New York: Putnam, 1871.
"This Is Why Not. Literary Man Should Not Write Dialect Verse Because He Can't." *Baltimore American,* 26 June 1909, 11.
Thomas, Lorenzo. *Extraordinary Measures: Afrocentric Modernism and Twentieth-Century American Poetry.* Tuscaloosa: University of Alabama Press, 2000.
Thompson, Clara Ann. *Songs from the Wayside* (Rossmoyne, OH: n.p., 1908). In *Collected Black Women's Poetry,* vol. 2, ed. Joan R. Sherman. Oxford: Oxford University Press, 1998.
Thoreau, Henry David. *A Week on the Concord and Merrimack Rivers.* Boston: Osgood, 1873.
"Today in History: Anniversary of the Birth of Bret Harte in 1839." 25 Aug. 1919, 4.
Toolan, Michael. "The Significations of Representing Dialect in Writing." *Language and Literature* 1.1 (1992): 29–46.
Trachtenberg, Alan. *The Incorporation of America: Culture and Society in the Gilded Age.* 1982; New York: Hill and Wang, 2007.
Tracy, Steven C. *Langston Hughes & The Blues.* Urbana: University of Illinois Press, 1988.
Triggs, Oscar Lovell. "A Century of American Poetry." *The Forum* 30 (Jan. 1901): 630–40.
Twain, Mark. *Mark Twain in Eruption.* Ed. Bernard DeVoto. New York: Harper and Brothers, 1940.
Van Allen, Elizabeth J. *James Whitcomb Riley: A Life.* Bloomington: Indiana University Press, 1999.
———. "The Signifier and the Signified." *Traces of Indiana and Midwestern History* 11.1 (Winter 1999): 29.
Van Dyke, Henry. "James Whitcomb Riley as a Person." *The Book News Monthly* (March 1907): 427–30.
Van Vechten, Carl. Introduction to *The Weary Blues* by Langston Hughes, 9–13. 1926; New York: Knopf, 1947.
Venable, W. H. *John Hancock, PhD.* Cincinnati: C. B. Ruggles & Co., 1892.
Vicinus, Martha. *The Industrial Muse: A Study of Nineteenth Century British Working-Class Literature.* New York: Barnes and Noble, 1974.
Wagner, Jean. *Black Poets of the United States: From Paul Laurence Dunbar to Langston Hughes.* Urbana: University of Illinois Press, 1973.
Wallin, J. E. Wallace. "Researches on the Rhythm of Speech." In *Studies from the Yale Psychological Laboratory,* ed. E. W. Scripture, vol. 9, 1–142. New Haven: Yale University, 1901.
Warren, Kenneth. Panel titled "Paul Laurence Dunbar: The Racial Politics of the Nadir." Accessed Jan. 1, 2012. http://www.youtube.com/watch?v=07Y01f1NcSQ.
Washington, Booker T. *Up from Slavery.* Ed. William L. Andrews. Oxford: Oxford University Press, 2008.
Webster, Noah. *Dissertations on the English Language.* 1789; Menston, England: The Scolar Press Limited, 1967.

Wegner, Laura Christine. *Riley Readings with Living Pictures.* Chicago: T. S. Denison, [c. 1921].
Weirick, Bruce. *From Whitman to Sandburg in American Poetry: A Critical Survey.* New York: Macmillan, 1924.
Wesling, Donald. *Bakhtin and the Social Moorings of Poetry.* Lewisburg, PA: Bucknell University Press, 2003.
Wheeler, Lesley. *Voicing American Poetry: Sound and Performance from the 1920s to the Present.* Ithaca: Cornell University Press, 2008.
White, Richard Grant. *Every-Day English: A Sequel to "Words and Their Uses."* Boston: Houghton Mifflin, 1880.
Wiggins, Lida Keck. *The Life and Works of Paul Laurence Dunbar: Containing His Complete Poetical Works, His Best Short Stories, Numerous Anecdotes and a Complete Biography of the Famous Poet.* Naperville, IL: J. L. Nichols and Company, [c. 1907].
Williams, Heather. *Self-Taught: African American Education in Slavery and Freedom.* Chapel Hill: University of North Carolina Press, 2005.
Williams, Raymond. *Keywords: A Vocabulary of Culture and Society.* New York: Oxford University Press, 1983.
Wister, Owen. *How Doth the Simple Spelling Bee.* New York: Macmillan, 1907.
———. "What Is True Spelling? One of the Foremost of our Younger Writers Does Not Think It Is the Kind Recommended by the Simplified Spelling Board." *New York Times,* 5 Oct. 1906, BR614.
Wolosky, Shira. "Poetry and Public Discourse, 1820–1910." In *The Cambridge History of American Literature, Volume 4: Nineteenth-Century Poetry, 1800–1910,* ed. Sacvan Bercovitch, 147–80. Cambridge: Cambridge University Press, 2004.
Wolters, Raymond. *The New Negro on Campus: Black College Rebellions of the 1920s.* Princeton: Princeton University Press, 1975.
"The Woman Suffragists." *Lancaster Daily Intelligencer,* 22 Feb. 1890, 6.
Wonham, Henry. *Playing the Races: Ethnic Caricature and American Literary Realism.* Oxford: Oxford University Press, 2004.
Worcester, J. E. *A Pronouncing Spelling-Book of the English Language.* Boston: William Ware and Company, 1879.
Wyatt, Edith. *Great Companions.* New York: D. Appleton, 1917.
Young, Art. *Author's Readings.* New York: Frederick A. Stokes Company, 1897.
Zlotnick, Susan. "'A Thousand Times I'd Be a Factory Girl': Dialect, Domesticity, and Working-Class Women's Poetry in Victorian Britain." *Victorian Studies* 35.1 (1991): 7–27.

index

A.M.E. Church Review, The, 234n23
actors and acting, 5, 31–32, 37, 40–41, 45, 55, 99, 123, 156, 183, 191, 222n82. *See also* performance, poetry
Ade, George, 82
Adventures of Huckleberry Finn, The (Twain), 11, 33, 246n12
advertising and advertising verse, 4, 36, 68, 71, 74, 77–79, 121, 126–27, 131, 135–37, 173, 184, 185, 213, 215n11, 221n60, 228n33, 245n82
African Americans: authorship and publishing, 94, 96, 124, 132, 144–46, 184–85; clubs and literary societies, 94, 146, 147, 165, 186; consumption of dialect poetry, 15, 93–94, 96, 111, 146, 155, 184–86, 195, 234n24, 236nn53–54; education, 110–13, 155, 165–67, 169–71, 176–78, 239n83, 250n88, 252n18; literacy, 9, 101, 110–12, 147, 154–55, 185–87, 192, 247n30, 248n39, 254n43; periodicals and, 94, 119, 124–25, 126–27, 132, 242n26; regionalism and, 15, 90–91, 92–94, 164, 232n2; "representative," 165, 166–67, 169–70, 171, 175–76, 178, 182, 250n84, 250n88; social class and, 110, 112–14, 130–31, 138, 144–45, 146, 157, 158, 159, 164, 165, 166, 167, 168, 175–77, 178, 245n79, 247n21, 249n62. *See also* historically black colleges and universities
"Ah Sin's Reply to Truthful James" (anonymous), 63
Aldrich, Thomas Bailey, 209
American Philological Society, 19
Anderson, William Wanless, 20–21
Andrews, Bruce, 16
"Angelina" (Dunbar), 98
annotation, 16, 172–73, 179, 183–84, 187–91, 194, 197–98, 205, 206, 254n57, 257n114
"Ante-Bellum Sermon, An" (Dunbar), 97, 99
anthologies, 26, 30, 32, 42, 98, 99, 135, 158, 173, 230n69, 236nn53–54, 246n5
Anthony, Susan B., 156
Appleton-Century Company, 34
Appleton's Journal, 3, 230n69
Ashton, Susanna, 128
Ask Your Mama (Hughes), 179, 254n57
"At 'The Literary'" (Riley), 114
Atlantic Monthly, 3, 35, 111, 115, 119, 131, 176, 213, 221nn54–55
Attridge, Derek, 72

audiences of American dialect poetry, 4, 5–6, 10, 14, 16, 17, 19, 21–22, 36–41, 43–45, 48–50, 55–56, 64, 65–66, 71, 90, 93–95, 96, 99, 100, 108, 131, 141, 155, 157, 173–74, 175, 182, 183, 184, 185, 188, 190, 192, 194, 195, 198, 201, 206–7, 210, 211, 220n38, 220n40, 235n44, 244n64; adults as target, 30, 33, 76, 77, 79–80; African American, 15, 93–94, 96, 111, 146, 155, 184–86, 195, 234nn23–24, 237n54, 246n9, 253n40; book versus magazine, 124–25, 128; children as target, 26, 30, 43, 76, 77, 79–80; coterie, 145, 165, 234n24, 246n6, 250n78; as high-brow, 34, 35, 36, 40, 128, 146, 157, 219n28; international, 22, 35, 59, 62, 71, 213; literacy and, 10, 11, 32–33, 36, 84, 155, 178, 184, 185–87, 192, 207; as low-brow, 33, 35, 134–35, 137–38, 139; as middle-brow, 33, 35; response and expectations of, 3, 8, 10–11, 14, 15, 72, 92, 94, 95, 97–98, 100, 119–20, 135, 137, 138–39, 144, 156–57, 169, 204, 235n28, 235n42, 235n44, 236n46; size of, 3, 9, 10, 19, 32, 35–36, 40, 97, 114, 138, 191, 212, 213, 214, 246n6; women, 146–47, 157

"Aunt Cloe's Trip to See Miss Liza Kyle" (Johnson), 162–64, 196

authenticity, 2, 7–8, 41, 58, 136, 172, 173–75, 200, 202, 210, 211; Dunbar and, 15, 91–98, 99, 100–101, 105, 107–8, 119, 131, 138, 147–48, 173–74, 192, 195, 233n9, 234n20, 234n22, 235n44, 237n54, 238n64; Harte and, 39–40, 61, 65–66; Hughes and, 172, 174, 193; McKay and, 172, 194, 195–96, 198, 199, 200, 203, 204, 205, 235n37; Riley and, 36, 77, 94, 95, 100, 219n28, 230n66

authorship: amateur and semi-professional, 2, 23, 122–24, 127–29, 131–34, 135, 136, 145, 165, 201; coterie, 145, 234n24, 246n6, 250n78; professional, 13, 35–36, 123, 126, 128–31, 137–38, 145

Baldwin, Rebekah, 121–22, 124
Balhorn, Mark, 200, 204, 229n43
Banana Bottom (McKay), 199
Barnes, Walter, 26, 228n41
Beam, Dorri, 210
Benjamin, Walter, 45
Bennett, Michael, 156
Bennett, Paula Bernat, 153, 246n6, 249n68
Bernstein, Charles, 7, 13, 16, 151–52, 172, 195, 197, 198, 199, 200, 205
Bibb, Henry, 198
Biblical World, The, 77–79
Bierce, Ambrose, 209, 219n28
Big Sea, The (Hughes), 182
"Big Timer, The" (Hughes), 175, 183, 254n57, 255n58
Biglow Papers, The (Lowell), 9
Billings, Josh, 19–20
Bizzell, Patricia, 151
Black Arts Movement, 236n53, 237n54
"Black Clown, The" (Hughes), 192, 194, 204, 255n58
Blair, Walter, 20, 21, 209
Blanck, Jacob, 227n22
Bobbs-Merrill Company, 48. *See also* Bowen-Merrill Company
Bok, Edward, 3, 120, 121, 127–28
Book of Joyous Children, The (Riley), 75–76, 229n41
Book News Monthly, The, 36
Bookman, The, 4, 234n22
Borus, Daniel, 97
Boston Transcript, 42, 96, 99
Bourdieu, Pierre, 209
Bowen-Merrill Company, 41. *See also* Bobbs-Merrill Company
Boyd, Melba Joyce, 147, 148, 153, 157
"Boyhood in Jamaica" (McKay), 195
Boys of the Old Glee Club, The (Riley), 51–52
Bramen, Carrie Tirado, 94
Brawley, Benjamin, 98, 99, 112
"Bric-À-Brac." *See* "In Lighter Vein" (*Century Magazine*)

British Simplified Spelling Society, 229n47
Brodhead, Richard, 5, 33, 63, 221n54
Brody, Jennifer DeVere, 2, 182
"Broke" (Hughes), 204, 255n58
Bronson, Walter C., 232n8
Brooks, Fowler D., 193
Brooks, Tim, 55
Brooks, Van Wyck, 35
Brown, Sterling, 176, 237n54
Browning, Robert, 48, 51, 54, 68
Bruce, Dickson D., 94, 95, 96, 110, 164, 235n26, 245n79
Buell, Lawrence, 123
Bullock, Henry Allen, 186
Bullock, Penelope L., 186
Burdette, Robert, 18
Burlingame, E. L., 80
Burlingame, Roger, 126, 132
Burns, Robert, 113, 130, 237n56
Bush, Harold K., 37
Butterfield, S. Attwood, 250n78
Byerly, Alison, 41, 191

Cable, George Washington, 97
cacography, 19–20, 143
Camlot, Jason, 48, 50, 53–54, 55
Campbell, James Edwin, 90, 200
Canning, Charlotte, 223n87
Carey, William, 34, 80
caricature, 1–2, 6, 15, 39–40, 55, 64, 71, 91–92, 96–97, 98, 102, 106, 107–8, 111, 116, 122, 132, 144, 164, 233n9. *See also* minstrelsy; plantation tradition
Carpenter, Charles, 231n83
"Casabianca" ("The Boy Stood on the Burning Deck") (Hemans), 184
"Cat and the Saxophone (2 A.M.), The" (Hughes), 179–82, 188
Cawein, Madison, 34, 242n28
celebrity, 3, 10, 13, 14, 19, 26, 35–36, 38–40, 41–42, 43–44, 48–50, 57, 95, 96, 97–98, 113–14, 173, 174–75, 178, 209, 213
Century Magazine, 1, 3, 15, 34, 35, 76, 79–80, 81, 89, 119–20, 122, 126, 131–37, 139, 141, 142, 212, 221nn54–55, 241n8, 242n28, 243n52, 244n67, 245n75
Certeau, Michel de, 31–32, 59, 68, 121, 151–52, 205
Chakkalakal, Tess, 7
Chall, Jeanne S., 26–30
Champney, Lizzie W., 246n5
character. *See* personae, stage
Charvat, William, 13, 35–36, 129, 167, 175, 251n90
Chautauqua, 18, 41, 220n32, 223n87. *See also* lecturing; lyceum
Cheney, Warren, 61, 227n17
Chesnutt, Charles, 193
Chichester, Charles F., 126
Child-World, A (Riley), 75, 229n41
children: "child dialect" (Riley), 56, 76–77, 79–80, 228n41; "child writing" (Riley), 11, 14, 31, 32, 71–76, 81, 82, 100, 103, 116, 143, 200; education of, 9, 24–26, 30–32, 85, 88, 230n69, 231n76; effect of literary dialect upon, 23, 25, 80, 134–35, 218n17; as fans of Riley, 43, 45–48, 77, 79–80; literacy acquisition, 14, 31–32, 57, 72–74, 76, 209, 210; poetry for, 26, 30, 75, 76, 77, 79, 80, 186, 199, 209; spelling and, 8, 25, 72–74, 75, 83–84, 87–88, 114, 150, 152, 153, 231n74; as subjects of poetry, 26, 50, 54, 72, 75, 76–77, 79–80, 82, 84, 87–88, 161–62, 192, 229n50
Chinese Americans, 58, 59, 63–66, 67, 71, 116, 226n3, 226n8, 227n26
Christmann, James, 154, 164, 247n21
"Cicely" (Harte), 208
Clorindy, or the Origin of the Cakewalk (Dunbar), 236n47
Cmiel, Kenneth, 3
Cohen, Michael, 120
Colfax, Schuyler, 222n82
Collins, Philip, 191, 223n87
Colored American Magazine, 94, 118, 234n23
"Colored Band, The" (Dunbar), 98
"Colored Soldier, The" (Hughes), 175, 188–90, 191, 194, 254n57, 255n58
Complete Poems (Dunbar), 195

Complete Works of James Whitcomb Riley (Riley), 77–79
Cook, Will Marion, 236n47
Cooper, Wayne, 205, 255n71
Cornelius, Janet, 247n30
"Cornstalk Fiddle, The" (Dunbar), 95
Corrothers, James David, 90, 117, 118, 234n18, 241n8
Cosmopolitan, 131, 136
"Cost of a Song, The" (Riley), 238n75
Cotter, Joseph Seamon, Sr., 97, 113–14, 240n94
"Country Girl, A" (McKay), 201
"Cowards from the Colleges" (Hughes), 177, 178, 185
Cox, John Harrington, 10–11, 24
Critic, The, 127, 234n22
Crowder, Richard, 229n53
Cullen, Countee, 179
Culler, Jonathan, 26, 135
cultivation: appearance of, 39, 138–39; children and, 77, 79–80, 85; Dunbar and, 15, 118–19, 120–21, 122, 123–24, 126, 129, 131, 132, 133, 135–36, 137, 138–39, 141–42, 156, 241n5, 245n82; etymology of the word, 12, 125–26, 127–28, 240n4, 245n82; Harper and, 156, 157; Harte and, 35, 39, 67; lack of, 82, 157, 162–64, 173, 178, 243n48; Longfellow and, 129–30; magazines and, 79–80, 124–25, 128–29, 133, 134–35, 136, 137, 141; McKay and, 196–97, 199, 205; Pears soap and, 137; women and, 146–47, 169, 171. See also leisure
cummings, e. e., 74
Cunningham, Virginia, 98, 112
Curry, S. S., 211

Daggett, Mabel Potter, 38
Daily Inter Ocean (Chicago), 157
Dale, Edgar, 26–30
Dandridge, Rita B., 250n81
"Dark Youth of the U.S.A." (Hughes), 192, 255n58
Davey, Elizabeth, 184, 187, 188, 190
Davidson, Cathy N., 209, 242n24

Davis, Charles T., 113
de Castell, Suzanne, 85
"De Men Folks ob Today" (Johnson), 160–61
"De Wintah Styles" (Johnson), 161, 162, 163–64
Deutsch, Babette, 253n27
Dial, 20
"Dialect in Literature" (Riley), 230n66
"Dialect Store, The" (Loomis), 1–3, 8, 164, 211, 214
dialects: African American, 1, 2, 15, 64, 91, 93–96, 97, 100, 108, 113, 131, 132, 147–48, 144, 164, 165, 167, 171, 173–74, 176, 178, 204, 223n86, 233n9, 233n13, 234n26, 235n44, 237n54, 245n3, 255n58; child, 23, 56, 72, 76–77, 79–80, 134, 228n41; Chinese American, 63–64, 65, 68, 71, 227n26; English, nonstandard (England), 33, 60–61, 62, 65, 115, 144, 200, 204; English, nonstandard (U.S.), 2, 3–4, 20, 57, 84, 85, 87, 104, 213, 214; English, standard (England), 1, 2, 16, 21, 85, 195, 196, 198, 201, 203, 204, 205, 206, 213; English, standard (U.S.), 4, 30, 37, 65, 67, 72, 74, 76, 77, 81, 83–84, 85–86, 87, 92, 94, 95, 102, 103–4, 115, 119, 131, 141–42, 148, 154, 162, 164, 171, 181, 200, 204, 221n55, 237n54, 245n1, 247n21, 249n65, 251n2, 255n58; French, 8; French-Canadian, 1; German, 1, 95, 227n21; Hoosier, 15, 74, 81, 93, 94, 96, 211, 214, 221n55, 222n83, 228n41, 230n66, 232n3; Irish, 1, 95, 235; Jamaican, 16, 195, 196–97, 198, 201, 255n71; nonstandard, general, 6–7, 72, 77, 81, 103, 199–200, 204, 257n99; Scottish, 1, 21, 113; Southern U.S., 91, 92–94, 100, 218n17, 237n54, 245n3; Western U.S., 1, 12, 39, 60–61, 63–64, 65, 66; Yankee, 1, 63; Yiddish, 1, 235
Dickens, Charles, 9, 60–61, 200
dictionaries and lexicography, 3, 20, 21, 84–86, 89. *See also* Webster, Noah; Worcester, J. E.

"Dilettante: A Modern Type, The" (Dunbar), 122–24, 126, 132, 134, 137–38, 165
dime novels, 12
"Discovered" (Dunbar), 141
Dissertations on the English Language (Webster), 83–84, 85
Dodd, Mead and Company, 117
doggerel. *See* light verse
domesticity, ideology of, 144–45, 158–59, 249n62
Douglass, Frederick, 154, 157, 192, 234n26, 236n46, 248n39
Douglass, Helen, 234n26
dramatic monologue, 5, 99, 100, 108, 172, 175, 182, 213, 224n108
"A Dream" (McKay), 201–2, 203
Dreiser, Theodore, 50, 55, 217n6
dress, 39, 44, 45, 139, 145, 146, 156, 157–58, 159–64, 169, 188, 249n68, 250n70
"Drunkard's Child, The" (Harper), 249n63
"Drunkard's Dream, The" (Johnson), 159
Du Bois, W. E. B., 94, 110, 111, 254n55
Dunbar, Paul Laurence: in anthologies, 40, 98, 99, 236nn53–54; appearance, 96, 139; audiences, 55, 93–95, 97–99, 100, 108, 111, 119, 131, 135, 137, 141, 146, 195, 201, 204, 206–7, 234n23, 235n28, 235n42, 235n44, 244n64, 246n9; authenticity, 15, 91–98, 99, 100–101, 105, 107–8, 119, 131, 138, 147–48, 173–74, 192, 195, 233n9, 234n20, 234n22, 237n54, 238n64; in the *Century*, 3, 15, 35, 119–20, 122, 126, 131–35, 136, 137, 139, 141, 142, 241n8, 243n52, 245n75; cultivation and, 15, 118–21, 122, 123–24, 126, 129, 131, 132, 133, 135–36, 137, 138–39, 141–42, 156, 241n5, 245n82; dramatic form and, 98–99, 100, 101, 108, 172, 236n52, 237n57; education and, 93, 101, 110–13, 119, 122, 123, 138, 165, 169, 176; epistolary dialect poems, 15, 92, 99–110, 116, 162, 237nn56–57; Harper and, 15, 147–48, 156; Hughes and, 93, 172, 173, 174–77, 192, 235n28, 237n54, 251n2, 252n9; income, 121–22, 124, 126, 138; influence upon Maggie Pogue Johnson, 16, 159, 169, 249n65, 251n93; labor, 15, 93, 112, 116, 117–19, 120–21, 124, 128, 129, 130–31, 132, 139, 239n88, 241n21; in literary history, 13, 15, 92, 95, 96, 98, 99, 173, 174, 175, 185, 195–96, 232n8, 236nn53–54, 251n2, 252n9; minstrelsy and, 55, 92, 94, 96–98, 106, 234n26, 236nn46–47; performance and, 15, 55, 90, 91, 95, 97–99, 100, 108, 114, 119, 121, 131, 137–39, 141, 213, 235n42, 236n45, 236n47; popularity of, 55, 95, 97, 98, 108, 232n7; regionalism, 15, 90–91, 92–94, 95–96, 98, 100, 105–8, 115, 131, 144, 232nn2–3, 232n8, 233n13, 236n54, 245n3; Riley and, 15, 33, 91, 92, 93, 94–96, 97–98, 99, 100, 101, 102–3, 105, 108, 109, 110, 113, 114, 115–16, 122, 123–24, 126, 130, 138, 142, 144, 173, 232n3, 232n7, 234nn18–19, 240n93, 242n25, 244n61, 251n5; social class and, 110, 112–14, 129, 130–31, 138, 176–77, 239n88, 245n79; spelling and, 75, 89, 112, 141. *See also titles of individual Dunbar works*
Dunbar-Nelson, Alice, 16, 40, 97, 121, 124, 131, 134, 144, 245n3
Dunne, Finley Peter, 58

Easthope, Antony, 136–37
Eastman, Max, 195–96
education: African Americans, 101, 110–13, 138, 155, 165–167, 169–71, 176–78, 185, 186, 239n83, 250n88, 252n18; children, 9, 24–26, 30–32, 85, 88, 230n69, 231n76; dialect poetry and, 6, 13–14, 16, 19, 20, 23, 25–26, 30–31, 56, 77, 79–81, 84, 135, 144, 165, 174, 196, 208, 209, 213, 214, 237n54, 256n78; elocu-

tion and, 24, 25, 175, 191; silent reading and, 10, 19, 24–25, 193–94; spelling and, 20, 21, 24, 75, 86, 87, 88, 89, 112, 209, 212, 218n10, 230n69
educators: African American, 110, 138, 166–71, 177, 178, 250n88; on literacy, 25, 111–12, 149–50, 151, 152, 154–55, 209, 210, 247n30; on poetry, 24, 26, 50–51, 77, 193–94, 208, 209, 211, 212, 219n28, 230n69; poets as, 111–12, 129, 167, 213, 242n28, 251n90; represented in literature, 8, 21, 82, 83, 85, 86, 115; on speech, 85, 202; spelling and, 20, 21, 82, 85, 86, 88, 209, 212, 218n10, 230n69
Eggleston, Edward, 61, 85, 86, 87, 88, 246n12
Eitel, Edward, 224n109
Eliot, T. S., 178
elision, 2, 104, 202, 203–4, 257n102
Elliott, Kamilla, 43
Ellsworth, William W., 126
elocution. *See* performance, poetry
elocution and recitation manuals, 30, 98, 115, 230n69
Engelsing, Rolf, 242n24
ephemera, 4, 42, 68–71, 215n11, 227n30
epistolary dialect poems, 15, 92, 99–110, 116, 162–63, 237nn55–56
"Etchings." *See* "In Lighter Vein" (*Century Magazine*)
"Everybody Loves My Baby" (Palmer and Williams), 180–81
extensive reading, 123, 242n24
eye dialect, 20, 72, 74, 143, 200, 211, 229n43
Eytinge, Sol, 67–71

Fallen Blossoms (Johnson), 162, 251n93
"Farmer Spittle's Spellin' Bee" (Dunbar), 240n95
fashion. *See* dress
Favor, J. Martin, 93
Fearing, Kenneth, 175
Ferguson Brothers, 145
"Fetchin' Water" (McKay), 197

Field, Eugene, 26, 98, 213, 232n7
film, 14, 19, 42–48, 56, 214, 224n94, 224n96
Fine Clothes to the Jew (Hughes), 178, 182–83, 185, 193, 253n39
Fish, Stanley, 202, 256n99
Fishkin, Shelley Fisher, 119
FitzGerald, Edward, 33
Forman, P. Gabrielle, 248n33
Foster, Frances Smith, 156
Frank, Perry, 214
"Free Labor" (Harper), 157
"Free Silver at Angel's" (Harte), 65
free verse, 13, 182, 251n5. *See also* meter; rhyme
Frost, Robert, 212
Fultz, Michael, 176
Furman, Lucy, 235n31

Gabler-Hover, Janet, 132
Gaines, Kevin K., 130–31
Galaxy, The, 22
Galow, Timothy W., 43–44
Garland, Hamlin, 36, 37, 38, 71, 77, 134–35, 141, 251n4
"A Garret" (Dunbar), 109
Gartner, Matthew, 130, 243n42
Garvey, Ellen Gruber, 136
Gates, Henry Louis, Jr., 7–8, 99, 176, 205–6, 236nn53–54
Gayle, Addison, Jr., 134
Gebhard, Caroline, 144
Genette, Gerard, 183, 188
genteel poetry, 94, 122, 123, 134, 226n3, 246n9
Gilder, Jeanette ("The Lounger"), 127
Gilder, Richard Watson, 134, 137, 209, 242n28
Gitelman, Lisa, 11
"Goin' Back" (Dunbar), 105, 107
"Gold Bug, The" (Poe), 182
Golden Stair Press, 185
Gray, Janet, 155, 246n5
Gray, Lillian, 25
Gray, Paul H., 32–33
Gray, Thomas, 34, 199
Greathouse, Charles A., 208
Griffiths, Eric, 213

Guest, Edgar, 212, 213

Hall, Donald, 213
Halttunen, Karen, 41
Hampton Institute, 165
Hancock Democrat, The, 52–53
"Happy! Happy! Happy!" (Dunbar), 101–5, 108, 111, 138, 162, 177, 206, 238n63
Harlem Renaissance, 93, 173–74, 236n53, 242n26
Harlem Shadows (McKay), 195, 199, 201, 205
Harper and Brothers, 77
Harper, Frances Ellen Watkins: audiences, 145, 155–57, 246n6; cultivation and, 156, 157; as dialect poet, 15–16, 145, 147–49, 154, 155, 171, 247n21; dramatic monologue, 172; dress and, 156, 157, 160, 169; Dunbar and, 15, 147–48, 156; femininity and, 155–57, 169; literacy and, 16, 147, 148, 153–55, 171, 248n33; performance and, 155–57, 169; racial uplift and, 147, 153–54, 155, 166; on temperance, 249n63. *See also* "The Drunkard's Child"; "Free Labor"; *Iola Leroy*; "Learning to Read"; *Sketches of Southern Life*
Harper's, 3, 19, 35, 111, 114, 131, 221nn54–55, 244n67
Harris, Joel Chandler, 50, 131, 137, 144, 225n114, 232n8, 246n12
Harris, Lee O., 221n60
Harris, W. T., 111
Hart, Matthew, 6
Harte, Francis Bret: advertising and, 135, 213; in anthologies, 26; appearance, 39, 67; *Atlantic Monthly* contract, 35, 213; audiences, 39–40, 213, 222n82, 226n3; authenticity, 39–40, 61, 65–66; cultivation and, 35, 39, 67; as dialect poet, 8, 17, 23, 57, 60, 61, 67, 81–82, 101, 102–3, 115–16, 147; in literary history, 15, 26, 57, 89, 212, 213, 226n1; in magazines, 35, 42; the *Overland Monthly* and, 42, 60, 62, 71, 226n3, 227n17, 228n39; performance and, 14, 39–40, 213, 222n82; "plain language" dialect, 14, 16, 57–58, 60, 61, 62, 63, 65–66, 71, 89, 115, 147; popularity of, 13–14, 22–23, 57, 98, 213, 246n12; Riley and, 40, 222n83, 227n21; satire and, 14, 57, 58, 59, 64, 65–67, 71, 226n3; spelling and, 57, 89, 102–3; spelling bee poems, 14–15, 82, 115, 196. *See also* "Cicely"; "Free Silver at Angel's"; "His Answer to Her Letter"; "The Latest Chinese Outrage"; *The Luck of Roaring Camp and Other Stories*; "Plain Language from Truthful James [The Heathen Chinee]"; "The Spelling Bee at Angel's"; "Truthful James to the Editor"
Hartford Courant, 42, 219n26
Hathaway, Heather, 195, 199, 203, 204
"Haunted Oak, The" (Dunbar), 126, 141
Hay, John, 8, 22, 23
A Hazard of New Fortunes (Howells), 58
Hazen, George H., 126
A Heap o' Livin' (Guest), 212
"Heartless Rhoda" (McKay), 197, 199
Heath, Shirley Brice, 10, 24–25, 87, 186
"Heathen Chinee, The." *See* "Plain Language from Truthful James"
Henkin, David, 215n11
"Hermit, The" (McKay), 203
Herrick (Dunbar), 99
Heywood, J. C., 62
Hibbitt, Charles W., 50
Hind, C. Lewis, 39
"His Answer to Her Letter" (Harte), 60
historically black colleges and universities: 55, 94, 110–11, 112, 165–66, 176, 177–78, 185, 252n18. *See also* Hampton Institute; Lincoln University; Tuskegee Institute; Virginia Normal and Collegiate Institute
Holmes, Oliver Wendell, 11–12
Holz, Arno, 17
"A Homesick Memory" (Riley), 80
Hoosier Holiday, A (Dreiser), 50
Hoosier School-Master, The: A Story of Backwoods Life in Indiana (Eggleston), 61, 85, 88, 246n12

Hopkins, Gerard Manley, 202, 204
Horton, Eliza Ann, 238n73
How Doth the Simple Spelling Bee (Wister), 83, 231n72
"How Persimmons Took Cah ob der Baby" (Champney), 246n5
"How They Brought the Good News from Ghent to Aix" (Browning), 54
Howells, William Dean, 19–20, 32, 41, 58, 61, 72, 91, 94, 96, 97, 111, 113, 114, 117, 128–29, 130, 131, 133, 137, 141, 146, 195, 196, 211, 242n28, 243n48
Hudson, Gossie H., 236n52
Hughes, Langston: audiences, 173, 174–76, 182, 183–84, 185, 186, 191, 192, 253n37, 253nn39–40; authenticity, 172, 174, 193; as dialect poet, 16, 171, 172–73, 174, 175, 176, 178, 204, 255n58; dramatic monologue, 172, 175, 182; Dunbar and, 93, 172, 173, 174–77, 192, 235n28, 237n54, 251n2, 252n9; education and, 174, 175, 176, 177–78, 185, 186, 191–92, 252n18; epistolary dialect poems, 99, 237n55; literacy and, 178–79, 184, 185, 186–87, 192, 194, 206; in literary history, 15, 93, 172, 173, 174, 175, 178, 237n54, 253n27; paratexts, use of, 183, 188, 254n57; performance and, 16, 171, 175, 179, 182, 183–84, 185, 186–88, 190–91, 193, 194, 206; publishing and, 182–83, 185, 253n37, 253n39; revisions, 192–93, 255n64; social class and, 175–77, 178, 184; as spokesman, 174–75, 178, 195; Whitman and, 173, 174, 251n3. See also titles of individual Hughes works
Hull, Gloria T., 148
Hull, Joseph, 67, 68–71
humor, 1, 3, 8, 15, 18, 20, 22, 37, 38, 50, 58, 66, 73, 76, 82, 83, 84, 86, 104, 107, 124, 132, 148, 162, 174, 196, 226n9, 228n39, 230n69, 234n24, 235n28, 237n54
Humphrey, Harry E., 50
Hutcheon, Linda, 43

"I Wish I Was a Grown Up Man" (Johnson), 161–62
I Wonder as I Wander (Hughes), 186, 187
illustrations, 45, 63, 67–71, 185, 187, 188, 189–90, 224n103, 227n30, 228n39, 253n40
immigrants, 3–4, 58, 63–64, 66, 83–84, 226n8, 231n74
"In Lighter Vein" (*Century Magazine*), 3, 15, 76, 133, 134–35, 136, 244n67. See also *Century Magazine*
Indiana State Teacher's Association, 26
intensive reading, 120, 123, 242n24
Iola Leroy (Harper), 151, 152–53, 154–55, 164, 247n21, 250n88
"Is Higher Education for the Negro Hopeless?" (Dunbar), 101, 111, 112, 239n88
Ives, Sumner, 216n17

Jackson, Cassandra, 250n88
Jackson, Virginia, 5
"James Hugo Johnston" (Johnson), 166
"James Whitcomb Riley" (Dunbar), 33, 122–24, 138
James, William, 31
Jarrett, Gene Andrew, 92, 95, 119–20, 234n20, 236n46, 243n52
Jekyll, Walter, 16, 172, 179, 194–95, 196–99, 200, 201, 204, 205, 206
Jenkins, Lee M., 200–201
Jesperson, Otto, 202
jingles. See advertising and advertising verse
John, Arthur, 132, 134, 244n67
Johnson, Charles S., 124–25, 242n26
Johnson, James Weldon, 7, 17, 97, 98, 131, 148, 172, 173–74, 235n44, 237n54, 241n8
Johnson, Maggie Pogue: audiences, 145, 246n6, 250n79; as dialect poet, 15–16, 145, 147, 164, 167; domesticity and, 158–59; dramatic monologue, 172; dress and, 157, 158, 159–64, 169, 249n68; Dunbar and, 15, 16, 159, 162, 165, 169, 249n65, 251n93; education and, 16, 165–71,

176; leisure and, 16, 159, 165, 166, 250n79; in literary history, 145, 172; performance and, 162; racial uplift and, 158, 165–66; social class and, 165, 166, 168; on temperance, 159; on women's rights, 250n84. *See also titles of individual Johnson works*
Johnson, Robert Underwood, 79–80, 243n52
Johnson, Rosamond, 98, 236n47
Johnston, James Hugo, 166–67, 170
Jones, Gavin, 3, 5, 21, 31, 58, 64, 95, 98, 107, 218n17, 233n9, 235n29, 238n64, 251n2
Jones, Meta DuEwa, 254n57
Joyce, James, 67, 218n23, 226n1

Keats, John, 130, 240n4
"Keep A-Pluggin' Away" (Dunbar), 121, 242n21, 242n25
Kellner, Bruce, 253n39
Kesterson, David B., 226n9
Kilton, Tom D., 68
Kinnamon, Keneth, 237n54
Kiparsky, Paul, 256n99
Kipling, Rudyard, 184, 212
Kirkham, Samuel, 217n1
Kittler, Frederich A., 1, 17, 54, 151, 183, 206
Knopf, 183, 185
Kowalewski, Michael, 227n26
Krapp, George Philip, 61
Kreilkamp, Ivan, 14, 51
"Krismas Dinnah" (Johnson), 159–60, 161

labor: Chinese Americans and, 59, 67, 226n8; Dunbar and menial, 112, 121, 130–31, 132, 139, 239n88; reading as, 5, 11–13, 15, 23, 31–32, 116, 120–21, 151–52, 153, 155, 200, 202, 206–7, 210, 211, 214, 231n71; representations of, 93, 117–19, 124, 139, 151–52, 157, 158–59, 165, 170, 241n21, 243n42; women's, 144–45, 158–59; writing as, 11–12, 13, 35–36, 71, 116, 118–19, 120–21, 124, 126, 127–28, 129–31, 205, 206–7, 210, 214, 250n78
"Lad without a Name, The" (Johnson), 251n93
Ladies' Home Journal, 3, 121
"Lake Isle of Innisfree, The" (Yeats), 198
"Latest Chinese Outrage, The" (Harte), 65
Laughlin, Clara, 230n66
Lauter, Paul, 148
Lawson, Edward H., 233n13
"Learning to Read" (Harper), 149–55, 166, 207
lecturing, 9, 10, 26, 39, 40, 81, 134, 138, 155–57, 222n82, 236n46. *See also* Chautauqua; lyceum
leisure, 15, 16, 32, 119, 121, 124, 125, 128, 129–31, 146, 159, 165, 166, 170, 250nn78–79. *See also* cultivation
Lerer, Seth, 230n71
"Letter, A" (Dunbar), 101, 105–9, 237n57, 238n66
"Letter from Spain" (Hughes), 191, 237n55
letter writing, 15, 92, 99–100, 102, 103, 108, 109, 116, 237n57. *See also* epistolary dialect poems
Levenston, E. A., 257n102
Levine, Caroline, 5
Levine, Lawrence W., 35
"Life-Lesson, A" (Riley), 208, 224n94
Lifting as We Climb (Johnson), 165
light verse, 3, 8, 15, 35–36, 125, 126–27, 133, 134–37, 142, 146, 212, 221n60, 244n67
Li'l Gal (Dunbar), 107
"Lincoln Lyrics" (Markham), 230n69
Lincoln University, 178
Linley, Margaret, 14, 213–14
Lippincott's, 243n52
"Lisping in Numbers" (Riley), 72–76
literacy rates, increases in: African American, 9, 147, 155, 185, 186; Southern U.S., 186; U.S., general, 9–10, 21, 209; white American, 9, 185, 186
literary histories and canon formation, 13, 15, 26, 30, 57, 90–91, 93–94, 96, 99, 145, 172, 173–74, 195–96,

199, 212, 213, 219n28, 223n91, 236nn53–54. *See also* anthologies; popular literature
"Little Breeches" (Hay), 22
"Little Orphant Annie" (Riley), 14, 30, 42, 43, 45, 48, 50, 74, 79–80, 81, 223n91, 224n100, 228n39
Little Orphant Annie (film), 14, 43–48
local color. *See* regionalism and local color
Locke, Alain, 174–75, 252n9
Long Way from Home, A (McKay), 199
Longfellow, Henry Wadsworth, 32, 35, 41, 123, 126, 129–31, 135, 167, 213, 223n91, 243n39, 243n42, 251n90
Loomis, Charles Battell, 1, 3, 9, 12, 83, 164, 211, 214
"Love Letter, A" (Dunbar), 237n57
Lowell, James Russell, 9, 12, 126
Luck of Roaring Camp and Other Stories, The (Harte), 246n12
Luke, Allan, 85
Lull, Herbert G., 193
lyceum, 38, 41, 88. *See also* Chautauqua; lecturing
lyric poetry, 4, 5, 6, 12, 26, 98–99, 101, 135, 175, 242n28
Lyrics of Lowly Life (Dunbar), 93, 117, 195–96

Macon, J. A., 241n7
magazines. *See* periodicals
Majors and Minors (Dunbar), 93, 97, 111, 113, 124, 133, 141, 240n1
Mance, Ajuan Maria, 158
Markham, Edwin, 230n69
Martin, Jay, 236n52
Matthews, Brander, 19–20, 24, 120, 128, 217n6
Matthews, James Newton, 91, 121, 122, 130, 241n5
McClure's, 37, 38, 131
McDowell, Deborah E., 164
McGee, Daniel T., 203
McGill, Meredith L., 5
McGuffey's Readers, 9, 30, 72, 112
McHenry, Elizabeth, 145, 146, 186

McKay, Claude: audiences, 173, 195, 198, 204; authenticity, 172, 194, 195–96, 198, 199, 200, 203, 204, 205, 235n37; cultivation and, 196–97, 199, 205; as dialect poet, 16, 152, 171, 195, 200–201, 203–5, 206; dramatic monologue, 172; education and, 198–99; epistolary dialect poems, 99, 237n55; Jamaican accent, 195, 255n71; Jekyll and, 16, 172, 179, 194–95, 196–99, 200, 201, 204, 205, 206; in literary history, 13, 15, 172, 173, 195–96, 199; poetic diction and, 16, 198, 200, 201–4, 205, 257n102. *See also titles of individual McKay works*
"Me 'n' Dunbar" (Corrothers), 117, 118
"Meal Time" (Johnson), 249n65
memorization of poetry, 9, 26, 30, 40, 54, 68, 77, 98, 99, 150, 199, 223n91
Mencken, H. L., 20, 24, 217n6
Merrihew & Son, 145
Merwin, Henry Childs, 61
meter, 13, 58, 96, 109, 136–37, 152, 173, 194, 205, 220n39, 220n47. *See also* free verse
Milburn, Nellie Frances, 41–42
Mill, John Stuart, 5
Miller, Joaquin, 89
Miller, Joshua L., 6
Miller, R. Baxter, 254n57
minstrelsy, 55, 92, 94, 96–98, 106, 155–56, 203, 234n26, 236nn46–47, 237n54. *See also* caricature; plantation tradition
Mitchell, Minnie, 89
modernist literature, 6, 13, 44, 74, 89, 98, 133, 218n23
Montage of a Dream Deferred (Hughes), 179
Moody, Christina, 143–44, 165
Moore, Colleen, 43
Morgan, Monique, 5
Morgan, Thomas Lewis, 119, 243n52
Morrisson, Mark, 191
Moscow Gazette, 35
Mott, Frank Luther, 30, 41, 135, 212, 223n90, 246n12

286 • Index

Mukarovsky, Jan, 256n99
Mullen, Harryette, 163, 214
Munsey's, 131–32, 136, 243n52
"My Grandfather Squeers" (Riley), 50
Myers, Reverend James A., 55

Nagley, Lester C., 45–48
"Name of Old Glory, The" (Riley), 221n55
Nation, The, 219n28
National Cash Register Company, 139
"Negro Artist and the Racial Mountain, The" (Hughes), 176, 235n28
"Negro Has a Chance, The" (Johnson), 166
"Negro Life in Washington" (Dunbar), 110, 112–13
"Negro Love Song, A" (Dunbar), 99, 136, 137, 139–41
"Negro Love Song, A" (Harris), 137
"Negro Mother, The" (Hughes), 175, 187–88, 192, 255n58
Negro Mother and Other Dramatic Recitations, The (Hughes), 16, 172–73, 175, 178–79, 182–85, 187–88, 190–92, 193, 194, 204, 206, 253nn39–40, 254n57
"Negro Society in Washington" (Dunbar), 110, 138, 245n79
"Nellie White (An Answer to the Foregoing)" (McKay), 237n55
Nelson, Cary, 191
Nesbit, W. D., 18
Newcomb, John Timberman, 212
newspapers. *See* periodicals
Nicholson, Meredith, 221n55, 222n83, 230n66
Nielsen, Aldon, 210
Nissen, Axel, 226n8
North, Michael, 3, 106, 195, 196, 197, 205, 233n13, 256n78
Northrop, Henry Davenport, 251n92
nostalgia, 9, 11, 14, 19, 25, 32, 45, 56, 72, 76, 77, 79, 84, 91, 93, 105–8, 116, 127, 189–90, 199, 207, 210, 220n39, 223n91, 233n13, 249n62
Nye, Bill (humorist), 53, 226n9
Nyong'o, Tavia, 158

"O-U-G-H" (Loomis), 8
Oak and Ivy (Dunbar), 93, 240n1
"Object Lesson, An" (Riley), 55
Okeke-Ezigbo, Emeka, 113, 240n93, 251n5
"Ol' Tunes, The" (Dunbar), 98
"Old England" (McKay), 199, 203, 205
"Old-Fashioned Couple, The" (anonymous), 228n33
"Old-Fashioned Roses" (Riley), 50
"Old Sweetheart of Mine, An" (Riley), 30, 54, 105
"Old Swimmin'-Hole, The" (Riley), 30, 105
Old Swimmin'-Hole and 'Leven More Poems (Riley), 212, 223n90, 246n12
Olson, Charles, 109, 212
"On Hearing James W. Riley Read (from a Kentucky Standpoint)" (Cotter), 240n94
"On the Banks of Deer Crick" (Riley), 54
Onderdonk, James L., 219n28
Ong, Walter, 9–10, 25, 32, 65, 182
Orphant Annie Book, The (Riley), 43, 48
orthography. *See* punctuation; spelling
"ortographt" (word), 16, 18–19, 55, 84
"Our Hired Girl" (Riley), 76
"Our Wonderful Society: Washington" (Hughes), 177–78, 185
"Out to Old Aunt Mary's" (Riley), 225n109
Overland Monthly, The, 42, 60, 62, 71, 226n3, 227n17, 228n39

Page, Thomas Nelson, 94, 131, 132, 144, 233n8
Palmer, Jack, 180
Palmieri, H., 227n30
"Party, The" (Dunbar), 97, 99, 159
Pattee, Fred Lewis, 230n66
"Paul Laurence Dunbar in the Tenderloin" (Reed), 251n5
Pawley, Christine, 218n22
Pawley, Thomas D., 236n52
Pearce, Roy Harvey, 208–9, 212
Pears Soap, 135–36
Pearson, Paul M., 232n7

"peculiar language" dialect, 14, 19, 57, 71–72, 80, 89, 115, 214
Pemberton, T. Edgar, 22
Penry, Tara, 226n3
performance, poetry, 4, 5, 17, 18–19, 24–25, 26, 31, 32–33, 36, 40–41, 51, 53–55, 88, 97, 150, 190–91, 193–94, 211–12, 223n87; amateur, 9–10, 14, 16, 30, 40–41, 58–59, 68, 146–47, 182, 184, 187, 188–90, 192, 194, 199, 206, 219n28, 219n32, 220n38, 223n91, 231n72; Dunbar and, 15, 55, 90, 91, 95, 97–99, 100, 108, 114, 119, 121, 131, 137–39, 141, 213, 235n42, 236n45, 236n47; Harper and, 156–57; Harte and, 14, 39–40, 213, 222n82; Hughes and, 16, 171, 175, 179, 182, 183–84, 185, 186–88, 190–91, 193, 194, 206; Johnson, Maggie Pogue, and, 162; professional, 40–41, 50, 55, 158; Riley and, 14, 15, 36–39, 40, 41, 42, 43, 45, 50, 53, 54–55, 74, 94–95, 97–98, 100, 110, 138, 178, 213, 219n28, 220n32, 220n38, 223n86, 223n91, 226n9, 240n94. *See also* actors and acting; celebrity
periodicals: African American, 94, 124–25, 127, 234n23, 242n26; children's, 80; circulation of, 4, 12, 131; dialect poetry in, 1, 2, 3, 4, 15, 20, 22–23, 32, 35, 36, 41–42, 58, 59, 71, 119, 125, 141, 142, 211–12, 220n38, 221n55; elite, 15, 35, 119, 128, 129, 131–32, 135, 141, 142, 211–12, 221n54, 243n52; layout and format of, 126–27, 136; poets' income from, 126, 242n28; readers of, 10, 35, 42, 124–25, 128–29, 136, 146, 221n54. *See also individual periodicals*
Perkins, David, 133–34, 242n28
personae, stage, 14, 26, 35, 36–38, 39–41, 44–48, 53–55, 59, 91, 94–95, 96–98, 99, 100, 138–39, 156–57, 158, 169, 175, 178, 188–89, 190, 192, 194, 211, 222n82, 223n86, 224n103, 232n3, 235n29. *See also* caricature; celebrity; performance, poetry
Peterson, Carla L., 156
Petrino, Elizabeth A., 148
Phelps, William Lyon, 50–51
Philological Society of England, 19
phonograph, 14, 48–55, 56, 74, 214, 224nn108–109, 225n114, 225n123, 230n69, 255n71
"Phonograph, The" (Riley), 52–54
"phthisis" (word), 83, 86, 87, 230n69, 231n71
Picker, John M., 48, 51, 224n108
Pidgin, Charles Felton, 238n73
"Plain Language from Truthful James [The Heathen Chinee]" (Harte), 9, 12, 14, 186, 220n47; Ah Sin in, 22, 58, 59, 60, 62–67, 68–71, 227n30; illustrations, 67–71, 227n30, 228n33; influence upon language, 22, 23; Osgood edition, 67; in *Overland Monthly*, 42, 60, 62, 71, 226n3, 228n39; parodies of, 63, 227n21; popularity of, 9, 14, 22, 23, 40, 42, 58, 59, 60, 65, 71, 213, 226n9, 228n37; racial politics of, 14, 57–60, 62–71, 82, 226n3, 226n8; Rock Island and Pacific Railroad edition, 68, 228n33; satire and irony in, 14, 57–58, 59, 62, 64, 65–67, 71, 82, 226n3; Truthful James in, 22, 59–61, 62–64, 65, 66, 71, 220n47; use of "which" in, 60–62, 63, 65; violence in, 59, 67–71, 227n30; Western News Company edition, 67
"plain language" dialect, 14, 16, 57–58, 60, 61, 62, 63, 65–66, 71, 82, 115, 147
plantation tradition, 91, 105–8, 235n26. *See also* caricature; minstrelsy; regionalism and local color
"Pleading" (McKay), 198
Plotkin, Cary H., 202, 204
Poe, Edgar Allan, 182
"Poet and His Song, The" (Dunbar), 117–19, 121, 124, 134, 139, 141, 142
"Poet of Our Race" (Johnson), 169, 249n65

poetic diction, 16, 198, 200, 201–4, 205, 255n58, 256n99, 257n102
Pope, Alexander, 22, 201
popular literature, 12–13, 14, 32–33, 35, 82, 88, 145, 146, 173, 174, 191, 209, 213, 214, 223n91, 231n72, 246n12; dialect poetry as, 3, 6, 7, 9, 10, 12, 13, 19, 20, 21, 22–23, 25, 30, 36, 40, 82, 146, 157, 207, 209, 212, 214
"Postcard from Spain" (Hughes), 237n55
Pound, Ezra, 178, 179, 201, 253n27
Powell, Richard J., 157
Price, Leah, 253n40
Prins, Yopie, 5, 68
Proctor, Richard A., 115
pronunciation, 7, 8, 19, 20–21, 34, 55, 72, 73, 74–75, 83–84, 85–87, 103–4, 115, 181, 182, 196–97, 198, 199–200, 206, 217n1, 229n47, 230n66, 231n71
punctuation, 2–3, 62–63, 74–75, 102, 103, 104, 108, 147, 174, 181–82, 189, 209, 219n28, 255n64
Pygmalion (Shaw), 115

"Quashie to Buccra" (McKay), 197, 205, 257n114

racial uplift, 94, 144, 145, 147, 153–54, 155, 158, 165–66, 176, 252n18
Radway, Janice, 13, 136, 214
"Raggedy Man, The" (Riley), 40, 50, 76, 77, 79
Rampersad, Arnold, 251n3, 253n39, 254n57
Randall, Dale B. J., 75
Ransom, John Crowe, 178, 179, 253n27
Read, Allen Walker, 85, 114
Read, Charles, 73
readability, as defined by Edgar Dale and Jeanne S. Chall, 26–30, 58, 148, 255n58
reading, methods of teaching, 25, 150
reading aloud, 2, 10–11, 16, 24–25, 31–32, 34, 75, 100, 147, 181, 184, 185, 187, 191, 193–94, 214, 218nn22–23, 223n91, 253n27. *See also* silent reading; subvocalization
realism, 40–41, 92, 210, 211, 213, 219n28, 234n20, 235n31, 236n46, 251n4
reception. *See* audiences of American dialect poetry
"Recipe for a Poem 'In Dialect,' A" (Strong), 12, 23
recitation. *See* performance, poetry
Redding, J. Saunders, 95, 147–48, 234n24
Reed, Ishmael, 251n5
Rees, John O., 60–61
regionalism and local color, 1, 3, 12, 15, 22, 30, 33, 37, 57, 60–62, 63, 65, 81, 82, 85, 86, 90–91, 92–94, 95–96, 98, 100, 105–8, 115, 131, 144, 148, 188, 211, 213, 214, 218n17, 222n83, 227n26, 228n41, 230n66, 230n71, 232nn2–3, 232n8, 233n13, 236n54, 245n3
"Representative American Negroes" (Dunbar), 167, 171, 175
Revell, Peter, 93, 95–96, 114, 234n19
Revue des deux Mondes, 35
Reynolds, Paul Revere, 126, 243n52
rhyme, 8, 13, 54, 74, 83, 103–4, 109–10, 135, 173, 184, 187, 198, 205, 220n39. *See also* free verse
"Rhymes of Riley, The" (Nesbit), 18
Riley, James Whitcomb: in anthologies, 26, 30; appearance, 37–38, 39; audiences, 14, 32, 33–34, 35, 36–39, 41–42, 43, 45, 49, 55, 56, 77, 79–80, 94–95, 96, 100, 220n40; authenticity, 36, 77, 94, 95, 100, 219n28, 230n66; Benjamin F. Johnson character, 38, 75, 81, 103; blankness of, 36–38, 54, 94–95; "child dialect," 56, 76–77, 79–80, 228n41; "child writing," 11, 14, 31, 32, 71–76, 81, 82, 100, 103, 116, 143, 200; as dialect poet, 17, 18–19, 23, 34–35, 66, 80–82, 84, 89, 99, 102–3, 105, 108, 115–16, 144, 147, 211, 214, 220n39, 220n46, 228n41, 235n31, 237n54; Dunbar and, 15, 33, 91, 92, 93, 94–96, 97–98, 99, 100, 101,

102–3, 105, 108, 109, 110, 113, 114, 115–16, 122, 123–24, 126, 130, 138, 142, 144, 173, 232n3, 232n7, 234nn18–19, 240n93, 242n25, 244n61, 251n5; education and, 25–26, 30, 56, 75, 76, 77, 80, 89, 208; in film, 14, 19, 42–48, 56, 214, 224n94; Harte and, 40, 222n83, 227n21; honors, 26, 48, 77, 208, 219n26; as "Hoosier Poet," 36, 37, 48, 95, 234n18, 236n45; income, 36, 113, 240n93, 241n19; in literary history, 11–12, 15, 16, 30, 35–36, 41, 44, 57, 95, 173, 208–9, 212–13, 219n28, 221n60, 223n91, 224n108, 251n4; Longfellow and, 32, 35, 41, 213, 223n91; in magazines, 3, 35, 40, 41, 76, 79–80, 219n28, 221n55, 221n60; as mass poet, 35–36; performance and, 14, 15, 36–39, 40, 41, 42, 43, 45, 50, 53, 54–55, 74, 94–95, 97–98, 100, 110, 138, 178, 213, 219n28, 220n32, 220n38, 223n86, 223n91, 226n9, 240n94; "peculiar language" dialect, 14, 19, 57, 71–72, 80, 89, 115, 214; phonographic recordings of, 14, 48–55, 56, 74, 214, 224n109, 225n114, 225n123; popularity of, 3, 13, 19, 21, 23, 30, 32, 35, 36, 41–42, 43–44, 48, 57, 95, 97, 173, 212, 223nn90–91, 246n12; social class and, 33, 37; spelling and, 19, 57, 66, 75, 76, 80–81, 82, 84, 89, 211, 229n53. *See also* titles of individual Riley works
Roadside Meetings (Garland), 37
"Rossville Lectur' Course, The" (Riley), 18–19, 54–55, 84
Rubaiyat of Doc Sifers, The (Riley), 33–35, 110
Rubaiyat of Omar Khayyam, The (FitzGerald), 33–34
Rubin, Joan Shelley, 10, 219n28
Russell, Irwin, 94

sales and marketing of printed dialect poetry, 2, 11, 32–36, 38–39, 41, 77–80, 91, 108, 111, 126, 134–37, 141–42, 146–47, 182–83, 184, 185, 186, 212, 223n90, 232n7, 241n19, 243n52, 246n12, 253n39. *See also* audiences of American dialect poetry
satire, 2, 14, 57, 58, 59, 64, 65–67, 71, 82, 83, 105, 124, 226n3
Saturday Evening Post, 126, 136
Scharnhorst, Gary, 13, 14, 39, 42, 58, 59, 67, 68, 222n81, 227n22, 227n28
Schatt, Stanley, 192
Schneirov, Matthew, 244n63
"School-Teacher Nell's Lub-Letter" (McKay), 237n55
schoolbooks, 9, 24, 26, 30, 32, 72, 77, 85, 86, 87, 112, 114, 152, 176, 199, 212
"Schoolboy Silhouettes—No. 1" (Riley), 72
Scott, Donald M., 81
Scott-Childress, Reynolds J., 132
Scribner's, 80, 126, 221n60
Scripture, E. W., 50–51
Sedgwick, Ellery, 126
Selig Polyscope Company, 43, 224n94
"Session with Uncle Sidney, A" (Riley), 75–76, 82
Shakespeare in Harlem (Hughes), 182, 187
Shoptaw, John, 6
silent reading, 10–11, 14, 15, 16, 17, 19, 24–25, 31, 41, 42, 43, 68, 82, 88, 100, 109, 147, 171, 181, 183–84, 190, 191, 193–94, 210, 211–12, 218n22. *See also* reading aloud; subvocalization
sincerity, 41, 50, 58, 61, 66, 123, 139, 174–75, 211, 230n66, 237n54
Sketches of Southern Life (Harper), 16, 145, 147–48, 154, 155, 157
slang, 3, 12, 60, 62, 181, 241n17
Smethurst, James, 15, 92, 204, 255n58
social class, 17, 22, 32–33, 37, 40, 57, 85, 93, 94, 110, 112–14, 129–31, 138, 144–45, 146, 154, 157, 158, 159, 164, 165, 166, 167–68, 175–77, 178, 184, 186, 220n40, 221n54, 239n88, 245n79, 246n5, 247n21, 249n62, 245n79
Soltow, Lee, 9, 229n50

Somerville, Siobhan B., 157–58
Songs from the Wayside (Thompson), 157
Songs of Jamaica (McKay), 16, 172–73, 179, 194–99, 201, 203–6
Sooy, Harry O., 49, 50, 51
Sorby, Angela, 13, 33, 35, 37, 53, 220n39, 223n86
Southern Workman, 234n23
"Spellin'-Bee, The" (Dunbar), 75, 114–15, 240n95
spelling: children and, 8, 25, 72–74, 75, 83–84, 87–88, 114, 150, 152, 153, 231n74; dialect, 2, 7, 8, 9, 11, 14, 16–17, 18–21, 23, 30, 31, 32, 33, 36, 65, 66, 72, 75, 76, 80–81, 82, 84, 87, 92, 102–4, 115, 141, 147, 149, 170, 174, 175, 178, 192, 201, 206, 208, 209, 210, 211, 214, 233n9; illogic of conventional, 8–9, 19, 21, 72, 83–84, 87, 89; morality of, 87–88, 89, 212; pronunciation, 86–87; valorization of, 14, 20, 21, 57, 75, 86–88, 112, 209, 212, 218n10, 230n69, 231n83
spelling bees, 15, 31, 82–89, 114–15, 150, 196, 230n69, 231n71, 232n87
"Spelling Bee at Angel's, The" (Harte), 82–88
Spelling Bee poems, 14–15, 31, 82, 87, 89, 114, 115, 196, 230n69
spelling reform, 9, 19–20, 21, 24, 31, 73, 74, 83–86, 87, 89, 115, 229n47, 231n74
St. Nicholas, 79, 80
Stanzas in Meditation (Stein), 61
Stein, Gertrude, 13, 61, 184
Steiner, George, 217n34
Stepto, Robert, 111, 195, 198
Stevens, Edward, 9, 229n50
Stevenson, Robert Louis, 120
Stewart, Garrett, 6
Stewart, Susan, 5
Stone Printing and Manufacturing Company, The, 246n6
Stowe, Harriet Beecher, 164
"Strokes of the Tamarind Switch" (McKay), 205
Stuart, Ruth McEnery, 131, 144

subvocalization, 31, 193–94, 200. *See also* reading aloud; silent reading
"Sukee River" (McKay), 200–201
Swinburne, Algernon Charles, 220n47
"Sympathy" (Dunbar), 236n53
syntax, 8, 21, 30, 31, 60–62, 63, 65, 66, 102, 147, 175, 192, 255n57

"Tale of the Airly Days, A" (Riley), 208
Taylor, Prentiss, 185, 188, 189, 253n39
Tennyson, Alfred, Lord, 21, 213, 224n108
Terrell, Mary Church, 145
"Terrible Threat" (anonymous), 1
theater, 40–41, 156, 183, 191, 223n87
Thomas, Lorenzo, 94
Thompson, Aaron Belford, 90
Thompson, Clara Ann, 90, 157
Thompson, Priscilla Jane, 90
Thoreau, Henry David, 241n4
Thoughts for Idle Hours (Johnson), 145, 165, 251n93
"To E.M.E." (McKay), 201
"To My Dear Reader" (Moody), 143–44, 165
"To Professor Byrd Prillerman" (Johnson), 168–69, 171
"To See Ol' Booker T." (Johnson), 169–71
"To the Eastern Shore" (Dunbar), 105
Tobey, Henry A., 119, 130, 142
Toolan, Michael, 64, 200, 204
Toronto Mail, 39
Trachtenberg, Alan, 33, 220n46
Tracy, Steven C., 182, 187, 255n64
"Tradin' Jim" (Riley), 54
Triggs, Oscar Lovell, 223n91
"Tropics of New York, The" (McKay), 106
"Truthful James to the Editor" (Harte), 65
Tuskegee Institute, 111, 169
"Tuskegee Meeting, The" (Dunbar), 110
"Tuskegee's Sorrow" (Johnson), 251n93
Twain, Mark, 11, 23, 33, 37, 39, 53, 54, 61, 83, 96, 97, 200, 213, 226n9, 238n74
typewriting, 74, 109–10, 238n75
typography, 17, 179, 181

"Uncle Rube to the Young People" (Thompson), 157
Uncle Tom's Cabin (Stowe), 158

"V.N. and C.I., The" (Johnson), 166
Van Allen, Elizabeth J., 26, 36, 48
Van Doren, Mark, 178, 179, 253n27
Van Dyke, Henry, 36, 214
Van Vechten, Carl, 176, 180, 182, 184, 185, 193, 253n39
Variety, 43
Venable, W. H., 88
vernacular. *See* dialects
Vicinus, Martha, 33
Victor Talking Machine Company, 14, 49
Virginia Dreams (Johnson), 16, 145, 165
Virginia Normal and Collegiate Institute, 165, 166
voice: dialectal, represented, 15, 63–66, 71, 79, 91, 95, 108–9, 148, 200, 213, 247n21; disappearing, 5, 84, 92, 233n13; narrative, 4, 254n57; performing, 41, 45, 53, 95, 98, 109, 138, 139, 156, 158, 175, 187, 191, 213–14, 236n45; poetic, 42, 62–66, 71, 101, 104, 108–9, 148, 174, 175, 182, 187, 199, 213–14, 224n108, 244n64; reading, 31, 68, 153; recorded, 14, 48–51, 53–55, 56, 74, 214, 224nn108–109, 225n114, 255n71; silenced, 43, 63–64, 71

Wagner, Jean, 113, 241n7
"Wait" (Hughes), 179
Ward, Artemus, 19
Warren, Kenneth, 167
Washington, Booker T., 111, 165, 166, 167, 169–71, 251n93
Watts, Isaac, 231n72, 241n21
"We Wear the Mask" (Dunbar), 92, 233n9
Weary Blues, The (Hughes), 174, 179, 185, 193
Webb, Mary, 158
Webster, Noah, 21, 72, 83–87, 89, 114. *See also* dictionaries and lexicography

Weirick, Bruce, 220n32
"Welcome Address to the Western Association of Writers" (Dunbar), 90
Wesling, Donald, 201
Western Association of Writers, 90, 91, 97
"What Task Must the Woman Fulfill" (Johnson), 250n84
"What's Mo' Temptin' to the Palate" (Johnson), 158–59
Wheeler, Lesley, 30
"When De Co'n Pone's Hot" (Dunbar), 95, 99
"When Malindy Sings" (Dunbar), 64, 98, 99, 110, 137
"When the Frost is on the Punkin" (Riley), 96, 234n18
"Where is Mary Alice Smith?" (Riley), 43
"Whistling Sam" (Dunbar), 97, 114
White Dialect Poetry (Andrews), 16
White, Richard Grant, 24, 86, 115
Whitman, Walt, 39, 156, 173, 174, 199, 251nn3–5
Whittier, John Greenleaf, 35, 41, 126
Wiggins, Lida Keck, 111
Willard, Frances E., 156
Williams, Heather Andrea, 152
Williams, Raymond, 12, 125
Williams, Spencer, 180
Wilson, Francis A., 126
Wilson, H. B., 193
Wister, Owen, 83, 231n72, 231n74
Wolosky, Shira, 6, 37
Wolters, Raymond, 252n18
women: as dialect poets, 15–16, 144–46, 148, 157, 245n1, 246n5, 250n84; domesticity and, 144–45, 158–59, 249n62; dress and, 145, 146, 156, 157–58, 159–64, 169, 249n68; racial uplift and, 144, 145, 147, 153–54, 155, 158, 165–66; as readers of dialect poetry, 146–47; sexually immoral, condemned as, 119, 144, 156; social class and, 144–45, 146, 157, 158, 164; on the stage, 155–57, 158, 165
Wonham, Henry B., 58, 92, 211
Worcester, J. E., 84–85, 86, 87. *See also* dictionaries and lexicography
Wordsworth, William, 72, 174, 199, 205

"Worn-Out Pencil, A" (Riley), 109
Wright, Edward Sterling, 55
Writer, The, 2
Wyatt, Edith, 220n38

Yeats, William Butler, 198

Young, Art, 224n103
Youth's Companion, 126

Zlotnick, Susan, 144–45, 249n62
Zon-o-phone, 50, 54, 225n114
Zukofsky, Louis, 13

www.ingramcontent.com/pod-product-compliance
Lightning Source LLC
Chambersburg PA
CBHW030107010526
44116CB00005B/140